ON TOUCHING—JEAN-LUC NANCY

CW00551719

MERIDIAN

Crossing Aesthetics

Werner Hamacher

Editor

Translated by Christine Irizarry

Stanford
University
Press

———————

Stanford
California
2005

ON TOUCHING—JEAN-LUC NANCY

Jacques Derrida

Stanford University Press
Stanford, California

English translation © 2005 by the Board of Trustees of the
Leland Stanford Junior University. All rights reserved.

On Touching—Jean-Luc Nancy
was originally published in French in 2000
under the title *Le toucher, Jean-Luc Nancy*
© 2000, Éditions Galilée.

Assistance for the translation was provided by the
French Ministry of Culture.

"*Salut* to you, *salut* to the blind we become" (p. 313)
was originally published in French under the title
"Salut à toi, salut aux aveugles que nous devenons,"
© 2004, Éditions Galilée / Jean-Luc Nancy.
Translated and published by permission.

Printed in the United States of America on acid-free,
archival-quality paper

Library of Congress Cataloging-in-Publication Data

Derrida, Jacques.
[Toucher, Jean-Luc Nancy. English]
On touching—Jean-Luc Nancy /
Jacques Derrida ; translated by Christine Irizarry.
p. cm.—(Meridian, crossing aesthetics)
Includes bibliographical references and index.
ISBN 0-8047-4243-X (cloth : alk. paper—
ISBN 0-8047-4244-8 (pbk. : alk. paper)
1. Nancy, Jean-Luc—Criticism and interpretation.
2. Touch. 3. Sense (Philosophy)
I. Title. II. Meridian (Stanford, Calif.)
B2430.N364D4713 2005
194—dc22 2005008743

Original Printing 2005

Last figure below indicates year of this printing:
14 13 12 11 10 09 08 07

Typeset by James P. Brommer
in 10.9/13 Garamond and Lithos display

Contents

Foreword

The first version of this essay was written in 1992. Peggy Kamuf translated it into English, and her translation was published the following year in *Paragraph*, which had dedicated a special issue to Jean-Luc Nancy at the time.[1] This international tribute clearly showed once again that the measure of an idea is often taken, first and last, "abroad," in "foreign" countries.

What I wrote then stands as a modest, partial, and provisional introduction to Nancy's work. It was my intention to develop it or pursue it elsewhere when the right time came. I have certainly not given up on that; many new developments are the mark of this. But I must admit that I have had to follow the motifs, at least, of my first attempts, as far as the topical heart of the matter is concerned.

While the choice of the guiding thread, and especially of the original title—*Le toucher*—seemed to impose itself, it never ceased to worry me. In the grammatical form of the French phrase and its indecision—between the noun *toucher* and verb *toucher*, the definite article *le* and personal pronoun *le*—it is easy to recognize two indissociable gestures: if one analyzed the way in which a great philosopher treated touch, how he handled this profound question of the sense that is apparently the most superficial, the question of the very surface itself, touching, was it not necessary also to touch *him*, and thus touch someone, address oneself to him *singularly*, touch someone *in him*, a stranger perhaps? Never to this degree have I felt how enigmatic, how troubling idioms are in their necessity, in expressions such as "touch to the heart," "touch the heart," whether their value is properly literal or figurative, or sometimes both, beyond all decidability.

However, by thus privileging one perspective, let us even say one *sense*, one of the senses, don't we undertake to choose, to unfairly leave in the shadows everything excluded by that one sense, indeed, by the senses in general, in and of themselves? Don't we risk losing sight of the measure of the work we are claiming to open up?

The risk is all the greater in that this topical vein, barely visible at first, perhaps hidden until then, has since been Nancy's to mine; and he has ceaselessly been expanding the reach of its influence, increasing the wealth of its stratifications, and thus confirming its resources—at the risk (to me) of venturing with this toward the unpredictable, or losing it there. Nancy's *Le sens du monde* (*The Sense of the World*), for example, first published shortly afterward during the same year, 1992, already bore witness to that, and "Toucher" ("Touching") became the title of one of its chapters. No lucky vein, then: what I had proposed risked appearing not only dated (it undeniably and purposely is) but also increasingly deficient, faltering, or obsolete.

Unable today to transform the central topic of this essay and make it less unworthy of Nancy's thought, and particularly of the powerful books he has published during the past few years,[2] I have contented myself here with changes in the form of the text, interpolated passages—some of them admittedly long ones—and notes added retrospectively.

The age of this text is thus multifold. It sometimes skips several years from one sentence to the next. And so, together with the reader, I could have played at coloring in the strata of an archive.

To admit these risks and accept them without shame is not enough, of course, to contain them.

In spite of all these shortcomings, if this attempt at interpretation, among so many other possible ones, at least persuades others to read one of the immense philosophic works of our time, this publication will not have been altogether unjustified.

                                                            Jacques Derrida

Translator's Preface

Two days after Jacques Derrida died, while this book was in production, Jean-Luc Nancy published an article in the newspaper *Libération* titled "Salut à toi, salut aux aveugles que nous devenons." I thank Jean-Luc Nancy for allowing it to be translated and published in this book.

I thank Peggy Kamuf, Jean-Luc Nancy (again and again), Helen Tartar, Norris Pope, Werner Hamacher, Avital Ronell, Kim Lewis Brown, Amy Jamgochian, Angie Michaelis, Mariana Raykov, Marc Froment-Meurice, Kalliopi Nikolopoulou, Edward Batchelder, Lee Moore, Ludwig Reichhold, Brigitte Vanvincq (in memory), Sophie Bissonnette, Stephan Reichhold, Mila Reichhold, Alice Irizarry Froment-Meurice Reichhold, Eddy Irizarry, Gil Mendez, Pascal Massie, Beate Schuh, Ronald Bruzina, Dieter Lohmar, Alan Bostick, and David Dwiggins.

Peter Dreyer deserves my extensive gratitude for his editorial work on this translation. His superb editing skills have contributed very significantly to the final result.

I thank the staffs of the Hong Kong Public Library, the San Francisco Public Library, the Nashville Public Library, and the Vanderbilt University libraries.

By permission of the Edinburgh University Press and Peggy Kamuf, this translation incorporates Jacques Derrida, "*Le toucher*: Touch / To Touch Him," translated by Peggy Kamuf, in *On the Work of Jean-Luc Nancy*, edited by Peggy Kamuf, *Paragraph* 16, 2 (July 1993): 122–57. Copyright: Edinburgh University Press (www.eup.ed.ac.uk)

Christine Irizarry

ON TOUCHING—JEAN-LUC NANCY

"When our eyes touch . . ."

Signing a Question—from Aristotle

One day, yes, one day, once upon a time, a terrific time, a time terrifically addressed, with as much violence as tact at its fingertips, a certain question took hold of me—as if it, or "she" [*la question*], came of me, to me.

To tell the truth, "she" didn't come to me—putting it that way is inaccurate. "She" didn't come to pay me a *visit*. In other words, "she" didn't *alight* to *see* me, as if I had *invited* "her." No, as I said, "she" took hold of me, "she" invaded me even before I had seen "her" coming: "she" touched me before letting "herself" be seen. In this sense, yes, although there wasn't any visit paid to me, it really was—before any invitation—a visitation. A genuine test of hospitality: to receive the other's visitation just where there has been no prior invitation, preceding "her," the one arriving.

Now as soon as I have nicknamed "her"—"her," let's say, this question— I may lose the right to say "one day" ("One day . . . a certain question took hold of me," or took me by surprise, or grabbed me) and thus to tell a story.

For the question just nicknamed was precisely one about the day, an enquiry on the subject of the day—the question of the day, if you will. By right, "she" thus came to light before the light of day.

"She" saw the light of the day, one might say, a priori: "she" came the evening before. A younger, earlier riser than the day, "she" henceforth has to keep watch over it—and therefore over the phenomenon. "She" remains prephenomenological, "she" does, unless we can say that "she" is transphenomenal as well.

And I would have even lost the right to say, sensu stricto, that "she" came to or from *me*—as if I assumed that a question come to me thus came *from* me. This question could not happen to *me* except by being *said* as much as *touched* upon—by the other—belonging first to the other, come to me from the other, who was already addressing it to the other.

First, "she" beholds, and is beholden to, the other.

Here it is, transcribed: "When our eyes touch, is it day or is it night?" ["Quand nos yeux se touchent, fait-il jour ou fait-il nuit?"]

I then tried to have it out with "her"—I mean to say with it, the said question. I was determined to show a limitless patience, ready for the infinite, the time of experience itself: let's see, can eyes manage to touch, first of all, to press together like lips?

To which surface of the eye do lips compare? If two gazes look into each other's eyes, can one then say that they are touching? Are they coming into contact—the one with the other? What is contact if it always *intervenes between x and x*? A hidden, sealed, concealed, signed, squeezed, compressed, and repressed interruption? Or the *continual* interruption of an interruption, the negating upheaval of the interval, the death of *between*? If two gazes come into contact, the one with the other, the question will always be whether they are stroking or striking each other—and where the difference would lie. A benediction bordering on the very worst, as always? Would a benediction be beneficent otherwise, without the threatening possibility of some perversion?

Now, in the first place, this presupposes that these eyes see *each other*.

—These eyes or these gazes? You're going from one to the other. For two gazes, more than two eyes are often needed. And then there are eyes that no longer see, and eyes that have never seen. Aren't you also forgetting those living without any eyes? All the same, they don't always live without any light.

—Where we are—this night—seems even darker, then. Don't we have to make a choice between looking or exchanging glances or meeting gazes, and seeing, very simply seeing? And first between seeing the seeing and seeing the visible? For if our eyes see what is *seeing* rather than *visible*, if they believe that they are seeing a gaze rather than eyes, at least to that extent, to that extent as such, they are seeing nothing, then, nothing that can be seen, nothing *visible*. Away from all visibility, they founder in the night. They blind themselves so as to see a gaze; they avoid seeing the visibility of the other's eyes so as to address themselves only to his or her gaze, to his or her sight that is merely seeing, to his or her vision.

At this instant, here, is it daytime? And does this instant belong to time? To the time of the earth? To time tallied by this turning around the earth known as the finite course of a sun? Is it a day? Is it night? Would one have to *make* it night, make the night *appear* in order to see oneself looking at the other or see oneself beheld by the other? In order to see the other seeing us, that is, provided we'd no longer see the other's eyes' visibility, then, but only their clairvoyance? Is that what night is, our *first night*—in the first sense, the strong sense of the word "night"? The first for which we'd need a taste to hear it, before seeing or touching?

—Let's repeat this question; however, let's displace it while taking note of its straying deportment: "At this instant, then, is it daytime? Is it night?"

If one answered "night," wouldn't it then seem that the eyes blindly *touch*, in the constancy of this contact and the consent of the interruption holding them together?

But "she"—the one I nicknamed the question—objected to me, or I myself objected to myself: "Unless this is precisely how they begin to hear and understand each other."

—But precisely, when my gaze meets yours, I see *both* your gaze *and* your eyes, love in fascination—and your eyes are not only seeing but also visible. And since they are *visible* (things or objects in the world) as much as *seeing* (at the origin of the world), I could precisely touch them, with my finger, lips or even eyes, lashes and lids, by approaching you—if I dared come near to you in this way, if I one day dared.

—Insisting tirelessly, someone is still repeating: at the moment of touching your eyes with mine, like lips, is it daytime or are we already inhabiting our night? Still and always our first night always? Is there still room, place, space, or an interval, *chōra*, for the day's phenomenality and its diaphanous visibility?

For, like an image in a pupil, everything can also turn itself around, where it is not yet daylight, at the point where the origin of its possibility is dawning. As long as you haven't touched me with your eyes, as long as you haven't touched my eyes, like lips, you won't be able to say "one day." Nor "adieu." Hello, goodbye, so long, take care of yourself, I pray that one day you'll outlive me. But this prayer already shames me, as if I were also admitting that I'm afraid—afraid of being a survivor and bearing death. Because, to admit to one last resignation, I expect the only chance of a reconciliation with death, I mean to say my own, from the good fortune thus promised of no longer seeing those whom I have loved—like myself, more than myself—die.

I barely dared sign such a question, not to mention its gloss (it comes down to tact, tactility, the caress, the sublime, when what is most discreet borders on the most indecent, unless it touches it), and for a moment I thought of inventing a history or, in fact, since we have said goodbye to history, of pretending to *invent* a true story.

This one: unlikely though it may seem, I thought I deciphered this anonymous inscription on a wall in Paris, as if it had journeyed there from the shores of another language: "Quand nos yeux se touchent, fait-il jour ou fait-il nuit?" ("When our eyes touch, is it day or is it night?"). It inspired me with the desire, pure and simple, to trot it out, to make it an epigraph to what I had long wanted to write for Jean-Luc Nancy, the greatest thinker about touching of all time, I tell myself.

—Of all time, really?

—Let's put it differently, to avoid sounding pathetic and excessive, even when speaking the truth—precisely for want of tact: not of all time, perhaps, but ever since Aristotle suddenly hit on the manifold aporia of touch (*aporia*, he said then, and *aporēseie*); ever since he, Aristotle, foresaw all the obscurities of the tangible: touch isn't clear, *ouk estin endēlon*, he says furthermore; it's *adēlon*, inapparent, obscure, secret, nocturnal.

Let's not put this off but say it: it is often the case in Aristotle that the diaporetic exposition, or within the exposition the moment that is properly diaporetic, is not necessarily a moment that can be passed or surpassed. By definition, one is never through with aporias worthy of their name. They wouldn't be what they are—aporias—if one saw or touched their end, even if there were any hope of being done with them. It is thus necessary to treat them differently, and decide otherwise, where they couldn't care less about our decision, and to let go, leaving ourselves in their hands in *such* a fashion, rather than any other, without any hope of stepping across them, or coming out on top, on the bottom, or by sidestepping—and even less by stepping back, or running to safety before them.

In Aristotle's *Peri psuchēs* (*On the Soul*), what touches on touch always comes down to the *unit or unity of one sense* and its appearing *as such.*[1] Yes, it comes to, first, the unit of sense of the sense termed *touch*; second, the unity of sense of the *tangible*; third, the unity of sense, *between the two*, of what refers touch to the tangible; fourth, the credit that we philosophers may here bring to common opinion, to *doxa*, with regard to this sensible unity of a sense.

Let's start over as clearly as possible, then, and quote the texts that lead onto the pathless path of these four obscure aporias:

1. "It is a problem [*aporia*]," Aristotle says, "whether touch is a single sense or a group of senses. It is also a problem, what is the organ of touch; is it or is it not the flesh (including what in certain animals is analogous [substituted for "homologous"—Trans.] with flesh)? On the second view, flesh is 'the medium' [*to metaxu*] of touch, the real organ being situated farther inward" (*Peri psuchēs* 2.11.422b).

2. "Nevertheless we are unable clearly to detect [*ouk estin endēlon*] in the case of touch [*tē haphē*] what the single subject [*hupokeimenon*] is which underlies the contrasted qualities and corresponds to sound in the case of hearing" (ibid.).

3. "[Since] that through which the different movements [causing the sensations for the senses other than touch—J. D.] are transmitted is not naturally attached to our bodies, the difference of the various sense-organs is too plain to miss. But in the case of touch [*epi de tēs haphēs*] the obscurity [*adēlon*] remains. . . . no living body could be constructed of air or water; it must be something solid. . . . That they are manifold is clear when we consider touching with the tongue [*epi tēs glōttēs haphē*]" (ibid., 423a).

4. "The following problem might be raised [*aporēseie d' an tis . . .*]. . . . does the perception of all objects of sense take place in the same way, or does it not, e.g., taste and touch requiring contact (as they are commonly thought to do [*kathaper nun dokei*]), while all other senses perceive over a distance? . . . we fancy [*dokoumen*] we can touch objects, nothing coming in between us and them" (ibid., 423a–b).

Aristotle is going to exert himself in questioning this *doxa* and, to a certain extent, in calling it into question. But only to a certain extent, there where what follows could take on the form of a "clear" thesis. Now, this is not always the case; at times the clarity of a proposition conceals another enigma. For example, though it is obvious or "clear" [*dēlon*] that, first, the "organ" of touch is "inward" or internal; second, flesh is but the "medium" of touch; third, "touch has for its object both what is tangible and what is intangible [*tou haptou kai anaptou*]" (ibid., 424a), one keeps asking oneself what "internal" signifies, as well as "medium" or "intermediary," and above all what an "intangible" accessible to touch is—a still touchable un-touchable.

How to touch upon the untouchable? Distributed among an indefinite number of forms and figures, this question is precisely the obsession haunting a thinking of touch—or thinking as the *haunting* of touch. We can only touch on a surface, which is to say the skin or thin peel of a limit (and the expressions "to touch at the limit," "to touch the limit" irresistibly come back as leitmotivs in many of Nancy's texts that we shall have to interpret). But by definition, limit, *limit itself,* seems deprived of a body. Limit is not to be touched and does not touch itself; it does not let itself be touched, and steals away at a touch, which either never attains it or trespasses on it forever.

Let's recall a few definitions, at least, without reconstituting the whole apparatus of distinctions holding sway in Aristotle's *Peri psuchēs.*

Let's first recall that sense, the *faculty* of sensation—the tactile faculty, for example—is only *potential* and not *actual* (ibid., 417a), with the ineluctable consequence that of itself, it does not sense *itself*; it does not auto-affect itself without the motion of an exterior object. This is a far-reaching thesis, and we shall keep taking its measure with regard to touching and "self-touching."

Let's also recall that feeling or sensing *in general,* even before its tactile specification, already lends itself to being taken in two senses, potentially and actually, and always to different degrees (ibid., 417a).

Let's mostly recall that touch was already an exception in the definition of sensible objects [*espèces du sensible*] (each being "in itself" or "accidentally"; "proper" or "common"). Whereas each sense has its proper sensible object [*idion*] (color for vision, sound for the sense of hearing, flavor for the sense of taste), "Touch, indeed, discriminates more than one set of different qualities": its object comprises several different qualities (ibid., 418a). Let's be content with this initial set of signposts by way of an epigraph. Down to this day, these aporetic elements have not stopped spelling trouble, if one can put it like that, in the history of this endless aporia; this will be borne out at every step we take.

For, with this history of touch, we grope along no longer knowing how to set out or what to set forth, and above all no longer able to see through any of it clearly. An epigraph out of breath from the word go, then, to what I renounced trying to write, for a thousand reasons that will soon become apparent. For, to admit the inadmissible, I shall have to content myself with *storytelling*, admitting to failure and renunciation.

Hypothesis: it's going to be a lengthy tale with mythological overtones —"One day, once upon a time . . . " Pruning, omitting, retelling, lengthening, with little stories, with a succession of touches touched up again, off on one tangent and then another, that's how I'm going to sketch the recollections of a short treatise dedicated to Jean-Luc Nancy that I have long been dreaming of writing *peri Peri psuchēs*, which is to say, *around, on the periphery,* and *on the subject of Peri psuchēs—De anima*—a murky, baroque essay, overloaded with telltale stories (wanting to spell trouble), an unimaginable scene that to a friend would resemble what has always been my relation to incredible words like "soul," "mind," "spirit," "body," "sense," "world," and other similar things.

How can one have spent one's life with words as defining, indispensable, heavy and light, yet inexact, as those? With words of which one has to admit that one has never understood anything? And to admit this while discharging oneself of any true guilt in the matter? Is it my fault if these words have never made any sense, I mean to say any *exact* sense—assured or reassuring for me—and have never had any reliable value, no more than the drawings deep in a prehistoric cave of which it would be insane to claim one knows what they mean without knowing who signed them, at some point, to whom they were dedicated, and so forth?

The difference is that I have never been able or dared to touch on these drawings, even be it just to speak of them a little; whereas for the big bad words I have just named (spirit, mind, soul, body, sense, sense as meaning, the senses, the senses of the word "sense," the world, etc.),[2] I dream that one day some statistics will reveal to me how often I made use of them publicly and failed to confess that I was not only unsure of their *exact* meaning (and "being"! I was forgetting the name of being! Yet along with touch, it is everywhere a question of "being," of course, of beings, of the present, of its presence and its *presentation,* its *self-presentation*), but was fairly sure that this was the case with everybody—and increasingly with those who read me or listen to me.

Now, we never give in to just "anything whatever": rigor is de rigueur; and, to speak like Nancy, so is exactitude. "Exactitude" (we'll come to it) is *his* word and *his* thing. He has reinvented, reawoken, and resuscitated them. That in a way is perhaps my thesis. It is thus necessary to explain—and that may be this book's sole ambition—how Nancy understands the word "exact" and what he intends by it. I believe this to be rather new—like a resurrection. "Exact" is the probity of his signature.

PART I

This Is—of the Other

§ 1 Psyche

"Around her, with such exact and cruel knowledge"

My narrative with its mythological overtones—One day, once upon a time . . . —might thus revolve *around* an event, as it should, but an event both virtual and current, more or less than real. Around something but also somebody, a person or mask, a role, *persona*, a woman no doubt, and both the thing and she would answer to the name Psyche.

Psyche: stake between Aristotle and Nancy, in and on the margin, in a circumspect and circumferential approach to the soul such as Jean-Luc Nancy's "De l'âme" [On the Soul], corresponding and responding to, re-plying to without naming it, Aristotle's *De anima* (or *Peri psuchēs*).

This is also a gift for Nancy, who, as we know, has written a "Psyche"— a female Psyche [*une* Psyche], because Psyche figures there under a femi-nine proper name, on a single page, first in *Première livraison*,[1] then in *Le poids d'une pensée* [The Weight of a Thought],[2] and finally in *Corpus*.[3]

The prime reference of Nancy's "Psyche," its point of departure, is al-ways a sort of Freudian aphorism. A point of departure, but it's as if Nancy, the better to launch himself forward, stopped short one day, para-lyzed by emotion, confronted with Freud's sentence "Psyche ist aus-gedehnt, weiss nichts davon" [Psyche is extended, knows nothing about it]. He starts off, then begins again, more than once, compulsively, always beginning by freezing, by gathering together his body, like a runner at the starting block. *Corpus* reinstates Freud's dictum more faithfully in the course of one of the numerous revivals of the same meditation—tireless, aston-ished, admiring—that this late note by Freud (for which he never gives the reference) sparks in Nancy.[4] He quotes the last sentence in a note comprising only four, four lines in all. Freud wrote it on a single sheet, on

August 22, 1938, one year before his death. Nancy thus tirelessly quotes the last sentence of a sick man's penultimate note, which almost looks like that of a dying man. Later on we shall read it *in extenso*. Freud's very last note, the one that follows, comprising fewer than two lines, was written on the same day. It terms "mystic," or perhaps it defines in this way *anything* "mystical," the obscure self-perception of the realm outside the ego, the id, unless it is, as the Standard Edition translates it, the realm outside the I and the id: "Mysticism is the obscure self-perception of the realm outside the ego, of the id" (Mystik die dunkle Selbstwahrnehmung des Reiches ausserhalb des Ichs, des Es).[5]

Would these aphorisms interest us as much as they do if they were not elliptical, and more than ever testamentary, as aphorisms almost always appear to be? And above all, if like the *Psyche* of whom they speak and whose extension they couch in words, they did not also keep silence, in their very words, on a bed? On the extension of a deathbed? On an extension extended [*une étendue étendue*] on its deathbed?

In the three cases, in Nancy's three texts, it all begins with what is extended, and more precisely with Psyche's being extended. Psyche *is extended*, stretched out (*ausgedehnt, étendue*). In her essence, she is *some* extension [de *l'étendue*] (*extensio*). She is made extended, made of extension. She is the extension/extended—noun and attribute. To express in his language something that would probably make Descartes spin in his grave, extension is the essence, the substance or essential attribute, of the soul that answers to the proper name Psyche.

Let us quote *in extenso* the first occurrence, the *princeps*—the first edition, as it were—in *Première livraison*.

Psyche

"Psyche ist ausgedehnt, weiss nichts davon," reads a late [*posthume*] note of Freud's. The psyche is extended, knows nothing about it. Everything thus ends with this brief tune:

Psyche ist ausgedehnt, weiss nichts davon.

Psyche [*Psyche*] is extended, *partes extra partes*; she is nothing but a dispersion of indefinitely parceled-out locations in places that divide themselves and never interpenetrate. No fitting inside anything, no overlap; everything is outside another outside—anyone can calculate their order and report on their relations. Only Psyche knows nothing of this; for her, there are no relations between these places, these locations, these pieces of a plane.

Psyche is extended in the shade of a walnut tree, as the daylight fades. She lies at rest; the slight movements of sleep have half exposed her bosom. Flustered and mischievous, all at once, Eros contemplates her. Psyche knows nothing of this. Her sleep is so deep that it has even robbed her of any abandon in her pose.

Psyche is extended in her coffin. Soon it is going to be shut. Among those present, some are hiding their faces, others are keeping their eyes desperately fixed on Psyche's body. She knows nothing of this—and that is what everyone knows around her, with such exact and cruel knowledge.[6]

Thus the first apparition, in *Première livraison*: "extended," Psyche "lies at rest," asleep or dead, *as if* dead, before Eros, who "contemplates" her. Apparently *without touching her*.

Soon she is dead: "extended in her coffin. Soon it is going to be shut."

Let us bear in mind the component *tôt* ("early, soon") in this *bientôt* ("soon, soon enough"). What does *tôt* mean? Before *bientôt* or *aussitôt* ("at once, all too soon"), what does *tôt* convey to us? This is one of the strangest words—or rather [*plutôt*] a lexical beehive—in our [French] language. Precocity, promptitude, precipitation, haste, or imminence—*bientôt* seems to signify an *advance*, and we cannot be sure that it gives us time for the future. *Tôt* is said to be an adverb of time. It is, but it so little says the time, it gives so little time—almost none—that one would think it is gobbled up in advance by time's other, which is to say, space: burned, overtaken, parched, consumed by what is extended. And incidentally, in the case of the last of the five sequences beginning with (twice) "Psyche ist ausgedehnt" or (three times) "Psyche est étendue" ("Psyche is extended in her coffin. Soon [*bientôt*] it is going to be shut"), it is too soon to read any future into the *bientôt* that follows. "It is going" ("soon *it is going* to be shut") is a present tense first of all, grammatically speaking: "it is going" [*on va*], "let's go" [*on y va*], *presently*. What is going to happen then, what won't be long in happening, what appears imminent, that indeed will no longer happen to Psyche, who is already dead. For if something happens presently that was already on the verge of happening, it's the end. "Soon" [*bientôt*] neither allows nor leaves time. Here "soon" [*tôt*] would mean death, even the end of a dead woman.

Look up its etymology, in fact: the usual sources most often refer to absolute speed, to the instant, to the timeless time of a flame (*tostus* means burned, and toasted, from *torreo*, consumed by fire, or incinerated—in a blazing immediacy that pulls out all the stops; and that is why one has *arrived all too soon*, in a present not yet present but no longer a future); or less often, as Friedrich Diez's etymology suggests, discrediting the former etymology but finding itself discredited in its turn by Littré [*Dictionnaire de la langue française* (1859–72)], the reference will be to *totus* and *cito*, that is, with all speed. With quasi-infinite speed, without leaving any time for motion.

In any case, that is what *tôt* means to say, whatever its etymology may be—absolute speed going faster than time, precipitation that brings us to the point of arrival before a finished sentence can finish anticipating, before anything has had time to happen. No sooner said, time is no longer given. Nor left: too late. All at once it is too late. Doesn't Psyche also speak to us posthumously of a certain belatedness?

Psyche's co-appearance in these three works would call for an interminable analysis. It is the same—threefold—Psyche, a woman, and each time there is a reminder, as Freud puts it, that she is extended (*ausgedehnt*). But each time (and three times the first sentence resonates in French, "Psyche est étendue . . . " ["Psyche is extended . . . "]) the mise-en-scène differs, as do the tableau and the implicit narrative.

Here, in *Première livraison*, is Psyche's impassiveness, all extended: she is not only extended, she is extension itself, the reclining one, woman laid up on her bed, neither analysand nor lover, but almost a recumbent statue, in the setting sun: "Psyche is extended in the shade of a walnut tree, as the daylight fades."

This impassiveness pertains neither only to the pure *exteriority* of her being nor only to the absolute outside where she maintains herself: "everything is outside another outside," Nancy says, plying the formula of a folding that has to be taken into account: the being outside another outside forms the fold of the becoming-inside of the first outside, and so forth. Hence, by reason of this folding, here are the *interiority effects* of a structure made up of nothing but surfaces and outsides without insides. The superficies of these surfaces, as noted earlier, are limits—exposed, as such, to a touch that can only ever leave them intact, untouched and untouchable.

Psyche's impassiveness does not only pertain to the *exposition* of her being *partes extra partes*. It is not only from her disseminal divisibility (" . . . places that divide themselves and never interpenetrate each other"), an irreducible *divisibility*, that all the rest, it seems to me, will have to follow. It is essentially, and for those very reasons, from a *nonknowledge*, her own unknown, self-ignorance—the unconscious. Four times on this short page—for this piece of writing covers less than a page—it is said that she *knows nothing* of this: "The psyche is extended, knows nothing about it. Everything thus ends with this brief tune: 'Psyche ist ausgedehnt, weiss nichts davon.' . . . Only Psyche knows nothing of this. . . . Psyche knows nothing of this. . . . She knows nothing of this—and that is what everyone knows around her, with such exact and cruel knowledge."

If Psyche remains alone, it is first because she is alone in knowing nothing of this. There again the meaning of the sentence bursts. Into bits, I mean. Psyche is the only one who knows nothing (nothing of herself, of her extension, of her recumbent being-extended); but further, by being alone *in* knowing nothing of this, she is also alone *for* not knowing anything of this. She finds herself alone without knowing it; her solitude is radical *because* she knows nothing, nothing of herself, of her extension, of *that which* others know; she doesn't know *what* they know and *that* they know, that is, the content and the fact of their knowledge. *On the subject of herself.* Indeed, she is the submissive subject (extended object), the support or subjectile of their knowledge but not of hers because on her own she knows nothing of herself—on the subject of herself.

In other words, those around her, peripheral to her, who are not touching her while gazing at her all the same—they know something about her. They know it and their knowledge is *exact* (one of Nancy's master words, which we'll come back to frequently: *exactitude* is this thinker's thing, his big deal—he thinks *exactly* something other than what one thinks in general or ponders too easily under the word "exactitude," and yet . . .). They know this with exact and cruel knowledge. "Exact" is not the last word, just one of the last. What do they know? Is this "they" masculine or neuter? Is Psyche only a feminine figure surrounded by men, and first exposed to Eros? Perhaps "they," "those present" know *the very selfsame thing* that she doesn't know, but know above all *that* she doesn't know, the very fact that everything taking place is *unknown to her*: indeed, everything is taking *place*, that is to say, extends, "in places that divide themselves," "between these places, these locations. . . . " And thus "they" know *that* she doesn't know about herself *that* very thing *which* is to be known without her knowing it, namely, that she is extended. They know her unconscious, her being-unconscious, Psyche's unconscious. They see her not seeing herself, that is to say, not seeing herself extended; they know her where she neither knows herself nor knows herself to be seen.

But the vision of this extended body becomes almost intolerable to them. She—she has no self-relation: she doesn't see, hear, taste, or touch herself;

in a word, she doesn't feel herself. She lacks the sense of herself, which amounts to saying that the sense is what she lacks. And no doubt sense. And the insensate (as much as insensible) support of this subjectile that knows nothing and sees nothing of itself becomes almost insupportable to them.

Can we imagine an extension that is untouchable? Imagining is neither thinking nor knowing, to be sure, but it is in no way a complete absence of thought or knowledge. Can one *figure* for oneself an untouchable extension, if you will? It is difficult, except (as Descartes, Kant, and a few others would have it) if an intelligible extension without a body is at issue, precisely there where the understanding passes imagination and sensibility; and except for some *insensible sensible* (Hegel, Marx, and so on). But inversely, is any touching imaginable that might touch something not extended? And further, to announce questions that will come back to us like boomerangs, what is the way to organize together the following four concepts or philosophemes: *extension, partes extra partes, to touch,* and *to touch oneself*? Soon enough, in a combinatory play closing up around a vacant center, their association and dissociation will compel us into a dizzying ambulation. If commonsensically I can only touch some extended *thing* (what is termed "body" and "material body"), it does not follow that every extension is touchable (as I said a moment ago about intelligible extension); nor that any extension is structured following the intrinsic exteriority, which is essential, of *partes extra partes*. Certainly, the living body, for example, comprises some *partes extra partes*, but it also has a relation to itself that is often thought no longer to be divisible in this way. Should I touch a living body, should a living body touch itself, then there is no assurance that extension is transcended—but there is even less assurance that the touching or self-touching touches in the way of *partes extra partes*. Soon, blows or caresses will force us to leave suspended any hasty conclusion on the subject at hand.

Among those present, some are hiding their faces, others are keeping their eyes desperately fixed on Psyche's body.

Psyche the untouchable, Psyche the intact: wholly corporeal, she *has* a body, she *is* a body, but an intangible one. Yet she is not only untouchable for others. She doesn't touch *herself,* since she is wholly extended *partes extra partes*. Those who are "present" to her refuse to see her or behold her desperately, and if their "knowledge" is so "exact and cruel," then it's not only because they know that she knows, sees, or touches nothing, not even her own body or anything properly her own. It's because this scene appears while a song of mourning resounds. Twice the "brief tune" resonates in German, for Psyche's name is written in German, without an accent, and moreover this is a "late [*posthume*] note of Freud's": "Psyche ist ausgedehnt, weiss nichts davon." This is about a passage, it is *after* Psyche's death, and the scene rather looks like an entombment.

Psyche is extended in her coffin.

This incarnation, this incorporation of Psyche's, a corporeal yet untouchable Psyche, is "posthumous." It is telling us perhaps, whether or not Nancy meant to say it, that *Peri psuchēs* (the title of Aristotle's text that dominates all our philosophical thinking about touch and every psych-ology as a discourse on the life of the living) must be reread or rewritten in this "posthumous" situation, in which Psyche must be regarded—if this is possible and if this death is not too unbearable—as an extension that is untouchable and from the outset intangible for herself. And those who bring themselves to be "present" to Psyche—

> Among those present, some are hiding their faces, others are keeping their eyes desperately fixed on Psyche's body. She knows nothing of this—and that is what everyone knows *around her,* with such exact and cruel knowledge. [I am emphasizing *around her,* of course.—J. D.]

—take a stand *around her, Peri psuchēs.*
They are there *subject* to her. They now *hold* onto her subject. They *hold* a session, a council, a conference on the subject of her. Just as they take up the places *around* this locus where nothing takes place but place, that is, extension, one can also sense that they *take the place of*—but of whom? Of what? What does this metonymy announce? For whom and for what is it in mourning, if every metonymy remains a sign of mourning?

(Metonymies are in mourning, at least, for a proper sense or name. And we shall see that this book is also about the metonymies of touch. It started out as an offering for Jean-Luc Nancy, for him alone, quite uniquely for him, and by running the risk of publication, it is already exposing itself to so many other metonymies. Hence the worrying in this unsteady gesture, in its tonalities and affect.)

It remains that she, Psyche, is the subject. She remains the subject inasmuch as it is rest ("rests," "lies"—reposing, lying, resting itself).[7] As for them, they are holding on, standing by her subject, not by her bedside [*à son chevet*], as we might say, but at the edge of her being-extended, of her cot, or her coffin. Knowing but one thing about her, which is that she knows nothing of it, they watch her and seek, just as we do, to give thought to the subject of the subject, and think about and around psyche (*peri psuchēs*), and think about "touching" and what it means to say. But touching is what they are not doing, since they are thinking; and they are thinking—that is their postulate—that in order to think touching, this thinking about touch must not touch. They are also asking themselves what this (that is, touching) might see in seeing and have to do with it, a seeing that some accept resolutely whereas others are "hiding their faces." They are asking themselves what touching might have to do with seeing and the other senses.

But they already know that this thinking of touch, this thought of what "touching" means, must touch on the untouchable. Aristotle's *Peri psuchēs* had already insisted on this: both the tangible and the intangible are the objects of touch (*hē haphē tou haptou kai anaptou*) (*Peri psuchēs* 424a). Once this incredible "truth" has been uttered, it will resonate down to the twentieth century, even within discourses apparently utterly foreign to any Aristotelianism, as we shall see.

How can this be? To ponder touching while touching on, or tampering with, the untouchable—would this be the absolute injunction? Doesn't this injunction dictate the impossible? Does it pertain to a posthumous history of Psyche or *Peri psuchēs*? And does posthumous here signify that Aristotle's legacy, no matter how undeniable, is really dead? Or does it mean that it is time to inherit it differently? What could this history of touch have to do with inheritance?

In any case, it was time to start with a tableau of mourning, not mourning for someone, male or female, some determined living being, some singularity or other, but mourning life itself, and what in life is the very living thing, the living spring, the breath of life. Psyche is also a common proper name, designating the principle of life, breath, the soul, the animation of the animal. That is why everything begins and must begin there. And it is indeed there that *Peri psuchēs*—so often translated in our tradition in Latin as *De anima*—begins. This treatise begins by explaining to us, at the very outset, what one is to begin with. For, if knowledge is among the most beautiful and most dignified things, if knowing one thing is worth more than knowing another by reason of its accuracy or by reason of the admirable quality of its objects, then knowledge of the soul must properly be entitled to the highest rank—this can be read at the beginning of *Peri psuchēs*. Knowledge of the soul greatly serves the knowledge of all truth. First, it serves the knowledge of nature because the soul is the principle proper to living beings (*esti gar hoion archē tōn zōiōn*) (*Peri psuchēs* 402a). Aristotle thus proposes to study, on the one hand, the traits "proper" to the soul, the ones that define the essence or the substance (*ousia*) of the psyche, and on the other hand, those traits pertaining to entire living beings. This beginning of *Peri psuchēs* assumes that the soul (*psuchē*)—at least the soul of the living being named man—can have self-knowledge. When one then comes to the part of the soul that "thinks" and "knows," one will deal with the intellect that is separable and is "able to think itself" in its eternity or immortality (ibid., 429b). Certainly, Aristotle's psyche, like Nancy's, is impassive (*apathēs*), insensitive, and indifferent to suffering, within its noetic and active principle, there where it thinks, thinks itself, and knows. But it is also separable, and when it is severed—which is also the moment of death, but here a death that doesn't happen—it re-becomes "immortal and eternal" (ibid., 430a).

It is appropriate, at this point, to recall what is evident: Aristotle's *Peri psuchēs* is a treatise on the pure life of the living.

Now, Nancy's Psyche sees herself treated as a dead woman.

This will have some consequences, both close and distant ones, for *psycho*-logy, *psycho*-analysis—that goes without saying—but also for a number of "modern" languages and our current discourses on the "living body" (*Leib*), whether the ear grasps it as "body proper" or the "flesh." The principle or drive to expropriation introduced there forthwith by death, the other or time, is certainly hard to tolerate, but, as we shall see, it's less resistant to thought than what complicates an *incarnation* even more, which is to say, the prosthesis, the metonymic substitute, the autoimmune process, and *technical* survival.

The *technē* of bodies, ecotechnics, and the intrusion of *L'intrus* are, for example, among the names that Nancy bestows on these.[8]

§ 2 Spacings

*The Incommensurable, Syncope,
and Words Beginning with 'ex-'*

May I, even before starting out again, be permitted the space and the freedom of a long parenthesis here to announce, at some remove, a possible destination? It is justified precisely by the attention accorded to *space*, or rather to *spacing*, the absolute condition of any extension and any *partes extra partes*, as well as the condition of this strange Psyche. A further justification for the parenthesis is the link between the spacing motif and an unusual thinking of *freedom*.

One of Nancy's rare references to Aristotle is an even rarer one to *Peri psuchēs*, in which he reminds us, without alluding to touch himself, that "Aristotle's *psuchē*—a substance [in the sense of form] of a living body—was united with the body like 'wax and the shape given to it.'"[1] And it is also in these last pages of his *Ego sum* that Nancy first revisits (so to speak) his own reference to Freud's note.[2]

Indeed, this point is quite significant, and accordingly, no doubt, we shall have to give sustained attention to it later on. Naturally, although the word "touch" does not appear there, the stakes of his demonstration do touch on what "touching" may mean. It deals with a subtle but firm distinction between *orality* and *buccality*, between *os* and *bucca*, the latter being more "primitive" than the former. The mouth *speaks* but it does so *among other things*. It can also breathe, eat, spit. It has "not always been speaking," not always been an *oral* agency: "the instant speaking begins, an unstable and mobile opening forms. For a few instants, nothing is discernible; ego will not say anything. All that ego does is open up this cavity" (Nancy, "Unum quid," p. 162). The mouth that can scream, the closed mouth at the breast, thus opens up before the "oral stage." The mouth attaches itself to the breast in an "identification more ancient than any identification with a face," the "mouth slightly open, detaching itself from the breast, in a first smile, a first funny face, the future of which is thinking" (ibid.).

At this point, a footnote refers us to "Psyche" and to Freud's "posthumous" note. Now, although the mouth is touching (but let me stress once again that then, in 1979, Nancy does not make use of the word "touch" in this context and thematically),[3] it is also detaching itself from the breast. It interrupts the contact in order to speak-think, in a first opening, an initial and original *spacing*: "And there, what comes to pass is that [the ego] spaces itself out [ce qui s'y passe c'est qu'il s'y espace]. 'Spacing brings about the free, the open, [the spacious,] for man's settlement and dwelling' (Heidegger).[4] But man is that which spaces itself out and never dwells elsewhere, perhaps, but in this spacing, in the *areality* of the mouth" (Nancy, "Unum quid," pp. 162–63).[5]

At this moment, then, the point where he puts in place a concept of *areality* that will organize a new logic of space (the logic of the ego's "exteriority" as well: "spacing of places," "distancing and strangeness that make up place," "tracings," and so forth), we have just come across a guarded and uneasy reference to Heidegger—almost an objection. It seems to me that this sets up, ten years in advance, Nancy's great problematic in *L'expérience de la liberté* (*The Experience of Freedom*).[6] This work will also be one of the strongest to have it out with Heidegger, in a debate (*Auseinandersetzung*) that is among the most necessary, that is to say, a debate that harries and worries things so as to question them or call them into question, *most closely*, efficiently, and effectively, *in effect, indeed,* starting from a comprehensive, understanding, patient, and tireless reading—a generous reading.

Generous? Yes, generous: this word is all the more compelling since a certain "generosity of being" becomes the ultimate justification of his "experience of freedom." This generosity is no longer simply the virtue of a subject, or what Descartes might have grasped by this word. This generosity allows one to *configure*, and indissociably think together, the *gift* (or rather the *offering*), *decision, spacing,* and *freedom*:

It is a generosity of *ethos* more than an ethic of generosity. . . . It gives freedom, or *offers* it. For the gift is never purely and simply given. . . . It is thus *kept* [*se garde*]. . . . One must *keep* [*garder*] the singular present in which the gift as such is *kept* [*gardé*], that is, offered. . . . The offering is the inestimable price of the gift. The generosity of being offers nothing other than existence, and the offering, as such, is *kept* [*gardée*] in freedom. All this means: a space is offered whose spacing, each time, only takes place by way of a decision. But there is no "the" Decision. There is, each time, my own (*a singular mine*)— yours [*la tienne*], his or hers, ours. And this is the generosity of being. (Nancy, *Experience of Freedom*, pp. 146–47; slightly modified—Trans.)[7]

I have emphasized the four occurrences of the verb *garder* [keep, guard, keep guard, ward off—Trans.] that are essential in my eyes. They point at the same time toward truth's *verity* [*veritas, Wahrheit*], which is a *guard,* as the word indicates, and to *economy*. Must a gift be kept? In truth? *Must* one keep or guard, as the text says? And is this keeping compatible with the "withdrawal," "retreat," "holding back," and "retaining," which are also in question? Questions.

And yet, when I reread this fundamental chapter, "Decision, Desert, Offering," followed by "Fragments," with admiration (some will say, another Cartesian word!); when I follow through, step by step, with grateful recognition at every instant, I wonder. Doesn't my timid, reticent concern about the *word* "generosity" (it is the word I worry about and not necessarily the concept at work in it) pertain to the very reserve that the *congenial* motif and the *good movement* of "fraternity" always inspire in me? I mean to say fraternity in the greatest tradition, certainly, and all its restorations, but still, in spite of the differences, in Levinas, Blanchot, and others.[8] In this conclusion of *The Experience of Freedom,* incidentally, the reference to fraternity is as insistent as it is cautious and awkward. While Nancy is very conscious of what may appear to be "ridiculous" or suspect in the French republican motto, and of what makes one "smile" in the word "fraternity," he nevertheless makes the suggestion that "thought" should be given to fraternity in another way, to "fraternity in abandonment, of abandonment" (Nancy, *Experience of Freedom*, p. 168). Briefly, what embarrasses me in the word "generosity," as in the word "fraternity," finally amounts to the same thing. In both cases, one acknowledges and nods to some genealogy, some filiation, a principle having to do with "birth," whether or not it is "natural," as it is often thought to be. Above all, the word privileges some "virility." Even if he is an orphan, a brother is a son and therefore a man. In order to include the sister or woman or daughter, one has to change words—generously—and then change the word "generosity" itself while one is at it. Indeed, if one gives or offers because one is naturally, genially, congenitally, or ontologically *generous*, at birth; if it's because one has to give or has something to give, because *one can* give, thanks to a power, a force, or a capacity related to giving, to having what it takes to give, with sovereign power; once giving is *possible*, or there is a "generosity of being"; then does one offer, does one still give? Here, like the gift, like spacing, "freedom" or "decision" perhaps presupposes the interruption of generosity as well as fraternity. To give, out of *generosity* or because *one can* give (what one has) is no longer to give. Giving is possible only where it remains *im-possible*, and not even im-possible *as such*.⁹ It here comes down to the impossibility of the "as such," to the fate of phenomenology as much as ontology.

Besides the insistence on *keeping guard*, a suspension of the constative utterance as the enunciation of a thesis gives way to an address in the familiar form [*tutoiement*] ("yours [*la tienne*], his or hers [*la sienne*], ours," and so on) at the heart of Nancy's demonstration will have been noted. The indicative mood of the thesis is suspended, not abandoned; the address is embedded in the analysis. But in the allocution, there is a certain challenge, which will have some importance for us later on. This movement does not proceed rhetorically. It often carries with it (and already recalls, with a change of scenes) an essential displacement in the gesture of the thinking. To bring this point home, it helps (though it does not suffice) to underscore to what degree philosophical discourse has excluded (one might even say prohibited) this strophic turn of the apostrophe, as well as "thou" and "you," from Aristotle to Kant, from Descartes to Hegel and to Heidegger. Even today, this prohibition extends to many others. Exceptions—if any—are rare; we would learn much from their inventory.

"The free" [*das Freie*] is the motif (the "semantic root") that Heidegger keeps until the end, whereas he has left by the wayside the theme, at least, of the essence of freedom. This leaves a gap, into which Nancy proceeds with his original meditation on a freedom that is no longer a subject's or someone's freedom (he says daringly: "In this sense, the stone is free" [Nancy, *Experience of Freedom*, p. 159]). In many places, but more particularly in the chapter titled "The Space Left Free by Heidegger" (ibid., pp. 39ff.), Nancy directly or indirectly questions the paradox of this "free space" that Heidegger maintains as a motif after he has let go of the motif of "freedom." Is it the space, or the place, in which it would be appropriate to engage thought?

End of this long parenthesis.

While *Peri psuchēs* is thus a treatise on the pure life of the living, it recurrently accords to touch a status that sets it apart. Touch may well exist apart from the other senses, but Aristotle stresses that without it, no other sense would exist. As has been noted, all animals possess this sense, which is also the sense of nutrition.

Why is it that, unlike ten years later, Nancy does not seem to have been preoccupied with touch—at least not as a theme and by this name—at the time when he wrote *Psyche* (1978) and *Ego sum* (1979), or even in briefly alluding specifically to the problem of life in Aristotle's *Peri psuchēs*?

The major question, at the end of *Ego sum* as well as in *Psyche*, seems to come together under the heading of one noun, namely, *extension*, and it is an incredible extension, that of the soul or thought. Underscoring what is paradoxical and unique, that is, incommensurable, in such an extension is at issue then. It seems that one can only touch an extended body or some part of it, but not every extension is necessarily touchable. There is an intelligible or *pure, sensible* extension, a nonempirical extension.

Psyche's extension—that is, that of Psyche the character in *Psyche*—has no measure in common with anything, and above all not with any other extension. And yet, as the term indicates and demands, must "Psyche" not share at least some trait with what one commonly terms "extension," with the everyday sense of extension? The conceptual passage, if one may say so, in this argumentation between the extension of the body (which is easy for common sense to apprehend, which is an essential attribute of the corporeal substance for Descartes and the eidetic component of any material thing and any transcendent and tangible *res* for Husserl) and the extension of the psyche or thinking (which is a paradoxical extension resisting intuition, perception, and consciousness) is what exceeds any measure in them both—and therefore exceeds common measure. That is their common incommensurability. This incommensurability—as incommensurability of extension, as incommensurability between two ways of being extended, two spaces or two spacings—goes through a thinking of *place* [*lieu*], as a place or locus that is reduced neither to objective extension nor to objective space. This place must be *spacing* before it is space; it must open an opening, as it were, an interval, which is to say an apparently incorporeal, though not intelligible, extension—thus neither sensible nor intelligible.

The mouth would here be this place, this unique place: cavity, gaping place, chasm, abyss, opening (these words are part of Nancy's lexicon in these pages); hole [*trou*], orifice (these additional words that do not appear, it seems, at least not here, might point toward other resources). As a unique place, even before one distinguishes between *bucca* and *os*, the mouth would thus be the common place of the incommensurables in question, that is, body and soul (spirit or mind or thought), and so forth. "The incommensurable extension of thinking is the opening of the mouth" (Nancy, "Unum quid," p. 161).[10]

Let us not forget the final demonstration that orients *Ego sum* (a work that can be read both as a new meditation on fiction, fictitiousness, or fictionality at work within the *cogito* [i.e., of Descartes][11] and as an experience, an experiment, and an abyssal "provocation" of what is called the mouth): without the mouth, one cannot conceive of the union of the soul and the body—of the "comme un seul tout" in the duc de Luynes's translation (that is, "seemingly a single whole," "a quasi-single whole," or [in the Haldane and Ross translation] "seem[ing] to compose with it one whole"), of the "conjunctum et quasi permixtum," or of the "quasi permixtio."[12] Nancy will make this the obsessive motif of his book—in truth, of the very *ego sum* itself—while to the "quasi," to the fable of this quasi-fiction, he will accord a decisive authority or a daunting pertinence.

Since I am playing at tracking down all the tropological uses of touch, all the times Nancy resorts to it—this tactile metaphor or metonymy, which some may find hackneyed and weakly invested—it may be appropriate here to point out that, just as he lends all the requisite attention to the duc de Luynes's translation of the famous passage in Descartes's Sixth Meditation, notably when it transfers—and effaces—the *quasi* from "quasi permixtum" to "unum quid," yielding "comme un seul tout,"[13] here Nancy quasi-touches, if I can put it that way, the figure or trope (metaphor or metonymy) of touch as if with a distracted, barely grazing hand:

> As for the Latin text, it says: I am quasi-intermixed with my body, so that along with it, I make up a certain unity—something like a "unum quid." The displacement [of *quasi*] does not *touch* on anything important, and it is in dependence on *quasi* that the Latin *unum quid* is thought, if not [grammatically] constructed. Indeed, Descartes wrote this *unum quid*, and we shall, so to speak, keep our eyes fixed on it. (Nancy, "Unum quid," p. 133)

The emphasis on "touch" is mine. Here, "to touch" means to say to tamper with, to change, to displace, to call into question; thus it is invariably a setting in motion, a kinetic experience. I would further note that the metaphor of sight may not be more strictly appropriate here than the metaphor of touch, yet it is only with respect to the "eyes fixed" that Nancy considers that he can decently make a concession: " . . . we shall, *so to speak*, keep our eyes fixed on it."

We are not through with this question, which is to say, with knowing whether the "quasi" of the "quasi permixtio" of the soul and the body is seen, or whether it is rather touched or lets itself be touched. As a close game will play itself out between these orifices, that is, the mouth and the eyes, these quasi-placeless places, these bordered openings, these girdled spacings, that's one of the reasons why we began with the scene of the kiss on the mouth—or on the eyes, between single eyes only, making eyes, eye to eye, eye on eye.

The common incommensurability (if this expression makes sense), common to thinking and extension, this incommensurability of which they partake and which will allow one to say that the *psyche is extended*, comes down to the "quasi permixtio" of the union. What is it? The mixing or the "quasi"—the "as if" of this mixing? Shall I be going too far myself in rendering or feigning to render the full value of the figure of the *exorbitant* that impresses itself on Nancy when he describes the effects of the incommensurable, an incommensurable that is absolutely unique, singular, and irreplaceable, all at the same time—and yet common to more than one incommensurable, here to the soul and the body?

So let us read, let us see, and let us listen to the "exorbitant," to exorbitant thinking. We shall often be able to verify that Nancy is the thinker of the *exorbitant* and *exactitude* at the same time, even if these two values seem antagonistic, at times, to anyone in a hurry. If there is any antagonism, then it is *tense; it is that toward which* Nancy's exigency or his very ethics *tend*. Exactitude is extreme exigency: let us term it an exorbitant exactitude—his own, his signature—or rather, exactitude faithful to the excess of the exorbitant. With the strictest probity, he goes to the exorbitant's appointment [il se rend . . . au rendez-vous de l'exorbitant]. We recall that the concept of the "ex-scribed" (a word that Nancy formed or coined) finds itself increasingly inscribed at the heart and inmost core of this writing that thinks: there remains a need to wonder about the body, the force, the compulsive drive that sets this syllable *ex* in motion and keeps it alive. Of course, we shall have to configure this syllable in accordance with a whole thinking of ex-pulsion, ex-pression, outward ex-cretion—this thinking itself conditions the "sense of the world"—and with the thinking of "excess" that "inexorably" pushes outwardly, until it is *throwing* or *jettisoning* (eject-ing, dejecting, objecting, abjecting) the ego's subjectivity into *exteriority*.[14] The outline of this discourse adjoins certain propositions by Paul Valéry, in "Bouche" [Mouth],[15] as well as Heidegger's thinking on *Geworfenheit*, on an "opening in and through which *I* is indeed properly *thrown*" (Nancy, "Unum quid," pp. 162–63). Here Nancy underscores the trait, or more ex-actly the traced outline or *tracings*, of this exteriorization of exteriority. Al-ready, the movement in *ex-* is scored as a sort of writing, and the concept of the *ex-scribed* in rehearsal, although it will only appear under this name later on, to unsettle every phenomenology of touch:

> The subject gives way in this abyssal chasm. But ego utters itself in it: ego ex-teriorizes itself there, which does not signify that it carries to the outside the visible face of an invisible interior. This literally signifies that ego makes or makes itself *exteriority*, spacing of places, distancing and strangeness that make up place, and thus space itself, first spatiality of the *tracings* of a veritable out-line in which—as in no other—ego may come forth, trace itself out, and think itself. (Nancy, "Unum quid," p. 163)

As we shall note in a moment, it is in this reflexive fold ("trace *itself* out," "think *itself*") that the question of touch, of "self-touching," has taken up residence beforehand. And on the score of *ex-*, let me also refer to the remarkable passage that draws away the "modern subject," that is, the Cartesian subject, from any faculty and any substantiality: "Cartesian experience is the experience of *sub* without any stasis or stance. Up to the end and without any reserve (*experior*), *sub* tests what it can be. Ego is the proof of *subex*" (ibid., p. 158).

This comes down to (and goes without saying—but that will be said later) another way of approaching ex-istence.

In the passage that I was preparing to quote, these last words in *ex* come precisely to correspond with the logic and the topological setup of the *ex-orbitant*, of the "inexorably" exorbitant:

> There is no *measure* to expect here. The incommensurable is what makes pos-sible the "quasi permixtio" of the union, making it a thinking that is incom-mensurable itself, that is exorbitant in relation to thinking. In the "quasi per-mixtio," thinking *is extended.*
> This may have been what Freud sensed when he wrote in a posthumous note: "The psyche is extended, knows nothing about it." Such a thought could

come to Freud only because he was thinking against the Cartesian subject. But this thought also "came" to Descartes, and in Descartes as in Freud, it inexorably tips over, falling outside, exceeding any psycho*analysis*. (Nancy, "Unum quid," p. 161)[16]

Henceforth there are two questions, *two beats in time* at least, for the same question.

First, how do two incommensurabilities—of psychical thinking and of the body—unite in an extension that is itself incommensurable? At this stage of the question, Nancy's answer is original yet clear and developed, and even insistent. It is contained in a single word (itself obscure and gaping): mouth—embouchure of the mouth, originary spacing of a mouth opening (*itself*) between the lips and at the other's breasts. It may be necessary here to distinguish between *extension* and *spacing*.

But *secondly*, as the question is generated a second time (that is, what about touch in all this? How does this double extension touch or *self*-touch? Is it opened by being touched/touching *itself*?), its answer still appears elliptical, virtual, and prethematic in *Ego sum*. That's my hypothesis, and I would like to support it with a few quotations.

First again, therefore: the mouth's answer to the first question is held between a nonspeaking mouth (*bucca*, without the orality of *os*) and a mouth that starts detaching itself from the breast and is ajar even before the "oral stage." Beating time, the opening of the mouth responds to the lips moving—the other's lips, the mother's lips at birth, then mine, if I may say so—always nearest to birth into the world, and from a mother, a noun and name Nancy never pronounces. Isn't birth into the world the first ex-pulsion? The word "mother" does not appear, despite Nancy's obvious, explicit reference to her (at the time of birth and nursing), despite his reference to the edges of the orifice, to the lips parting and opening the passage for the newborn (the labia between the mother's legs as well as the infant's lips in their first cry), despite his reference to the breasts parting the nursling's mouth. (Note the earlier reference to a silent photograph of the stretched-out, *extended* mother [in "When Our Eyes Touch," n. 2].)

Why? If it is the mother, in any case, who opens the bordering edges as well as the lips of a mouth first described as an opening, then this happens before any figure—not before any identification, but before any "identification with a face," as a later remark specifies.

It is the opening that incommensurabilizes—there where it [*ça*] spaces itself out. The mouth is *at the same time* place and nonplace, it is the locus of a dis-location, the gaping place of the "quasi permixtio" between soul and body, which is to say the incommensurable extension between them and common to both, since the mouth—any mouth, before any orality—opens an opening. More specifically, as a self-opening, it spaces itself out, "opens (*itself*)" and "distends (*itself*)" (my emphasis):

> The incommensurable extension of thinking is the opening of the mouth. The mouth that opens (itself), forming "ego" (other lips had already opened to deliver into the world this "me," when it gave a first cry), is the place or locus of the union, inasmuch as this union opens (*itself*) and distends (*itself*)—and thus "unum quid" comes about. This place is not a place and yet it is not out of place. Within place, in the extension of a face, it makes up a gaping nonplace, a gaping noncase [*la béance d'un non-lieu*]. In this nonplace and noncase, figure (that is, extension, measure) and figurelessness (that is, thought without measure) adjoin and distinguish themselves; they are adjoined through their distinction. The locus of the uttering is formed by the internal dis-location of this reunion. (Nancy, "Unum quid," p. 161)

I don't believe that the said opening *of self* ("opens [*itself*] and distends [*itself*]") signifies autonomy or auto-affection. The nonplace-noncase of this place is also opened by the other. *All at once* auto-affected and hetero-affected, uniting both affections like two lips, it lets itself be opened—hence "thought without measure," hence the incommensurable, hence that which seemingly comes to pass, here, between Aristotle and Descartes. Nancy goes on, making his only reference to Aristotle's *Peri psuchēs*:

> The *psuchē* of the ancients was localized—whichever its bodily organ might be. Aristotle's *psuchē*—a substance [in the sense of form] of a living body—was united with the body like "wax and the shape given to it." The Cartesian soul (whose detailed study would furthermore show several traits carried over from those traditions), as the soul of the one whose being it is to utter, takes up this place-nonplace-noncase of the mouth opening and closing upon "ego sum," then opening and closing a second time at once, repeating, not repeating, "ego existo." This double beat utters the subject; it utters itself as subject.
>   But a mouth is neither a substance nor a figure. *Bucca*—a later, more trivial term—is not *os*. (Nancy, "Unum quid," pp. 161–62)

Here Nancy works on several figures, among several figures of the figure, which is to say of a kind of fictionality and a kind of facticity of *fingere*. Four figures of the figure, at least, belong to this semantic configuration:

1. Figure as the form of extension: Nancy has just said: "figure (that is, extension, measure) and figurelessness (that is, thought without measure)";

2. Figure as fashion—way of fashioning, fashion of the making and doing [*façon de faire, façon du faire*];

3. Figure as trope;

4. Figure as visage [*face*] or face [*visage*].

These figures are inscribed within one another, as when the face becomes a metonymy for the mouth, for example: "But a mouth is neither a substance nor a figure. *Bucca*—a later, more trivial term—is not *os*. *Os, oris*, the mouth of orality, is the face itself taken as metonymy for this mouth it surrounds, carries, and makes visible, the place through which all kinds of substances pass, and first of all the airy substance of discourse" (ibid., p. 162).

Similarly, the self-relation of a mouth that "opens (itself)" or "spaces itself out" draws the figure of the mouth before any figure as visage (orality) and before any identification with a (maternal) face:

> The Freudian child (I won't say the subject) is not initiated in an "oral stage." First of all he or she opens into a mouth, the open mouth of a scream, but also the closed mouth at the breast, with which it is attached in an identification more ancient than any identification with a face—as well as the mouth slightly open, detaching itself from the breast, in a first smile, a first funny face, the future of which is thinking. The mouth is the opening of ego; ego is the opening of the mouth. And there, what comes to pass is that it spaces itself out [*ce qui s'y passe c'est qu'il s'y espace*]. (ibid., p. 162)

Secondly. Nowhere in the analysis that we have just followed (in the last pages of *Ego sum* and the reference to Freud's "The psyche is extended, knows nothing about it"), do we encounter any allusion to touch, at least under this name, since all that the mouth does before orality, all that is abundantly evoked here (eating, sucking, spitting, and so forth) is hardly foreign to tactility. But the word "touching" is not mentioned and "self-touching" even less. It further seems to me that this is the case throughout this book, from beginning to end, despite its preoccupation with the problem of *sentir*, "feeling," "sensing," and not just in the Cartesian sense of the word (see, e.g., ibid., p. 136). This is a decisive point, since Nancy daringly (isn't it risky?) inscribes Descartes's *sentir* and his "properly speaking it is what is in me called feeling" under the heading of fiction:

> . . . *et* [*sic*] *certe videre videor*—"*properly* speaking it is what is in me called feeling":[17] proof that this *feeling most proper*, most *properly* speaking (evidence itself, as opposed to any syllogism), resting on feint or consisting entirely of it, also implies nothing but the fiction that lets it be established. More especially, it thus implies nothing as to the real nature of the subject of this feeling; it thus implies neither the "spirituality" nor the "corporeality" of this subject. (ibid., p. 136.)

So it may be. But, from Descartes's point of view, can one say the same of this "feeling oneself feel" [*se sentir sentir*], the target here, no doubt, of the "properly" and the "most proper," which I felt I had to emphasize? Isn't this the place where it all plays itself out? Isn't it in this place of reappropriation that the simple, phenomenological dimension of "sensing," of "feeling that one feels," of "feeling oneself feel," spiritualizes or decorporealizes experience? It follows that—at least for Descartes—pure feeling, "feeling oneself feel," would indeed be spiritual and not at all corporeal. Mutatis mutandis, this would be the same for the analogous moment in Husserl's phenomenology.

And Nancy is thus not naming touch here. And yet—can it be insignificant that once in this book (only once, if I am not mistaken), as if distractedly or rhetorically, he seems to let escape a "touches itself" that looks like one of those dead or hackneyed metaphors whose appearance I have vowed, in a way, never to neglect here? It all leads one to think that Nancy—here at least—does not attribute any decisive *thematic* or *problematic* importance to this. The expression appears only once; Nancy neither underscores nor analyzes it; he neither interrogates nor relaunches it in any way. And yet—is it fortuitous that this "touches itself" should appear here regarding the "mouth," whose "place," spacing, locus without locus, place without place, we have just considered? Is it fortuitous that the subject of this "touches itself" is precisely the very subject itself, *I*, but a faceless *I*, even a bodyless *I*, *except* for what is mouthlike in it?

Before we ask ourselves what happens then, let me quote an excerpt, at least, from these pages and their ample, tight webbing, which one should reconstitute each time (once and for all, let us here recall this duty, which is as imperative as it is unworkable). Around a certain "I" that "touches itself" (or himself or herself) or "is touched" [*Je* se touche . . .], here is a "faceless mouth," but also the words: "But that is still saying too much," which, with the next stroke [*trait*], seem ready to retract each word—retracting it either by effacing it or in order to neutralize its literality by dint of tropes. And here again, it is the predicate open/closed that is decisive overall (the "mouth" thus becomes that which, by opening, has "the look or the shape of a mouth"):

> Unum quid, a something that is neither-soul-nor-body, opens its mouth and pronounces or conceives "ego sum." But that is still saying too much. Unum quid *has* no mouth that it could manipulate and open, any more than an intelligence that it could exercise to reflect upon itself. Yet something—unum quid—opens (it thus has the look or the shape of a mouth) and this opening is articulated (it thus has the look of a discourse, hence of thought), and this articulated opening forms *I*, in an extreme contraction.
>
> At one blow, it forms *itself* as *I* in a convulsion; it experiences *I*; it thinks itself *I*. *I* touches itself, is touched; it fixes itself, going—saying—*I* [faisant—disant—*je*]. (ibid., p. 157)

Before carrying on with the reading of this passage and seeing the moment of auto-affection, the tactile figure of pure auto-affection, the "*I* self-touches," come forth, one must take note of *three* things at least:

1. "Extreme contraction": it turns the articulated opening into an auto-affection, a retraction into oneself, an economic self-gathering. This economy circumscribes the opening and forces it to determine itself and not be just anything whatsoever or whosoever. The "I" owes as much to the *contract* and the gathered stroke or *trait* of this contraction of oneself (with oneself) as to the opening itself, that is, of what is called the mouth, here, before the face. The word "contraction" is important. Shortly afterward, the word "contracture" takes over. Between the occurrences of these two words, this same movement is described as a "convulsion." At the beginning of this chapter devoted to unum quid, Nancy announces a "convulsion of Cartesian thought," "*his* convulsion"—a convulsion that, "starting with Descartes, philosophic thinking has refused to confront," as "its own convulsion," he eventually concludes (ibid., pp. 131, 164).

The terms "spasm" and "syncope" are regularly associated with the word "convulsion." These words say what happens to the body and affects it, but not necessarily as a disorder or disease or to signify disjunction or simple defeat of what then becomes unhinged, unjoined, but, on the contrary, where: "The question of the joint makes up the last question in Descartes: it concerns the soul and the body adjoining" (ibid., p. 131). Then, in this self-commotion resembling a (diastolic/systolic) heartbeat as much as a syncope, a rhythmical violence concentrates. It is a gathering in an interruption, the cut that opens and shuts the mouth. Three years earlier, in 1976, Nancy had published *Le discours de la syncope: 1. Logodaedalus.*[18] Unless one mobilizes this entire earlier work, one might find it somewhat difficult, it seems to me, to read what Nancy says here about the convulsive contracture of the mouth that *touches itself* when it "forms *itself* as *I.*"

2. The discourse on the "contracture around the noise 'I,'" "ego," or even "*o,*" does not seem more artificial or forced than this entire thematics involving the mouth. It suffices to keep in mind Descartes's insistence on pronunciation, on the ineluctable pronouncement of "Ego sum, ego existo"—and on time, on this "each time" of the proffered utterance [*profération*], which cannot be reduced to a merely enunciated utterance [*énonciation*]. Words seem to be carried [*portée*] by the mouth beyond their mere discursive reach [*portée*]. Not only does Nancy place this passage of the Second Meditation (in Latin) at the beginning of his book in an epigraph (" . . . denique statuendum sit hoc pronuntiatum. *Ego sum, ego existo,* quoties a me profertur, vel mente concipitur, necessario esse verum"), he also proposes an explanatory translation for it, the whole pedagogical signification of which is self-evident: the effective proffering of an utterance [*profération*; *profertur*] is what has to count the most (according to Nancy, because his interpretation is special in this, and more canonical readers will no doubt be tempted to resist it), and not the mere conception of something "in my mind" [*dans mon esprit*; *mente concipitur*], although Descartes seems to have considered the latter equivalent to the former ("quoties a me profertur, vel mente concipitur"). Nancy's explanatory translation deliberately and massively throws any equivalence or symmetry off balance, it seems to me, and favors the proffering. He privileges the proposition inasmuch as it *comes forth outside of the mind* and there where Descartes, in a decision performed by another performative, might want to confer upon it some philosophical status or legitimacy—as if conception within the mind were a double or a copy, or in any case something dependent on the proffered uttering act [*acte profératoire*]. Here, then, is Nancy's eloquent translation, which speaks for itself: " . . . finally, one must rule, establish, decide, erect as a statue and found as a statute

that this pronouncement, this pronounced utterance, this enunciated utterance, *I am, I exist*, is necessarily true every time that I proffer and utter it, propose and pronounce it, or that I conceive it in my mind, or that it is conceived in my mind, or by my mind" (ibid., p. 5).[19]

3. Finally, there is the passage to "*I* self-touches" (which I shall quote in a moment, at long last). It explains the genesis of the "I," auto-affection in its tactile figure ("*I* touches itself . . . "), addressing itself to *toi*, "you," "thou." Simultaneously, there is a passage to the second person and the familiar use of *tu*, "you" (which is difficult to translate into English, for example). This familiar apostrophe, *tu*, signs, all at once, the general singularity, the plural singularity of any possible addressee, an abrupt familiarity, which interrupts the habitual neutrality of philosophical discourse at the very moment when "I" makes its entrance; and above all, it signs the possibility or the need for the said "I" (as soon as it touches itself) to address itself, to speak to itself, to treat of itself (in a soliloquy interrupted in advance) *as an other*. No sooner does "I [touch] itself" than it is itself—it contracts itself, it contracts with itself, but as if with another. It addresses itself to itself and says *tu* to itself. How not to use the familiar "you" with oneself? Thou tryest it, you try it. We could say that the contracture of the contract, the contraction and the convulsion (these being the words that dominate this whole analysis of unum quid) feature the *treatment* of [*ont trait . . . à*], trace out, and give its singular trait to, this unavoidably familiar address of oneself—of oneself as the first or the last other. An *I*, there where it is (self-)*touched* [Là où ça *se touche*, un *je*]. But *I* self-touches spacing itself out, losing contact with itself, precisely in touching itself. It switches off the contact, it abstains from touching, so as to touch itself.

"Ça se touche, un Je":[20] here the French *se* and its grammar remain eternally untranslatable. This accident is all the more interesting since it touches on the idiom, precisely—on the untranslatable singularity at the very heart itself of translation. "Il se touche" means that it or he self-touches itself or himself (in a loop, with the mouth lip-synching the looping—of a circle, literally of an *o* or a zero). It also means that it or he is touched, touchable (by any other whatsoever). "Il se tutoie" signifies that he is saying *you* to himself or itself, or he or it is being addressed in this way—he is *tutoyable*, addressable with *tu* (by any other whatsoever). He is already, as "I," like "I," the other's muted, still "you," and his properly own still you. "Se toucher toi": "to self-touch you," Nancy will write. Later.

The syncopated convulsion, this contraction of the inside and the outside, is also this (still and spoken [*tu et dit*]) discourse, a difference at the heart of the *I*, the articulation that can be disarticulated of an ego, an ego capable of touching it to the heart in touching its heart. Isn't the heart memory? Isn't it thinking *of* memory? Thinking *as* memory? We shall safeguard the recollection, the cardiogram of this cardio-logy from one end of this book to the other—as it also writes itself or is written on the heart and on the hand, if not with a wholehearted hand or a freehanded heart —especially when we lend an ear to a certain heart sensation in Husserl, his *Herzgefühl*, in the haptological moment of *Ideas II*.[21] In the meantime, here is a first diaphragm:

> . . . and this articulated opening forms *I*, in an extreme contraction.
>
> At one blow, it forms *itself* as *I* in a convulsion; it experiences *I*; it thinks itself *I*. *I* touches itself, is touched; it fixes itself, going—saying—*I* [faisant— disant—*je*]. Imagine a faceless mouth (which is to say the structure of a *mask* once again: open holes, and the mouth opening in the middle of the eye; locus of vision and theory, diaphragmatically traversed—open and shut simultaneously—by a proffered utterance), a faceless mouth, then, mouthing the ring of its contracture around the noise "I." "You" [*tu*] experience this daily, each time you are pronouncing or conceiving ego in your mind, each time (and this happens to you daily) you are forming the *o* of the first person (indeed the *first*: there is nothing before it): "eg*o* cogit*o* exist*o*." An *o* forms the immediate loop of your experience. Truly, it is of *that* which it is and that it undergoes the experience it makes—that it *makes* or *forms* because it cannot *be* it. (ibid., p. 157)

This difference between *making* or *forming*, on the one hand, and *being*, on the other; the excess of *fashioning* over *essence*, with one making up for the other; one coming in lieu of the lack or impossibility of the other; all that, no doubt, is the law of *fiction*, at the origin of *feeling oneself* as *touching oneself*: there where it is not, one will have had to *make*, to *fashion*, to *feature*, to *figure*. Where the taking-place of the event doesn't find its place —a gaping locus, indeed, a mouth—except in *replacement*; where it doesn't find room except in replacement—isn't that the trace of metonymy or the technical prosthesis, and the place for the phantasm as well, that is to say, the ghostly revenant (*phantasma*), at the heart of (self-)feeling? The revenant, between life and death, dictates an impossible mourning, an endless mourning—life itself. Barely visible scene of this mourning: it pertains to a *spacing* that is irreducible or even heterogeneous in relation to an "extensio" from which, however, one should not dissociate it.[22]

§ 3 This Is My Body

*Points Already: Counterpoint, Mourning Psyche,
and the Hand of . . .*

How is one to take up again the "proper" of "unum quid"?[1] The debate
necessarily unfolds around an "inextension of the mind," or a "nonextension of the mind," thus *around* Psyche, inasmuch as she can be "united to
the whole body," extended, stretched out, subjected—and she lies down
on her couch in the course of this union, or even with a view to this
union, which will always look like a fiction, "quasi permixtio."

An animated debate around the animation of inanimate Psyche: it is
with Descartes that Nancy thus organizes this *Auseinandersetzung*—with
him, wholly alongside and against him, repeating *against him*, but through
this mouthpiece and about the mouth, what the inventor of the modern
"subject" and its "truth" thought, without thinking, in the very utterance
of the *cogito*.

There are several voices, therefore, in this serene and subtle altercation
with Descartes thus ventriloquized. Although Psyche is in mourning and
the mourning barely acknowledged, she collects herself, making a pronouncement. The pronouncing of a final judgment goes through the opening [*embouchure*] of the mouth, to be sure, but we could say that, besides
the places thus identified, it goes through a singular point, and the point
named *point*. For the soul is united to the *whole* body, and it could not be
circumscribed in one *part* of the body, be it a point. Accordingly, Nancy
analyzes the *double contradiction* jeopardizing the hypothesis of a *punctual*
spatialization of the mind such as the theory of the pineal gland and the
animal spirits inhabiting it. It is contradictory to think of the mind as an
extension, but it is also contradictory to think of extension as a point.
Hence the voluminous figure of a gland whose soul does not inhabit the

inside, steering it like a pilot. Hence, also, the "incredible theoretical con-
tortions Descartes engages in so as to *subtilize* the body in the gland and
the 'animal spirits,' in order to *permix* body and mind." If "the gland is this
improbable somewhere, also an 'unum quid,'" and if "'unum quid' pronounces 'ego'" (Nancy, "Unum quid," pp. 144–45, 156), then the altercation with Descartes finds its space here (at least here in this book, *Ego sum*),
that is, not in the question of the heart or of the body, but on a strange trajectory between an improbable pineal gland and a mouth from before
speech [*parole*], an opening still anoral and already touching.

Digression. Why this altercation with Descartes (rather than with Aristotle or Kant?) It could be explained by the needs of a strategy, with reference to the *subject*, this concept of modern tradition, if one can put it like
that, and more precisely to *the truth of this subject*, which one often associates with Descartes (though the word "subject," sensu stricto, is not
Cartesian but rather Kantian), notably in discourses marked by Heideg-
gerianism or Lacanism. Nancy's strategy seems clear: "The nonextension
of the mind appears, therefore, as what the union demands as much as
what the distinction guarantees. What is demanded and guaranteed in this
way is the unity of the subject as its truth" (ibid., p. 145).

Altercation with Descartes—as we were saying—rather than with Kant,
or Aristotle.

Why not with Kant, who paid more attention, no doubt, to any subjectivity of the subject than Descartes did, and to what we call touching
[*le toucher*]?

Is it because Kant is fundamentally mute, taken aback, when confronted
with the body, confronted with the union of the soul and the body? This,
at least, is what Nancy proffered three years earlier in *Le discours de la syncope: Logodaedalus*,[2] a luminous, inventive book, so cheerful it leaves one
breathless; it bursts with the laughter of thought—at the very place where
it leads us to think the thinking of laughter and of syncopes and syncopation, the contretemps, and also the counterpoint that gathers and upholds, in order to keep it all together, dissociation itself.

Thus, "Kant the philosopher" has nothing to say about the flesh, about
the philosopher's flesh, about his "union of the soul and the body": in a sequence that we shall have to reconstitute, Nancy names "a connection between the body and thought about which Kant the philosopher, in truth,
has *nothing* to say" (Nancy, *Logodaedalus*, p. 145).

"Kant the philosopher," he says. Doesn't this cautious pinpointing suggest that this Kant is distinct from another one, a Kant without cover, yet to be discovered? The context of this demonstration is important for us. For even if touching or self-touching as such is not mentioned in it, even if Nancy doesn't appear expressly to draw from this rich vein (which I shall call "French" here to save time, and to which we shall return later),[3] it deals with a syncope of contact, a quasi-masturbatory auto-affection, and it comes down to autoerotism lost in pleasure, sinking in syncopated laughter. And so it is a certain way of self-touching without touching, or touching oneself and interrupting the contact, but a contact, a tactility, that nevertheless *succeeds in interrupting itself.* It succeeds in setting up contact, in setting itself up *as* contact, in thus touching itself *in interrupting itself,* at the moment when it's suspending—or even forbidding or abstaining—itself, to such a point that it's holding its breath, so as to give itself, still, within the syncope, the pleasure of which it is depriving itself. This is what makes laughter laugh—laughter, "the fictive notion (or literary tool) for the philosopher's presence to himself or herself" (ibid., p. 146):

> Laughter can ensure the conditions of possibility for contentment (consciousness *for* reason) only through a sinking [*perte*] into pleasure, the syncope *of* and *in* pleasure itself. One cannot identify this jolt or shaking with the continual and progressive throb of a discourse machine [*machine de discours*], precisely: instead, the jolt disinsures such a discourse—and laughter communicates (?) with literature. (If autoerotism is constitutive or figurative of metaphysical autology, then one has to say that the *auto* both rebounds and ruptures in Kantian laughter, that an *other* comes forth who is not necessarily the other sex but the same, perhaps, undeciding itself[4]—ambivalent, or petrified [*médusé*], or both at once, self-petrified and deprived of Self. . . . This alteration game takes place each time *Witz* [wit] intervenes.
>
> We have agreed that Kant, too, invented the "thing-in-itself"—unknowable according to him—on the basis of the castration complex, in which onanistic anguish and hermaphroditic complexes play a role as well. The thing-in-itself would thus be the thing-unto-Kant. . . . (Georg Groddeck, letter to Sigmund Freud, May 9, 1922)[5]

> What is at issue is not only a syncope described and discoursed upon, but a syncope *of* discourse: indeed, the salutary property of laughter can only be understood *approximately*; to explain it, one must invoke a connection between the body and thought about which Kant the philosopher, in truth, has

nothing to say ("For if we admit that with all our thoughts is harmonically combined a movement in the organs of the body . . . ").[6]

The union of the soul and the body (this union giving itself sexual airs here), this union which is also the sublime union of thought and the unthought (the nonrepresented)—this union which isn't one, and isn't the reunion of two orders or two substances, but is, if it *is* something, the philosopher's *flesh*—, this union of the heterogeneous is not the object of some knowledge: "What is your opinion about the union [*Gemeinschaft*] of soul and body, about the nature of mind, about creation in time? I have no opinion whatsoever about that. . . . Whence this question is necessary and, in regard to the object, can only be answered subjectively—this I know."[7]

Let us accept as a working hypothesis that Nancy is right. "Kant the philosopher" has nothing to say about the union of the soul and the body. This hypothesis does not exclude two others; and it is tempting to formulate them in the following way:

1. No philosopher, as such, has ever had anything to say, philosophically, about the theme formulated in this way: the union of the soul and the body—Descartes no more than any other.[8] And on this point, Kant mocks Descartes, just at the point when—and this is the second hypothesis:

2. No longer as a philosopher, this time, but as an anthropologist (supposing, then, that this delimitation is reliable and pertinent, like the delimitation between his *Critiques* and his *Anthropology from a Pragmatic Point of View*), Kant speaks of the union of the soul and the body, for example, of sensibility and, singularly, of touch. Certainly, in *Logodaedalus*, Nancy evokes the *Anthropology* here and there—we'll get to this—and always in a rather acute, original, and elliptical fashion. But since this is a time when the question of touch as such does not yet interest Nancy, he refers neither to Kant's irony about Descartes's roving speculation nor to a sort of Kantian short treatise of the five senses, and therefore of touch in particular.

Let us resume and sketch an analysis that might this time be titled "Kant's Hand," before Husserl's[9] and Heidegger's:[10] the hand that signs, and the hand that he analyzes, and first of all the hand of Kant pointing to Descartes and deriding him. Kant distinguishes between man's *physiological* knowledge and pragmatic knowledge, that is, between the study of what *nature* has made of man and what man has *freely* made of himself, beyond racial or national peculiarities, as a citizen of the world (*Weltbürger*),[11] and he hands down an unappealable verdict regarding the former, namely,

alleged physiological knowledge: the discourses one may attempt within
it about the union of the soul and the body are pure speculation, they are
pointless ratiocinations, uninteresting and unprofitable quibbles, "a sheer
waste of time." Here a verb keeps coming up like an accusation; it is
vernünfteln, that is, to speculate, split hairs, ratiocinate. And in this in-
dictment, Descartes is the accused:

> He who ponders about natural phenomena, for example about the causes for
> the faculty of memory (*das Erinnerungsvermögen*), can speculate to and fro (in
> the Cartesian fashion) (*hin und her [nach dem Cartesius] Vernünfteln*) on the
> traces of impressions which keep lingering in our brain; but, in doing so, he has
> to admit that he is a mere spectator in this game of his imagination and that he
> has to leave everything entirely to Nature, since he knows neither the cerebral
> nerves and filaments nor their operation when they carry out his intentions.
> Such speculative theorizing is a sheer waste of time (*mithin alles theoretische
> Vernünfteln hierüber reiner Verlust ist*).[12]

On the other hand, where physiological anthropology must hold back
from saying anything whatsoever (as Descartes would have done), anthropology from a pragmatic point of view has much to teach us. But is-
n't this finally what Descartes told Princess Elizabeth in the letter that
Merleau-Ponty cites and that I have just quoted [in n. 8]? In particular,
pragmatic anthropology informs or teaches us, since this is our concern
here, on the subject of the sense of the five senses—not only on the subject of sensibility (*Sinnlichkeit*), as faculty [*faculté*] to know through intuitive representation, comprising both sense and imagination (the latter,
and the last-mentioned connection, is what matters most of all to Nancy
in *Logodaedalus*); not only on the subject of an inner sense; not only on
the subject of corporeal sensations known as vital (*Vitalempfindung*) or
sensus vagus; but on organic sensation (*Organempfindung*) or *sensus fixus*.
Now, it is precisely in this latter category, that is to say, *external* corporeal
senses assigned to bodily *organs*, on the subject of this *human* body *not
without organs*, that Kant thinks that there are things to say, and has things
to say, from a pragmatic and, above all, anthropological point of view.

Hence the hand, and the fingers—and we are coming to them. The
senses should be five in number—no more and no fewer, he confirms—
the objective ones (*tactus, visus, auditus*) and the subjective ones (*gustus, ol-
factus*). The former contribute more to knowledge, and among them touch
(*Betastung*) comes *first*, at least in accordance with certain criteria. Which

ones? To the extent that touch is the only sense of *immediate* external perception and thus the one bringing us the greatest certainty, it is the most important or the most serious one (*wichtigste*), although it is the clumsiest (*gröbste*) among the external senses. In a way it is the foundation of the other two objective senses, sight and hearing. These must "originally be referred" (*ursprünglich bezogen werden müssen*) to touch in order to "produce empirical knowledge" (*um Erfahrungserkenntniss* [sic] *zu verschaffen*) (Kant, *Anthropology*, p. 42).

Such a hierarchical arrangement is without any doubt part of the great tradition that accords an absolute privilege to touch and does not let itself be encroached upon by the possibility (briefly and poorly evoked by Kant) of any vicariousness of the senses (*Vicariat der Sinne*). This "tactilist" or "haptocentric" tradition extends at least until Husserl and includes him— his original part will be discussed later. The tradition becomes complicated, with the risk of being interrupted, in Merleau-Ponty, as we shall also see, when the latter seems to reinstate a symmetry that Husserl challenges between the touching-touchable and the seeing-visible.

Now, in the Kantian period of this tradition, it is indeed suitable for a pragmatic *anthropology* to know the fundamental, founding, and originary signification of touch, for the only organ to which Kant ascribes this organic sense is the hand, the human hand—the fingers and the fingertips, in truth. The sense of touch has its appropriate place in the fingertips and the nerve endings, the papillae. These nerve endings inform us, human beings, about the form of a solid body. Indeed, one could ask oneself which way the difference between the physiological and pragmatic points of view goes here. This way, no doubt: if it is nature that has provided the hand, so to speak, it has given it to human beings only; and by thus making human beings, it has then allowed them freely to make themselves, particularly through objective knowledge, the guiding thread of this analysis. And what Kant analyzes is not the structure of the papillae and the nervous system, or the link with thought, and so forth; rather, it is what *human beings make with their hands*. It comes down to their phenomenal experience of the hand, as it were. And one is tempted to suggest that Kant outlines or prefigures, within the limits of an anthropology, a phenomenological or prephenomenological reduction that requires a comparison with Husserl's gesture in *Ideas II*, to be discussed later. The hand's finality; what nature puts within reach of the human hand, and only the human hand; what it allows human beings to make *by hand*, with the hand, thanks to the hand:

all that is the proper object of a pragmatic anthropology. For Kant, as Heidegger and so many others will repeat later, animals possess nothing that can be compared to a hand: "Nature seems to have endowed man alone with this organ, so that he is enabled to form a concept of a body by touching it on all sides. The antennae of insects seem merely to show the presence of an object; they are not designed to explore its form" (Kant, *Anthropology*, p. 41).[13]

Kant insists precisely on "form." Since the privileged position of touch is defined here from the point of view of objective knowledge, it is advisable to set apart from it all that has to do with "vital" impressions (*Vitalempfindung, sensus vagus*), that which is not specific to an organ (*Organempfindung, sensus fixus*) and that, through touch, leads us to sense something other than forms: coldness and heat, softness and roughness.

Let us note in passing that although Nancy does not make any allusion to this anthropology of touch in Kant in *Logodaedalus*, it seems to me, here he already underscores a trope of touch. As a mere rhetorical figure, it is a mark that the problematic or thematics of touch have not yet been broached, as such, at this date; but their point already appears, and it is pointedly there, above all, like the pointy tip of an antenna, a scout at the forefront, in this very acute place where it always comes forth subsequently: still very close to a point, and upon a limit. For Nancy, it is always a matter of touching what is well-nigh at the limit not to be touched— namely, the limit itself, and the point's extreme, pointed tip. Thus, the sentence quoted just below is all the more remarkable because, in evoking Kant's *Anthropology* (but at the same time ignoring its theory of touch), it has to do precisely with the figure and with sensible figuration in *Dichtung* [poetry]. Let us read these lines, which describe a coupling and what then "touches" with its "pointed tip." They also follow a remarkable, abyssal development about the "fraternal" (Kant *dixit*) or even an "incest" (Nancy *dixit*), between the understanding and sensibility, locus of schematism, place of "art concealed" in the depths of the soul, of *Dichtung*, sensible power or sensible figuration of this power, and so forth. "But for the time being this operation is more narrowly interesting for us: here, in the *Anthropology*, it couples understanding with sensible imagination. Now, while the power of *Dichtung* remains, to the letter of the text, limited to sensibility, it nonetheless *touches* on understanding, with its pointed tip" (Nancy, *Logodaedalus*, p. 108).[14]

Here ends the digression, or anticipation.

Having taken note in 1976 that Kant "the philosopher" had nothing to say about the union of the soul and the body, nothing about the flesh, about *meum corpus*, or the body proper, Nancy, for whom it is the thing itself, turned toward Descartes's *ego sum* for this polyphonic and ventriloquized altercation—between the mouth and the pineal gland.

Yet Kant is the one to whom Freud turned, against whom he turned, in the aphorism bequeathed by the moribund man who proclaimed on his deathbed, "Psyche ist ausgedehnt," the leitmotiv of Nancy's "Psyche." Freud first formed a hypothesis, in four lines; he called up a possibility, a merely probable one. But no matter how dense and elliptical the logic of this mere probability, its aim is not to put the soul outside, to expel the soul into a space or onto an extension that would be first and irreducibly given to us—familiarly there, on the outside, exterior. On the contrary, the spatiality of space, its *exteriority* would only be an outside projection of an *internal* and *properly speaking psychical* extension. In short, the outside would only be a projection! It is in this sense, in this direction (from internal extension toward external extension, toward the spatiality of space —the only exteriority worthy of the name), as enigmatic as this remains, that the Freudian (that is, purely *psychological*) derivation is irreversibly oriented. It would be difficult, apparently, to push psychologism any further. Is this different from what Nancy imports from this when he inversely puts the outside inside? And when he says that Psyche is extended, and thus outside, is he thinking of a "projection" effect, as Freud, literally, seems to be doing? Or, on the contrary, of an exteriority resisting any projection even if it makes possible some projection *effects*?

Is this a good question? What difference is there between the two, and is there one, first of all? Is Freud more or less psychologizing than Nancy? Does one still psychologize when one asserts that the psyche is extended though not yet spatial, and that there is an internal extension? What would a nonspatial extension be, one still without an outside—the psychical extension from which, *by projection*, one would derive space? Must one put the entire weight of the argument on the word "apparatus," which Freud wrote twice? Indeed, before saying "Psyche," he repeats "psychical apparatus." Is it the apparatus that *extends (itself)*? Is that which is extended a topological structure rather than pure psychic life? I am multiplying these questions so as to suggest that they are carried away, on their own, touching on their loss of sense. In any case, Freud writes (these are the first two sentences in this "posthumous" note comprising only four in all): "Space may be the projection of the extension of the psychical apparatus. No other derivation is probable."[15]

The grammar of this last proposition deserves a pause. In a negative mode—or one of denial, some would unhesitatingly say—Freud thus suggests that there is no other "likely" or "probable" derivation. He does not say that the latter is clear, distinct, true, or certain. He presents it only as a possibility, plausible or probable. That is the least one can say, for on the contrary nothing is more unlikely and contrary to common sense than this derivation of space or spatiality, which is to say, of the outside, starting from a projection of psychic interiority. What is projection, and what does the figure of a *projection* signify where there isn't any space yet? In truth, nothing is more paradoxical and incredible. Now, this is the provocative schema of this strange hypothesis and this derivation termed "probable," which Freud seems to oppose to Kant at that point.

But is it really a question of opposition? What if, far from going against Kant, Freud only wished to interpret and refine the Kantian model by substituting for it, while remaining within the same logic, a kind of improved formalization? To wit, in the next sentence, he makes explicit what he has just said and writes "instead of" (*anstatt*): "Instead of Kant's a priori determinants of our psychical apparatus. Psyche is extended, knows nothing about it."[16] This last reading (entailing a more adequate or more consequential substitution, but remaining within the *same* perspective) would imply that transcendental psychologizing, or more precisely transcendental psychoanalysis, or better yet transcendental psychoanalytic aesthetics, might account for spatiality starting from a psychical apparatus that would indeed have to be extended in order to comprise, among the two pure forms of sensible intuition, an a priori form of external sense. Kant might in fact be seen as prefiguring a certain Freudian line of argument when he states, not in any *Anthropology* this time, but in the *Critique of Pure Reason*:

> The representation of space [*die Vorstellung des Raumes*] cannot, therefore, be empirically obtained from the relations of outer appearance. On the contrary, this outer experience is itself possible at all only through that representation.
> Space is a necessary *a priori* representation, which underlies all outer intuitions.[17]

Wouldn't Freud be more amenable than it seems to the logic of a "metaphysical," then a "transcendental," "exposition" (*Erörterung*) of the concept of space? Doesn't Freud confirm that pure intuition [here of space] "must be found in us prior to any perception of an object" and that consequently, it must be a "pure, not empirical, intuition"?[18] Therefore, wouldn't it be a kind of pure sensibility, the insensible sensibility reappearing as a motif in Hegel and Marx? And here, following our thread, a kind of sensibility touching nothing? Or a kind of touch without empirical contact, a self-touching or being touched without touching anything? For it is known that the recognition or attribution of extension to *something* or *someone* (for example, to Psyche, which and who is both) does not suffice to make a body, a tangible body. The pure form of sensibility, pure intuition, "even without any actual object of the senses or of sensation, exists in the mind (*im Gemüthe*) a priori as a mere form of sensibility."[19] Kant insists on it: in the representation of a body, when one has detached what comes from the understanding (substance, force, divisibility) and what comes from sensation (impenetrability, hardness, color), there still remains something of empirical intuition: extension (*Ausdehnung*) and figure (*Gestalt*).

It will not have escaped the attention of anyone interested in touch, as we are here, that among properties accessible to sensation are the properties that are tangible par excellence, that is to say impenetrability (*Undurchdringlichkeit*) and hardness (*Härte*), tangible properties that Kant's *Anthropology from a Pragmatic Point of View* excludes from organic sensibility in order to lock them into a vital receptivity (*Vitalempfindung, sensus vagus*), without organs, without objective knowledge. These sensible givens of sensation do not fall within pure sensibility, as figure and extension do. Here, even if there is no touchable body that does not *also* appear extended, extension is not touchable through the senses—no more than in Descartes, though for radically different reasons. It is well known that this motif of transcendental ideality is joined to an empirical realism interrupting the reduction of appearances—that is, phenomena—to mere illusion. Certainly it allows one to understand the movement of the "good Berkeley" who foresaw the absurdities to which a realism of space and time as properties of things in themselves leads. But it also allows one to avoid Berkeley's absolute idealism.

I am recalling these well-known yet always enigmatic matters for a number of contextual reasons. On the one hand, it is in order to try to understand Freud's brief allusion to Kant, its ambiguity, and how difficult it might be to inflect it toward any materialization, or incorporation, or even incarnation of Psyche (the word "extended" in itself means neither accessible to sensation nor—especially not—tangible). On the other hand, it is in order to approach the knot of a certain tension. Even if one understands that the link between this "transcendental idealism," or this (transcendental, for Kant; psychologizing, for Freud) subjectivism, and a thinking of finitude (*intuitus derivativus* and so forth) defines a finitist tradition in which the author of *Une pensée finie* [A Finite Thinking][20] may recognize himself up to a certain point; even if this same alliance of "empirical realism" and "transcendental idealism" allows one to give every opportunity to the movements of interpretation and appropriation in sensible perception, including touch (and this perception is never raw; rather, it invests or *interprets* the tangible starting from a "desire," a "drive," or in any case a "my body"), the fact remains that the motif of greatest obstinacy, for Nancy and in the name of touch, consists in resisting any idealism or subjectivism, be it transcendental or psychoanalytical. What would drive out this whole tradition, no matter how strong and necessary, is the insistence on touch. For Nancy, touch remains the motif of a sort of absolute, irredentist, and postdeconstructive realism. The spacing of space he exposes to touch remains irreducible to any mathematizable extension and perhaps to any knowledge—an absolute realism, but irreducible to any of the tradition's realisms. The Thing touches itself, is touched, even there where one touches Nothing. Henceforth this is what we shall have to try to understand, as well as how touch and nontouch are *really* touched and self-touching—with infinite tact, into which Nancy's writing, his exact hyperbole, engulfs, sinks, exhausts, and ex-scribes itself.[21]

If one were intent on elaborating these Kantian dealings in a more consequential fashion, one would have to turn to the (metaphysical and transcendental) exposition of the concept of time; one would have to go where time is not only the form of an inner sense, but the "*a priori* formal condition of all appearances whatsoever,"[22] *all* phenomena, be they internal or external. And there, following in the footsteps of Heidegger,[23] among others, we would find again the great question of pure auto-affection, pure "self-touching," in the movement of temporalization. There, around Psyche (*peri psuchēs*), which is to say around the great question of "pure" self-touching and preempirical auto-affection, the doctors Kant, Husserl, Freud, Heidegger, Merleau-Ponty, and so many others closer by too (whose opinions will be asked for later) hold what is called a consultation, doubtless calling on their precursor Aristotle. They ought to, in any case—they should either follow him or have done with him.

Aristotle has not left us for a moment, even though Nancy does not invite him to speak. Let us stress again the singular place that touch has in Aristotle's discourse on the living—in such a zoology. Touch is the only sense that the existence of the living as such cannot dispense with. The purpose of the other senses is not to ensure the being of the animal or of the living, but only its *well*-being (Aristotle *Peri psuchēs* 435b20–25). But without touch animals would be unable to exist; the sense of touch alone is necessarily the one whose loss brings about the animal's death: "It is evident, therefore, that the loss of this one sense alone must bring about the death of an animal. For as on the one hand nothing which is not an animal can have this sense, so on the other it is the only one which is indispensably necessary to what is an animal" (ibid., 435b4–7). Aristotle measures this essential coextensivity of animal life and touch; he also explains it by putting it to the test of death. When an animal is deprived of sight, hearing, or taste, it does not necessarily die. Should it come to a lack of touch, however, it will die without delay. (This follows the set of distinctions recalled earlier.[24] Among the senses, touch is an exception, because it has as its object more than one quality—in truth, it potentially has *all* sensible qualities.) Conversely (but it is the other side of the same phenomenon), animals also die when an excessive intensity of touch touches them. Tangible excess, "hyperbole," comes to destroy the organ of this touching, "which is the essential mark of life" (ibid., 435b).[25] Couldn't one say that this *measure*, this moderation of touch, remains at the service of life to the sole *extent*, precisely, that some kind of reserve holds it on the brink of exaggeration? A certain tact, a "thou shalt not touch too much," "thou shalt not let yourself be touched too much," or even "thou shalt not touch yourself too much," would thus be inscribed a priori, like a first commandment, the law of originary prohibition, in the destiny of tactile experience. Ritual prohibitions would then come to be determined, *afterward*, and only on the background of an untouchability as initial as it is vital, on the background of this "thou shalt not touch, not too much," which wouldn't have awaited any religion, ritual cult, or neurosis of touch. In the beginning, there is abstinence. And without delay, unforgivingly, touching commits perjury.

Touching, then, is a question of life and death. One cannot say as much, and it is not true, of the sense of the senses in general. Now, whether or not Nancy aimed at the opening of *Peri psuchēs*, whether he did it deliberately, explicitly, or elliptically, or even maliciously (like Eros who "contemplates"

Psyche, "flustered and mischievous, all at once"), it turns out that, in the brief, discreet page, the quasi-mute *tableau*, the powerful, reserved allegory that Nancy, the author of "Psyche," affects to dedicate to a kind of deploration (Psyche's deathly sleep and her imminent interment), we can decipher a stubborn, ironic, discreet, and overdetermined challenge to Aristotle, to the one who, at the beginning of *Peri psuchēs*, lays down or implies this double possibility, that is, knowledge and self-knowledge of the soul.

Hypothesis: would Nancy have chosen the words "around her" for his last sentence if at this point he had not had Aristotle's *Peri psuchēs* in view, even though he virtually never mentions it? He insists on this, with cruel exactitude, and I emphasize: "She knows nothing of this—and that is what everyone knows *around her*, with such exact and cruel knowledge."

For according to Nancy, the knowledge of "those present" with Psyche, around her (let's say, *peri psuchēs*), is the knowledge so "exact and cruel" of which (and that) Psyche, for her part, knows nothing, nothing herself, of herself—of (and from) her extension, in any case. We have noted it—it is repeated, in more than one language, four or five times within a few lines. The scene goes on—it certainly places itself, if one may put it this way— under Freud's authority, or at least it goes with the guarantee, or the security, of his "posthumous" note (for there is also another, more Aristotelian Freud: psychoanalysis intends to be knowledge that is *peri psuchēs* and accessible to a psyche knowing itself, in a certain way).

Let us be attentive to this writing, which is so exact, and above all to the unfolding in time, to the rhythm, to the four beats in time of this *tableau vivant*. Any picture, *tableau*, or portrait is called a *zōgraphia*, or *tableau vivant*—in short, a "living painting" or "painting of the living"—in Greek. But for this once, here is the *tableau vivant* of a death—of an imminence, of a coming death, of a dying woman who will be dead before the end of the sentence. But a corpse that has not been buried yet. And even if this were her entombment, she has not yet been conveyed into the ground.

Later in the year during which I wrote the first version of this text (1992), Nancy gave an extraordinary conference about Caravaggio's painting *The Death of the Virgin* at the Louvre. The text, "Sur le seuil" ("On the Threshold"), was reissued first in *Po&sie*,[26] and then in *The Muses*,[27] a book that comes back forcefully to the question of touch and the "primacy of touch" (Nancy, *Muses*, p. 11ff.). From then on—since Nancy refers then to the first version of my text, among other things—in our gestures we keep meeting, even touching each other, at all points where there is a question of our touching. And from this point of view, I no longer dare, I hardly dare approach Nancy's numerous writings published after 1993.

It remains that one should no longer dissociate two "apparitions," two "visions," however singular: "Psyche" (1978) and "On the Threshold" (1993–94). What I venture to term a vision or an apparition, the one inspiring this last reading of *The Death of the Virgin*, so beautiful it leaves one breathless, here looks like "Psyche" in a troubling fashion—but without authorizing the slightest analogy. I may try to make them co-appear some day, word by word, in their ineffaceable difference, but also in their reciprocal convocation or annunciation—a little like the two Marys, the Virgin and the Sinner or the Penitent, of whom the last text speaks: "Mary is the model of Mary, but no figure is common to them both. Doubtless they together refer to a third, who, however, is not or is barely a figure. . . . In the *Entombment* by the same painter, the two Marys are side by side" (Nancy, *Muses*, p. 65).

I shall not quote here every sentence that would have suited "Psyche" fourteen years earlier. I let myself go and imagine that this scene, this woman in truth, never leaves him: she remains for him, in front of him, forever immobile, impassive, intangible. Christianity's indeconstructible? What a scene! What scene? What woman? Why *she*, when he thinks—so far and so powerfully—that thought is extended, when on this subject he quotes an enigmatic sentence by Freud? Why this hallucination of one who would be extended, a woman, and a beautiful one, so beautiful, beautiful for being neither dead nor alive, eternal yet perpetually dying, and surviving, belying death itself, death's ever being there? Psyche as Mary, Psyche as Mary and Mary, as two or three Marys: the virgin, the sinner, the penitent.

Just one example, but it is not an answer. And it is not in "Psyche," but in *The Muses*. As always, *exactitude* keeps its appointment (I am emphasizing: " . . . she is not *exactly* dead"):

> She did not die here. They have carried her to this makeshift bed where they deposited her body, slackened in a posture not yet arranged, to wash it before the funeral. . . . And yet, this body is firm, whole, intact in its abandon.
>
> It is not here that this woman died, but here she is not exactly dead. One might also say that she is resting, as if she were still on this side of death, or else already beyond it. . . .
>
> And is it not for this reason that there is not, there is never "death *itself*"? (Nancy, *Muses*, pp. 58–59)

About Psyche's nonknowledge, the notations are numerous—twice in German, four times in French. But different, each time. Each paragraph sets forth one of them—in French. But each of the four paragraphs ascribes or identifies another theme, another object, as well as another time, to this nonknowledge.

Psyche does not know anything, to be sure. This is understood and enunciated in multiple ways (Aristotle would further say: *pollakōs legomenon*). Psyche knows nothing:

1. about the fact that she is "extended";

2. about the fact that, of her dispersion *partes extra partes*, everyone save her—safe she—can calculate the order and report on the relations;

3. about the fact that in her sleep and the abandon of her pose, "flustered and mischievous, all at once, Eros contemplates her";

4. about the fact that later (but is it not *already* "later," or "later" soon?), in her coffin, which is soon going to be shut ("Soon it is going to be shut"; she is dead but, like disappearance, inhumation seems imminent; she is dead but remains visible; she is dead but not yet a departed [*une disparue*]; she is on the verge of disappearing but is still visible, though she does not know herself to be seen)—well, the others, in their presence *peri psuchēs*, see her or avert their eyes—but in any case they *know* her [*la savent*].[28] Exactly.

If *psuchē* is Life itself, then mourning Psyche is not just any mourning among others. It is mourning itself. It is absolute mourning, mourning of life itself, but mourning that can neither be *worn* and *borne* (no life can put on such mourning any longer) nor go through the "work" of mourning. Mourning without work of mourning, mourning without mourning. Mourning on the threshold of mourning. Our life itself—isn't it? To represent Psyche as a dead woman, "extended in her coffin," is to represent Life as a Departed woman [*comme une Morte*]—dead in her sleep already. What is dying *in* one's sleep? A transition of which we are told nothing, as if on purpose, but of which the temporality interrupts itself. Within the blank that marks the passage from one paragraph to the next,

Her sleep is so deep that it has even robbed her of any abandon in her pose.

Psyche is extended in her coffin. Soon it is going to be shut.

. . . the passage is from one rest to the other. One has gone from the sleeping woman to the corpse—or the recumbent figure. From the transient repose of sleep ("She lies at rest; the slight movements of sleep have half-exposed her bosom"), a pose seeming to seduce Eros as much as Psyche's nonknowledge, one has insensibly become engaged in the endless repose of death. From the repose of the pose, one has slid toward the extended extension in the coffin.

But across the interruption, across the blank on the page, one has moved from one imminence to the other. No sooner asleep (asleep almost all at once), no sooner dead (dead almost all at once), all at once, "soon" locked into her coffin. Precipitated time of imminence, a "soon" announcing the end rather than the future, this is the announcing of an apocalypse, which is to say an unveiling or revelation.

Now, what this apocalypse reveals is not so much a truth as the night of nonknowledge in which every desire gathers momentum. Eros's flustered, mischievous contemplation seems to have to do with this nonknowledge and Psyche's own unknown. Eros seems seduced by that which, in her, no longer affects itself. And by that which, in her, can no longer say "I touch myself." *I* seduces there where *I* does not self-touch. It is she. She, Psyche, is desirable, infinitely, as death, as a dead woman coming, and only a Psyche lets herself be desired, where she knows nothing, feels nothing of herself, where she partakes of the discontinuous duration, the precipitation of a dying [*mourance*] in which she finds herself without finding herself already, in her rest as a sleeping and a dying one, *soon* in her deadly rest, and *soon* invisible and inaccessible still: *ex-posed* to the other and *surrendered* [*livrée*], but *already* inaccessible and *just before* becoming invisible. Exposed, surrendered but *all too soon* denied to the other's eyes after having been prey to the other's hands. Maybe as a dead woman, as only the dead may be. Between the hands of the other, surrendered into the other's hands. *The other's hands*: this could have yielded a title for all the scenes that are henceforth going to engage us.

This *tableau* condenses the narrative ellipsis of an allegory. Psyche is exposed, surrendered to the word of the other *around her—and about her*. For Psyche, for a psyche altogether exposed to the outside and the other, there is no autobiography, there has never been any "I touch myself." No point in a signed autobiography for the one who, untouchable to herself, feels or knows nothing of herself. Mourning autobiography is not just any mourning among others, any more than Psyche's mourning lets itself be preceded or properly figured by any other. One might as well say that, being unimaginable, it can only give rise to images, phantasms, and specters, that is, figures, tropes, allegories, or metonymies opening a path to *technics*. Being undeniable, it can only leave room for denial. And so this mourning without mourning will never be overcome by any—failing or successful—"work of mourning."

At the time when he attempts to rethink the question of "sense" between the name of death and the verb for being born [*naître*], Nancy draws the line, exactly, between "work of mourning" and death, between the work of mourning and absolute mourning. In doing this, he shows the direction for a representation of the unrepresentable—and this could well be a way of inviting us to *read*, of telling us how to read, in other words and beyond any representation, of seeing without seeing his allegorical painting named *Psyche*.

> *Death* is the absolute signified, the sealing off [*bouclage*] of sense. The *noun* is what it is (and even this *proper name*, "Death"), but the *verb* is "bear," to be born [*naître*].
>
> It is certainly neither false nor excessive to say that all production of sense—of a sense making sense *in this sense*—is a deathwork. The same goes for all "ideals" and "works," and the same goes, remarkably, for all philosophies. Philosophy distinguishes itself by the unique way it profits from death [*jouir de la mort*]—which is also a way of assuring its own perdurability. Philosophy is ignorant of true mourning. True mourning has nothing to do with the "work of mourning": the "work of mourning," an elaboration concerned with keeping at a distance the incorporation of the dead, is very much the work of philosophy; *it is the very work of representation*. In the end, the dead will be represented, thus held at bay.
>
> But mourning is without limits and without representation. It is tears and ashes. It is: to recuperate nothing, to represent nothing. And thus it is also: to be born to this nonrepresented of the dead, of death.
>
> *To come forth and be born*: to find ourselves exposed, to *ex-ist*. Existence is an imminence of existence. [29]

This sets off a dream: what if *Psyche* also described the picture of an imminent "being born"? Of a coming into the world? What if the work of

mourning, philosophy perhaps, philosophy precisely, far from only dealing with "keeping at a distance the incorporation of the dead," were, *by
way of this*, working on such an incorporation, on a denying avoidance,
by way of the incorporation of the dead?

Following Aristotle and those beyond him, let us suppose that the haptical, unlike the other senses, is coextensive with the *living body*. Let us
further suppose that eating, as Aristotle also says, has to do with touch.
What does incorporation become, then, and what does it signify, in concert with mourning? Still a living moment of life? Of course—how could
it be otherwise? Still, one would have to include death within life. Would
this living moment of life be an interiorization or an expulsion? A be-
coming-tangible of the untouchable or on the contrary an idealization, a
spiritualization, an animation that produces an intangible becoming of
the tactile body, of the touching and touched?

In what way would this matrix of questions give birth to the question
of the *world*? And to the question of *finitude*? For the haptical is not just
a sense among others, and in a way it is not even a sense, sensu stricto
(we'll come back to this), because, to every *finite* existence, it recalls what
is coming—so as to present it with something, whatever it may be, whatever being it may be, but while marking, with the gift of this presentation,
the limit at which or from which the presentation announces itself.

Fifteen years later, in 1992, a paragraph in Nancy's *Corpus* is dedicated
to "Psyche's extension." This time, "touch"—that is, the word *toucher*—
comes forth in a strange way, a mode that doesn't let one decide whether
or not it is a figure. This needs to be emphasized again, since in the 1978
text, namely, a single page titled "Psyche," the word *toucher* never appears,
never as such, nor does any word from this lexical family. This time, in
1992, figuratively or not, touch now designates nothing less than the self-
relation of "our world."

"Notre monde *se touche*": our world touches itself, can be touched, is
touched; our world *is in touch*.

Would this mean to say, as French grammar allows, that one touches
the world and that it is touchable and tangible? No, not only that. "Our
world" *self*-touches itself; it flexes, inflects, and reflects itself; it auto-affects
and hetero-affects itself in this way; it folds itself, onto itself and yielding
to itself. To be sure, it touches itself so as to become world, but also to exit
from itself. And it is the same thing, the same world. It self-touches so as
to exit itself. It touches "something" in itself. But this "something" is not

a thing and this "in itself" is no longer an interiority. Let us rather quote, and emphasize: "If only our world were to understand that it is no longer time to want to be Cosmos, no more than Spirit oversizing Nature, it seems that it could do nothing except *touch in itself* the abjection of festering immundity [*l'abjection de l'immonde*]."[30]

(A parenthesis for a matter to be developed later, elsewhere, unless it has long been done already: at this time in the "history" of the "world," with a discourse—rather, the world's *doxa*—spreading so powerfully, easily, irresistibly, as well as violently, on the subject of the said *globalization* (*mondialisation* in French; *Globalisierung* in German); at the time when Christian discourse confusedly but surely informs this *doxa* and all that it carries with it, beginning with the world and the names for its "mundiality," and its vague equivalents globe, universe, earth, or *cosmos* (in its Pauline usage), Nancy's propositions may be intersecting with a strand of Heidegger's project (though his trajectory is quite different), which is to dechristianize the thinking of the world, of the "globalization of the world" [*mondialisation du monde*], of the world insofar as it mundifies or mundanizes, worldifies or worldizes (*weltet*) itself. What Nancy announces today under the title "The Deconstruction of Christianity"[31] will no doubt be the test of a dechristianizing of the world—no doubt as necessary and fatal as it is impossible. Almost by definition, one can only acknowledge this. Only Christianity can do this work, that is, undo it while doing it. Heidegger, too —Heidegger already—has only succeeded in failing at this. Dechristianization will be a Christian victory.)

What "our world" touches *in itself,* then, is nothing else but this rejection. Self-expulsion is precisely what it produces. This thinking of "touch," of the world's "self-touching," of "our world" inasmuch as it is rejected and rejects itself as foul and festering "immundity," is going to develop amply at the point when Nancy writes *Le sens du monde* (*The Sense of the World*),[32] published one year later. Indeed, it comprises a chapter on "Touch"—to which we shall return—and another, "Painting," that proffers essential, powerful things about "the threshold between intactness and touching" (*Sense of the World*, p. 81). But above all, within its very axiomatics ("The End of the world"; "There is no longer any world: no longer a *mundus*, a *cosmos*. . . . In other words, there is no longer any sense of the world" [ibid., p. 4]), it *corresponds,* in a way, with the discourse orienting *Corpus,* about rejection, abjection, expulsion.

What happens in it? And why does it fall to a work titled *Corpus* to put in place a post-Aristotelian and non-Aristotelian thinking of touch, a thinking that nevertheless continues to graze Aristotelianism where *Peri psuchēs* established that all of touch and all living beings as such are indissociable—an indissociability (let us emphasize this once again) that doesn't hold true for any of the other senses? Why does this fall to a work titled *Corpus*, a terrible, terribly *sarcastic*, book—I mean to say, a book having it out with the *flesh*, with what is termed the flesh (*sarx*), and first of all the flesh of Christ, in an implacably thinking way, an expert, ironic, interior, and biting way, all at once? (Along the way, it's not hard to imagine languages in which touch is not coextensive with all the other senses of sense, and gives rise neither to the presupposed unity of a sense named touch nor to this nondelimitable rhetoric, this endless proliferation of figures for the tangible or the tactile. In no way would I be able in these languages to write what I am writing here, or to read any of the texts we are reading here, on touching, *le toucher*: the untranslatable. Right from the title—just like *Corpus*, incidentally—it causes one to touch the untranslatable.)[33]

In its fashion, the major referent of *Corpus* is the body of a living being or a mortal, which comes down to the same thing here. It is the body of a being in the flesh, which is to say, more precisely, a being of flesh and blood. Blood, the sign and condition for *this* animal's life (and not for every living being), is also the very element of this originary rejection, its opening or passageway. There, too, at the very place where the signs *Corpus* makes in the direction of the Christic or mystic body are manifold, there will or would be a need to ward off any rechristianization of blood. For it is easy to describe Christianity as a religion of blood—beyond the point where any religion, no doubt, begins with the experience of blood.

Here, I mean in Nancy, it is as if "touch in itself" were touching blood —touching or tampering with the relation between sense and blood, between a "stroke of sense" and a sanguineous "stroke" of blood[34] (with a proximity or affinity, in French, between the former, *sens*, and the latter, *sang*, of which I ask myself, there again, how other languages would translate it, not to mention the play on "without," *sans*—devoid of privation or negativity—and "the infinite of '100' [*cent*]": creation "*without* a creator," "*without* principle and end" [*Corpus*, pp. 94, 93]).[35] Indeed, Nancy insists on this movement of rejection or self-expulsion immediately after asserting that "our world" can only "touch in itself the abjection of festering immundity." Such a movement would have no cessation, no age, no rest; in sum, it would be originary, the origin of the world. (The necessary "figure of ecotechnics," such as one sees it appear and reappear here, will later introduce us to what, it seems to me, singles out Nancy's thinking among all other modern ideas about the body proper, the flesh, touch, or the untouchable, which is to say, the taking into account of technics and technical exappropriation on the very "phenomenological" threshold of the body proper. And there, this thinking of touch, of the world and of rejection, of the possibility of the world as possibility of "its own rejection," seems both necessary and impossible, in equal measures—*mad*, fittingly; fittingly and justly mad; just to be mad; just like a certain kind of madness.)

> This exudation and this intimate agitation of the world's corpus are Psyche's *extension*. . . . This is not only the ambivalent effect of all narcissisms. *In fact*, as soon as the world *is world* it produces *itself* (it expels itself) also as foul immundity. The world *must* reject and be rejected (as) a festering im-mundity, *because its creation without a creator cannot contain itself.* Creators contain, they retain their creation and bring it to bear on themselves. But the creation of the world of bodies comes to nothing, and falls to no one. *World* means to say without principle and end: and that is what *spacing of bodies* means to say, which in its turn means nothing except the in-finite impossibility of homogenizing the world with itself, and the sap of sense with the sap of blood. Openings of the sanguine are identically those of sense—*hoc est enim* . . . —and *this* identity is made only of the absolute self-rejection that the world of bodies *is*. The subject of its creation is this rejection. The figure of ecotechnics, which propagates, in every sense and way, global swarming and the foul contagion of immundity, is the figure of this identity—and in the end, no doubt, it is this identity itself.
>
> A body expels itself, that is, as corpus, distended spastic space, rejection-of-the-subject—"immundity," if the word is to be retained. But that is how the world takes place.
>
> In a sense, the creation of the world of bodies is the impossible itself. And in a sense, in a repeated stroke of sense and sanguinity [*de sens et de sang*], the impossible is what takes place. That the sensical and the sanguine have no common schema (notwithstanding the sound and scent of their *sans* and the infinite of "100" [*cent*]); that creation is an uncontainable distancing, a fractal and architectonic catastrophe; and that coming into the world is an irrepressible rejection—all that is what body means, and what *sense* means, henceforth. The sense of the world of bodies is the *sans*—without-limit, without-reserve; it is the assured extreme of *extra* partes. In a sense, that is what sense is, in *one* sense—always renewed, always spaced out, in *one* sense and *an* other, in *a* corpus of sense and thus in all senses, but without possible totalization. The ab-

solute sense of the world of bodies, its *very* [*mêmes*] mundiality [*mondialité*] and corporeality: the excretion of sense, sense exscribed.

Thinking this makes one mad. . . . the world is its own rejection, the rejection of the world is the world. (Nancy, *Corpus*, pp. 93–95)[36]

The insistence and playfulness are remarkable here, and first, among other things, the insistent, mechanical, machinelike, and quasi-mechanistic return (understood as an introduction to ecotechnics) to the structure of *partes extra partes*,[37] the "assured extreme of *extra* partes," which had ensured or even organized Psyche's very body; and then, the playful game based on the word "sense." The plurality of the senses of the word "sense" affects each of its two principal senses: on the side of signification, of course, when one speaks of the sense of a word or the sense of the world, and so forth, but also on the side of the said sensible faculties and sensitivity, each side remaining essentially multiple, resisting community, resisting it precisely by virtue of *partes extra partes*, a contiguity without contact, or a contact as artificial, and thus technical, as superficial.

By definition, this spaced-out multiplicity can only "renew" itself— whence this concept of creation ("creation of the world of bodies," for example), which Nancy will never give up, at the very place where this creation is said to be "without a creator" and even "impossible," the impossible of an impossibility that is in truth what takes place: "the impossible is what takes place." Madness. I am tempted to say of this utterance, itself impossible, that it touches on the very condition of thinking the event. There where the *possible* is all that happens, nothing happens, nothing that is not the impoverished unfurling or the predictable predicate of what finds itself already there, potentially, and thus produces nothing new, not even accidents worthy of the name "event." The spaced-out multiplicity of senses, and of the senses of sense, and of the sense of the senses—the condition of creation as well as of the event—is also (if one may further say so) what sanctions this just madness of thinking or language, the madness aroused by phrases such as "in *a* corpus of sense and thus in all senses, but without possible totalization."

All the concepts of Nancy's new *corpus*, all the concepts that he "created," in this new sense of the word *create* (creating the world, the sense of the world, mundiality, the ex-scribed or ex-creted, sense, "the excretion of sense, sense exscribed," and so forth) are born of this just madness, and they call for a different thinking of the just.

We said that they are "born," for these *catastrophic* theses ("creation . . . is a fractal . . . catastrophe") are also thoughts of birth. They make us give thought to the birth of the body, of the *corpus*, a birth to distinguish here from plain origin. They let us think of a delivery into the world as a rejection, but also of the possibility of *rejection* in general, the rejection of the body at birth as well as the rejection of one of its essential parts—a transplanted heart, for example—by the body itself. In itself ejectable, disposable, rejectable. Immune disorder is also *in order*.[38] All that Nancy will later say about the "exscribed" essentially springs from this, it seems to me. And since it is also a matter of *self*-rejection, this source does remain essentially autobiographical. But this is true only at the point where, as we have noted, Psyche's pure autobiography is impossible, and the possibility of transplantation puts its instituting signature there. The return of "Hoc est enim . . . " in this book is more than just a mise-en-scène setting the table for transubstantiation, which is *sarcastic*, that is, mordant—a fierce transubstantiation tirelessly biting, morsel by morsel, and biting again, mortally setting upon the flesh, putting it to death; a transubstantiation of the Eucharist itself, agitating the whole *Corpus*, shaking it sometimes until it bursts out laughing. The one who speaks here presently has an experience of death, and therefore of the living body, that cannot be invoked by any of those who are like me and never stop thinking about death without having yet had a change of hearts—and without knowing, without knowing within their bodies, within their "my body," that a heart can be thrown off or rejected. Of course, they do know it, but isn't their knowledge so very poor, abstract, shameful, protected, and shamefully cozy, compared to his knowledge—that of the one who is able to put his signature to *Corpus*, who *happened* to be able to sign that *Corpus*?

To each his or her own "Hoc est enim . . . " to sign.

We have recalled one, and here is the other, on the facing page, with another accent; it is the continuation of the interrupted quotation:

Thinking this makes one mad. This thinking, if it is a thought, or the thought that it behooves one to think *that*—and nothing else. This thought: "Hoc est *enim*," here it is, the world is its own rejection, the rejection of the world is the world. Such is the world of bodies: it has in it this disarticulation, this inarticulation of *corpus*—enunciating the whole, wide-ranging *extension of sense*. In-articulating utterance [*énonciation*]—that is to say, *signification no longer, but instead, a "speaking"-body that makes no "sense," a body-"speak" that is not*

organized. At last, material sense, that is to say, madness indeed, the imminence of an intolerable convulsion in thought. One cannot think of less: it's
that or nothing. But thinking that, it's still nothing.

(It may be *laughter*. Above all, no ironizing, no mockery—but laughter, and
a body shaken by thinking that can't possibly be.) (Nancy, *Corpus*, p. 95)

From the opening pages onward, things are clear: the title, *Corpus*, first
of all rings out like such laughter, like a sort of thinking burst of laughter,
fierce and implacable before Jesus, in truth within the very evangelical
word and the Christic body. The whole book *preys* and sets upon "Hoc est
enim corpus meum," thereby announcing his work in progress, whose announced title is "The Deconstruction of Christianity." But Nancy believes
he can identify the power or reach of "Hoc est enim corpus meum" well
beyond Christian culture strictly speaking and hear in Buddhism, Islam,
and Judaism an "obstinate, or sublimated paganism."

Unless—whispers the spoilsport that I have remained, at the point of
lighting votive candles, still, in all the Catholic churches in the world, in
the role of incorrigible choirboy, and Jewish, no less—unless there is no
true beyond, beyond what I just imprudently termed "Christian culture
strictly speaking"; unless Christianity carries in itself—and all but *constitutively* consists in carrying in itself—the resource, and the law, of this de-
stricturation, of its passage beyond itself, of this ability to part without
parting, of universal abandon while remaining with oneself, in a word of
death without dying, without this "death itself" ever coming about. Then,
the deconstruction of Christianity would have its infinite task cut out for
it as its daily bread. "Hoc est enim corpus meum." Bread for the (Last
Supper) stage would safeguard the very memory of all deconstruction.
Evangelical and apocalyptic. Luke and John. Saint Augustine recalls this
clearly in *The City of God*, which also quotes Peter and John. And knowing how to read would be enough, if one can put it like that. It would be
enough to hear, but hear well, the injunctions about reading at the end of
John's Apocalypse, the terrible threats flung at those who will not hear or
do not know how to read, and at anyone tempted to add or subtract something in the witnessing text, in the "martyrdom" describing the punish-
ment reserved for those who, instead of reading and receiving, would like
to enrich the text further, or deplete it, and then write otherwise, something else—in a word, deconstruct or sign. Nancy does not want to believe
in this—nor be a believer—and neither do I. But all the same. If there is

deconstructing to do, Christianity is it (period). And Plato, predisposing one to Christianity. And Hegel, in order to sublate Christianity into absolute knowledge and so forth.[39] And Marx, in order to sublate Hegel. And Heidegger, who is never done with Luther, with Hegel, again, and Kierkegaard. For a certain Christianity will always take charge of the most exacting, the most *exact*, and the most eschatological hyperbole of deconstruction, the overbid of "Hoc est enim corpus meum." It will still make the sacrifice of its own self-deconstruction. Hey, Sade—go for it! For there is deconstruction and deconstruction. Let us never forget the Christian, in fact, Lutheran, memory of Heideggerian deconstruction (*Destruktion* was first *destructio* by Luther, anxious to reactivate the originary sense of the Gospels by deconstructing theological sediments).[40] Let us never forget this, lest one mix up all the "deconstructions" of this time. And of the world. But in truth, one can never forget this Christian (Lutheran, Pascalian, Hegelian, Kierkegaardian, Marxian, and so forth) memory when one reads Heidegger, when one also questions his denials. A "deconstruction of Christianity," if it is ever possible, should therefore begin by untying itself from a Christian tradition of *destructio*.

I shall not even attempt to comment, paraphrase, or gloss the first chapters of this *Corpus*. They are too rich, and their stitches too tightly woven. My sole ambition is to invite reading, inevitably, directly, and without interposition. I am content to track the metamorphic displacement of touch, there where the trail is in danger of disappearing.

Indeed, "touching," the lexicon of touch, strikes a grammatical pose and heads off on quite diverse rhetorical side paths. It carries a semantic tenor whose specter seems to obey a subtle and ironic play, both discreet and virtuoso. As if a master of language airily made believe he wasn't touching any of it. And by the way, is he doing it on purpose? Or is he letting a treacherous symptom show an obsession too strong to be dominated or formalized? A dread that is within language before it haunts an individual subject? And within a language that changes sense, that *touches* sense, one could say, reaching the presumed core of sense, passing from the verb "to touch" to the noun "touch," or from the noun to the adjective and the participle "touching"?

ONE. Thus, for example, just within the limits of the first three pages of the book, here is *toucher* at first, a *verb*, "touching" as a verb. From the first page, and despite a certain Thomas, there is a suggestion that this "Hoc est enim . . . " ends up forbidding us to touch, or in any case seeks to keep its body away from anything that could *touch* it: "[I]t is our obsession to show a *this* [*ceci*], and to be convincing (ourselves) that this this [*ceci*], herewith [*ici*], *is* that which one can neither see nor touch, neither here nor elsewhere—and that this is *that* [*cela*], not in whichever way, but *as its body*. The body of *that* [*ça*] (God, the absolute, whatever one wishes), that *having a body*, or that *being* a body (and thus, one may think, 'that' being *the* body—absolutely): that is what haunts us" (Nancy, *Corpus*, p. 8).

TWO. But just after that, here comes a *noun*. In order to describe the idealization that keeps the body from touching, in order to see to the sublimating subterfuge or the magical sleight of hand that makes the tangible disappear, Nancy resorts to the pictorial figure of the *touch* [*la touche*].[41] The magician's finger, which makes the tangible untouchable—this is a painter's paintbrush. He must know how to put the finishing "touch" to his simulacrum so as to make the body vanish in producing it, and so as to reduce it in affecting its production: "'Hoc est enim . . . ' defies, appeases all our doubts about mere illusions, giving to the real the true finishing touch of its pure Idea, that is, its reality, its existence. One would never be done with modulating the variants of these words (randomly listed: *ego sum* [the title of that other great book by Nancy, thus dealing with egological fiction], nudes in painting, Rousseau's *Social Contract*, Nietzsche's madness, Montaigne's *Essais*, Antonin Artaud's 'nerve-meter' [*Pèse-nerfs*])" (ibid., p. 8). If one reads what follows, it goes the way of the whole culture, "the whole texture interweaving us": "*Body*: that is how we invented it. Who else in the world knows it?" (ibid.).

THREE. Now, just after the verb and the noun, here comes the attribute of a past participle or *adjective*, introduced by a "soon" [*sitôt*] that is more troubling than ever: "As soon as it is touched. . . . " As for this desensitizing operation, indeed, this anesthesia, this sublimating idealization that produces the body, the "this" and "here" of the body, while making it inaccessible to touch, we know that it engenders anguish—anguish before death, as it were, but protecting itself against itself, a sort of anesthesia of anesthesia, a euthanasia contract after the terms of which, while pretending one is dealing out death to oneself until the end of time, one ends up succeeding.

We ask, What is *this* [*ceci*]? And why does the "this" of famous "sense certainty" evaporate in the very indetermination of all here-and-now and all this? One does not have to wait for Hegel's *Phenomenology of Spirit* to suffer the wounds of the said "sense certainty." In order to describe the point at which the latter is all at once attained and wounded ("attained" in the sense of "reached," become accessible, but also reaching out toward an "attaint," and the sense of a harm that is "sustained"), Nancy says of it that it is "touched": no sooner has one attained it, no sooner has one touched it, no sooner does one believe one is touching it, than one wounds it, finding it harmed already, attainted, cut into, vulnerable at once, and even sick. It is not what it used to be, nor what one believed it to be. Waking from this anesthesia, sense certainty becomes mad. It mixes up everything. What makes sense, Rimbaud says, are the senses in disarray. Adjective, attribute, past participle: "As soon as it is touched, sense certainty turns to chaos, to tempest, and every sense to disarray.[¶] Body is certainty startled and shattered. Nothing is more properly of our old world, nothing more foreign to it" (ibid., p. 9).

FOUR. Retouching the verb. What in fact happens just after that—after the verb, the noun, the past participle, or adjective have had their turn? We turn to the verb *toucher*, "to touch," again. Paradox: we shall now be shown that if one has sought (as in ONE) not to "touch," to keep the body from touching; if one has longed for the untouchable; if one has had to add a "finishing touch" (as in TWO) to the idealization and the conjuring away of touch; if sense certainty is thus "touched" by this (as in THREE) until the senses are in disarray, it is because of a desire or a hyperbolic hunger to "touch," to be what one wants to touch by eating it. "Touch" turns around, and everything seems to be decided. All of Nancy's new conceptuality (*Begrifflichkeit*), a seizing put-upon or at grips with one's grasp,[42] receives the mark of this, beginning with another thought of the body, of the mundane and "immund" world, and of freedom, and first and foremost, of what from now on *excribes* itself as the *ex-scribed* (as expulsion, originary abjection, and so forth).

At this turning point (though one could find other metonymies), one seizes again the resource or springlock of Nancy's thinking—his *weighing*, as we shall say later—and in it, let's say, that which might make a *beam* of the scales—or a "flail," or even "scourge," the "flail" proper, which is to say every sense of the French word *fléau*: an instrument for threshing or flagellating; evil; calamity; cataclysm or disaster; baneful wound; sometimes, precisely, the scales or scourge or flail *of* God; or as God; but especially an implement of justice with scales that *weigh exactly, necessarily, the unthinkable and unweighable [l'impe(n)sable], the impossible, the unbear-*

able, and give the immense its exact measure. A question of hearts, and of foreign bodies, a question of exappropriation of the ownmost and most proper, as autoimmune desire of the proper, I would say. An implacable deconstruction of modern philosophies of the body proper and the "flesh." So it should surprise no one that this turning around of touch should produce the concept of *ex-tirpation, expulsion* of the desirable, of the *exscribed* and the *body far-flung* or *lost*, during the course of a sequence with the Last Supper busy eating the body—in truth, eating God's heart out, the Sacred Heart:

> But instantly, always, it is a foreign body that shows itself—monstrance of a monster impossible to swallow. There's no getting away, one is caught up in a vast waste of images stretching from a Christ who daydreams over his unleavened bread to a Christ who extirpates from himself a throbbing, bloody Sacred Heart. This, this . . . *this* is always too much, or not enough, to be *that*.
>
> And all the ways of thinking the "body proper," the laborious efforts to reappropriate what was believed to be unfortunately "objectified," or "reified"; all the ways of thinking about the body proper are contortions of comparable scope: they end up with nothing but the expulsion of what one wished for.
>
> Being in anguish, wishing to see, touch and eat the body of God, to *be* this body and to *be nothing but that*, all that makes up the principle of (un)reason of the West. At a stroke, the body, any body, any of the body, *never takes place there*, and *especially not when one names or summons it there*. For us, the body is always sacrificed—holy host.
>
> If "Hoc est enim corpus meum" says anything, it is outside and beyond any words [*hors de parole*], it isn't said, it is exscribed—the body lost in a mindless thrust [*à corps perdu*]. (Nancy, *Corpus*, p. 9)[43]

One is never done with an analysis of the variations, and keys touched upon, in playing this hymn to touch, to tactful fingering, which is to say to con-tact as interrupted contact. After the passage I have just quoted, over ten short pages: "the body *must* touch down" (p. 11); "Writing: to touch on extremity" (p. 12); "Nothing else happens to writing, then, if something should happen to it, except *touching*. More precisely: touching the body. . . . Writing touches the body, by essence . . . that's where it's touching" (p. 13); "points of tangency, touches . . . " (p. 14).[44]

Shall one join him when he says that this history of the world and the body is merely Christian, or even Abrahamic, and limited to the West ("principle of (un)reason of the West")? And to the body "for us," implying "we," the Jewish, Christian, or Muslim heirs of "Hoc enim corpus meum," as the beginning of the text suggests it? Or is it a universal "history"? Or further, in greater likelihood, the history of the production of every "universalism" and "globalization"—through the obligatory passage of a surreptitious, autoimmune, and globalatinizing[45] Christianization? And therefore to be begun in Latin, with "Hoc enim corpus meum" (Matt. 26: 26), rather than the Greek τοῦτό ἐστιν τὸ σῶμά μου.[46]

Is Psyche a beautiful Christian woman? Is she one or the other, one and the other, of the two Marys whose fascinating hallucination inspired us with a few questions some time ago? And what if there were several "bodies" in the world, and what if this body or that other one resisted the Christian corpus, sometimes within the very heart, the very body of a Christian? At the very same time when a non-Christian can conversely inhabit, without knowing it, a Christian body? Other cultures, perhaps every culture, could have produced this idealizing anesthesia, this neutralization, this euthanasia of the body, even before being touched (be it indirectly) by any virtual Christianization.

To avoid any confusion, is it necessary to change words, then, in order to tell the difference of bodies? Is it necessary to resort to another term instead of "corpus"? And instead of "touch," or "touching," by the same token?

Nancy may be suggesting this, and here one can measure what is at stake in a translation. One wonders who will be able to tell us what happens when one translates *corps.* Let us just think of the difficulties that already await us in the snuggest Western domesticity: how is one to translate in one word the difference between *Körper* and *Leib*? And as for *body* in English (in all the places, for example, where it is an obsession for American culture and academia), who could one lead with a straight face to believe that it is a trustworthy equivalent of all that we term *corps, corps propre,* or *chair* [flesh]? And once it has been subjected to the euthanasic test of anesthesia of which we speak, doesn't it rather, sooner, all too soon, very soon turn into a sort of "corpse," the more or less glorious body of a cadaver?[47] In a word, when Freud seems to lay the psyche upon the horizontality of a surface, on a bed or a "couch," when he speaks on the subject of psyche as body, on the subject of this submissive and subjected subjectivity, and extension, is he referring to the Christian body?

To say of Psyche that she is "extended," even if Eros has enough tact not to touch her, is to recall that she remains or should remain tangible, as a body—against Descartes and against Kant, against extension without body, against intelligible extension and against the extension of pure sensibility devoid of any empirical sensation. It is also to recall what Freud had said about this, precisely, in this "posthumous" note, the "brief tune" quoted first: "Psyche ist ausgedehnt, weiss nichts davon."

She knows nothing of this, at the point when one speaks of it; she is bound to a secret; she knows nothing of herself—in particular, of herself extended, and therefore always far off, self-distanced, no matter how close she is. Tangible, to be sure, yet untouchable. For Eros, at least. At least when Eros is tactful. And experienced—or even an expert—in caresses.

What is still needed from here on? An explanation as to why the *Peri psuchēs* of our time is now called *Corpus*, by Jean-Luc Nancy.

§ 4 The Untouchable, or the Vow of Abstinence

*The Exorbitant, 1—Tact "beyond the possible"
—Stroking, Striking, Thinking, Weighing:
Mourning Eros and the Other Hand of . . .*

Wem gefiele nicht eine Philosophie, deren Keim ein erster Kuss ist?
Who would not like a philosophy whose kernel is a first kiss?
—Novalis

What to give him, and how? Would it have to be? Does it have to be?
I did not know what to present as an offering to Jean-Luc Nancy in order to tell him of my gratitude and admiration, whose limits I cannot even
measure, which I have felt for him for too long—and have seen revived or
rejuvenated too often—even to attempt to tell myself their story. There is
no declaration for these things, they shouldn't be declared, either publicly
or privately.

For there is a *law of tact.*

Perhaps the law is always a law *of tact.* This law's law finds itself there,
before anything. There is this law, and it is the law itself, the law of the
law. One cannot imagine what a law would be in general without something like tact: one must touch without touching. In touching, touching
is forbidden: do not touch or tamper with the thing itself, do not touch
on what there is to touch. Do not touch what remains to be touched, and
first of all law itself—which is the untouchable, *before* all the ritual prohibitions that this or that religion or culture may impose on touching, as
suggested earlier. And this enjoins us to respect, and above all to respect in
the Kantian sense, so to speak, where it is first of all respect for the law, respect for which is precisely the *cause* of respect, that is to say, in the first
place, to respect the law rather than the person. This only gives an example of it. Respect commands us to keep our distance, to touch and tamper
neither with the law, which is respectable, nor—therefore—with the un-

touchable. The untouchable is thus kept at a distance by the gaze, or *regard*, in French (meaning *respect* in its Latin provenance), or in any case at an attentive distance, in order to watch out carefully, to guard (as in *achten, Achtung*, in German) against touching, affecting, corrupting. One is not to touch the law commanding that one not touch. Hasty conclusion: tact, one could say, is what *confines* to the origin and the essence of law. And one should understand tact, not in the common sense of the tactile, but in the sense of knowing how to touch *without* touching, without touching *too much*, where touching is already too much. Tact touches on the origin of the law. Just barely. At the limit. By essence, structure, and situation, the endurance of a limit as such consists in touching *without* touching the outline of a limit.

There is a law of tact.[1]

Before any vow of abstinence, before any self-imposed interdict, is there an untouchable, are there untouchables? And what is more, quasi-transcendental ones? One might think so, for such a vow of abstinence could hardly retain us and impose any restraint except where some untouchable remains at least possible, already possible. Conversely, what would such a vow of abstinence be if *there* touching were not always possible, effectively possible or promised? What if this possibility of the promise, this promised possibility, were not already *there*, not here but *there*, haunting abstinence itself, sometimes to the point of intensifying its transgression, the unforgivable perjury at the heart of the interdict? Is this double, undecidable logic (Eros in mourning at the most intense of Eros's living desire) already a logic of the unconscious? Perhaps.

There is a law of tact there.[2]

Touching, in any case, thus remains limitrophe; it touches what it does not touch; it does not touch; it *abstains* from touching on what it touches, and within the abstinence retaining it at the heart of its desire and need, in an inhibition truly constituting its appetite, it eats without eating what is its nourishment, touching, without touching, what it comes to cultivate, elevate, educate, drill [*dresser*] (*trephein*).

But what *mēchanē*, what trick, what fatal machination does such a law always keep in store? Between two given orders—yes, given as given as much as ordered (do touch but *do not* touch, in no way, do touch *without* touch-ing, do touch *but* do watch out and avoid any contact)—it in effect installs a kinship that is at the same time *conjunctive* and *disjunctive*. Worse than that, it brings into contact both contradictory orders (do do and do not do), thus exposing them to contamination or contagion. But what it thus brings into contact, or rather into contiguity, *partes extra partes*, is first of all con-tact *and* noncontact. And this contact without contact, this barely touching touch is unlike any other, in the very place where all it touches is the other.

There is no facile thinking or formulation whatsoever in this—rather, it is madness. It is certainly always possible painlessly to produce and re-produce these paradoxical formulas. It is certainly always possible to speak as a somnambulist, to handle symbols stripped of any intuition,[3] to pro-nounce apparently paradoxical syntagmas such as, to define "tact" or "fin-gering" [*doigté*], for example, "touch without touching," "contact without contact," or "contact without contact between contact and noncontact."

But one certainly feels (as will be verified, and verified precisely by test-ing the very senses of the word "sense," of the French *sens* or *sentir*, which tend to come down, though not reductively, to the word "touch") that from Aristotle to Nancy, aporias (originally Aristotle's word), as aporias of touch, lead us to think the essence of touch only through language that paradoxi-cal, more than contradictory and hyperdialectical (x without x, x = non-x, x = conjunction and/or disjunction of x plus and minus x, and so on).

Whereabouts of the impossible: is tact (tact that would know how to touch without touching, a contact without contact) knowledge or know-how? Isn't this an impossible knowledge or a thinking of impossible knowl-edge? Yet one recognizes in it the figure of the Law, capital Law, led by its uppercase letter. Here, before any other (religious, ethical, juridical, or other) determination, we hear and understand law as commandment, which is to say the interruption in the contact or continuity with what we have learned to call "nature." Now, one can speak of tact (for example), and con-tact without contact, only where there is a law dictating or prescribing, and enjoining what is not (natural). And this is produced in "nature," well be-fore man, and always before the distinction between the beings and the liv-ing. And that is enough to discredit every opposition fundamentally: na-ture/culture, nature/mind or consciousness, *physis/nomos*, *thesis* or *technē*, animality/humanity, and so forth.

Now in this regard it is no longer possible to ask the question of touch *in general*, regarding some *essence* of touch in general, *before* determining the "who" or the "what," the touching or touched, which we shall not too hastily call the subject or object of an act. There is not in the first place *the* sense of touch, followed by secondary modifications that allow the verb to be completed by a subject or a complement (that is, what touches whom or what, who touches whom or what).

There is little doubt that Aristotle took into account a differential transformation of touch depending on the diversity of tangible things, and perhaps on what this grammatical distribution may specify. However, for lack of sufficient indications on this subject,[4] one wonders whether in Aristotle's *Peri psuchēs*, his treatise on touch, there was room for *blows* (for striking blows in all their multiplicity, a multiplicity that may not be reducible to any general blow) or *caresses* (all stroking caresses, which may not be accessible either by way of any subsumption under one concept of the caress in general). A blow is perhaps not a kind of destructive touching, indeed, of the excessive tangibility that, as Aristotle already noted, can have devastating effects. Likewise, stroking is not only a species of soothing, beneficial, and pleasant touch, pleasure enjoyed by contact. Striking and stroking address a "who" rather than a "what," "the other" rather than some other in general. Such a living "who" is no more necessarily human, moreover, than it is a subject or an "I." And above all it is not a man any more than a woman.

What, then, is a treatise of touch that says nothing about this: "Who touches whom? And how?"; "Who strikes whom? Who strokes whom? And why? And how?" Let us insist again that various causes or qualities do not come and modify or modalize one single, selfsame, presupposed generality of what we conveniently term the "caress" and the "blow." There again, they constitute a multiplicity without the horizon of a totalizable unity. For, let us not hide this from ourselves, by this stroke, and with a caress—a caress may be a blow and vice versa—it comes down to the conceptual condition of concepts. And let us not exclude either that certain experiences of touching (of "who touches whom") do not simply pertain to blows and caresses. What about a kiss? Is it one caress among many? What about a kiss on the mouth? What about a biting kiss, as well as everything that can then be exchanged between lips, tongues, and teeth?[5] Are blows wanting there? Are they absent in coitus, in all the penetrations or acts of homosexual or heterosexual sodomy? Is a "caress," more so than a "blow," enough of a concept to say something of this experience of "touching" of which Aristotle, followed by all those who came after him in the great traditional philosophy of touch, hardly breathed a word?

As for Nancy, he does not fail to name the caress and the blow, or more precisely—for *verbs* and gestures are what counts—*stroking* and *striking*, among a nonfinite number of other experiences, in what he terms the "tactile corpus," under the heading "Weighing" [*"Pesée"*]. Of course, I am underscoring the words *striking* and *stroking*, as well as a point that will be important for us later on, in that there is no sexual difference marked here as a dual or dissymmetric opposition, which does not mean that sexual difference is not taken into account—on the contrary: "Tactile corpus: skimming, grazing, pressing, pushing in, squeezing, smoothing, scratching, rubbing, *stroking*, palpating, groping, kneading, massaging, embracing, hugging, *striking*, pinching, biting, sucking, wetting, holding, letting go, licking, jerking, looking, listening, smelling, tasting, avoiding, kissing, cradling, swinging, carrying, weighing."[6]

Why does he end his list here? What right has he to do so? Are there operations that are completely independent of any tactile semantics and rhetoric? And that would rightfully be excluded from this series? This question will remain with us, under this form or another; it concerns what this corpus has left out. But the opposite question also looms: it concerns inclusion no less than exclusion. And so, by classifying "looking" and "listening" in a tactile corpus, does one follow this traditional or even classical gesture (a gesture we shall keep recognizing later on), which consists in including sight and hearing, as well as *all* the senses, in the general or fundamental sense of touch? This hypothesis is confirmed just afterward by the inclusion of "smelling" and "tasting," the sense of smell and the sense of taste. Or, on the contrary, is it a matter of challenging in that tradition that which would pertain to retaining only the most proper and most literal in what is called touching? What could make one lean toward the second hypothesis in this list would rather be the inclusion of verbal expressions such as "letting go" [*lâcher*] or "avoiding" [*éviter*], which rather than touching seem, on the contrary, literally to signify noncontact, interruption, spacing, a hiatus at the core of contact—tact, precisely! And the heartbeat, with its syncopal interruptions, which gives its rhythm to pulse, pulsion, or even haptical compulsion, the *cum* of con-tact, coming to link or conjoin only where disconnection remains at work, as well as a possible disjunction. Not to mention, in this reckoning, that the French grammar of this corpus and the series of transitive verbs referring to an object of sense lead to the discovery of more undecidable ones, undecidably transitive and/or intransitive ones, "wetting," for example, but especially "weighing," which we have yet to examine.

I have something like a vision of the future, then. I imagine generations of philosophers. Do you see them, as I do, soon leaning over this page by Nancy, over this *tactile corpus* as over a table of categories? A corpus, upon a table without operations or anatomy lessons, but with so many problems! And as with all tables of categories, from Aristotle to Kant, one would ask oneself whether this list is truly grounded and closable, or here or there rhapsodic.

First of all, what has entitled me, too—why have I underscored two verbs in this corpus, *stroking* and *striking*? Why this privilege—if not as a concession to a logic that I had called into question a little earlier? Suppose that I did it for sheer pedagogical or provisional convenience, so as to tie in again, in a barely visible, elliptical, and virtual fashion, with a problematic and texts that Nancy does not mention and that we shall soon try to recognize, in this chapter and the following ones.[7]

Then comes a question for Nancy, as I just said: why close this list? Why this way of punctuating? And for a corpus or table, what do the suspension points signify if not a concession to a vague "et cetera"? And why not a deduction, then? Why an *enumeration*, a *juxtaposition* (*partes extra partes*, precisely, as he likes to say so often), there where one experience finds itself implicated in advance in another one, and conjoined to another one, whatever the originality or even the acute independence of each one may be? For in the end, can one be caressing without doing— after a fashion, to be sure—so many other things that pertain to the same "tactile corpus," and making other gestures such as "skimming, grazing, pressing," and so forth? Moreover, doesn't Nancy himself subtract from the list one concept, which he turns into a sort of transcendental of all the other ones, namely, to weigh, the act of "weighing," the one that comes last? Doesn't he state immediately afterward that this multiplicity converges in the end, be it beyond any synthetic composition? "Even without synthesis, everything communicates with weighing in the end. A body weighs always, or lets itself be weighed, weighed out" (*Corpus*, p. 82).

This is another way of saying that, in this *tactile corpus*, one is dealing less with a categorial list of operations that consist in touching than with *thinking*, which is to say pondering, *weighing* that which gives itself over to tact in a thousand ways, namely, the body, the *corpus*, inasmuch as it weighs—and therefore, in a certain way, *thinks*. Whether thinking is extended or weighs, along the way, we have apparently moved from the extension of a Psyche (the soul or thought "is" extended) to weight, body weight ("a body weighs always"), as well as the weight of thought.

Now, this changes something as far as tact and touching are concerned. Extension can remain intelligible (with Descartes) or sensible-insensible (with Kant and a few others), and thus intangible. The extension of a body, a body inasmuch as it is extended, can thus remain untouchable. Can one say as much about a body or thought that *weighs*?

Let us note in passing that "The Weight of a Thought," a section of the book *The Gravity of Thought*,[8] works out a *double question*, with a breadth, a precision, and a force that I will not try to reconstitute here. First, it is the question of the etymology that "relates thinking [*pensée*] to weighing [*pesée*]";[9] then, by the same stroke, the question of the "figure of speech" seeming to have a stake in an "intimate co-appropriation of thinking and weighing" (p. 76). Nancy does not give up the "etymologist's desire," nor does he give in to it, or to any of the temptations that Jean Paulhan so rightly denounced in his book on "etymological proof":[10] " . . . to have us accede," Nancy says, "at least by reason of a trace deposited in language, to a weighty/weighing property of thought, which would be identical to a thinking property of the weighty thing" ("Weight of a Thought," p. 76).

He questions the postulation of this irrepressible desire, and this leads him to a series of undecidable or contradictory propositions, of which he then accepts, formalizes, and (let's say) powerfully *thinks* the necessity. It goes without saying that we shall find this necessity to be identical or analogous, again with the same problems, on the subject of touching. Here is just one example of these dense formulations:

> This is not to say that the intimate co-appropriation of thinking and weighing is a mere figure of speech, or the phantasm of a somewhat alchemical materialism. On the contrary, this appropriation is certain and absolute. The act of thinking *is* an actual weighing; it is the very weighing of the world, of things, of the *real* as *sense*. . . . the co-appropriation of sense and the real is precisely that by which existence always precedes itself, as itself, that is to say, insofar as it is without essence—insofar as it *is* the without-essence.
>
> This absolutely indubitable point of the reciprocal and archi-originary appropriation of weighing and thinking (which is truly the creation of the world) is equally, identically, the absolute point of inappropriability: we have no more access to the weight of sense than (consequently) to the sense of weight.
>
> And it is not having such an access that makes us thinking as well as weighty beings, and that strikes the chord within us, as our*selves*, of this discord of weight and thought that constitutes the whole weight of a thought.
>
> (This does not mean that such access would be available for other beings:

the co-appropriation of weighing and thinking, just as it is reached in etymology only through a metaphorical reversal [*bascule*] that always precedes itself, is in and of itself inaccessible, and definitely so; its terms define it in this way, just as they command it to occupy its place-without-access.) (ibid., pp. 76–77)

This place without access seems to overdetermine itself, if I am not being imprudent or flighty here, in belonging to a sense of the *world* as *earth*, which is to say a certain law of gravity—to be pondered.[11]

In this context, as he does elsewhere and so often, Nancy repeatedly has recourse to the lexicon of *exactitude* ("exact," "exactly," and so on), words that are so strangely familiar to him. And we shall come back again to these words, which here seem particularly appropriate (notwithstanding the usual reservations that have just been recalled), if not reserved for the affinity between thinking and weighing: "Thinking weighs *exactly* the weight of sense," or "*The weight of a thought* is *quite exactly* [*très exactement*] the inappropriability of appropriation, or the impropriety of the proper (proper to the proper itself, absolutely)."[12] At the very moment when he superlativizes exactitude ("*quite* exactly"), a hyperbolic overbidding comes to characterize—precisely, exactly—an impropriety, an inappropriability, something like an inexactitude. It would seem as if all of Nancy is signing this gesture (the minute difference of a letter, *n*, is poised [in French] between thinking and weighing, *penser* and *peser*): never to give up the summons of exactitude, the most *exacting, demanding* petition,[13] as one would say in English (the most exigent, astringent, enjoining), at the very moment when limits become inaccessible, contradictory or undecidable, and apparently despairing of any exact determination. Always, Nancy remains determining and determined—that is his "probity"—within the thinking-weighing of what best resists determination, which he determines in a determined and determining fashion precisely in that, in this place, to this limit, at this point —be it a vanishing point. Let's just say that he works on weighing-thinking the unthinkable-unweighable [*l'impe(n)sable*] exactly; he gauges (thinks-weighs) the impossible as exactly as possible, whereby he remains a rigorous philosopher at the very moment when the limits of the philosophic come to tremble. It is without trembling, then, that Nancy submits himself to the trembling.

And so he is at work on the concept and works at the concept, and first the concept of what he terms the *exscribed*, which needs to be analyzed exactly in its relation to the concept, to style, and to the Nancean ethos of *exactitude*.

While these texts have often been translated, they remain untranslatable, no doubt. They speak to us of this untranslatability, of this "trace deposited in language." How is one to translate into English or German the affinity in French between *penser* and *peser*? One might wish more often to have at one's disposal a set of analyses as sobering as these, as vigilant and fair with regard to etymologistic desire or metaphoric power, to undecidable and nondialecticizable contradictions, when such an affinity inscribed in another family of languages is at issue—for example, concerning thought, the affinity between *denken* and *danken* and "thinking" and "thanking." Even in French, we often refer to it, at the precise moment when, in Heidegger's wake, we seek the specificity of a *thinking* that can be reduced neither to poetry nor to philosophy nor to science. And some are often content with an admiring, trusting, even incantatory reference to the miracle of language: German or English, in which the same gift may be recognized in "thought" and "thanks," and here, in the first place, a gift of languages, the good luck, as Hegel put it, of an idiom that is originally speculative.

If one gave in to the same wonder, one would point out that the verb *peser* ("to weigh") is conjugated in French *simultaneously* as both transitive *and* intransitive, precisely like the verb *penser* ("to think"). This "simultaneously" at a stroke bestows its genius, its stroke of genius, upon this sentence of Nancy's: "La pensée pèse exactement le poids du sens" (literally, "Thinking [or thought] weighs exactly the weight of sense"). The event of this sentence takes place once only. It signals an invention, signed but reassigned to the account of language, the language one speaks, appropriates, yet never possesses. Thus, one can well see that his sentence, "Thought weighs exactly the weight of sense" plays out, while respecting it exactly, an unstable grammar, a syntax that is untranslatable in its duplicity:

1. Transitivity: thought *weighs*, and by weighing it examines and weighs out what it is weighing, evaluating sense exactly; it indicates its exact weight.

2. Intransitivity: thought *weighs*: it is weighty as much as pondering or thinking; it has the weight of sense; it weighs, itself, what sense weighs, neither more nor less, exactly.

What, then, is the hypothesis worth that Nancy on his own does not juxtapose modalities of tactility? And the hypothesis that the theme, in his tactile corpus, is corpus as much as it is tact? I believe it to be confirmed by another piece of evidence. In this open series, since it is a matter of thinking the body sooner than tactility, we can also find—and I have underscored—sensible perceptions not ordinarily associated with touch, for example *looking, listening, smelling, tasting*. All the senses are included in this *tactile corpus*, not only touching, but also seeing, hearing, smelling, and tasting.

—Weren't you asking, even before the beginning, whether we could caress or stroke each other with our eyes? And touch the look that touches you?

—We are slowly approaching the *figure* of touch. Earlier, I spoke of a contamination or a contagion that would have the peculiarity of putting in contact (without contact) contact *and* noncontact. Contamination then becomes what it is not; it disidentifies itself. It disidentifies everything even before it disidentifies *itself*. It disappropriates, it disappropriates itself, it attains what it should never signify, namely, an interruption of relations and the ex-propriety of the proper.

The law in fact commands to touch *without* touching it. A vow of abstinence. Not to touch the friend (for example, by abstaining from giving him a present or from presenting oneself to him, out of modesty [*par pudeur*]), to not *touch him* enough is to be lacking in tact; however, *to touch him*, and to touch him too much, to touch him to the quick, is also tactless.

Yes, one will have to talk about the caress, which cannot be reduced to simple contact, be it contact with the other, nor to any of the other experiences that have been evoked, before and after "stroking." The caress gives *or* takes. And/or it gives *and* takes. In giving it takes; it gives to take; it takes up giving—what one calls pleasure a little hastily. In pleasure, the caress besieges us, it invests us with a nontheoretical and besetting question, with a worry constitutive of pleasure itself: "What is this pleasure? What is that? Where does it come from? From the other or from me? Am I taking it? Am I giving it? Is it the other who gives it to me? Or takes it from me? The time of this pleasure—is it that I am giving *it myself*?" And so forth. And if all these hypotheses were not contradictory or incompatible, how would one need to think them? Declare them? Even confess them? Confessing them and touching them as the stakes of touch itself, as if the grammar of the response to acknowledged gratitude ("Thank you for what you give me") remained undecidable ("But no, I'm not giving you anything, I'm giving *myself* . . . ," etc. "You're saying, I'm giving myself. Is that so? Do you mean to say, 'I'm giving myself' or 'I'm giving myself *to* myself'?" etc.).

The caress finds itself no less affected by this and divided in truth by this salvo of contradictory injunctions. The order, the command is no longer altogether that of tact: to touch without touching; to press without pressing, always more, always too much, never enough; to give without holding back or retaining, but with restraint; to give to hold without holding on; to give without imposition: "Tiens!" [There! Hold on to this! Take it! Have it!—Trans.]. What is one saying, what is one giving to understand, when one says "Tiens!"[?] Is what is wanting here the virtual shadow, at least, of a hand gesture ("Tiens!": "Take this!"), a touching hand or a handing one, a hand given to touch the other, an extended hand held out or extending something to the other? "Tiens!" Take this! But tact's command is neither to tender nor to grasp ourselves and each other without trembling, without some relinquishment at the heart of the seizing. Tact enjoins not to touch, not to take what one takes, or rather not to be taken in by what one takes. Tact beyond contact. Which does not necessarily mean to say a *neutralization* of touching.

One of our concerns incidentally bears on this enigmatic hypothesis of neutrality. Could there be a touch or tactile experience that is neutral? And this can be understood in multiple ways—three at least:

1. The way of a *theoretical touch*, that is to say objective, knowing, exploratory in the epistemic sense of this word: touching in order to know, *in view of* the knowledge of an *object*: that which is *before oneself* but can thus also present itself to sight (the theorem) or that which *resists* and seems more appropriate for haptical objectivity; the privilege of the theoretical touch has always been central in every philosophy of touch.

2. The way of a touch preceding any drive, invested or committed; *before caresses or blows*, and even before this prehensile and comprehensive grasping that one can detect in the most "theoretical" of touches.

3. The way of a *phenomenological neutralization*, a "phenomenological reduction," which would leave intact—in order to analyze them or describe their constitution—all the intentional modalities that we have just mentioned.

Contradictory injunctions, thus, at the heart of touch. Can they still give rise to a phenomenology, or to what Emmanuel Levinas termed a "phenomenology of voluptuousness" as early as in the years 1946–47, in the first edition of *Time and the Other*?[14] One day, together and separately, one will indeed have to reread these two thinking approaches to the caress, Levinas's and Nancy's, and from the outset follow this theme within each of their trajectories, more particularly in order to pinpoint their respective differences in relation to phenomenology, beyond the discrepancies that keep them apart.

In Levinas's work, long before *Totality and Infinity* (1961)[15] and its "Phenomenology of Eros," *Time and the Other* includes a chapter, "Eros," which tells of the caress as contact beyond contact: "The caress is a mode of the subject's being, where the subject who is in contact with another goes beyond this contact. Contact as sensation is part of the world of light" (*Time and the Other*, p. 89). Which is another way of saying that the caress carries beyond phenomenality, indeed beyond any contact sensation, or any contact as sensation, and does not share with sight this being enclosed within a totality, this belonging to the immanence of the world. Voluptuousness is not a "pleasure like others," it is not "solitary." Somewhat recklessly, Levinas then states that eating and drinking, on the other hand, are solitary pleasures, whereas the caress takes away erotic experience from any "fusion" and recalls "the exceptional place of the feminine."

Let us not linger here over this aspect, which I have touched on elsewhere;[16] let us just keep it company for a step beyond the stop, the one carrying this analysis of caressing further than touching, though *still in accordance with the hand, the hand only*: "Contact as sensation is part of the world of light. But what is caressed is not touched, properly speaking. It is not the softness or warmth of the hand given in contact that the caress seeks. The seeking of the caress constitutes its essence by the fact that the caress does not know what it seeks. This 'not knowing,' this fundamental disorder, is the essential" (Levinas, *Time and the Other*, p. 89).

The limit seems unequivocal, but it is subtle. Levinas, Levinas's hand, is proposing it. From the outset, we are clearly told that the caress does not fall under the sense called touch, not even under contact or the sensation one relates to contact: "what is caressed is not touched," "not touched, properly speaking." Is this clear enough? One could be tempted to put this proposition side by side with Maurice Merleau-Ponty's when the latter, without however naming the caress, speaks of a certain *untouchability* of the other, or rather of the other inasmuch as the other comprises some untouchable and thus gives me access to this thinking of the untouchable as such.[17]

But this same language immediately acknowledges that it is hostage to rhetoric. Levinas specifies that it is only with regard to touching "properly speaking" that the caress remains alien or heterogeneous. It is only with regard to sensation as world of light, with regard to "knowing" and knowing what one "seeks" that the caress goes *beyond*. The caress transcends touch, sensibility, and knowing "properly speaking." But Levinas makes believe that here we know what speaking means to say properly speaking, and what touching, sensation, light, and knowledge signify "properly speaking."

At the time of *Time and the Other*, and perhaps later still, Levinas maintains and keeps this discourse within an ontological code. He blames Freud for not understanding this pleasure "in the general economy of being." But already he matches the experience of the caress and its "not knowing" accordingly with the apprehension of time, with pure temporalization as absolute anticipation. One is tempted to say of this (though this is obviously not Levinas's language here)[18] that it is quasi-messianic: "The caress is the expectation of this pure future (to come), without content" (*Time and the Other*, p. 89). More insistently: "My thesis, which consists in affirming voluptuousness as the very event of the future, the future purified of all content, the very mystery of the future, seeks to account for its exceptional place" (ibid., p. 90).

It is this attention given to the future that is the keynote of the analyses devoted to love and Eros in *Totality and Infinity*. But the word "future" could still mislead us if we heard in it merely the modality of a time beyond the now present that will form the horizon of another possible, virtual, and promised present. The chapter devoted to the "Phenomenology of Eros" specifies in this respect and underscores again what Levinas had just written on the score of "The Ambiguity of Love," which is to say, "through the face filters the obscure light coming from beyond the face, from what *is not yet*, from a future never future enough, more remote than the possible" (Levinas, *Totality and Infinity*, p. 254).[19] There where "the caress aims at the tender," it carries toward the future beyond the future, which here simultaneously means beyond a future present and the very possibility of a being-able, of every "I can." That is why I am tempted to say, in a language that is no longer Levinas's but does not necessarily betray him either, that there where I touch without touching, in caressing, the order of the promise itself is what finds itself thereupon exceeded or disqualified, and with it the order of what one quietly thinks and fits under the category of performatives, of an "I can" that would have the power to produce an event through a legitimized speech act, in a sure context, and following agreed-upon conventions. The event as such, if there is any, couldn't care less about the performative or the constative. In caressing, and even when the one doing the stroking is being stroked, without there ever being the least symmetry or the common measure of some reciprocity, this event affects us, before and despite any possibility and any power of being-able, any legitimacy of an "I can," and even an "I know." Should the caress be an event, that is what happens with it.

Levinas does not say it in this way, to be sure, and surely what I just suggested is (perhaps—I can't be sure; some terminological decision should still arbitrate here) valid for any event worthy of the name, beyond what we might wish to circumscribe as a narrow, literal sense of the caress. But if this defeat (which is not necessarily an unfortunate one) of the performative facing the event remains the rightful consequence of what Levinas tells us about the caress, about the "*regime* of tenderness" and the "future never future enough, more remote than the possible," in truth, the "obscure light coming from beyond the face," then what finds itself exceeded is not only the order of power, of knowledge, of temporality ordered in the present, the order of the theoretical constative or the praxic and productive performative, it is the order of the face itself. Hence the extraordinary "equivocal" or "equivocation" (which is the terminology Levinas uses repeatedly) marking this whole approach of the voluptuous caress. Equivocal—for what "filters" through the face exceeds the face. Like the flesh ("The carnal, the tender *par excellence* correlative of the caress"; "In the carnal given to tenderness, the body quits the status of an existent" [Levinas, *Totality and Infinity*, p. 258]),[20] the caress, in Levinas's analyses, is unsettling for all that is ordered in keeping with the face, which is to say almost everything. And doesn't what we suggest of the "equivocal" also suit the "exorbitant," Levinas's other predicate, which he accords on a regular basis to this experience of the carnal caress? The *exorbitant* makes a sign toward what we recognized in Nancy on the score of hyperbolic excess and what is *exactly excessive* and rigorously paroxysmal, while not passing over everything toward whatever thing in whichever way. As for Levinas, he speaks of "extreme fragility" "at the limit of being," of "*exorbitant* ultramateriality," concerning the "regime of tenderness" and the "epiphany of the Beloved" (and about the Beloved or *Aimée*, we shall be asking: why only this feminine form?). "These superlatives, better than metaphors, denote a sort of paroxysm of materiality." Further, it is "the exhibitionist nudity of an *exorbitant* presence" or the "*exorbitant exhibitionism,* which is a production of being" (ibid., pp. 256–57).[21] What becomes exorbitant does not only exceed or disturb the onto-logic that Levinas calls in question on a regular basis. It *threatens* the very ethics to which Levinas appeals so powerfully.

Threat: the word is not too strong, for all this also describes the threatening par excellence, as a good number of Levinas's formulas let it come across. We have to insist on this for *three reasons* at least, each being of quite a different order.

On the one hand, it comes down to the limits of the ethics and axiomatics of the face that are in command of Levinas's discourse on this subject.

On the other hand, where promise carries beyond the possible or the future while remaining a promise, an aim, an expectation of a *"not yet* more remote than a future"; where promise comprises a threat, it is the concept itself of the promise, in its classical definition, that finds itself *automatically* deconstructed.

At last, where Levinas courageously takes it into account, sexual difference can be analyzed here within an expressly dissymmetric space. Its analysis is signed by a masculine signature. There is a resolutely virile *point of view* there, or a *point of contact* (contact that touches without touching the untouchable), and this discursive privilege in its turn seems untouchable. As a discursive, philosophic, and phenomenological privilege, it is all the more untouchable, unchangeable in that the feminine threatens even the order of discourse and language: "The feminine is the Other refractory to society, member of a dual society, an intimate society, a society without language" (Levinas, *Totality and Infinity*, p. 265). Indeed, the touching touch of the caress is touching (without touching) on the untouchable as inviolable, and the one stroking is always masculine and the stroked one (the untouchable) feminine.

Let us be quite specific about these three points and for clarity's sake proceed as if we could distinguish them, although they are truly indissociable, as the quotations will show.

1. First, that which seems to extend past the limits of ethics and the face, therefore threatening them, from the side of the feminine. On this side, the voluptuous caress indeed runs the risk of locking things up in secrecy, clandestinity, the asocial, but also in animality. The question of the secret and secrecy is at the center of these analyses, a secret *at once, simultaneously*, good and bad, untouchable and touched, inviolable and violated, sacred and profane. As we will see, this *at once, simultaneously* defines profa-

nation itself and equivocation, "the simultaneity of the clandestine and the exposed" [*découvert*]. This equivocation of negation without negativity, which is marked in the analysis by the recurrence of "as if" and "without" (*x* without *x*, "essence of this non-essence," "appears without appearing," and so forth), will therefore have been the accepted ambiguity of this discourse with regard to what is called truth, phenomenon, appearing, ontology, and phenomenology. Nothing less. That is what is touched upon, one might say, without, on the face of it, any semblance of a touch.[22] Stroking thought. "Exorbitant ultramateriality," of which we spoke earlier

> . . . designates the exhibitionist nudity of an exorbitant presence coming as though from farther than the frankness of the face, already profaning and wholly profaned, as if it had forced the interdiction of a secret. *The essentially hidden throws itself toward the light, without becoming signification.* Not nothingness—but what is not yet. Without this unreality at the threshold of the real offering itself as a possible to be grasped, without the clandestinity describing a gnoseological accident that occurs to a being [slightly modified—Trans.]. "Being not yet" is not a this or a that; clandestinity exhausts the essence of this non-essence. In the effrontery of its production this clandestinity avows a nocturnal life not equivalent to a diurnal life simply deprived of light; it is not equivalent to the simple *inwardness* of a solitary and inward life which would seek expression in order to overcome its repression. It refers to the modesty it has profaned without overcoming. The secret appears without appearing, not because it would appear half-way, or with reservations, or in confusion. The simultaneity of the clandestine and the exposed precisely defines *profanation*. It appears in equivocation. (Levinas, *Totality and Infinity*, pp. 256–57)[23]

Equivocation of the caress: in the untouchable's touching, the inviolable's violation, the caress threatens the ethical, since it carries beyond the face. But what goes "beyond the face," always following the same "contradiction" of "formal logic," is still a face, a "face that goes beyond the face." "*Eros* hence goes beyond the face" (ibid., p. 264). Light that goes beyond light—not only beyond light and vision, but even beyond expression and signification. And this is decidedly seen making an inscription on the side of the feminine, seemingly *modifying*, then verily *defeating*, intentionality. It is as if the passage quoted next moved all but insensibly from an "intentionality without vision" to what would be an altogether different thing, namely, a "model of being irreducible to intentionality." One goes, therefore, from a strange kind of intentionality to what would no longer be intentional at all. Touching on the untouchable, a caress not only brings about what comes about each time one says "touching the untouchable" (or touching *without* touching, with or without caresses), that is, one no longer quite knows what one is saying or wanting to say, one no longer quite knows what touching is, in its proper sense, in its essential predicate. Once more, though in a sense differing from the one we interpreted with Kant as a starting point, we are dealing with insensible sensibility, beyond all sensibles or on this side of them: "The caress, like contact, is sensibility. But the caress transcends the sensible" (ibid., p. 257). By the same stroke, the same stroking, rather, the caress is also enough to send shivers throughout a whole idea of phenomenology, and precisely there where the caress might be experience itself, pure experience, experience before any concept—as one can read it here:

> Voluptuosity profanes; it does not see. *An intentionality without vision*, discovery does not shed light: what it discovers does not present itself as *signification* and illuminates no horizon. The feminine presents a face that goes beyond the face. The face of the [feminine (*aimée*)] beloved [I am emphasizing the feminine *aimée* to underscore my perplexity: why not a masculine *l'aimé*, or Eros?—J. D.] does not *express* the secret that *Eros* profanes—it ceases to express, or, if one prefers, it expresses only this refusal to express, this end of discourse and of decency, this abrupt interruption of the order of presences. In the feminine face the purity of expression is already troubled by the equivocation of the voluptuous. Expression is inverted into indecency, already close on to the equivocal which says less than nothing, already laughter and raillery.
>
> In this sense voluptuosity is a pure experience, an experience which does not pass into any concept, which remains blindly experience. Profanation, the revelation of the hidden as hidden, constitutes a model of being irreducible to intentionality, which is objectifying even in praxis, for not taking leave of "numbers and beings." Love is not reducible to a knowledge mixed with affective elements which would open to it an unforeseen plane of being. It grasps nothing, issues in no concept, does not *issue*, has neither the subject-object structure nor the I-thou structure. Eros is not accomplished as a subject that fixes an object, nor as a pro-jection, toward a possible. Its movement consists in going beyond the possible.
>
> The non-signifyingness of erotic nudity does not precede the signifyingness of the face as the obscurity of formless matter precedes the artist's forms. It already has forms behind it; it comes from the future, from a future situated beyond the future wherein possibles scintillate. (ibid., pp. 260–61).

2. What announces itself in this way, beyond the future and the possible, is also what introduces the threat into the promise. Equivocation, profanation, indecency, indiscretion are not good. And if "To be for the Other is to be good," as Levinas says a little further on, it is indeed evil or wickedness, as the face's beyond, that winds itself into the face itself and the promise of erotic movement, its good movement of love. This does not forbid the promise but makes us call into question again, once more, all the analyses of the promise and its performative virtue. According to these classic analyses and common sense itself, the promise, the performative of the promise, does make the assumption that one will promise only what is good, the good things—and that a promise, in its essence, in its pure signification as promise, be pure and free of any threat. One promises to save, or give, to give life first and foremost; one threatens to kill or take away, to take away life first and foremost. According to the good sense of common sense, one should never promise to give and deal out death. I recall this here again,[24] in its principle and sketchily, solely to show that, insofar as they are convincing, these analyses comprise a logic that is itself threatening: both for sense and onto-phenomenology, as well as the theory of speech acts (which incidentally takes for granted a whole implicit or explicit onto-phenomenological axiomatics, and often a philosophy of intentionality).

3. An evident dissymmetry organizes this "phenomenology of eros." It is Eros's phenomenology, the phenomenology *of* Eros—a subjective genitive, which is to say produced and led from Eros's point of view, the masculine [*le*] stroking one, and not from hers, the feminine loved one, femininity, the feminine tender one. He is stroking, she is stroked. He is touching, caressing, but does not touch. As for her, she remains untouchable even when she is being stroked. One has the feeling that she never caresses. In order to confirm this and justify our astonishment, and even perplexity, let us choose, from among a great number of equivalent or converging propositions, the ones likely to provide nourishment for a virtual dialogue with Jean-Luc Nancy. In his *tactile corpus*, where he speaks of *stroking*, the latter does not seem to grant a privilege to any one side of sexual difference—and I should rather say sexual difference*s*. From this, some would hastily conclude that he neglects or neutralizes the said sexual difference. But, in order to do justice to this difference, in order to avoid neutralizing it in the name of the neutral (precisely what Levinas

wants to avoid doing), should one favor a dissymmetry, as well as the presumed sexual identity of the signatory?

Levinas habitually names the more or less mythological Eros, or rather "l'Éros" [*the* Eros] (*Totality and Infinity*, pp. 256ff.), a designation that hesitates between *someone* and *something*. But here it is always the figure of an Eros with desires, desiring the femininity of the tender one. One is tempted then to proceed "as if," to pretend, in a brief *tableau vivant*, to couple the Levinassian Eros (Nancy never names Eros, I think, outside of the text titled "Psyche") and the Nancean Psyche (Levinas never names Psyche, I think). In order to do this, and for the *tableau* to lack no finishing touch, one would have to restage mythological sequences of such complexity, overabundance, and diversity that one would never be done with the aftereffects. It is true that Psyche (the original Psyche but also Nancy's) bears some resemblance to the femininity at whose side Levinas's Eros busies himself: excessive beauty, vulnerable and passive self-exhibition, inviolable virginity prey to Venus's jealousy, Venus whom she resembles, who puts her son Love in charge of her vengeance: his marrying death, then the young woman's sleeping, the husband's forbidden, inaccessible face: "my face, which if thou once fortune to see . . . thou shalt see no more";[25] then her recognizing Cupid, at the cost of the irreparable, his burning, and at last, yes, their legitimate union as a couple when the healed Cupid wakes Psyche from her lethargy after locking up sleep into a box again and pleading with Jupiter.

Let us give up this restaging of the scene.

I recall it here only so as to dream a little, in reading two thinkers, two friends. What if the one's Psyche had met the other's Eros? How would I have been able to bear witness to that?

Still another reason for warding off this incredible scene without delay: among so many additional complications, it is necessary to take into account Orphic theology, which makes Eros coming out of the primeval egg into a bisexual being (Phanes-Eros), a close relative of Aristophanes' androgynous being—which Levinas, let it be noted, incidentally interprets in his own fashion, in "The Ambiguity of Love," before his "Phenomenology of Eros," when it all begins. He interprets Aristophanes' myth precisely as an interpretation, an interpretation moreover justified, but also as the very disaster of Eros or the defeating of desire in incest. But it is necessary also to meditate on the fact, on which Levinas touches in passing, that what *justifies* this interpretation and thus describes this defeat in the "most egoist and cruelest of needs" is nothing other than "enjoyment," sexual pleasure [*jouissance*]! Pleasure itself, should there be any! The enjoyment of pleasure that "is broken" there where it "is satisfied." It is in this context, this time, that Levinas names the "soul"—Psyche, therefore, but a sister soul ready to touch there where one should not, an incestuous soul mixing up desire and need:

> Love as a relation with the Other can be reduced to this fundamental immanence, be divested of all transcendence, seek but a connatural being, a sister soul, present itself as incest. The myth Aristophanes tells in Plato's *Symposium*, in which love reunites the two halves of one sole being, interprets the adventure as a return to self. The enjoyment justifies this interpretation. It brings into relief the ambiguity of an event situated at the limit of immanence and transcendence. This desire—a movement ceaselessly cast forth, an interminable movement toward a future never future enough—is broken and satisfied as the most egoist and cruelest of needs. It is as though the too great audacity of the loving transcendence were paid for by a throw-back this side of need. (Levinas, *Totality and Infinity*, p. 254)

Levinas broaches his analysis where this incestuous connaturalness, the return to self of this unique, bisexual being interrupts itself. There is femininity and she is femininity, at least what "we shall term *femininity*." What do we call this way? And what does he? Since we are favoring a virtual dialogue with Nancy, the thinker of thinking-weighing whom we evoked earlier, let us remark that in *Totality and Infinity*, "femininity" denotes the weighing of a certain *weight*, a heaviness, a gravity heavier than real weight, a charge heavier than the weight of the real—a "subterranean" gravity. That is why the feminine is not simply the graceful which it resembles and with which one always associates it. Here, it is gravity without grace. Levinas has just mentioned "wanton nudity," "erotic nudity": "Let us note in passing that this depth in the subterranean dimension of the tender prevents it from being identified with the graceful, which it nevertheless resembles. The simultaneity or the equivocation of this fragility and this weight of non-signifyingness [non-significance], heavier than the weight of the formless real, we shall term *femininity*" (ibid., p. 257).

Never will any contact breach the virginity of this femininity of the

Aimée, the feminine Beloved (Levinas never, I think, speaks of the Aimé, the masculine Beloved). One can indeed violate her but only to run aground before her inviolability. For this Eros (though some could say that Levinas here only describes the point of view, the desire or fantasy of Eros, his phenomenological fantasy, experience, what appears *for him*), femininity is only violable, that is, like the secret that it is, inviolable. "Feminine" signifies the locus of this "contradiction" of "formal logic": violable inviolable, touchable untouchable. It is *epekeina tēs ousias*—"beyond being"—but this time, it is not good, it is not the Good:

> The Beloved, at once graspable but intact in her nudity, beyond object and face and thus beyond the existent, abides in virginity. The feminine essentially violable and inviolable, the "Eternal Feminine," is the virgin or an incessant recommencement of virginity, the untouchable in the very contact or voluptuosity, future in the present. . . . The virgin remains unseizable, dying without murder, swooning, withdrawing into her future, beyond every possible promise to anticipation [slightly modified here—Trans.]. Alongside of the night as anonymous rustling of the *there is* extends the night of the erotic, behind the night of insomnia the night of the hidden, the clandestine, the mysterious, land of the virgin, simultaneously uncovered by *Eros* and refusing *Eros* —another way of saying: profanation. (ibid., pp. 258–59)

Touchable-untouchable, violable-inviolable: these are general forms of formal "contradictions." Without necessarily following Levinas at this point, one may think that their field is in principle not reserved for the "femininity" of which he speaks. The question would then no longer concern the said contradiction itself—the touchable-untouchable, violable-inviolable—but rather the way in which Levinas feminizes the contradiction (feminine-*la* touchable untouchable; feminine-*la* violable inviolable) and in doing this determines the figure of the feminine. I insist on this so as to mark that, starting from the same experience, namely, touching of the untouchable or the touchable-untouchable, one may infer differing, even divergent and incompatible, discourses. Nancy's, for example, differs from Merleau-Ponty's,[26] which differs from Levinas's—who, starting from this general, contradictory predicate (to be touchable-untouchable, to be violable-inviolable, and so forth), as if this were a good consequence, identifies feminine-being, femininity as "irresponsible animality," "infantile," the "young animal," "non-signifyingness," or "signification that signifies falsely." And above all nonrespect, the "disrespect" of "you shall not commit murder." Indeed, such are the traits of what Levinas tells us "we shall term femininity." The latter, at least inasmuch as she is the one stroked by the caress, is neither a thing nor a person, but animality, childhood, a young animal, barely a human life, barely even a life, almost the death of a life ignorant of its death:

> The caress aims at neither a person nor a thing. It loses itself in a being that dissipates as though into an impersonal dream without will and even without resistance, a passivity, an already animal or infantile anonymity, already entirely at death. The will of the tender is produced in its evanescence as though rooted in an animality ignorant of its death, immersed in the false security of the elemental, in the infantile not knowing what is happening to it. . . . The tender designates a *manner*, the manner of standing in the *no man's land* between being and not-yet-being. A manner that does not even signal itself as a signification, that in no way shines forth, that is extinguished and swoons, essential frailty of the [feminine] Beloved produced as vulnerable and as mortal [slightly modified here—Trans.]. (ibid., p. 259)[27]

There is an implacable configuration there: femininity, infancy, animality, irresponsibility. It is in no way transient, it is insisting like the insignificant, or rather the "non-signifyingness of the wanton," "inverted signification" of a "signification that signifies falsely" (ibid., p. 261).[28] If we are insisting on this insistence, it is because it has paradoxical implications regarding life and death, or murder and ethics—the sense of duty—as well as the ethics of social organization and lifestyle. What implications? Before coming to this, let us point out in these regions the double entendre, the ambiguous use, of "as" (*comme*). This word hesitates in a significant-insignificant fashion between the rhetorical "as" of risky comparisons and the phenomenological "as" of appropriate description (the in*as*much *as* of a German *als . . . Struktur*). This oscillation is regular, if not constant, in Levinas. The emphasis is mine, of course:

> The [feminine] beloved is opposed to me not *as* a will struggling with my own or *as* subject to my own, but on the contrary *as* an irresponsible animality which does not speak true words [slightly modified—Trans.]. The beloved, returned to the stage of infancy without responsibility—this coquettish head, this youth, this pure life "a bit silly"—has quit her status *as* a person. The face fades [*s'émousse*], and in its impersonal and inexpressive neutrality is prolonged, in ambiguity, into animality. The relations with the Other are enacted in play; one plays with the Other *as* with a young animal.

The non-signifyingness of the wanton is therefore not equivalent to the stupid indifference of matter. *As* the reverse of expression of what has lost expression, it thereby refers to the face. (ibid., pp. 263–64)[29]

Paradoxical implications, then. The tact of a caress, thus turned toward *this* untouchable inviolability (the femininity of the Beloved *as* the irresponsible infancy of the young animal), according to the face beyond the face, also plays with death, and not only with death as the absence of life or the negative absence of whatever it may be, but with murder. Death at one's fingertips—that is what the movement of this hand is. Far from saying "You shall not commit murder," the first of the commandments and the opening of the ethical according to Levinas, far from calling for respect of the face that is as one with this commandment, the femininity of the tender invites profanation, "at the limit of the obscene," "disrespect," in this "inversion of the face" and in accordance with this "disfigurement" (see n. 28): it is not the absence of good, it is evil. There is—let us use a word that is not Levinas's—a perversion there. As for him, he says "inversion of the face" and "disrespect," a profanation that "presupposes the face," indeed, but no longer relates to it with straightforwardness.

> Language, source of all signification, is born in the vertigo of infinity, which takes hold before the straightforwardness of the face, making murder possible and impossible.
> The principle "you shall not commit murder," the very signifyingness of the face, seems contrary to the mystery which *Eros* profanes, and which is announced in the femininity of the tender. In the face the Other expresses his eminence, the dimension of height and divinity from which he descends. In his gentleness dawns his strength and his right. The frailty of the feminine invites pity for what, in a sense, is not yet, disrespect for what exhibits itself in immodesty and is not discovered despite the exhibition, that is, is profaned.
> But disrespect presupposes the face. (ibid., p. 262)

Is one straining the point by inferring murder from this? Or by concluding that, at the very least, death is already at work in this violence inviting profanation, in this violence of profanation itself, where, right through the face, the caress carries beyond the face toward the disrespect of "You shall not commit murder"? Can't we say that, through his epiphany, in the very experience of *this* caress, the caress thus described or "lived," this beyond of the face announces a mortuary mask? At the heart of this "phenomenology of Eros," here is the beyond of the face as it threatens the epiphany of the face, a dead woman, desirable still, perhaps, dead and stretched out before Eros:

> [W]e have sought to expose the epiphany of the face as the origin of exteriority. . . . exteriority is signifyingness itself. And only the face in its morality is exterior. In this epiphany the face is not resplendent as a form clothing a content, as an *image*, but as the nudity of the principle, behind which there is nothing further. The dead face becomes a form, a mortuary mask; it is shown instead of letting see—but precisely thus no longer appears as a face. (ibid., pp. 261–62)

The nudity of the principle is the nudity of the face. It can only be threatened with death by this other nudity, the "mystery" of the "exhibitionist nudity" that "exhibits itself in immodesty" . . . "that is, is profaned." Two nudities: absolutely heterogeneous, and one being the reverse of the other, yet both and each announcing the one through the other and the one beyond the other.

Is one straining the point by restricting the traits of this truly hierarchizing discourse to this "masculine civilization," which is precisely in question here, which is *naturally* in question in this analysis of caressing, equivocation, and the "epiphany of the feminine"?

> Equivocation constitutes the epiphany of the feminine—at the same time interlocutor, collaborator and master superiorly intelligent, so often dominating men in the masculine civilization it has entered, and woman having to be treated as a woman, in accordance with rules imprescriptible by civil society. The face, all straightforwardness and frankness, in its feminine epiphany dissimulates allusions, innuendoes. It laughs under the cloak of its own expression, without leading to any specific meaning, hinting in the empty air, signaling the less than nothing. (ibid., p. 264)

We are not going far from our "subject," the touching of the untouchable, the caress, the [feminine] Beloved, and the epiphany of the feminine. The social and sexual hierarchy that we have just recognized is even too familiar for us, but it builds up around the vacuum or solitary vertigo of a radical asociality, and this asociality has its paradoxical place in a "community of feeling," in this "community of sentient and sensed" which is also a "non-sociality of voluptuosity." The feminine attracts toward separation, far from the social, the universal, far from language. While attracting by starting from voluptuousness as the community of sentient and sensed, the feminine does this also in the community of the touching and the touched. One will also notice how abruptly one is changing over from a sentence concerning the asociality of lovers (a man and a woman, supposedly) to "the feminine," suddenly, on her own, becoming "the Other":

> The relationship established between lovers in voluptuosity, fundamentally refractory to universalization, is the very contrary of the social relation. It excludes the third party, it remains intimacy, dual solitude, closed society, the supremely non-public. The feminine is the Other refractory to society, member of a dual society, an intimate society, a society without language. . . . This solitude does not only deny, does not only forget the world; *the common action of the sentient and the sensed* which voluptuosity accomplishes closes, encloses, seals the society of the couple. The non-sociality of voluptuosity is, positively, the community of sentient and sensed: the other is not only a sensed, but in the sensed is affirmed as sentient, as though one same sentiment were substantially common to me and to the other. . . . In voluptuosity the Other is I, and separated from me [slightly modified here—Trans.]. The separation of the Other in the midst of this community of feeling constitutes the acuity of voluptuosity. (ibid., pp. 264–65)[30]

"Separation of the Other"—for the recurring words "common" and "community" shouldn't delude anyone. The "community of feeling," "community of sentient and sensed," "the common action of the sentient and the sensed" only seal a double and triple solitude, at the very heart of the voluptuous caress: the lovers' solitude, separated from a third party and social relations, the solitude of the [feminine and the masculine] Beloved, separated from each other: in the "relationship between lovers" there is neither "possession," nor communal fusion, nor even "complementarity" (ibid., pp. 264ff.).[31] Nothing is *possible*, finally. With a caress, nothing is attained or touched.

But it remains to be seen where the borderline—if there is one—runs between the beyond of the possible exceeding the caress while making it possible as caress and the beyond of the possible opening up the ethical and making it possible.

What does our question signify? It questions that which, in the tender caress, comes to extend toward the beyond of the possible. Isn't this movement of transcendence already extended toward the ethical? Or must one interrupt the tender of the caress so as to tend toward the ethical, from one beyond of the possible toward the other—beyond the possible?

Is it possible? And what if the "profanation," the "beyond the face" (of which Levinas so often recalls that it *already* presupposes the face) already pertained to the ethical, at the point where one "beyond the possible" stays at a *tangent* to the other, one in *contact* with the other, in what remains, as an impossibility, the *same* impossible? And the *same* "desire"?

In what describes the caress, for example, in the lines quoted below, how can we not recognize the very structure of ethics? Our hypothesis, then, does not orient us less toward an "already-ethical" of the caress or profanation than toward a remainder of shame, profanation, treachery, and perjury in the respect of the ethical. In both cases, isn't it tragically the same caressing experience of two nearly indiscernible "impossibles" or two "unpowers" [*impouvoirs*]? Here again, unsurprisingly—this is the equivocalness of equivocation—everything pivots upon a "without," around its syntax without negativity. Tenderheartedness of the caress: he gives, extends, and takes pleasure, in one and the same movement—but it is also a "suffering *without* suffering," and first and foremost an "evanescence." Death is still promised there. There is a death threatening the promise, giving to see the mortuary mask in the face beyond the face:

> [I]n the evanescence and swoon of the tender, the subject does not project itself toward the future of the possible. The not-yet-being is not to be ranked in the same future in which everything I can realize already crowds, scintillating in the light, offering itself to my anticipations and soliciting my powers. The not-yet-being is precisely not a possible that would only be more remote than other possibles. The caress does not *act*, does not grasp possibles. . . . Wholly passion, it is compassion for the passivity [*toute passion, elle compatit à la passivité*], the suffering, the evanescence of the tender. It dies with this death and suffers with this suffering. Tenderheartedness, suffering without suffering, it is consoled already, complacent in its suffering [slightly modified here—Trans.]. . . . Voluptuosity does not come to gratify desire; it is this desire itself. . . . To discover here means to violate, rather than to disclose a secret. A violation that does not recover from its own audacity—the shame of the profanation lowers the eyes that should have scrutinized the uncovered. The erotic nudity says the inexpressible, but the inexpressible is not separable from this saying. . . . The "saying," and not only the said, is equivocal. (ibid., pp. 259–60)

This equivocation accommodates—"shame of the profanation"—the unforgivable perjury whose absolute precocity has been noted.

Law of tact: it all begins—fidelity itself, oaths—with an unforgivable perjury.[32]

§ 5 Tender

This Is My Heart, "the heart of another"

We have just followed a certain gesture of Levinas's. A scene, a face, a beyond of the face. These analyses of the caress, this "phenomenology of Eros," which touch on what touches another untouchable, an other *as* untouchable, also touch upon beauty. But verge on the sublime.

Whether beautiful or sublime, they [these analyses] remain unsettling.

We acknowledged their "truth," evidently, and recognized their pertinence with regard to the experience thus described, but we did this while sensing or finding again some invincible stratagems in the fact of this experience itself and its interpretative organization. We thought we could once again see in this something at work, perhaps, some ascent, or indeed more than one religious ascendancy, a filiation of virile, paternal, fraternal, always phallocentric fantasies, with a fraternity of only sons always, of each "only," "unique son" as the "chosen son."[1] We thought we recognized in this a sequence of movements as irreproachable as they are guilty; we recognized a series of properly shameful movements, their shame moreover confessed, as it were, in an avowedly shameful confession. But it is the avowal of an irrepressible profanation, and perhaps displaces and dissimulates, replaces or denies another culpability. Perhaps, while praising ethical dissymmetry and "good" heteronomy, it does not touch sexual dissymmetry and the androphallic position from where this "phenomenology" can be examined. The analysis is not so tender. This tender is not so tender. Yet this tender thing is at the nondeclared origin of the ethical or what Levinas finally has good reasons to term "metaphysics."

Is one right—will one ever have the right to have the desire, no matter how muted, to change climates and landscapes? Is it possible? I believe not; I don't really believe this, not simply, not in an instant, not with a loss of memory—but all the same.

I therefore return—I turn around, toward Jean-Luc Nancy. Is what he says about the caress, in his "tactile corpus," compatible with what we have just read? A change of climates or landscapes would not be enough to prove it. Moreover, what is a climate in philosophy, and what is a landscape? What about the pathos—declared or not—of a discourse? What about the scene of the signature that gives rise to it, in this place I just termed "landscape"? Does this resist analysis? Is there anything else to analyze, finally—and what could be more interesting? Furthermore, there may be a religious fund that the two thinkers share in more ways than would at first seem. Levinas sometimes plays a game (he did it right before me): he plays at confessing a Catholicism that Nancy, for his part, seriously disclaims.

"Tenderheartedness," says Levinas, and the tender: extending privileges to tenderheartedness and speaking of the "tender" as an original category implies putting the accent in love[2] and the erotic (in "The Ambiguity of Love" and the "Phenomenology of Eros") on a movement toward appeasement, a moment of peace, and a disarming, which insistently reaches into the violence of a violation—moreover impossible, the [feminine] Beloved's virginity remaining "inviolable"—or the violence of unfailing profanation. Levinas almost always says "tender" and "tenderheartedness," rarely (in fact, never, it seems to me) "tenderness." This may be because what he describes is less a shared state or feeling (such as the "ambiguity of love," for example) than an *eidos* (the invariant of the tender or the becoming-tender), the essential and ideal quality of an intentional experience, readable right on the other, or in me as other. One seeks this disarming and this peace (peace is the ethical itself for Levinas) more in the tender of the caress, where the caress would renounce possession, than in any erotic violence *pushing tooth and nail* to achieve pleasure [acharnée à jouir]. The caress does not set upon anything tooth and nail. It is tender in that it does not push to take anything. It won't even let itself be pushed by the flesh. Rather, it tends to give, extend, tender forth the tender: "Tiens," hold, take what I do not possess, nor you, what we do not and shall never possess. This will not be properly our own; of this, we shall never be the masters and owners. Gift or offering?

Let us not play with words—ever. Let us not place any bets on the homonymy, in French, between *tendre* and *tendre*, on the relations between, on the one hand, the immense semantic network and all the properly *intentional* senses of the *verb tendre*: in the dominant tradition in French, it connotes rather *oriented activities*, perhaps even *virility* (Latin, *tendere*, French, *tendre*: to tend, to hold out, to tender, to extend, to stretch, to lay out, to set up [*dresser*], to hold out one's hand or to set up a trap and attend to it, to give or to ensnare, to orient oneself toward, to intend to, intentionally to seek, and so forth); and on the other hand, the instance of the *attribute tendre*: the latter often connotes fragility, delicacy, a rather *passive* vulnerability that is nonintentional, exposed, and rather childlike or feminine in the same dominant tradition of its privileged figures. Thus, in extending privileges to the caress, Levinas no doubt put the accent upon the tender of the [feminine] Beloved. But in opening it up onto peace (an impossible peace, at any rate—beyond the possible), he also implied the gift or offering of that which tends or extends, or tends to hold out to the other. With the chance of quasi-homonymy, the haunting of the *tender* comes back, in an essential, irreducible, and necessary fashion, to visit the other. The other, the tender—extend her, extend him. The proof of the tender is only in tending.[3]

Without any play on words, ever, it would therefore be necessary to extend an ear and tenderly attend to these words—tender, tend, extend.

What does this say? To extend is to offer, or give; to give what is given without giving up, which is to say without exchange or waiting that the other returns it—or give (him- or herself) up. Tender it. Attendant upon tender, "Tiens!" can be heard. "Take!" Not "I give you" (a phrase made obscene by its assumed certainty and the recognition that it seems to expect), but "take," "receive," "accept," not from me, precisely, since recognition is made a party to this, as is the propriety of the proper, and economics, but "take," "accept," from whom one doesn't know, from "God" knows whom. From "God," perhaps, from "God knows who."

Let us then repeat the question: what is one doing when one is holding out to the other something that must not come from oneself, that must not belong to who is extending it, and saying "Tiens!" in French, and only in French, thus in a language, which is to say something that in principle cannot be touched? Literally, in saying "Tiens!" (as I would like to do here), one proposes that the other *touch* (literally or figuratively, it's always the same oscillation, and *toucher de l'argent*, "to touch money"—payment, profit, or capital gain—is the popular idiom), that the other *grasp*, or *seize*, or get a grip on him- or herself, but also, in receiving and accepting it, that the other *keep* what one *extends* to him or her. Saying "Tiens!," signifying "Tiens!" means holding out or extending, and giving to "touch." One is suggesting that the other take the gift of an offering for example, and receive and accept it, and thus touch it by taking it on, by taking it in him- or herself, by keeping it in or near oneself—as nearly as possible, in oneself or within reach of the hand. Touch, more than sight or hearing, gives nearness, proximity—it gives nearby. And if the two other senses, tasting and smelling, do this also, it is no doubt because of their affinity with touching, because they partake in it or lie near it, precisely, near the sense of nearness, proximity. In this regard, is it ever possible to dissociate the "near," the "proximate" [*proche*] from the "proper," the "propriate" [*propre*]? The proximate, the proper, and the present—the presence of the present? We can imagine all the consequences if this were impossible. This question will no longer leave us, even if it is in silence that we leave it to do its work. In it, the shares and dividing lines are announced, even if they cannot always be decided. . . .

If one begs the other to take in the gift of an offering, and therefore to touch it by taking it on, by keeping it in or near oneself, in the closest possible proximity, in oneself or within reach of one's hand, it is because, as always (irresistible tendency) one thinks first of all, and too much, about *hands*, that is, about the *manual*, the *manner*, *maneuver*, or *manipulation*: seizure, comprehension, prehension, captation, acceptation, reception—a plea [*prière*] that something be received that begins to seem like an order: "Tiens!" do take it, do touch. Hence, this "tender extending" may sometimes become violence itself—not even to mention the striking twist [*coup*] in the language that displaces the "Tiens!" (Take this!) of a gift to the "Tiens!" (Take that!) of a blow [*coup*]: "Tiens!" "Take that!" one sometimes says when dealing a blow—for, in French, a blow is also dealt, that is, given: one gives the blows one strikes. But this gift is not a present, then; it shouldn't be—so one thinks, at least—and an offering even less.

Nancy distinguishes between offering and gift, or rather the offering in the gift. A gift is an offering when at the heart of the donation of the gift there is a "withdrawal of the gift," the "withdrawal of its being-present."[4]

"Tiens!" Fittingly, it is on the subject of "The Sublime Offering" that Nancy enjoins the incredible. He lets himself be enjoined—but he seems to hold to this—to "change *sense*," no less!

This gesture looks like him: I know Jean-Luc Nancy to be always ready for everything, resolved to change everything, even sense, and more than anyone else, he still, always, even should he be the last one still doing it, talks sense, of sense in all the senses of the word sense, which does not prevent his *corpus* from remaining consistent and powerfully faithful to itself. And he is working on a book to be titled *Le sens du monde* (*The Sense of the World*), no less![5]

Now, in the aftermath, and after a few earlier allusions to this, isn't this the place to risk proffering the "periodization" hypothesis that is guiding us? It is worth whatever it is worth, it is nothing but a hypothesis, it is worth whatever such periodizations are worth. Certainly, there is no cutting, indivisible limit; there is no simple instant or agency between a *before* and an *after* wherever, with the nonlinear duration of a process, thinking-weighing-pondering, language and the "body," and the exscribed, come about. All aftereffects discreetly refer back to a few premises, a past from before the markable beginning; to find them announced, it suffices to sharpen one's reading. However, I wonder whether it may not be toward the end of the 1980s that touch touched down in Nancy's thinking and writing, let's say in an increasingly phenomenal way, increasingly less evitable—until the early 1990s, when touch invaded his lexicon by way of *every* rhetorical or logical mode. Let me repeat that none of this can have started just out of the blue, one fine—or bad—day. To be sure, some precursory signs were already there very early on. But it was between 1985 and 1991 (approximately—pending a more fine-grained statistical analysis) that the corpus was more than touched upon: it was summoned, almost violated, penetrated, dominated, by the operation that came to inscribe some "touching" at the heart of all writing. The operation in question did not take place in one single day, to be sure, at a particular hour, and if it did take place one day, it had a whole history preceding and following it, a history that is older than the body and thinking of Jean-Luc Nancy, as he said himself.

I have purposely just used the general term "operation." The operation of which I am speaking is contemporaneous with what is called a *surg*-ical one [surgery: Greek *cheirourgia*, from *cheir* (hand) and *ergon* (work)], done by hand, the hand of the other, and thus by touching, even if, as always, machines and technology are indispensable in this. (And in the following chapters, it is the thinking of a *technē* of bodies as thinking of the prosthetic supplement that will mark the greatest difference, it seems to me, between Nancy's discourse and other more or less contemporary discourses about the "body proper" or "flesh.") I am alluding to the heart transplant operation whose "subject" Jean-Luc Nancy was, in a way, more than ten years ago. I believe that Nancy does not know, and I do not know whether he is trying to find out, whether the heart of the other that he carries within him is the heart of a woman or a man. *L'intrus* (*The Intruder*) dates from January 1999:

> I have—Who?—this "I" is precisely the question, the old question: what is this enunciating subject? Always foreign to the subject of its own utterance; necessarily intruding upon it, yet ineluctably its motor, shifter, or heart—I, therefore, received the heart of another, now nearly ten years ago. It was a transplant, grafted on. My own heart (as you've gathered, it is entirely a matter of the "proper," of being one, or one's "own"—or else it is not in the least . . .)—my own heart in fact was worn out, for reasons that have never been clear.[6]

A searing testimony, admirable in its clear sobriety, exactitude, and probity, it is to my knowledge unique in the history of humanity and the history of philosophy—for reasons that he himself analyzes in an impeccable way. Now, this "text" (whereby the friend discreetly retreats toward his topic) twice *touches* upon the vocabulary of *touching*: once in order to tell the *uniqueness of the event* (the operation, incision, transplantation, ecotechnics, the coming of prosthetics or a foreign body at the heart of the body proper, a coming whose possibility will have been open forever); another time in order to tell about the contact between "I" and "I" in pleasure, in suffering, and in *rejection*. "I feel it distinctly; it is much stronger than a sensation: never has the strangeness of my own identity, which I've nonetheless always found so striking, touched me with such acuity."[7]

In other words, here he is touched by a strangeness that no longer has anything to do with the quasi-transcendental strangeness that refers us all to our "I's" or our own bodies. And yet, in their possibility, the two strangenesses keep making signs toward one another and implicating each other. They look alike; one shelters the other; one hides or shows the other's truth. Hence the possibility to speak about this and be heard, apparently, be it at the cost of an unfathomable misunderstanding. The same goes for the rejection that is also at issue in the second occurrence. This rejection remains, although it is not simply the quasi-transcendental rejection that one makes out in all the experiences with *ex-* mentioned earlier (expulsion, ex-scription, and so forth). One has trouble deciding, moreover, whether the rejection of which he speaks is the rejection of suffering in general or the "rejection" of a transplanted organ:

> The empty identity of an "I" can no longer rest in its simple adequation (its "I = I") when it speaks [*s'énonce*]: "I am suffering" implies that there are two "I's," each one foreign to the other (yet touching). So it is with "I am in ecstasy" [*je jouis*] . . . in "I am suffering," one "I" rejects the other "I," while in "I am in ecstasy" one "I" exceeds the other. The two resemble each other, doubtless like birds of a feather [*comme deux gouttes d'eau*], neither more nor less.[8]

One more word about "periodization"—possible yet impossible to prove, probable yet im-probable, only barely probable. Having taken these precautions, I would like to, if I may, bring up a few quick and superficial pieces of evidence. "The Sublime Offering," which I was preparing to discuss (this text was first published in 1985, but reappeared as part of a book, *Une pensée finie*, in 1990),[9] indeed proposes to "pass from sight to tact."[10] But what it behooves us to return to its concrete thickness, to the experience of resistant density, is by way of a figure this essentially abstract, insensible, invisible, and intangible thing that a *limit* is: "the singular mode of the presentation of a limit is that this limit must be reached, must come to be *touched*: one must change sense, pass from sight to tact."[11]

Before we return to what transpires in this passage dealing with such a "passage" of the limit, and especially this passing "from sight to tact," let us freely grant ourselves three retrogressions, which are also three virtual programs.

A. First, let us note that, mutatis mutandis—if this may still be said at such a gaping distance—this passing from sight to tact here again recalls Berkeley. In truth I never stop thinking of him while writing about touch, even if I cannot possibly here do justice to the fine complexity of his problematic. But out of its context a sentence such as "one must . . . pass from sight to tact" could belong to the Berkeleyan axiomatics that began with the rejection of any identity between a seen object and a touched object. One needs to leap from one to the other blindly, like someone born blind, across an infinite abyss. Even if it is the "same thing," what we see is one thing, what we touch is another, says Berkeley in *An Essay Towards a New Theory of Vision* (section 127) (in a *pre*phenomenological style: an *already* phenomenological style, already with a certain reduction, and still *at the threshold* of this reduction): "The extension, figures, and motions perceived by sight are specifically distinct from the ideas of touch called by the same names, nor is there any such thing as one idea or kind of idea common to both senses."[12]

Later on, these different objects will go by the same names, and thus, what Berkeley mobilizes to account for this is the whole question of language, its use and destination, and the question of theology ("the proper objects of vision constitute an universal language of the Author of Nature").[13] And that is the ultimate recourse grounding his philosophy. What this interpretation of the senses presupposes—and first of all of touch, of the haptical, that is, the least reducible among them, common to all living beings in the world, which is not the case with vision—lastly is a theology, and more precisely an ontotheology. But beyond so many obvious differences, a common gesture of thought takes into account the heterogeneity between the two senses, the two "phenomenologies of perception" that are dedicated to them, as well as a certain primacy granted to touch. If the ideas of space, distance, and therefore movement could not come from vision, as Berkeley tirelessly repeats and Nancy also seems to imply, then the figure of the limit, the approach of and to a limit, the "presentation of a limit" must push us, as Nancy says, indeed, to "pass from sight to tact." In addition, Berkeley often argues that the *physical* mechanisms of vision, "retina, crystalline, pupil, rays" traveling through it, and so forth, "are things altogether of a tangible nature."[14]

The remaining task (is it a task for today?) is to try to account for the "same names," common, for example, to both the visible and the tangible; almost, here, at the *limit* visible and tangible. The remaining endeavor is to follow their genealogy starting from another discourse altogether, another "knowledge" altogether, a knowledge less confident in its thinking of "common sense," or the fivefold root of the senses—in a body with five senses, no more, no less—without at once calling on God for help. A "deconstruction of Christianity," we can bet, will have to do battle between the visible and the tangible—and seek something else.[15]

B. For—and this is my second backtracking digression, my second retrovision, and also my second remark in view of a short theological treatise on touch—it is necessary to remind the author of *Corpus* of what he no doubt knows well,[16] he who replays the "Hoc est enim corpus meum" in an entirely different way: even before and beyond the eucharistic moment of this "corpus," all the Gospels present the Christic body not only as a body of light and revelation but, in a hardly less essential way, as a body *touching* as much as *touched*, as flesh that is touched-touching. Between life and death. And if one refers to the Greek word that translates this touching, which is also a divine power and the manifestation of God incarnate, one can take the Gospels for a *general haptics*. Salvation saves by touching, and the Savior, namely the Toucher, is also touched: he is saved, safe, unscathed, and free of damage. Touched by grace.

1. Jesus the savior is "touching," he is the One who touches, and most often with his hand, and most often in order to purify, heal, or resuscitate—save, in a word.

He heals or purifies the leper by touching him: "And he stretched out his hand and touched him, saying [*et extendens Iesus manum, tetigit eum, dicens . . . /kai ekteinas tēn cheira ēpsato autou legōn*], 'I wish it; be clean.' And immediately his leprosy was cleansed" (Matt. 8: 3).[17]

He heals Peter's mother-in-law by touching her hand with his hand: "He touched her hand [*tetigit manum eius/ēpsato tēs cheiros autēs*], and the fever left her" (Matt. 8: 15).

He heals the blind by touching their eyes: "Then he touched their eyes, saying, 'According to your faith be it done to you.' And their eyes were opened" (Matt. 9: 29–30). Healing the blind seems all the more initial, and initiating, since touch is what gives sight: the hand opens to the light of revelation and gives to see, and then makes one follow Christ: "And behold, two blind men. . . . Jesus stopped and called them, saying, 'What do you want me to do for you?' They said to him, 'Lord, let our eyes be opened.' And Jesus in pity [he was moved; *misertus/splagchnistheis*] touched their eyes, and immediately they received their sight and followed him" (Matt. 20: 30–34).[18] The allusion to Jesus's emotion (*misertus/splagchnistheis*) speaks of the essential movement of *heartfelt merciful* [*miséricordieuse*] compassion, of Christ's heart or entrails, the fleshly locus of pardon. The heart: that is where Christ is first moved and touched. And there, and then, he touches, since he has been touched. . . .

He heals and saves from fear (there is no mention *where* his touch reaches here): "But Jesus came and touched them, saying, 'Rise, and have no fear.' And when they lifted up their eyes, they saw no one but Jesus only" (Matt. 17: 7–8).

Ailments of the tongue and speech he doubtless heals even more strikingly. To an all but mute deaf man, he gives back the ability to speak. Laying his hand on him and touching his tongue, he listens to him: "And they brought to him a man who was deaf and had an impediment in his speech; and they besought him to lay his hand upon him. And taking him aside from the multitude privately, he put his fingers into his ears, and he spat and touched his tongue [*tetigit linguam eius/ēpsato tēs glōssēs autou*]; and looking up to heaven, he sighed, and said to him, 'Ephphatha,' that is, 'Be opened.' And his ears were opened, his tongue was released [*vinculum linguae/desmos tēs glōssēs*], and he spoke plainly. And he charged them to tell no one; but the more he charged them, the more zealously they proclaimed it" (Mark 7: 32–36).[19]

Touching a coffin, the coffin of the only son of a widow, he cures death itself. There again all begins with *heartfelt mercy* [*miséricorde*]. Jesus is touched to the heart before he touches: "And when the Lord saw her, he had compassion on her [*misericordia motus/esplagchnisthē*] and said to her, 'Do not weep.' And he came and touched the bier, and the bearers stood still. And he said, 'Young man, I say to you, arise.' And the dead man sat up, and began to speak. And he gave him to his mother" (Luke 7: 13–15).

Restoring life, restoring or giving speech in touching the child: those are reminders that these are first, or frequently, children (vulnerable, disarmed, innocent, and still without true speech) whom Jesus touches or who are offered to Jesus's touch: "Now they were bringing even infants to him that he might touch them; and when the disciples saw it, they rebuked them. But Jesus called them to him, saying, 'Let the children come to me, and do not hinder them; for to such belongs the kingdom of God. Truly, I say to you, whoever does not receive the kingdom of God like a child shall not enter it" (Luke 18: 15–17).

2. Not only is Jesus touching, being the Toucher, he is also the Touched one, and not only first in the sense that we have just identified (that is, touched in his heart by heartfelt, merciful compassion): he is there as well *for the touching*; he can and must be touched. This is the condition for salvation—so as to be safe and sound, accede to immunity, *touching*, the Toucher, Him. Or better yet, touching, without touching, that which would come in contact with his body, namely—like a fetish, or the origin of fetishism—his garment, his cloak. It is not the touch that is saving, then, but the faith that this touch signifies and attests. "And besought him that they might only touch the fringe of his garment; and as many as touched it were made well [safe] [*et quicumque tetigerunt, salvi facti sunt/kai osoi ēpsanto diesōthēsan*]" (Matt. 14: 36). For he had healed "many, so

that all who had diseases pressed upon him to touch him" (Mark 3: 10). . . . "And there was a woman who had had a flow of blood for twelve years. . . . She had heard the reports about Jesus, and came up behind him in the crowd and touched his garment. For she said, 'If I touch even his garments, I shall be made well [saved].' And immediately the hemorrhage ceased. . . . And Jesus, perceiving in himself that power [*virtutem/duna-min*] had gone forth from him, immediately turned about in the crowd, and said, 'Who touched my garments?' . . . the woman . . . told him the whole truth. And he said to her, 'Daughter, your faith has made you well [saved].'" Shortly afterward, Jesus saves a little girl who had died and makes her stand up, holding her by "the hand" (Mark 5: 25–34, 41).[20] "And wherever he came, in villages, cities, or country, they laid the sick in the market places, and besought him that they might touch even the fringe of his garment; and as many as touched it were made well" (Mark 6: 56). "And all the crowd sought to touch him, for power came forth from him and healed them all" (Luke 6: 19).

The faithless Pharisees themselves recognize the power that emanates from this "touch." In the overwhelming scene that the sinner Mary Magdalene opens up when she bathes Jesus's feet with her tears, wipes them with her hair, kisses them or anoints them with perfume, the Pharisee host declares: "'If this man were a prophet, he would have known who and what sort of woman this is who is touching him, for she is a sinner.'" (Luke 7: 36–50).[21]

It seems that these literal allusions to touching are rarer or even absent in the Gospel according to John. Why? On the other hand, if one may say so, Jesus becomes momentarily untouchable; and John is the one who gives a report of the "Touch me not" (*noli me tangere/Mē haptou mou*) intended for Mary Magdalene at the moment when she is still in tears, next to the grave, and has just recognized him ("Rabboni!" "Master!"): "Do not hold me [touch me not],[22] for I have not yet ascended to the Father; but go to my brethren and say to them, I am ascending to my Father and your Father, to my God and your God." In the evening of this same day, when Jesus has come and the disciples rejoice upon seeing him, Thomas Didymus is not among them. And so he doubts their testimony: "Unless I see in his hands the print of the nails, and place my finger in the mark of the nails, and place my hand in his side, I will not believe." Eight days later Jesus says to Thomas: "Put your finger here, and see my hands; and put out your hand, and place it in my side; do not be faithless, but believing. Thomas answered him, 'My Lord and my God!' Jesus said to him, 'Have you believed because you have seen me? Blessed are those who have not seen and yet believe'" (John 20: 16–29).[23]

C. The third retrospection turns to what seems to happen in Nancy's *The Experience of Freedom* concerning limits, precisely—the touch and touching of the limit—and what comes to pass when one has to touch on the untouchable. This book was published in 1988, precisely, after Nancy had worked it out, as a thesis, in the same years as "The Sublime Offering" and "A Finite Thinking."[24] In it, Nancy makes the figure of touch appropriate, if one can put it that way, to this thing without a thing that a limit is. And this touching of the limit is the very moment itself of the decision, the turn, that this great book *takes*, marks, recalls, and interprets in the thinking of freedom. Such a decision is not for us to make. Here are two examples:

> But in fact it is not we who decide whether this will be the task of philosophy, even if it is necessary for us to make a decision. It is not an option offered to our free will any more than philosophizing freedom as such or any of its "orientations" was ever a matter of freely choosing a "freedom of thought."
> If philosophy has *touched the limit* [my emphasis—J.D.] of the ontology of subjectivity, this is because it has been led to this limit.[25]

Nancy almost literally repeats this formula on the next page, and I'll cite it. There is thus, apparently, a *figure of touch* there, for philosophy, literally, has never touched anything. Above all, nobody, no body, no body proper has ever touched—with a hand or through skin contact—something as abstract as a limit. Inversely, however, and that is the destiny of this figurality, all one ever does touch is a limit. To touch is to touch a limit, a surface, a border, an outline. Even if one touches an inside, "inside" of anything whatsoever, one does it following the point, the line or surface, the borderline of a spatiality exposed to the outside, offered—precisely—on its running border, offered to contact. In addition, here in the case of this figure ("philosophy has *touched the limit* of the ontology of subjectivity," and so forth), another need comes to light as far as this figure is concerned, throughout the chain of a remarkable demonstration whose stages I cannot reconstruct here.[26] This surface, line or point, this limit, therefore, which philosophy might have "touched" this way, finds itself to be at the same time touchable and untouchable: it is as is every limit, certainly, but also well-nigh at and to the limit, and on the exposed, or exposing, edge of an abyss, a nothing, an "unfoundable" unfathomable, seeming still less touchable, still more untouchable, if this were possible, than the limit itself of its exposition. Philosophy will have "touched" (it has already happened, Nancy speaks of it as something past—what an event!) upon the untouchable twice, both on the limit and on the unfoundable abyss opening beneath it, beyond it—under its skin, as it were. And because this touching, this contact, this tact will have just been able to touch on something untouchable [*de l'intouchable*] (but it has done this! And this event was a transgression—exceedingly passing, passing the limit), literally there can only be a *figure* of touch. One only touches by way of a figure here; the object, the touchable's thing, is the untouchable. The touchable is what it is impossible to touch (to attain, to rape, to violate in its inaccessible immunity, in its soundness). The "thing itself" gives itself, opens (itself), opens an opening only in the history of this figure—some would say of this fiction. History of the untouchable, therefore—of the immune, the sound, the safe. Save or safe—*touching*. Is this "good news"?

Let us not forget the context and the stakes of the demonstration to which I am referring here: it comes down to freedom and decision, no less; freedom to think freedom, to a "thinking . . . free for freedom":

> Thus philosophy has always already given itself over to the thinking of what it can neither master nor examine: and this is also what we understand, simply, by "being-free." We are therefore not free to think freedom or not to think it, but thinking (that is, the human being) is free *for* freedom: it [thinking] is given over [*livrée*] to and delivered [*délivrée*] for what from the beginning exceeded it, outran it [*devancée*], and overflowed it [*débordée*]. But it is in this way that thinking definitely keeps its place in the world of our most concrete and living relations, of our most urgent and serious decisions.[27]

It is for *two reasons* that I quote this conclusion of the chapter in full.

1. One may ask oneself what could justify this parenthetical concession here: "(that is, the human being [*l'homme*, i.e., man])." It does not seem sustainable except where one transfers onto this *name (of) man* (but why this name, then? Or why not? In both cases, it seems arbitrary or merely justifiable through some pedagogical or strategic calculation) the excess, the overflowing, and so forth, which will come into question immediately afterward; and thereby one admits that one presently does not know what the term "man" means to say, if not this experience of the excess of all de-

termination, including the determination one believes to be recognizable in the term *anthropos*.

2. The excess in question is indeed the untouchable's; it is the excess of an inaccessible beyond, beyond a limit itself untouchable, although "philosophy has touched" it. This excess would indeed be the origin of the figural fiction of which we speak: *touching*, always by way of a figure.

Thus, it is on the subject of freedom, this new thinking of freedom, one more time, from one page to the next, that Nancy has recourse to the figure of touch, of a philosophy capable of touching the limit, and this time touching it in itself, within philosophy and as philosophy: "Thus philosophy, as soon as it touches within itself the limit of the thought of foundation, or as soon as it is carried by way of itself to the unfoundable border of this thought, can no longer represent its own beginning as the originary unity of a Subject-of-philosophy appearing to itself in its freedom, or of a Subject-of-freedom appearing to itself as philosophy."[28]

Let us now come back to "The Sublime Offering" and *A Finite Thinking*. Let us turn to the point where, again, on the subject of the limit, Nancy suggests then that one "change *sense*," no less, and "pass from sight to tact"; let us do it without really knowing whether by tact he intends to convey the tactile in general or this manner of touching *without* touching, characteristic of a certain politeness, the discretion of a certain contact, though an interrupted contact, a syncope. The truth is that he does not content himself with suggesting that one change sense and pass from sight to tact; he reminds us that, according to him, *it is necessary* to do this; that *it cannot not come about*; and that that is the *sublime*. Is there some *sublime*, or sublimation, wherever some untouchable is announced in a touch? And wherever touching is figuralized? Maybe so. "[T]he singular mode of the presentation of a limit is that this limit must be reached, must come to be *touched*: one must change sense, pass from sight to tact. This is, in fact, the sense of the word *sublimitas*: what stays just below the limit, what touches the limit (limit being conceived, in terms of height, as absolute height). Sublime imagination touches the limit, and this touch lets it feel 'its own powerlessness.'"[29]

If it "feels" "its own powerlessness," then the imagination *touches* upon its powerlessness. The imagination encounters that which it *cannot*, the impossible for it; it comes into contact with what remains impossible for it. It encounters, therefore, that which it *cannot* encounter; it accedes, as such, to the inaccessible as such; it attains and reaches there; it falls, upward, and comes onto that which it cannot touch, and thereby it touches *itself*, as we shall see; it feels *itself* (powerless) there where it touches (tangentially) what it cannot attain or touch: the point or the line, the flimsy, unsubstantial *limit*, here, there, whither and whence it can no longer touch. The imagination attains a limit, reaches a shore whither it can *come only in not coming about*. It thus tends toward that which it can only *hold out to itself without giving itself to hold*, and still without touching; whereby it becomes what it is by essence, imagination, possibility of the impossible, possibility without power, possibility auto-affecting its essence of a nonessence. It is not what it is—the imagination. It is touched, in a movement of withdrawing or re-treating to the fold, at the moment it touches the untouchable. The imagination confines without confining itself to itself.

In what sense and by what right can one say that it touches *itself* or that it *feels itself* touch, touched, touching, that it feels itself by touch or by touching itself? (Note parenthetically that, concerning what touches on the French language at least, where the latter touches itself closest to untranslatability, "cela se touche" can mean or be understood *reflexively* as either "it *itself* touches *itself*" or "*one* touches it, it lets itself be touched [by something or someone else] without necessarily touching *itself*.") And what is the phenomenological, ontological status, the logical or rhetorical legitimacy of that which we cannot without trepidation call the *figure* of "touch"? And what if this word, touching, *le toucher*, then became useless and unusable, and fell into disuse, in advance *im-pertinent*, and at the same time contingent, therefore, and not pertinent—incapable of "touching" the very thing itself that it comes to "touch" by accident, without any necessity whatsoever, simply through contiguity, the very thing that it pretends to aim at? And what if this word did not keep any value, or sense, precisely, any *justification*, except where a *solely* ontophenomenological status—in an absolutely *empirical* fashion and "in our eyes," *solely* loaded with verbal memory and logico-rhetorical culture—were what reassures us in the confident *use* of such a term? And so it is our very old habit in this or that historical culture, "at home" in the West, to make use of these terms (the "logic" and "arithmetic" of the five senses, and so forth) so as to adjust them more or less well (and often not very well at all, as we are experiencing it here, and that is all of philosophy) to suit some pretended ontophenomenological evidence in "our body." Empirical ontophenomenology + historical legacy + language of a culture: perhaps this makes a common habit, a way of being social, a praxis, a pragmatics, a consciousness, and so forth. But how is one to justify these "commodities" in view of a science of the body said to be proper and of inanimate bodies, in view of a physiology (physics, biology, neurology, and so forth) that would demonstrate that there is nothing that one could rigorously define as "senses," nothing that allows one to count them up to five, and above all nothing that lets one recognize in them each time an identity without contamination, an identity such that the "tradition" thus under suspicion—even when it admits some contamination, cooperation, substitution, and vicariousness—keeps presupposing an identity thus contaminated, remedied, replaced, and so forth?

—And in an aside you tell yourself: what a funny, admiring, and grateful salutation you're addressing to him, to Jean-Luc Nancy. What a peculiar way to pretend you're touching him while acting *as if* from now on you wanted to put his lexicon about touch out of service, or even banish it to the *Index librorum prohibitorum*. Or, as if you stubbornly kept reminding us that it should always have been out of service already, even if we like that—touching—precisely when it's impossible-prohibited; and we even love to call this loving—abstaining. Like the messiah. What a funny present, indeed! What an offering! Altogether as if at the moment of calling others so that they will become ecstatic before this great work and this immense philosophic treatise of touch, you whispered in his ear: "Now, Jean-Luc, that's quite enough, stop touching and tampering with this word, it's prohibited, you hear. You have to abstain from this 'touching,' and once and for all stop using this incredible vocabulary, this concept nothing can really vouch for, these figures without figure and therefore without credit. And besides, if I may remind you of this again, haven't you yourself said 'there is no "the" sense of touch'? Therefore, don't keep pretending, don't make believe, stop acting as if you wanted to make us believe that there is something one could call *the* touch, an understood 'thing itself' about which we could pretend to agree, there where, in touching upon the untouchable, this thing remains untouchable. Knowing you, I don't think this objection will stop you, I tell myself. No, you just go on, and so do I—thankfully in your steps."

"Sublime imagination *touches* the limit," he thus wrote by way of a figure; and I am adding the emphasis, "and this *touch* lets it feel 'its own powerlessness.'"

The emphasis is mine, of course. Before quoting the next few lines, let us already and very tersely point to three essential indications.

1. In this context, the "touch" is that of the imagination: sensible presentation or transcendental schema. The nondelimitable concept of touch is thus going to take in at once all that these words comprehend—so many figures and things at stake, the importance of which it is impossible to exaggerate: imagination, presentation, sensibility, passivity/activity, internal sense/external sense, time/space, *intuitus derivatus*, thus finitude, "finite thinking," schematism, transcendentality, and so forth.

2. To feel itself as touch will be immediately a "feel *itself*" and thus a "touch *itself*." We have not finished exploring the infinite and puzzling resources of this reflexivity. All the more so because in *our* grammar, as I noted a moment ago, *se toucher* strangely folds or unfolds its reflexivity according to the workings [*engagements*] of the sentence. Like *s'attendre, se toucher* can turn the subject toward itself (*s'attendre soi-même*, to expect or wait for oneself; *se toucher soi-même*, to touch oneself) or toward the other, according to a reciprocity that is easier to say than to attain (*se toucher— l'un l'autre, les uns les autres*, two touching each other, many touching each other): *se toucher toi*, "to self-touch you," he will say in a passage of *Corpus* of which for the moment I shall do no more than light the fuse. A thing that *se touche*, however, can also quite simply mean to say that it is touchable, without ever *self*-touching *itself*, without two or many others ever touching one another; it can mean that the thing is exposed to touch: in this way "a thing *se touche*" signifies "one can touch a thing," "one feels a thing at a touch": it is tangible.

—If I ask you now: What does *se toucher les yeux* mean? Does it mean "to touch one's own eyes with one's own fingers"? That's easy. To touch (for example) the eyes of the other and reciprocally? That's not impossible. To touch the eyes of the other with one's own eyes in order to see while losing one's sight [*à perdre la vue*], in a sort of reciprocity that is apparently immediate? That's difficult and rare but not at all impossible. And you may still remember that that's where we started from.

—And touching one's own heart? As the heart—like the heart—of the other?

—Let's wait.

3. All of Nancean thinking regarding the *syncope*, set in motion more than fifteen years beforehand,[30] finds itself taken up again here—reread, reinvested, relaunched. The passage we are reading at the moment concerns the "syncopated imagination" insofar as it opens the experience of the sublime. The latter is also the experience of the border and of overflowing, the trembling apprehension of that which, *touching* on the border, at once goes overboard and remains at the border, holding out and holding back, retaining itself or abstaining, on the border; but crossing over, then, perhaps in abstinence itself, and perhaps better than ever: "[T]he entire affair of the sublime occurs on the edges of works of 'fine art,' on their borders, frames, or contours: on the border of art, but not beyond art."[31]

One of our questions could take shape here: if there is indeed a figure of the limit as border, does it have an essentially *tactile* genealogy, tactile by privilege of birth? Does it *figure* itself on the basis of the properly or literally tangible? Can one ever speak of a thing, *x*, that is *properly* tangible? Isn't this latter the very place of the irreducible contamination of the proper, of contamination *itself*, of contact and contagion and impurification? This question, one senses, does not pertain only to itself. It is already a difficult and serious one. But it doubles and immediately proliferates itself: does one have the right, without accepting too many presuppositions, to wonder whether one of the senses (here, touch) is, as such and solely, more *proper* (as it has so often been asserted, from Aristotle to Berkeley and Maine de Biran to Husserl), more literally engaged in the constitution of anything whatsoever, here in that of a figure that would depend on it in a more necessary fashion? Also opened by Aristotle, when the latter wondered whether touch (*haphē*, contact, which also means tact, grasp, but likewise the place of the contact, line of joining, blow or wound) is *one*, a "unique sense" (*mia aisthesis*) or plural (*pleious*), this matrix of questions pertains also to the concept of *figure*, of course, since inevitable figurality has to do perhaps with this internal multiplicity that disperses the so-called literal signification of touch or the property of the tangible. But let us leave all that and go on now with the quotation:

Sublime imagination touches the limit, and this touch lets it feel "its own powerlessness." If presentation takes place above all in the realm of the sensible—to present is to render sensible—sublime imagination is always involved in presentation insofar as this imagination is sensible. But here sensibility no longer comprises the perception of a figure but rather the arrival at the limit. More precisely, sensibility is here to be situated in the imagination's *sentiment* of itself when it touches its limit. The imagination feels itself passing to the limit. It feels itself, and it has the feeling of the sublime in its "effort" (*Bestrebung*), impulse, or tension, which makes itself felt as such when the limit is touched, in the suspension of the impulse, the broken tension, the fainting or fading of a syncopation.[32]

What is he telling us, in a word?

A term, notion, concept, or figure? What does the word *effort* (*Bestrebung*) designate, appearing as it does in this singular context (of "sublime offering"), where effort, precisely, stalls in *making an effort*? At the point where effort *meets* the limit forcing it to *exert itself* in this *effort*? Where it touches upon this exertion itself and, from this resistance, comes back toward it, is felt or feels *itself* at the limit, is touched or touches *itself* at the limit, exhausts *itself* in exerting *itself*? What is this necessarily finite experience of forceful *exertion*? And is there ever any encounter without it?

As far as touching is concerned, does this finite thinking of resisting effort subterraneously meet—without getting mixed up or dissolving in it—with a manifold tradition, at the crossroads of filiations or trends both heterogeneous and affined, from Maine de Biran (the thinker of effort and exertion, as it were) to Merleau-Ponty or Gilles Deleuze, by way (of course) of Husserl's *Ideas II*?

Let us be patient, touch things up, and translate, if this is possible.

§ 6 Nothing to Do in Sight: "There's no 'the' sense of touch"

Haptics, 'technē,' or Body Ecotechnics

> . . . suddenly B.'s heart is in my heart.
> —Georges Bataille, quoted in Jean-Luc Nancy,
> *Being Singular Plural*

He is speaking to us of an experience, perhaps of experience in general, which consists in this: to feel *oneself feeling one's self touch*, of course, and therefore feeling one's (masculine or feminine) self touched [*touché(e)*]. (I am putting the [feminine] gender in parentheses because, as just noted, it may well be the sublime imagination [feminine in French] that is in question, but also in order to announce and respect sexual differences. *Se toucher*, to touch (oneself), is to touch upon all that can be translated, at least metonymically, in *se toucher le sexe*, that is, to touch one's own or one another's genitals—and therefore all sexual differences.)

But by the same token, experience in general would start there: it would begin by feeling itself touching a limit, feeling touched by a limit, and its own limit.

What is it to touch one's own limit thus? It is also not to touch, not to touch oneself enough, to touch oneself too much: impossible sublimity of tact, the diabolical machination of love when it dictates infinite renunciation. It is to lose the proper at the moment of touching upon it, and it is this interruption, which constitutes the touch of the *self-touching*, touch as *self-touching*, that Nancy calls *syncope*. When he was writing about the syncope, without speaking very much or even at all, perhaps, about touch, he was already speaking about it; and this could point to a good way of consequently rereading everything—of rereading him, Nancy, but the whole philosophical tradition as well. I'll try later to show that the motif of the syncope, which is to say, a certain interruption in contact, will sign all the interruptions, precisely, between the most powerful traditions of thinking about touch, on the one hand, and Nancy's thinking on the other. These interruptions will not always be obvious and easily accessible. We shall apply ourselves to analyzing them, at the point that is nearest or most "proximate" to the former and the latter, and that is where the "logic" of the syncope will play a determining part, under this name or another.

If tact and the caress cannot be given their measure or their law in a "more or less" of touch, then perhaps they have nothing to do [*rien à voir*] with the experience of touching and all the figures that it has procured for us. One would have to review everything in this lexicon and this rhetoric and take infinite precautions before touching on them. For example, what is one saying when one proposes [in French] to *toucher un mot* [literally "to touch a word," colloquially to have a word with, to mention]? What is one doing then? What is one intent on doing by "having a word" and touching one's friend with it, for example on the subject of this or that, which might be touch, touching him or her, or quite simply a word, but for example the word "touching"? To friends we speak and in them we confide—briefly, elliptically, closely—so as to inform them, no doubt, to have a word with them and "touch on it"; often, however, in order to warn them, to put them on their guard, alert them ("Get in touch with him? Oh yes. I'll have a word with him and touch on this, should the opportunity arise, to find out what he thinks of this, and by the same token I'll tell him, in a word, how I see the matter at hand—I myself, so as to avoid saying foolish things, and also, as a reminder, to recall a little of this enormous memory, the stuffed belly of a library of touch."). How is one to have a word and touch on it? And let oneself be touched by it? A visible, audible, readable word? We have long been struggling between the tactile and vision, the eye that does not touch and the eye that touches, like a finger or lips. It is about time to speak of the voice that touches—always at a distance, like the eye—and the telephonic caress, if not the (striking) phone call.

(Imagine: lovers separated for life. Wherever they may find themselves and each other. On the phone, through their voices and their inflection, timbre, and accent, through elevations and interruptions in the breathing, across moments of silence, they foster all the differences necessary to arouse a sight, touch, and even smell—so many caresses, to reach the ecstatic climax from which they are forever weaned—but are never deprived. They know that they will never find ecstasy again, ever—other than across the cordless cord of these entwined voices. A tragedy. But intertwined, they also know themselves, at times only through the memory they keep of it, through the spectral phantasm of ecstatic pleasure—without the possibility of which, they know this too, pleasure would never be promised. They have faith in the telephonic memory of a touch. Phantasm gratifies them. Almost—each in monadic insularity. Even if the shore of a "phantasm," precisely, seems to have more affinity with *phainesthai*, that is, with the semblance or shine of the visible.)

For at the heart of all the debates regarding the "body proper" or the "flesh"—ongoing debates as well as those that lie in wait for us—at the heart of the syncope, between touching and the untouchable (an absolute untouchable that is untouchable not because it is of the order of sight or hearing, or any other sense, but untouchable in the order of touching, untouchable touchable, untouchable right at [*à même*] the touchable), there is the originary intrusion, the ageless intrusion of technics, which is to say of transplantation or prosthetics. And on the groundless ground of this ageless originarity, what we have been speaking about since the beginning, is the history of events and their caesuras, the story of irruptions, mutations without measure and without common measure, the story of incommensurable singularities. But never again will the said "technical" intrusion of the other, the ecotechnics of other bodies let themselves be reduced.

And what is one doing when, to have (and touch) a word with him or her, one is laughing with a friend? When it is not Laughter that one shares with him or her but a singular burst of laughter? Now, what relation can this strange question have with the ones that have kept us occupied for some time—having to do with touching, limits, and syncope? It is by way of these questions (that Nancy is neither asking as such nor under this guise, but to which he does not fail to bring a sort of answer) that I attempt to prepare a sort of suitable lodging to accommodate the reading of a certain passage—one page only, in "Laughter, Presence."[1] In the name of touch, of course. It is a page around what Nancy announces, after opening a parenthesis, as the need for a "very long detour": ("No doubt [he says— J. D.], a very long detour should be made here").[2] Yes, we shall need to take a very long detour here.

Laughter, especially a peal or burst of laughter, is like a syncope. Of course, even if it shakes up the whole body, laughter is a thing of this mouth—and the open mouth, toward which the question of touch and self-touch incessantly leads us back. The mouth touches, touches itself, is touched, not only because the lips touch, and not only because one would not speak—to have a word with a friend, for example, to touch on a matter with him or her—if this auto-affection of a mouth, this contact interrupted and repeated between the lips, the tongue, the palate, and so forth, did not impart speech.

We must have a mouth for laughs and for laughing. Surely, we can laugh with our eyes, but it is difficult (even if it is not impossible) to imagine a living being laughing without something like an opening other than the eyes. The opening in question may be presently visible and significant in the burst of laughter, or it may not; it is indispensable. For laughter as for so many other things, more than one opening is needed.

That is also why "Laughter, Presence" lets us read "the laughter of a wide mouth, red and white and alluring . . . " in Charles Baudelaire's "The Desire to Paint." Now, this syncopated beat all at once scans a limit, an endurance of the limit, *and* an experience of *tact*, of touching without touching as "art"—not art in its manifest essence, in its presence, but precisely in the multiple bursting of singularities. Though laughter may be "the substance," or even the "subject" of art, it also makes the essence of art, and of each of the arts, disappear. This time, Nancy puts the "as/like" [*comme*]— which generally announces the presentation of an essence and an "as such" —at the service of a bursting diffraction, explosion, dispersion, and disappearing. But let us not forget that he also speaks, and justly so, with this sense of justice that respects absolute singularity, with a view to keeping in sight *this* text by Baudelaire, solely this one, rather than any other:

> Laughter of infinite mockery, of derision, and irony: the subject of art sees itself there *as* what bursts, explodes, is consumed, and disappears. But also, the laughter and smile of an "inexpressible grace," of the grace with which "art" slips away, and each art disappears into another only to bloom there again, a superb flower but impossible to recognize, to relate to its model—on the volcanic soil where there is never anything *like* art, where all essence is petrified.[3]

Nancy draws the consequences of this bursting of the laugh and is respectful of these multiplicities, which philosophy, the philosophy of art in particular, always seeks to "sublate, or to sublimate." He thus works out the logic of these multiple singularities, which are as many instances of "coming" into presence without presence ever presenting itself as the essence of the presence. "Multiple singularities": and so one can read these pages in *Une pensée finie* in 1990 [and *The Birth to Presence* in 1993—Trans.]. Years later, he will speak of *being singular plural.*[4]

Here I would like parenthetically to mention one of the numerous contretemps with which the encounter or crossbreeding of our texts, years
apart, appoints (and thwarts) some anachronistic rendezvous for us. In
Nancy's 1996 book *Être singulier pluriel* [*Being Singular Plural*], we can
follow more than ever, more strongly acknowledged than ever, the injunctions and even a "logic" of touch. Touching is the very experience of
"origin" as "plural singularity." The plural singular, originarily, is what
finds itself given to touch. The origin could be touched, or would have to
be, as—and like—touching itself as *self*-touching. To *self*-touch *oneself*;
(*self*-)touch *one another* (among two or many): *se toucher*, in good French,
can mean to say all that: to (self-)touch oneself, to be in touch, to touch
each other (feminine or masculine, among two or many). French grammar tolerates reflexiveness as much as flexing irreflexiveness, in the singular as in the plural; and this is beginning to look like the true subject of
this book. Moreover, fortuitously or not—we'll get there—there is also a
French tradition—an original one—of a certain problematic of touch.

In any case, Nancy insists on this plural singularity at the moment of
touching:

> To have the goal in sight, all but "touching home," is again to risk missing it.
> But the origin is not a goal. The End, like the Principle, is a form of the
> Other. To touch upon the origin is not to miss it: it is properly to be exposed
> to it. Since the origin is not another thing (an *aliud*), it is neither "missable"
> nor appropriable (penetrable, absorbable). It does not obey this logic. It is the
> plural singularity of the Being of beings. We touch on it to the extent that we
> are in touch with *ourselves* and in touch with the rest of beings. We are in
> touch with ourselves and each other [*nous nous touchons*] insofar as we exist.
> Being in touch is what makes us "us," and there is no other secret to discover
> or bury behind this touching itself, behind the "with" of coexistence. (*Being
> Singular Plural*, p. 13; translation modified.—Trans.)

On the following page, we go from the verb *touche* to the homonymous
noun *la touche*, "the touch": "Is this not what interests us or touches us in
'literature' and in 'the arts'? . . . What counts . . . is access to the origin set
apart [*écartée*], in its very distancing itself [*écart même*]; it is the plural touch
upon the singular origin" (Ibid., p. 14; modified.—Trans.). In this way,
touching would be—within Being, as Being, as the Being of beings—*contact* of the *with* (*cum* or *co-*) with oneself as well as with the other, the *with*
as contact, community as co-tact.

So be it. But how can he say that we are "properly . . . exposed" to an origin that is not "appropriable"? I'll have to ask him this. Just as I ask myself why I would never have dared write that. He knows in advance that I would undoubtedly put up a muted resistance there—fear, perhaps, in the guise of stiffness or philosophical rigor—against this frank assertion, this assurance regarding the *properness* of an exposition to the origin: to wit, an existence, a form of "self-touching," would (itself) be properly exposed, according to him, to what is "properly" the origin (itself), even if the latter were not "appropriable," in the sense of "penetrable, absorbable." But what about other modes of appropriation? And couldn't one still detect in the said exposition—*proper* to an origin that would properly be itself—a reserve, the ultimate resource of an appropriation? Of a reappropriation? The possibility of this affirmative statement ("To touch upon the origin . . . is properly to be exposed to it")—a statement that is possible for him, and not for me—may be what inspires, motivates, dictates, and compels the thinking and desire of "touching," and especially so when one can see this thinking and this desire of "touching" invade his corpus in an increasingly speedy and intense fashion, be it with so much caution, across so many complications, paradoxes, and hyperboles; be it in the abnegation, without negation, of touching within the "without touching"; and be it through the active or implicit reading of other thinkers. And this is how I further explain, without seeking too much to justify a virtual question or objection (it does not matter here), that the figure and lexicon of "touch" remain rather scant as far as I am concerned, at least on the rare occasions when, as it were, I speak in my own name. That is why those who have this easier "touch" fascinate me. I admire them, yet I cannot bring myself to believe in it very much—in touching, that is. Some ill-intentioned though well-programmed philosophers may conclude from this that I am more of an "idealist" than Nancy.

My defense attorney would not be long in responding, playing up two counterclaims:

1. What has conferred on "touch" its absolute privilege and its titles of philosophic nobility is a great "idealistic" tradition, from Berkeley's absolute idealism to Kant's or Husserl's transcendental idealism. Plato had already started this (as we'll later see).

2. As for idealists, isn't Nancy just another one, guilty rather because of his imprudence when he still credits the appropriation of a properness and when he quietly says: "To touch upon the origin is not to miss it: it is properly to be exposed to it"?

And idealism: before turning it into a philosophical combat weapon, here are so many preliminary questions to ask about the history of the *idea*—which is seen rather than touched, as its name indicates—and about the irrepressible and undeniable constitution of ideality; about idealization processes and the "idealistic" position inscribed in the history of sense and the senses, in the obscure trafficking between sense, common sense, and the senses, for example, between touch and sight. This enormous history has kept many among us busy for quite some time (elsewhere, what is more—and I'll come back to it).

Supposing I raised objections here, though I don't (I am merely astonished, or concerned), Nancy could specify that, in this passage, he does not simply speak in his own name. At this exact moment, he is thinking "with" Georges Bataille; he is actively reading and interpreting, explaining and exposing a certain Bataille, and keeping him company. In order to become involved in a fair and serious debate, one would therefore need to disentangle what falls to either one, and it is almost impossible to do so in this context. I should do no more than quote the passage and the accompanying note, which call for, motivate, and justify the lines into which I just pried, with some bafflement on my part. We shall see that Nancy does no more perhaps (but isn't it a great deal? isn't it enormous?) than subtly divert Bataille's lexicon, and admit he is doing it, precisely where Bataille himself names a certain diversion, to the letter.

Indeed, when on the subject of *truth*, Bataille says "accede" and "attain," Nancy, if one may say so, translates it by "touch," while speaking about *origin*, this time. This acknowledged diversion (as we'll read) must not be criticized or denounced; however, it permits identification of the drive to think-name-touch the sense of touch, rather than any other, as "properly" Nancean ("properly"? Come on . . .).

If I now think it necessary to quote this whole passage, including the note and a long fragment by Bataille, it is for another reason, which may be even more important; it has perhaps imparted its first movement to the analysis. At the end of the Bataille quotation, in italics of which I no longer know whether they are Nancy's or not [the italics are Georges Bataille's—Trans.], we can read these words: "Suddenly B.'s heart is in my heart." As for the "sudden" event of this utterance, nothing could have kept Nancy from hearing it beat in his very own heart. And here we are hearing it *with* him, in our heart altogether other and the same.[5] Here is the passage; it comes immediately before the paragraph around "To touch upon the ori-

gin . . . is properly to be exposed to it." The lexicon of touch, the under
scoring, bears Nancy's signature, of course, and not Bataille's. The insis
tence—so irrepressible—on a certain exactitude once more ("exact," "ex
actly": he even boldly writes "perhaps, exactly") is signed by Nancy as well
The movement finds itself launched, then relaunched, in an impeccably
calculated play on the equivocal syntax of an expression of truth, *à la vérit*
(a phrase remaining forever French, as if a tongue could be touched un
translatably—and on the following page Nancy evokes a certain "untrans
latable" forming "each time, an absolute point of translation, transmission
or transition of the origin *into origin*"):

> . . . being-*with*. The origin is together with other origins, originally parted. In
> truth, therefore, we accede to it. We reach [*nous accédons*], in exact accordance
> with the mode of access: we get there; we are on the brink, as near as can be,
> at the threshold; we *touch* on the origin [Nancy's emphasis.—J. D.]. "In truth,
> we accede . . ." [*à la vérité, nous accédons*] is Bataille's phrase,[6] and I repeat its
> ambiguity while diverting it from its reach—since in Bataille it precedes the
> assertion of an instantaneous loss of access. Everything comes to pass, perhaps,
> exactly between loss and appropriation—neither one nor the other, nor one
> and the other, but much more bizarrely and simply than that.
>
> In truth, my memory fails me: Bataille writes "we attain" [*nous atteignons*]:
> to attain, to accede—like the doubling of the approximate itself in touching
> at the origin. But I must cite the whole passage from Bataille: "We don't have
> the means of attaining at our disposal: in truth, we do attain; we suddenly at-
> tain the necessary point and we spend the rest of our lives seeking a lost mo-
> ment; but how often we miss it, for the precise reason that seeking it diverts
> us from it. Joining together is doubtless a means . . . of missing the moment
> of return forever. Suddenly, in my darkness, in my solitude, anguish gives way
> to conviction: it's insidious [*sournois*], no longer even wrenching [*arrachant*]
> (through constant wrenching, it no longer wrenches), *suddenly B.'s heart is in
> my heart*." (Nancy, *Being Singular Plural*, p. 13; p. 196n17; modified.—Trans.)

On whom is it bestowed, this terrifying grace—to hear, grasp, receive,
and even countersign the literality of these last words, "suddenly B.'s heart
is in my heart"? Undoubtedly not even on their author, not even on
Bataille.

End of the parenthesis. I resume: we were, as always, laughing with him.
What is "laughed by the poem" is therefore the logic of these "multiple singularities" that are as many instances of "coming" into presence, without

presence ever presenting itself as the essence of presence—as we were saying. There where it is "laughed by the poem," there where the poem is
laughing that [*le poème rit ça*], in a movement that is internal, immanent,
and yet bursting out, laughter becomes *at once*, therefore, transitive *and* intransitive.[7] We noted this earlier about weighing, which "weighs," and
which is weighing what it weighs, the other (transitively), or of its own
weight (intransitively), as *what* it thinks. It comes down to thinking weighing like laughter or tears. One is either weeping intransitively, period, or
one is weeping tears, transitively, (bemoaning the loss of) something or
someone—or because one no longer knows who or what, or oneself as
who or what, is weeping. To complain, period. Or to make a point to complain about. . . . To complain about someone—or because one has lost
someone. As many reasons or ways to weep. Whom or what.

Of these multiple singularities let us, for the moment, retain just one
trait. For our decision concerning the trait that is chosen and remarked, as
always, pertains to a contract—touching (him) in a word, and contract-
ing everything at the limit, the traced outline of a contact. Which trait?
This one: it is *on a limit* that these singularities burst out laughing, but
this limit, here, puts touch and the other senses in touch, and thus confirms the quasi-transcendental privilege of the tactile—of spacing, in
truth—and further, of spacing as what gives rise to *technē* and the prosthetic substitute. Indeed, contact does not carry out any fusion or any
identification, nor even any *immediate* contiguity. Once more we have to
dissociate touch from what common sense and philosophical sense are
forever according it, namely, *immediacy*—as evidence itself, as the first axiom of a phenomenology of touch.

The use Nancy makes of the expression *partes extra partes* seems obsessive at times, and yet it is truly necessary and determining. In addition to
an invincible principle of disseminal divisibility, it seems to me to signify
a ceaseless desire to mark this break with the immediacy or the continuity
of contact, this interval of spacing, this exteriority, at the selfsame moment, furthermore, when there is such insistence on contiguity, touching,
contact, and so forth. As if Nancy wanted to mark the interruption of the
continuous and challenge the law of intuition at the very heart of contact.
And in doing this, his "intervention" touches and tampers with the philosophic gigantomachy surrounding intuition and intuitionism—no less.

Indeed, are we going around anything other than intuitionism, in this
debate without a combat? Not this or that intuitionism as doctrine or

philosophical thesis, nor an intuitionism in the set field of a determined problematic that would face an opposing, adverse position—against formalism, conceptualism, and so forth. No. Rather, we endeavor to identify an intuitionism constitutive of philosophy itself, of the gesture of thought that consists in philosophizing—and even of the idealization process that consists of retaining the sense of touch within sight so as to ensure for the glancing eye the fullness of immediate presence required by every ontology or metaphysics. The fullness of immediate presence signifies above all the *actuality* of what gives itself effectively, energetically, *actually*. As the noun might indicate, we know that *intuition* gives a privilege to vision. But it is always to reach a point there, where the fulfillment, the plenitude, or the filling of visual presence touches contact, that is, a *point* that, in another sense, one could nickname blind spot; and there the eye *touches* and lets itself be touched—by a ray of light, unless it is (more rarely, and more dangerously) by another eye, the eye of the other. At least since Plato, no doubt, and despite his indebtedness to the eye that looks, intuitionism has *also* been a metaphysics and tropology of touch—a metaphysics as hapto-tropologic. This metaphysics fulfills itself and thus comes to its plenitude, its pleroma, which is to say, its limit, in betting on the elementary trick or *turn* of tactile fulfillment, the turn or bent of a language that is oriented in a quasi-natural fashion toward touch, there where, as language precisely, it loses intuition and no longer gives to see.

Let us at least recall Plato's *Phaedo*,[8] in which everything is already "prefigured." I mean to say that, in it, the figure of touch is prefigured. Socrates asks: when does the *psuchē* touch (*haptetai*) on truth and attain it? The answer: when it is troubled neither by vision nor hearing, nor any pleasure or displeasure of the body; in other words when it has dismissed the sensible, when it has been able to say "hello"/"goodbye" [*salut*] to the senses and the body (*chairein to sōma*) (65c), and when "she has as little as possible to do with the body" [i.e., as little intercourse, contact (*mēd'haptomenē*)], "and has no bodily sense or feeling," but is aspiring after being (it *desires* what is: *oregētai tou ontos*) (65c). Only by no longer touching on touching, namely, on the corporeal and sensible letter of the tangible, does the *psuchē* thus touch on truth; and attain the *aspect*, the visibility of the *eidos*, of what really *is*; and realize in idealizing. But then, by touching on it by way of a figure, *psuchē* really touches (*haptetai*) upon truth. It touches on it in giving up touching. Truth is not touched except where it is untouchable. In Plato's *Republic*[9] the same "haptic" figure describes the relation of the immortal soul with everything that it touches or attains (*hap-tetai*) in its love for truth—"philosophy" itself.

It is a great, endless history of haptics. If together with Pascal one were to imagine "Plato, to attract towards Christianity,"[10] one of the paths of the demonstration would go not only (and self-evidently, and all too obviously) through a thinking of truth as light, as revelation to sight, but also through the affinity of two haptics, two haptologies, the one in the Gospels, of which we spoke earlier, and the one of which a few examples in Plato have just been evoked.

From Plato to Henri Bergson, from Berkeley or Maine de Biran to Husserl, and beyond them, the same ongoing formal constraint is carried out: certainly there is the well-known hegemony of eidetics, as *figure* or *aspect*, and therefore as visible form exposed to a disembodied, incorporeal look. But this supremacy itself does not obey the eye except to the extent that a haptical intuitionism comes to fulfill it, fill it, and still the intentional movement of desire, as a desire for presence. For desire, of course, is of itself naturally intuition*istic*—as soon as it is weaned of intuition; and that is its first lethal contradiction and the precursory sign of its end, its *telos*. *Telos* is haptico-intuitionistic. Shall we say of philosophy in general that it is obediently under the thumb of the finger and the eye? For, as the *Republic* spells it out, what is at issue here is *philosophy* itself and the desire of pure *psuchē*.

We could trace the necessity and speak of the legacy of an analogous movement in Plotinus, who uses haptical terms both abundantly and decisively (*epaphē*: contact; *ephapsasthai*; *ephapteta*: touch; to be in contact; *thigein*: to touch; *thixis*: a touch, and so forth). First, touching yields *presence*: the One "is always present to anyone who is able to touch it."[11] Correlatively, this comes down to the indivisibility of the One and *psychical* experience, the relation of the knowing soul with the *indivisible*, for the soul agrees with the One, it is in contact with it, as it were, and touches it;[12] and with what is wholly simple, "it is enough if the intellect comes into contact with it."[13] This contact is more extraordinary, more hyperbolic—hyperbolic as *epekeina tēs ousias* (which is the hyphen, so to speak, between Plato and Plotinus)—and touches what exactly [*cela même*] stands beyond Being, the One as the Good, thus bringing it into presence: "there will not be a thought of it, but only a touching and a sort of contact."[14] We could then touch what is not! Which is to say, not only intelligible beings—beyond the senses—but also what does not even present itself any longer as a being, a being-present. In Aristotle, one finds an analogous figure, a figure beyond the figure, this time about *nous*, the *psuchē* inasmuch as it knows: "And thought thinks on itself because it shares the nature of the object of thought [*kata metalēpsin tou noētou*]; for it becomes an object of thought in coming into contact with and thinking its objects, so that thought and object of thought are the same [*noētos gar gignetai thigganōn kai noōn, hōste tauton nous kai noēton*]."[15]

Only if the haptical itself called to order (namely, the metonymic order of the *finger*, that is, of the *hand*) the order of presences would one be allowed to speak of strict obedience under the "thumb of the finger and the eye." All is thus decided in the passage of a metonymy, and the stakes may be there, perhaps, finally, as may be the singularity of Nancy's work: it inheres less in the recollection of touch than in another thinking of the body, the mouth, and the "hand" (the hand and the fingers), and especially of metonymy. It is another story and history of the body, presupposing also another experience of desire.

To this we have not yet come. Soon we shall be questioning certain texts by Maine de Biran and Husserl, regarding very precisely (especially from the *point of view of the hand*, if I may say so) a certain privilege of touch. Never mind Bergson, whose recommendation it is to multiply metaphors in order to exceed the deceitful rigidities of concepts, "abstract ideas, whether general or simple."[16] Never mind when he recalls us to the need of this disparate multiplicity of tropological figures: seeing fulfills itself in touching. Never mind that he is pleading for a strategy of dispersal and spendthrift rhetoric:

> No image will replace the intuition of duration, but many different images, taken from quite different orders of things, will be able, through the *convergence* of their action, to direct the consciousness to the precise *point* where there is a certain intuition to seize on. By choosing images as dissimilar [*disparates*] as possible, any one of them will be prevented from *usurping* the place of the intuition it is instructed to *call* forth, since it would then be driven out immediately by its *rivals*.[17]

(The emphasis is mine. What a beautiful philosophical program! And what a scene! So many well-chosen images, indeed, around this queen, Intuition, a *psyche*, as it were, a queen *called* upon to rule. And we can see the suitors, not to mention the *rivals* crowding around the throne: all of them—male and female—concepts! Usurping dames! Regicides!)

And so, at the moment when he tells of this *convergence* and this limit *point* of intuition itself, something he will so often term "coincidence" (as will Merleau-Ponty after him), Bergson is still hierarchizing. And then (shall we say, as Plato does?) he subjects vision to contact. *Incidence* can define the angle of a thing or a look, a ray of light striking a surface; whereas *coincidence* calls for an experience involving contact. When vision tends no longer to distinguish itself from the seen or the visible, it is *as if the eye touched* the thing itself—or better yet, in the event of this encounter, as if the eye let itself be touched by it. Intuitive vision does not just come into contact, as it is said; it *becomes contact*, and this movement would pertain to its nature. And further, its motion would go—its drive would extend, rather, from the optical (or the scopical) to the haptical. Thus, for example: "The intuition . . . then bears above all upon internal duration. It grasps a succession which is not juxtaposition. . . . It is the direct *vision* of the mind by the mind. . . . Intuition, then, signifies first of all consciousness, but immediate consciousness, a *vision* which is scarcely distinguishable from the object seen, a knowledge which is *contact* and even *coincidence*."[18]

We know that this becoming-haptical of the optical is one of the themes of Gilles Deleuze's and Félix Guattari's *A Thousand Plateaus*, even if the Bergsonian streak (to which Deleuze always laid a claim, incidentally) is not central in this context. Reference is especially made to Henri Maldiney and Aloïs Riegl: "It was Aloïs Riegl who, in some marvelous pages, gave fundamental aesthetic status to the couple, *close vision-haptic space*."[19] "Where there is close vision, space is not visual, or rather the eye itself has a haptic, nonoptical function."[20]

The hand is not far, there again—or more exactly *the finger of the hand*. The finger is not far, in fact, since this even deals with the "close range," with "close vision," and as in Bergson, as we just read, with *the mind*, the very mind. About nomad space or art we read: "[T]he whole and the parts give the eye that beholds them a function that is *haptic rather than optical*. This is an animality that can be seen only by touching it with one's *mind*, but without *the mind becoming a finger, not even by way of the eye*. (In a much cruder fashion, the kaleidoscope has exactly the same function: to give the eye a *digital* function.)"[21]

Who better than Hélène Cixous, as near as can be to her own experience, will have *written*, and described, the poem for this figure of the touching eye? Touching with the hand and lips—but as figure of the figure, precisely, and without letting us *believe* that a philosophical concept could literally, properly, measure up to it? In Cixous's "Savoir"—as well as elsewhere and differently, in so many places—what is given to see is given to touch, though henceforth, from the outset, it is given to read.[22] This thing happens after a *surgical*, that is, handmade, operation that has just restored Hélène Cixous's eyesight, just as another surgery had given another heart, the heart of another, male or female, to Jean-Luc Nancy—and so I associate my two miracle wonderfriends.[23] I have quoted from his *L'intrus*; here, now, is her "Savoir":

> But at this dawn without subterfuge she had seen the world with her own eyes, without intermediary, with the non-contact lenses. The continuity of her flesh and the world's flesh, touch then, was love, and that was the miracle, giving. Ah! She hadn't realized the day before that eyes are miraculous hands, had never enjoyed the delicate tact of the cornea, the eyelashes, the most powerful hands, these hands that touch imponderably near and far-off heres. She had not realized that eyes are lips on the lips of God.
>   She had just touched the world with her eye, and she thought: "it is *I* who can *see*." *I* would thus be my eyes. I the encounter, the meeting point between my seeing soul and you? Violent gentleness, brusque apparition, lifting eyelids and: the world is given to her in the hand of her eyes. And what was given to her that first day was the gift itself, giving. (Cixous, *Veils*, p. 9)[24]

Because of the *proximity* value, because this vector of *close presence* finally determines the concept and term "haptic," because the haptical virtually covers all the senses wherever they appropriate a proximity, Deleuze and Guattari prefer the word "haptic" to the word "tactile": "'Haptic' is a better word than 'tactile' since it does not establish an opposition between two sense organs but rather invites the assumption that the eye itself may fulfill this nonoptical function. . . . It seems to us that the Smooth is both the object of a close vision par excellence and the element of a haptic space (which may be as much visual or auditory as tactile)."[25]

What makes the haptical, thus interpreted, cling to closeness; what identifies it with the approach of the proximate (not only with "close vision" but any approach, in every sense and for all the senses, and beyond touch); what makes it keep up with the appropriation of the proximate, is a *continuistic* postulation. And this continuism of desire accords this whole discourse with the general motif of what Deleuze and Guattari (in following Antonin Artaud) claim as the "body without organs." Consequently, it is in the "smooth" and not the "striated" space that this haptical continuism finds, or rather seeks its element of appropriation, and it is there that it confirms and smoothes out its logic of approach: "The first aspect of the haptic, smooth space of close vision is that its orientations, landmarks, and linkages are in *continuous* variation; it operates *step by step* [*de proche en proche*]."[26]

I said continuistic *postulation*—for the continuous is never given. *There is never any pure, immediate* experience of the continuous, nor of closeness, nor of absolute proximity, nor of pure indifferentiation—no more than of the "smooth," or therefore of the "body without organs." Of all that, there is never any "immediate" given. Where has experience ever encountered (perceived, seen, touched, heard, tasted, *felt*) the purely smooth? Or some "body without organs," Artaud's great fantasy, his metaphysical and no doubt Christian fantasy? If one has never met them, if this has never given rise to an event or an experience, if this has never come or happened, does this then give us a contingent *fact*? And would this fact preclude neither the right of concept nor the right of desire? Or on the contrary, is this an essential phenomenological impossibility, an *eidetic* law of experience and event, a very condition of desire, which any conceptual construction—any "concept" "creation," as it were—should take into account? And thus every "philosophy," even if this acknowledgment counters an ineradicable intuitionism constituting the regulating idea of philosophy itself (as I suggested earlier)? A "deconstruction" begins in this very experience; it is, makes, and bears out the experience and experiment of this aporia.

The concept of smooth is not smooth—no more than there is any rigorous concept of the haptical here, for the haptical then depends on the smooth, in a correlative, determining fashion. The relation between smooth and striated, therefore, does not constitute a reliable conceptual opposition, but rather an idealizing polarity, an idealized tendency, the tension of a *contradictory* desire (for pure smoothness is the end of everything, death itself) from which only a mixed given, a mixture, an impurity comes forth in experience.

Would a distinction between fact and right save the pertinence of this conceptual opposition, as Deleuze and Guattari seem to think, at the very moment, right at the beginning of the chapter on the "smooth and the striated," when they are acknowledging the "mixes" of which we speak? I believe this to be all the less likely in that the "fact" in question is not an empirical, contingent fact, but an eidetic law of structure (and thus of stricture or striation); and above all, in that the distinction "de facto / de jure," like the distinction "smooth/striated," finds itself hierarchized; the distinction is finally kept under the de jure authority of law (and therefore of a pure conceptual opposition which never functions). Let us rather assess the following, and keep in mind that the haptical, still on the side of the smooth, is absolutely near to absolute proximity:

> Smooth space and striated space—nomad space and sedentary space—the space in which the war machine develops and the space instituted by the State apparatus—are not of the same nature. No sooner do we note a simple opposition between the two kinds of space than we must indicate a much more complex difference by virtue of which the successive terms of the oppositions fail to coincide entirely. And no sooner have we done that than we must remind ourselves that the two spaces *in fact* [my emphasis—J. D.] exist only in mixture: smooth space is constantly being translated, transversed into a striated space; striated space is constantly being reversed, returned to a smooth space. . . . But the de facto mixes do not preclude a *de jure*, or abstract, distinction between the two spaces . . . it is the *de jure* distinction that determines the forms assumed by a given *de facto* mix and the direction or meaning of the mix. . . . [27]

The authority de jure, here, is all the less authorized to make a decision since, *on the one hand*, it rather pertains to one of the two agencies (striated power, and often state power) and is already implicated in the problematic opposition (like a defining element in the defined or to-be-defined); and *on the other hand*, from a purely juridical-phenomenological point of view, the recourse to experience itself shows that the *sense* of this mixing never delivers anything that might be, de facto or de jure, pure and free from the said mixture.

Therefore, there is no pure concept, nor any pure intuition, of course, nor any immediate intuition of the haptical.

Nancy, for his part, departs. He departs, he marks his departure ("Corpus: Another Departure" is a chapter title in *Corpus*). He parts and shares and separates; he no doubt also departs from this fundamental problematic, as well as from this intuitionism of the continuous or the *immediate*, this more radical, more invincible, more irrepressible intuitionism than the one simply opposed to its contrary (conceptualism, formalism, and so forth). Nancy thus gives another *sharing out* and *parting* of the senses to think, in this place of the limit, *of plural* limits, where this tradition finds its resource. Marking and remarking the limits, rather, he spaces out the continuity of this contact between touching and the other senses, and even the immediate continuity at the heart of touching itself, if one may say so—the touching he will recall as "local, modal, fractal." Later, in *Corpus* (1992), after *Une pensée finie* (1990), it is on the subject of "exscription," of reading, and precisely of touching *as* reading, or reading *as* touching, that the "privilege given to immediacy" will find itself firmly challenged; and we have just evoked the inexorable tradition of this privilege, its invincible compulsion, and the endless resistance it will keep opposing to an interminable analysis. While Nancy, on the contrary:

> . . . (*here*, see, read, take, "Hoc est enim corpus meum" . . .). Of all writing, a body is the letter, and yet never the letter; or, more remote, more deconstructed than all literality, a "lettricity" that is no longer for reading. That which of a writing—*properly* of it—is not for reading, that's what a body is.
> (Or we clearly have to understand reading as that which is not deciphering, but rather touching and being touched, having to do with body mass and bulk. Writing, reading, a tactful affair. But there again—and this, too, has to be clear—only upon the condition that tact does not concentrate, does not lay claim—as Descartes's touching does—to the *privilege given to immediacy*, which would bring about the fusion of all the senses and of "sense." Touching, too, touching, first, is *local, modal, fractal*.) (Nancy, *Corpus*, p. 76)[28]

On the score of *body ecotechnics*, a world of bodies that has no sense, "neither transcendental nor immanent," *Corpus* pursues this dislocation of touch. Without ever letting go of his insistence on the tactile—he is keen on it and never gives it up—Nancy always associates it, *against* the continuistic tradition of immediacy, with the value of apartness, displacement, spacing, partition, parting, dividing, or sharing out. "There is no intact matter—if there were there would be nothing. On the contrary, there is tactility, posing and deposing, the rhythm of the coming and going of bodies in the world. Tact unbound, parting and imparting itself" (ibid., p. 102).

(One cannot be sure, of course—even if he wages a battle against this all the time, it seems to me—that Nancy hits it off, with every stroke, continually and simply, and dodges the continuistic and immanentist postulation about the "smooth" and the "body without organs" of which we spoke earlier. But who could finish with this tempting postulation? And one can always ask oneself why this is *necessary*: what or who embodies the figure of this Necessity here.)

As soon as tactility (like sense, like the senses) is thus *shared out, parted,* partaken of, divided, partitioned, pluralized—in a word, *syncopated,* for sharing out is a syncope and the syncope a sharing out—but as well given to others, distributed, dispensed, there is no longer anything one can designate by using the general singular preceded by a definite article in French: *le toucher,* "the" touching. The definite article in general—itself and properly—finds itself henceforth unemployed, perhaps, for anything whatsoever—as we were just saying a moment ago about the words *même,* "same," *propre,* "proper," and *proche,* "proximate." But how are we to write without them, without making believe we believe? Without each time asking the other to believe in that for the spell of a scratching that will come to sign the shared, imparted act of faith, and share out (divide, worry, put to pieces) the act of faith, and faith itself? This is how he exscribes, for example—and we shall understand him: "There is no 'the' body; there is no 'the' sense of touch; there is no 'the' *res extensa.* There is that there is: creation of the world, *technē* of bodies, limitless weighing of sense, topographical *corpus,* geography of multiplied ectopias—and no u-topia" (ibid., p. 104).

It is always the same break with immediacy and the indivisibility of the continuous. This break is not Nancy's, precisely; it is not his decision. It takes place. He recognizes it, weighs it, ponders it, thinks it. It is not so easy. But this break, which does not mean that touching is given a leave, or that the proximate is, or the next one, or the same, or the definite article, and so forth, restructures or reinterprets these significations. It would be necessary to quote all the pages dedicated to the "*technē* of bodies," but I have to limit myself to this extract pointing to the path, the path of another "here"—"ours," the here of our historic time, of our now, of our historic body: *here,* the path leading from the deconstruction of touching to a deconstruction of Christianity, its before as well as its beyond:

> Ecotechnics deconstruct the system of ends and makes them nonsystematizable, nonorganic, even stochastic. . . . Finally, *areality* gives a law and medium, in lieu of a transcendent/immanent dialectic, of a *proximity,* both global and local—one within the other. Finally, we are within the *technē* of the *next* one, the *fellow.*
>
> The Judeo-Christian-Islamic "fellow man" resided in the *particular* and the *universal*—in the dialectization of the two; and without fail, this ends in the

universal. But *here*, the neighborly fellow is *next*, what is coming, what takes place in approaching, what touches and also sets itself apart, localizing and displacing the touch [*la touche*]. Neither natural nor artificial (as he or she appeared by turns until now), the "next" "fellow man" as *technē* is the true "creation" and "art" of *our* world, moreover subjecting to revision these words "creation" and "art," not to mention, principally, the "next," "neighborly" "fellow man." And so I prefer to say that *technē* is the *technē* of bodies shared out, or of their co-appearance, that is, the various modes of giving rise to the tracings of areality along which *we are exposed together—neither presupposed in some other Subject*, nor *postposed in some particular and/or universal end*, but rather exposed, hand in hand, bodies laid out, shoulder to shoulder, edge to edge, *close for no longer having a common assumption, but only, of our tracings partes extra partes, what is between-us.* (ibid., pp. 78–80)

I believe that in such passages we must never dissociate, on the one hand, what touches upon technics or the prosthetic supplement (and which is what distinguishes in a determining way Nancy's corpus from other, more or less contemporary, discourses about contact, the "body proper," or the "flesh") and, on the other hand, his insistence on separation that spaces out: Nancy almost always says, as he does here, "touched and spaced out"—apartness in contact, the outside in the inside of contact.

Nancy would thus *share out* and part the senses, and touching, too. The conditional of this proposition does not only point to an interpretative hypothesis: it translates some conditionality in "things themselves," the obligation to reckon with the limits that a prevailing tendency (here, the intention to think, attest, and tell of such a sharing out) is all but forced to encounter—for reasons that are not contingent. For it can also happen, it can moreover *always* happen—we have to insist on it—that the intuitionistic-continuistic logic of immediacy shows itself to be as irrepressible as desire itself, as intractable as language constraints, grammatical violence, and all that we spoke of as shared-out faith a moment ago; it can always happen, it has always to be able to happen that the power of this law regularly allows some symptoms to crop up; not only here and there in Nancy's text, but massively elsewhere, as other quotations have lately reminded us.

This parting and sharing can be tracked following the trace, and *detour*, of the other (way of sense). Such a trace (but he does not say it like this—not he) would suffice to subtract sense, the senses, the senses of sense, the experience of sense and of the sharing out and parting of the senses, from any sovereignty of *presence*, immediacy, the proper and the proximate. Nothing, no presence whatsoever, without a detour. No logic of sense, and not even a logic of touch, not even an ultratactile haptics, would then yield, it seems to me, to an ontology of presence (if one still dares use this pleonasm).

Hence the need for the *long detour* still awaiting us. We turn and go continually from detour to detour, from one "turn" toward other "turns" and twists of touch (touching *itself* and *properly speaking*—which is no longer sayable, as I have lately indicated [in n. 28]):

(No doubt, a very long detour should be made here. What of the sharing [*partage*] of the senses? . . . Can they be felt? Do they feel that they can't be?— Is there a purity of each sense, or would there be no vision without a trace of touch, no touch without a trace of taste, and so on?—Is there a language without a trace of one or the other? But then: how are the senses shared with regard to art? How could one fail to observe that the three senses devoid of art "proper"—touch, smell, and taste—are also "most properly" the senses of sensual love? [a double "observation" that I am tempted to complicate, but it does not matter here . . . —J. D.]—And the "wide mouth, red and white," so close to the nostrils, is it not precisely, their locus in the poem? . . .)

Laughter bursts at the multiple limit of the senses and of language, uncertain of the sense to which it is offered—to the sight of color, to the touch of the mouth, to the hearing of the burst, and to the sense without meaning of its own voice. Laughter is the joy of the senses, and of sense, at their limit. In this joy, the senses touch each other and touch language, the tongue in the mouth. But this touch itself puts space between them. They do not penetrate one another, there is no "art," still less a "total" art. But neither is there "laughter," as a sublime truth withdrawn from art itself. There are only peals of laughter.

. . . "the common among men" and what is common to men; what they share above all else—and in which they are shared out—is being in the world by way of the difference of the senses, the differences of sense. Being in the world by strokes, by bursts, by shakes of rhythm and dispersion of rhymes, by a harsh dance and the delicacies of lava—by a certain death, an inconceivable star, and the loose grace of a girl shaking with laughter.[29]

Psyche's Other, perhaps.

The one whose mourning has to be worn, by either one and both. In oneself and itself.

At this point, my discourse was shaping up badly, and everything already had to be started over from the beginning. To settle forever in the "long detour." An endless contretemps: I've hardly taken a single step, and he's already running ahead of me, never out of breath, touching and retouching his text, taxing my belatedness in advance. What a heart! Better than mine. I multiply the rendezvous, but all I share with him is the jubilation of anachronism. Touching him! How is one to touch him, still? And how is one not to touch—the truth? And how is one to touch—one another, ourselves? One and the other at the same time?

The necessity of telling a story having to do with this affect and this affection, the compelling urge to pretend one is proffering a fable, and constantly to begin over again, stems no doubt from this impossible alliance of contact and the syncope. They suspend the process in simultaneity, but they also interrupt the synchrony promised by a touch, by the affect of a "self-touching" which, like the imagination, can only feel itself by feeling "its own powerlessness." (I'm using his words, again.)

The power of powerlessness, the possibility of the impossible.

So I began again, and I already know that I shall proceed here only by a series of tangents. Will it be necessary to tell the whole history of philosophy and append a confiding postscript? Can't we write anything without a story, without a stir, spelling trouble in the name of the history of philosophy?

A tangent touches a line or a surface but without crossing it, without a true intersection, thus in a kind of impertinent pertinence. It touches only one point, but a point is nothing, that is, a limit without depth or surface, untouchable even by way of a figure. Suppose one were to reach there, what would give one the right to touch it?

My impertinence will be my tact. Also my way of going off on a tangent, so to speak, so as to elude while playing a little, like someone struggling. How is one to avoid an impossible task, not to acquit oneself of too heavy a debt? I would like to think that the story of the baroque composition, and the flaunted taste for delirious profusion, is a—calculated but embarrassed, playful and elusive—response to the aporias of tact.

The preceding already had only a tangential relation to the work and the corpus of Nancy. But I felt the need—the duty, in truth—to draw a series of other tangents.

PART II

Exemplary Stories of the "Flesh"

§ 7 Tangent I

Hand of Man, Hand of God

Nothing to teach Jean-Luc Nancy, of course, and nothing to make known to him. How could I pretend to give, and give to think anything, to one of those thinkers in whose proximity it is always better to hold one's tongue and lend an ear? I wanted, without telling him anything, at least to *touch him*. But not without tact, from a respectful distance.

And, if it was still necessary to tell him something, that it be a sort of secret: something confided or confessed that, without teaching him anything, without bringing anything to his awareness, especially not the truth, would have had as effect to *touch him*.

But with tact. To touch him without moving him.

To impart to him, as it were—but without saying or announcing to him anything that obtains. To impart to him—all but nothing. A question of tact. To *partake* and share with him, as he would say, in this imparted announcement, in something that touches him. Without bothering him, without importuning him with my demonstrations of admiring friendship, almost imperceptibly, intangibly.

I sense but I still do not know what touch, to touch him [*le toucher*] means—I know it less and less. Of course, I cannot impart this—touching him—and make it known to him and share it, except by touching touch, and therefore by touching upon the question or the plea of touch, which themselves ought to touch *pertinently* on the theme, that is, on the *sense* of touch. How is one to touch, without touching, the *sense* of touch? Shouldn't the sense of touch touch us, for something to *come about* at last —an event, as some say, a little tiresomely, a *singular event* (!!), *before* any constative statement, any performative mastering act or convention, be-

135

fore any event that we would still produce by way of an act of language and on the background of a foreseeable horizon, *even before* we touch it, or perhaps, if it does not anticipate in this fashion, then *at the same time* at which we touch it, as if the idea itself of simultaneity, even continuity, were born for the first time in contact with the contact between two points of contact? Tangentially?

Should one have touching power (to touch him)?[1] Or *laugh* touching, as he would, perhaps, also say?

(As for me, I'd lean toward saying "weep" touching: to weep, to cry (for) it. But I sense that it comes down to the same thing. We agree when it comes to shedding tears of laughter, for this "touch," this poor dear—dissociated, spaced out, severed from itself, in a word.)

From now on, I'll let this formula float between its two senses, especially around the value of enabling *power* (possibility, faculty, sovereignty), which here and elsewhere is not less problematic than the value of touch: to have *the power* to touch him, to be capable of touching him; and to have "touching" power, the *capability* for touch, *potently* to be with this singular sense that is called touch. *Potent* [*en puissance*], in the double sense of the force of power (that is, freely, sovereignly) and of the indefinitely reserved virtuality, in retreat, of *dunamis.* I'll leave this indecision open because what I would like to attain—him, if you like—is this possibility, touching (it), all the while meditating with him, simultaneously, on what touching, touching-power, "is" or what it "does" to (tell) the truth.

Would there be synchrony, an idea of synchrony, and in general some *syn-,* therefore a very idea of presence, presentation, and the auto-presentation of presence, if we *could not touch it, if we were not capable of this very thing, touching (it)?* He said in the passage cited earlier: to present is to make sensible, and sensibility equals the touching of the limit, touching the limit, at the limit.[2] What does this mean?

Touching power: "*pouvoir*" *le* "*toucher.*" *Le toucher*: to touch / to touch it (him): to be capable of it, to have the potential or power. Not simply to touch this or that, for example him (*le* = personal pronoun answering the question "who," while waiting for the proper name—here, Jean-Luc Nancy), but to be capable of that very thing, this common thing termed "*le* toucher," that is, "touching," "touch," a noun preceded (in French) by the definite article, "*le* toucher"—no longer "who," this time, but "what"; no longer the personal pronoun but the definite article. To be capable of touch, thus simultaneously of that contact without which, hypothetically, the idea itself of the *simul* would never have been born in us, *between us.*

(I am dreaming of a demonstration that would translate in this fashion the Berkeleyan logic—oh, marvelous Berkeley, the indisputable one!— there where it links the privilege of touch, let us say the privilege of the haptical with regard to the optical, to the grounding in God, in the language that God speaks to us, of the language among us and of the institution of signs and knowledge, of everything that resists doubt and makes of idealism something other than a skepticism. Here one would have to convoke once again the whole theory of those born blind and operated on in the seventeenth century, their observers and their philosophers: William Cheselden and William Molyneux and Diderot, and so many others. Between France and England, a longer detour still. For one of the theses or hypotheses of this book (for laughs, of course) is that something took place—an *affair*, a plot, a sort of conspiracy, a philosophical intrigue of touch, in Europe, along certain boundaries (more figures of touch) and at the borders of France, between France and England, to which I just alluded, and between France and Germany—with Kant and Husserl on one side, and Maine de Biran, Ravaisson, Bergson, Merleau-Ponty, and Deleuze on the other—to mention the dead ones only and leave room for all the border crossings through customs, for convergences, coincidences, chiasmuses, and "long detours." De jure, the question of touch fully belongs to the history of the body, of course, and "my body," as I have said and will say it again; to the legacy of "Hoc est enim corpus meum"; to all the cultures of the body; but also and indissociably, to the history of Europe making itself, which is to say, perhaps, having it out with its "Christianity.")

But how can one still say anything that does not in advance get surrounded, invested, preoccupied, in all the historical places of these figures of touch, in their rhetorical circle, in their logical or hermeneutical twirling around?

Indeed, this question—one, singular, acute—belongs to an immense family (resemblances, common traits, genetic variations and mutations, elementary laws of kinship). Very old, even archaic, since it has given rise over twenty-five centuries to an immense philosophical literature that we can't even skim here.

No doubt, we remember him saying, "a very long detour should be made here." In order to respond to his invitation, or even injunction, his question, perhaps ("a very long detour should be made here. What of the sharing of the senses?"),[3] I shall merely—timidly, gropingly—sketch the ellipsis of such a detour. Along margins, marches, and boundaries, it would be a brief and tangential excursion, which the "modernity" of this "European" question of touch makes in the history of philosophy—a sampler, involving the *hand*, between France and Germany. The hand: it won't be more than a sample, more or less well sewn, following, like a guiding thread, the contour of the hand and especially of the finger. It will only be a question of recognizing what this contour, "tour," and "turn" (the linear drawing of this running border and the figure of this trope) commands, delimits, and circumscribes; and yet also, perhaps, what these same strokes let slip away; and thus virtually what this "medium," this "contour" of "modern" thinking—even when he isn't named or cited in it—could help us to determine in Nancy's work, in the very places where the latter exceeds or displaces that thinking.

—And in an aside you tell yourself: what a funny, admiring, and grate-ful salutation you're addressing to him, to Jean-Luc Nancy. What a peculiar way to pretend you're touching him while acting *as if* you wanted again to put his lexicon about touch at the service of a tradition, or worse, a filia-tion itself. Or, as if you reminded us that this lexicon and its usage should always already have been related to agelessly well-worn or even usurious ways; even if we like that—touching—anew, precisely, when it's impossible-prohibited; and we even love to call this loving—abstaining. What a funny present, indeed! What an offering! Altogether as if at the moment of calling others so that they will become ecstatic before this great work and this im-mense philosophic treatise of touch, you whispered in his ear: Now, Jean-Luc, that's quite enough, give this word back, it's prohibited, you hear. Leave it to the ancestors, don't make any compromises with it, don't let this *megalovirus* contaminate you, and once and for all stop using this incredi-ble vocabulary, this concept nothing can really vouch for, these figures with-out figure and therefore without credit. Don't keep pretending, as they do, don't make believe, stop acting as if you wanted to make us believe that there is something one could call touch, an understood thing itself about which we could pretend to agree, and say something new, in the very place where, in touching upon the untouchable, this thing remains untouchable. Touch is finitude. Period. Stop at this point. Haven't you yourself said "there is no 'the' sense of touch"? Knowing you, I don't think this objection will stop you, I tell myself.

—Nor you. Would you like to touch him, as you say, in the way the point of a buttoned tip touches, during a fencing duel? Also, Americans say *touché*, in French, with a funny accent, when a point is scored.

—On the contrary, here what matters most of all to me is his singularity, his "plural singular being," even when I speak of the others to the others. It's this absolute singularity of his signature that I exert myself in trying to attain.

—You exert yourself? What does that mean?

Let us start again from what we nicknamed earlier, that is, the effort of *forceful exertion* [*l'efforcement*]. We wondered what this necessarily finite experience of *forceful exertion* may signify. Force, of course (and even the mysterious one—*virtus*, *dunamis*—that Jesus, as we recall, recognizes in himself when someone touches him), but also "exerting oneself," in its self-relation. This self-relation institutes itself and is born to itself as exertion at the moment when a limit comes to insist, to *resist*, to oppose (itself) to the effort that this limit literally *determines*. I chose the word "exertion" [*efforcement*] because it bespeaks the effort as well as the limit next to which the tendency, the tension, the intensity of a finite force stops (itself), exhausts itself, retracts or retreats from its end back toward itself: at the moment, the instant, when the force of the effort touches upon this limit. (I spoke earlier of the *objectivity* of being(s) determined not only as that which is *exposed before* the gaze, but that which *opposes a resistance*— to touch. The hand (being-before-the-hand or at-hand [*sous-la-main*], or that which meets a resistance to manipulation) might well reconcile, conjoin, and adjoin these two *positional* values of the objectivity of the object.) Every thinking of effort comprises at least a phenomenology of finitude, even if, in the case of Maine de Biran and especially Ravaisson, this thinking accommodates the infinite (will or pure activity, grace, spiritual freedom) against the background of which a finite effort is set off. But an effort always signs a finitude.

It is there perhaps that touching is not a sense, at least not one sense among others. A finite living being can live and survive without any other sense; and this occurs with a host of animals that have no vision (it is possible to be sensitive to light without "seeing"), no hearing (it is possible to be sensitive to sound waves without "hearing"), no taste or sense of smell answering the physical or physiological modifications of which these "senses" are the usual effects. But no living being in the world can survive for an instant without touching, which is to say without being touched. Not necessarily by some other living being but by something = x. We can live without seeing, hearing, tasting, and smelling ("sensing," in the visual, auditory, gustatory, and olfactory senses), but we cannot survive one instant without being with contact, and in contact. Aristotle said this very well, as cited earlier. That is where, for a finite living being, before and beyond any concept of "sensibility," touching means "being in the world." There is no world without touching, and thus without what we just termed forceful exertion.

That is how I am tempted to interpret the privilege that Maine de Biran simultaneously accords to effort (force + limit), to tactility, but to the hand as well, the "organ of touch," in a more problematic mode this time. He ties together what these signify in an original fashion, even if his discourse forms part of an immense contemporary debate (the famous question, raised by Molyneux, Locke, Berkeley, Condillac, Buffon, Diderot,[4] Voltaire, the *Idéologues* [a circle that in addition to Cabanis and Destutt de Tracy included Ginguené, Daunou, and Volney], Charles Bonnet, and Barthez, among others, concerning the problems of those who are born blind), which won't be reconstructed here.[5] Some Cartesian sources of the same argument go back more specifically to the First Discourse in Descartes's *Dioptrics*, in which he compares the stick of the blind to the "organ of some sixth sense given to them in place of sight."[6] A German streak already comes to blend with the French or Anglo-French medium of this tradition. In his *Mémoire sur la décomposition de la pensée*, Maine de Biran cites Schelling and Fichte, following Joseph Marie de Gérando.[7]

One could say that the "Introduction" to Maine de Biran's *The Influence of Habit on the Faculty of Thinking*[8] begins with touching. While proposing to unite ideology with physiology, Biran pretends that he is following a physicist's example by not concerning himself with essences or first causes, but only with "effects" and "phenomena," and their relation and succession, "leaving behind one, and under the veil that covers them, first causes which should never become for man objects of *knowledge*." And he adds: "We know nothing of the nature of *forces*."[9]

We know only their "effects," and for that very reason it is pointless to seek out what the soul is and how it can be united with the body: "Physical science does not concern itself with essences—why should metaphysics?

It is our intimate sense that must lead us and not the false glimmer of imagination or abstract methods."[10]

To be sure, it is a limited analogy, but it is certainly analogous to a Kantian or Husserlian gesture. One starts with a received impression, or sensation, a word held to be synonymous with it here: "primary faculty" of the "organic living being" [*l'être organisé vivant*]. Each of these words counts—originarity, the life of the living, organic or organized faculty (as well as organ). Now, if impressions are divided into active and passive, motor and sensitive; if the activity and distinction of the *ego* immediately connect with motor activity, then, from a phenomenal or phenomenological point of view, the two types of impression cannot be disentangled. And this would hinge on the "nature of our organization," either necessarily or contingently, but in any case starting from a *fact* with which one must begin: "such is the direct correspondence, the intimate connection which exists between the two faculties of feeling and moving, that there is almost no impression which does not result from their mutual co-operation and which is not consequently active in one situation and passive in another" (Maine de Biran, *Influence of Habit*, p. 56).

The word "almost" stands out ("almost no impression"). Although it is difficult to fit an example in this category of the exceptional (that is, pure activity or pure passivity), it is clear that Biran requires this possibility in order to preserve the operating power of the conceptual opposition and to distinguish the *predominating* element in each case. This logic of predominance makes it possible at once to lift or soften the pure conceptual opposition (between activity and passivity—which Condillac would have recognized, but that he later forgot so that he "confuse[d] things") and to introduce axiomatics of force and effort; not force as cause in itself but force in its phenomenal *effects*. What will be called "sensation" is the *most* passive impression (where "feeling *predominates* up to a certain point" [my emphasis—J. D.] and where "the movement which occurs with it is as nothing": "as nothing," and not nothing) and what will be termed "perception" is the impression where "movement *takes the upper hand* [*prend le dessus*]" (my emphasis—J. D.). Therefore, there is always *a part* of activity and *a part* of passivity, though now the one takes the upper hand, now the other predominates. Differential of force or hegemony. Maine de Biran then proposes to examine the organization of these two parts, feeling and movement, in the exercise of "each of our senses," and he begins with the "organ of touch" [*l'organe du tact*].

Why? Indeed, the answer is not given at the beginning but only toward the end of the course, when it becomes necessary to tackle the other senses, and when, at the end of the analysis of tactility, there is praise for the sense of touch, which "combines the two faculties [passive and active, sensory and motor] in the most exact proportion." (Maine de Biran also likes the word "exact," though we may wonder here what an exact proportion might be, "the most exact," between passive and active, and where one might find its criterion and its measure.) Maine de Biran does not contradict those who content themselves with a comparison, those for whom "it is customary to compare the different sense impressions with those of touch proper." Without objecting to it, he relates this hearsay *doxa* ("it is said") which turns touch into the genus of which the other senses would only be the kind, the species: "all our *sensations*, it is said, are only a kind of *touch*. That is very true." And this comparatism or analogism banks on a logic of inclusion. All our sensations are comparable to touch; they are *as*, they are *like* species of it, because touch is the genus of which the other senses are the species.

But after Maine de Biran has thus assented to received opinion, he ventures farther out and praises touch and its incomparable excellence. If touch cannot be paralleled by any other sense organs, it is also from the point of view of activity, and therefore motor activity. The other senses will correspond to touch only in accordance with their *mobility*, which is what will make them *agree* with the motor activity that is appropriate to touch, what will *correspond* to or come to an *understanding* and cooperate with touch [*s'entendra avec le toucher*]. Motor activity is therefore the specific difference, if not the essence, of touch—whence (we'll get to this) a certain privilege for the hand. The analogy between the other senses on the one hand and touch on the other will depend on the proportion of movement (motor activity, mobility) found in them. But only touch comprises a motor activity that is properly its own—and hence turns it into something more, something other than simply a sense, more and other than simply the locus of a passive sensation.

> All our sensations, it is said, are only a kind of touch. That is very true if one thinks only of their sensory or passive function; but with respect to activity and movement, no other sense organs are similar [*ne supporte le parallèle*]. Only in proportion to their *mobility* are they more or less capable of corresponding to or of cooperating [*s'entendre*] with touch, of profiting by its warnings and

of associating their impressions with it. We shall make this clear in a rapid analysis of the senses. (ibid., p. 61)

The logic of this argument is remarkable—and paradoxical. The space allocated to mobility, motility, or motor activity deserves a pause. To a large extent this motif was already present in Destutt de Tracy, who was moreover the *rapporteur* of Maine de Biran's *Mémoire* on the subject of habit answering a programmatic question formulated in Charles Bonnet's *Psychologie*: "What are all the operations of the soul if not movements and *repetitions* of movements?" (Maine de Biran, *Influence of Habit*, p. 41).[11] To a certain extent at least, this question conditions both the contents and the form of the *Mémoire*.

Before returning to this, and to anticipate a more patient look at Merleau-Ponty, this may be the right place for a historical digression. Merleau-Ponty devoted at least one series of lectures to Maine de Biran (alluded to a little earlier). It was in 1947–48, that is, two years after the publication of Merleau-Ponty's *Phenomenology of Perception*. The book never refers to the author of the two *Mémoires sur l'habitude*,[12] it seems to me. In fact, these *Mémoires* are not studied in the lectures of 1947–48, which instead deal with Maine de Biran's *Mémoire sur la décomposition de la pensée*, the *Commentaire sur les Méditations métaphysiques*, and the *Essai sur les fondements de la psychologie*. Furthermore, it is on the subject of the latter *Essai* that Merleau-Ponty reflects the Biranian notion of effort and shows the whole reach of this philosophy of motor activity—the style and character of his rhetoric sharpen things up a little, so to speak:

We are quick to say "motor subject or thinking subject," as if they were terms of an alternative. Biran did not reduce consciousness to motility but he identified motility and consciousness. The primitive fact is consciousness of an irreducible relationship between two terms irreducible themselves. It is not a consciousness becoming movement, but a consciousness reverberating in movements. It is neither an interior fact nor an exterior fact: it is the consciousness of self as relationship of the I to another term.[13]

Beforehand, however, although Maine de Biran is not yet cited in *Phenomenology of Perception*[14] and the major references in it are altogether different, Merleau-Ponty's analyses already bestow a role that is just as decisive on motor activity (normal or pathological). To wit, this is the case, in the chapter "The Spatiality of One's Own Body and Motility," with the pages dedicated to deficiencies of "unsound" or pathological touching or "potential" [*virtuel*] touch, as well as, in the chapter "Sense Experience," with the "motor significance of colours" and "motor physiognomy" of all sensations, and even of this "synaesthetic perception" that "is the rule," of this "intersensory object," of the "intersensory unity of the thing" that makes up the most continuous theme of this book and seems inseparable from the concept of world, being in the world, or just being—a concept organizing this phenomenology of perception (see Merleau-Ponty, *Phenomenology of Perception*, pp. 210, 239, et passim).

A little earlier, in the passage cited just below, *sensation* presents itself as *communion*. Let us here note the return of the haptical figure of contact, primordial contact, to speak of the experience—no less—of being and the world. The logic of these phrases runs throughout the book; one often comes across the literal mark they leave:

> Every sensation is spatial; we have adopted this thesis, not because the quality as an object cannot be thought otherwise than in space, but because, as the *primordial contact with being*, as the *assumption* [*reprise*] by the sentient subject of a form of existence to which the sensible points, and as the *co-existence of sentient and sensible*, it is itself constitutive of a setting for co-existence, in other words, of a space . . . this *assumption* [*reprise*] implies also that I can at each moment absorb myself *almost* wholly into the sense of touch or sight . . . the unity and the diversity of the senses are truths of the same order. . . . it is *a priori* impossible to touch without touching in space, since our experience is the *experience of a world.* (ibid., p. 221)[15]

And so these firm declarations about "primordial contact with being," this belief in "co-existence of sentient and sensible" are on a par with a philosophy of *immediate coincidence* that will be relayed later—unstoppably, continually, without denial or admitted contradiction—by an increasingly insistent discourse about all the phenomena of noncoincidence or even noncontact with the untouchable. We could situate one of the places of the transitional transaction—still from the point of view, if we may say so, of tactility and its figures—for example in the conference about Bergson (May 1959) published in *Signs* and titled "Bergson in the Making." In it, Merleau-Ponty goes within one page from coincidence of absolute contact to "partial coincidence" and nevertheless comes back to *coincidence* with a "non-coincidence." This movement is all the more significant because Merleau-Ponty will have once again claimed his own reader's "preferences"

and "partialities," orienting the reading of Bergson not only toward a phenomenology—complete with "reduction" and so forth—but also toward
his own phenomenological bent:

> Now we can bear witness to the vitality of his works only by saying how he
> [Bergson] is present in our own, showing the pages of his works in which, like
> his listeners in 1900, we with our own *preferences* and *partialities* think we per-
> ceive him "in contact with things."
>
> . . . For if this is what time is, it is nothing that I *see* from without. . . . So
> time is myself; I am the duration I grasp, and time is duration grasped in me.
> And from now on we are at the absolute. A strange absolute knowledge, since
> we know neither all our memories nor even the whole thickness of our pres-
> ent, and since my *contact* with myself is *"partial coincidence"* (to use a term
> often used by Bergson which, to tell the truth, is a problematic one). In any
> case, when my self is at issue the *contact* is *absolute because* it is partial. I know
> my duration as no one else does because I am caught up in it; because it over-
> flows me, I have an experience of it which could not be *more narrowly or closely*
> conceived of. *Absolute knowledge* is not detachment; it is inherence. . . .
>
> Since it is *a non-coincidence I coincide with* here, experience is susceptible to
> being extended beyond the particular being I am. My perception [*l'intuition*]
> of my duration is an apprenticeship in a general way of *seeing*. It is the princi-
> ple of a sort of Bergsonian "reduction". . . .
>
> . . . Intuition is definitely not *simply coincidence or fusion* any more. It is ex-
> tended to "limits". . . . [16]

And since we have already paid so much attention to the *corpus* of "Hoc
est corpus meum," and to the Christian body and the Eucharist, and to
irony that thinks, troubled and troubling in the hands of Nancy, let us do
no more than situate here a certain connection between Merleau-Ponty's
thinking of motor activity and the Last Supper. His tone and intention are
quite different from Nancy's. The passage can be found in the first pages of
the chapter on "Sense Experience" in *Phenomenology of Perception*. Merleau-
Ponty has just insisted—notably on the subject of the perception of colors
—on "motor physiognomy," motor reactions, "motor significance," and
the amplification of our motor being. Here, now, is the analogy, the "just
as . . . in the same way," reminding us of more than one "my body," a "my
body" that I wholly "surrender" [*je livre*] in this way:

> In the same way I give ear, or look, in the expectation of a sensation, and sud-
> denly the sensible *takes* possession of my ear or my gaze, and I *surrender* [*je
> livre*] a part of my body, even *my whole body*, to this particular manner of vi-

brating and filling space known as blue or red. *Just as* the sacrament not only symbolizes, in sensible species, an operation of Grace, but is also the real presence of God, which it causes to occupy a fragment of space and communicates to those who eat of the consecrated bread, provided that they are inwardly prepared, *in the same way* the sensible has not only a motor and vital significance, but is nothing other than a certain way of being in the world suggested to us from some point in space, and *seized* and acted upon by our body [*que notre corps* reprend *et assume*], provided that it is capable of doing so, so that sensation is *literally* a form of communion. (Merleau-Ponty, *Phenomenology of Perception*, p. 212)

It is Husserl to whom Merleau-Ponty then refers, often as an authority. But a certain Biranian tradition is not incompatible with this thinking of motor intentionality as a thinking of power, of force in effort, and of an ego that relates to itself in the experience of the "I can" (the usual term in Husserl's unpublished writings): "These elucidations enable us clearly to understand motility as basic intentionality. Consciousness is in the first place not a matter of 'I think that' but of 'I can'" (Merleau-Ponty, *Phenomenology of Perception*, p. 137).

Here ends this anticipatory digression. A later chapter deals with touch according to Merleau-Ponty. This motif of motor activity here allows us to come back to Maine de Biran—whom, in truth, we had not really left.

After his analysis of touch, Maine de Biran announces, then, that he is going to deal with the other senses, saying: "We shall make this clear in a rapid analysis of the senses" (*Influence of Habit*, p. 61).

The analysis of the other senses will thus be "rapid." Among essential traits, it will select what relates to touch, *by way of an analogy*, that is, in accordance with *movement*, proportionally to mobility or motor activity. Now touch is also a fundamental *organ* and thereby not a sense properly speaking; or in any case, it is what it is properly—that is, distinct and superior—only there where motor activity, in it, exceeds pure sensation, namely, the "sensory or passive function." Touch is no doubt the highest of the senses, the first, the *incomparable* model: at most one can only *compare* something else to it. But this primordial excellence has to do with what makes it into something other than a sense, other than an organ of pure, passive sensation. This sense transcends the others; it also grounds them; it makes them possible, but to the extent that it is not quite a sense any longer. In a language that (for good reasons) is not Maine de Biran's, one could acknowledge its *transcendental* status—all the more so since it is first evaluated under the angle of knowledge and the relation to an object: "It is only, therefore, as a motor organ [specificity of tactility/touch— J. D.] that touch [*le tact*] contributes essentially to putting the individual in communication with external nature; it is because it combines the two faculties in the most exact proportion that it is susceptible of such nice, such detailed, such persistant [*sic*] impressions; in short, it is in virtue of this that it opens a feeding ground for intellect and furnishes it with its more substantial nourishment" (ibid., p. 61).[17]

The sensibility of sight is no doubt the most "delicate" but it could scarcely be "circumscribed" if one failed to take into consideration its relation to touch, which is to say the "mobility peculiar" to the gaze and especially its "association," its "close [*intime*] correspondence with touch": "It is only because of its mobility that the eye maintains such intimate relations with touch [*le tact*]" (ibid., p. 62). The analogical "[just] as" always commands the logic of this community of the senses: "How could the hands say to the eyes: *Do as we do*, if the eyes were immovable?" (ibid., p. 62n3). After "as" comes "almost" (the difference of the *almost* would open up the interval that we earlier risked nicknaming "transcendental": touch is not quite a sense—not a sense *as* or *like* the others): "For that matter, we can apply to sight *almost* all that we have said of touch. In the natural state and in the ordinary exercise of the organ, the two functions—sensory and motor—correspond with and balance each other with no mutual disturbance" (ibid., p. 63).

Maine de Biran seems more uneasy when relating hearing to touch, but his procedure is always the same: the recourse is to *analogy* by reason of or proportionally to *motor activity*. "In order to hear well," he notes, "it is necessary to *listen*" (ibid., pp. 63–64). And this presupposes "putting into action the muscles," a "tension," an "effort." If, in this case, the effort has become "imperceptible" owing to the ear's immobile passivity, a *supplement* of motor activity comes as the remedy, taking up with touch again. A natural supplement, of course, and a teleological one! "But nature herself has taken care to supplement these faults; she has restored equilibrium by associating in the most intimate way her passive impressions with the activity of an organ essentially motor" (ibid., p. 64). But it is especially to the vocal organ that this supplement of motor activity finds itself entrusted. Through the effect of a sympathy so habitual that it does not strike us at all, sounds transmitted to the ear and the cerebral center set in motion the vocal organ "which repeats them, imitates them, turns them back [*les réfléchit*]," "incorporates" them in the "sphere of the individual's activity." An interesting theory of *echo* and *double imprint* follows. The correspondence with touch goes through the echo. Passivity and activity are thus coupled, and this is what it takes to turn hearing, listening, and the voice into kinds of touching, modalities of haptical approach or appropriation. As always, the proper and the proximate are given (or rather, supposed to be given) in the same movement: "Thus, the individual who listens is himself his own *echo*. The ear is as if instantaneously struck both by the direct external sound and the internal sound reproduced. These two imprints are added together in the cerebral organ, which is doubly stimulated [*s'électrise doublement*]—both by the action which it communicates and by the action which it receives. Such is the cause of *têtes sonores* [literally, sonorous or resonant heads]" (ibid., pp. 64–65).[18]

Affinity and dependence: this double relation with touch thus determines hearing as well as sight. But according to Maine de Biran this is still more evident in the case of taste and smell. Tastes are "the touch inherent [*propre*] in the tongue and the palate," and the sense of taste is thus the one that is "most closely related to touch"; while what can be said about taste "applies still more directly to smell," these two senses being "closely [*intimement*] connected with each other as with their internal organs."

Maine de Biran never forgets the animal. He compares the passivity of smell (there again, the *movement* of respiration *makes up* for it, supplements it [*suppléée*]), or rather its role among the external senses, at the same rank as the polyp or the oyster "in the scale of animal life" (ibid., p. 67). Since smell is the most passive of the senses, it is as close as can be to the sixth category of impressions, *pure sensations*, which come to us from inside the body—no perception here, no effort, or at least "no perceived effort," "no activity, no discrimination, no trace of memory." And when, in order to qualify these pure sensations, these purely internal and passive sensations, Maine de Biran concludes: "all light is eclipsed with the faculty of movement," he confirms and gathers several axioms:

1. This analysis of the senses is ruled by the point of view of the perceiving *consciousness* and *objective* knowledge.

2. The figure of light finds itself as if naturally associated with that, at the very moment when sight is nevertheless interpreted as a kind of touch.

3. Above all, the reference to movement, the "faculty of movement," is

determining here as we have seen, in order to justify the absolute privilege of the tactile, and it is what *withdraws* touch from the order of sensibility, from "pure sensation." Sensu stricto, touch is not properly a sense. This exemplary sense is a sense above the other senses, which are not senses, in fact, except in reference to it; however they are—henceforth—more "sensitive," more *properly* senses than touch is. Maine de Biran is not saying it like this, but this formulation seems to me ineluctably to correspond to the premises that we have just rehearsed. The quasi-transcendental constraints of this paradoxy no doubt apply well beyond Maine de Biran's discourse, and it is also on this score that they call for our attention. Touch is more of a "sense" than are the others. The latter are senses only by way of touch and are therefore less "sensitive" than touch is. But for the same reason, because they are more passive, less active, less motor-driven, and therefore more "sensitive" than touch, they are more legitimately entitled to being termed "senses." One finds more and less sense, at the same time, on both sides of the analogy.

But in order further to remain with the *Mémoires sur l'habitude*, having traced the logic of the relation between touch and the other senses, let us come back to what necessarily privileges an organ of touch, the hand, in this philosophy of effort and the motor will. There is a Kantian hand, and there will be a Husserlian hand, and a Heideggerian hand,[19] and so forth, which have traits in common but do not overlap. And there is also a Biranian hand.

Motor activity remains the distinguishing trait of touch, marking its excellence; it is what makes the other senses resemble touch and relate to it, even if touch is in fact also characterized by the union of the faculties of feeling and moving. The faculty of moving is the one to which the ego is immediately attached, with its activity and its distinctiveness. Furthermore, this faculty of motion is a will, and the ego that moves and self-moves is a "willing subject." Since Maine de Biran's formulas here are at the same time precise and figurative, we should not proceed without remaining close to their letter. Maine de Biran wants at the same time to dissociate and associate just as rigorously the faculties of moving, self-moving, and feeling. And since it is to the first faculty that he *immediately* connects the ego—an ego whose identity has to be that of a willing subject—he stretches the rhetoric of his effort so as to dissociate what he associates, in fact *twinning* two faculties. Such a twinning provides the condition for a fundamental experience of effort, at the joint of two faculties. If there were nothing but a motor will (pure ego), there would be no effort, but there would not be any either if there were nothing but pure sensibility. I am not just conveniently inventing the schema of twinning. Here, for example, as early as the introduction to the *Mémoire*, is a passage, the passage of a certain "rather," that bears witness to the rhetoric exerted so as to justify the concept of effort itself: "We can already begin to perceive that activity, as that which is distinctive of the ego and its ways of being, is directly attached to the faculty of *moving*, which ought to be distinguished from that of *feeling*, as a main branch is distinguished from the trunk of the tree, or rather as twin trees are distinguished which cling together and grow into one, with the same stem [*dans la même souche*]" (Maine de Biran, *Influence of Habit*, p. 56; slightly amplified.—Trans.)

The stem [*souche*][20] of the effort, therefore, is the stem itself. The effort works the stem, in the stem of the ego, and since it is also the origin of the ego, it is an ego before the ego, ego without ego or ego before ego. This relation to oneself, this faculty to say I or to posit oneself, "self-identical," as I, can only institute itself, from the stem itself, in a memory, with persistence, in repeated efforts, and in self-retention. And so it should not surprise us that the clearest formulas on this subject appear at the moment when Maine de Biran deals with what he terms *réminiscence* ["memory"] and that the most interesting formulas discreetly put in communication a thinking of force, potential power, these temporalizing dynamics of the effort, with a thinking of the virtual:

> The motor determination is a *tendency* of the organ or the motor center to repeat the action or the movement which has occurred for the first time. When this tendency passes from the *virtual* to the *actual* [*effectif*], as a result of renewed external stimulation, the individual *wills* and executes the same movement. He is conscious of a *renewed effort*. . . . here are the elements of a relation, a subject which *wills*, always self-identical, and a variable term, *resistance*. . . .
>
> The motor being who has acted, and who acts now with greater facility, cannot perceive this difference without recognizing his own identity as *willing subject*. But this recognition necessarily entails that of the end of the action; they presuppose each other, and are closely united in the same impression of *effort*. (ibid., pp. 70–71)

This intimate union of two heterogeneous elements (which are *disassociated* in a way) constitutes the primitive fact of the effort in *mixed* fashion, and this primitive fact is anything but simple. As early as on the second page of the introduction, Maine de Biran has to speak of something "mingled" and of "first reflection" that "has discovered a compound." And there resides his faithful concern, but also and at the same time his first unfaithfulness with respect to the *Idéologues'* analytism and their craving for an ultimate, simple element or an originarity that will not break down.

And where does the first instance of the word *effort* occur—the word *effort* underscored? It seems to be, still in the introduction, in the course of the first analysis of touch, and more precisely *manual* touch. The expression "on my hand" comes up three times to scan a theatrical action, that is, going into action, and more literally into surgery, this manual operation that carries the hand forward and puts it in contact with a foreign body. *Resistance*, then *effort*—as if everything went by way of the hand, the human hand, the three beats of a human hand. Starting with *moi*, with the genesis of *moi*—as willing motor subject.

A. *First beat*: "If one places on my hand an object whose surface is rough. . . . " It is the moment of pure, purely passive sensation, the "part of feeling." The motor faculty is still "paralyzed," the ego is not distinct from its modifications.

B. *Second beat*: "If the object is left *on my hand,* supposing it to have a certain weight. . . . " (Here the concept of weighing, of which we spoke earlier, also carries over to the hand.) I feel a "force opposed to mine" but it is not yet the *ego* acting to raise or to hold back my arm, even if I already know that there is something outside of me [that] challenges all the "sophisms of idealism."

C. *Third beat*: "If—the object still remaining *on my hand* [my emphasis—J. D.]—I wish to close the hand, and if, while my fingers are folding back upon themselves, their movement is suddenly stopped by an obstacle on which they press and [that] thwarts [*écarte*] them, a new judgment is necessary; *this is not I.* There is a very distinct impression of solidity, of resistance, which is composed of a thwarted movement, of an *effort* [that] I make, in which I am *active.* . . .

Let us stop an instant on this impression of *effort* which comes from any thwarted [*contraint*] movement. We must learn to know it well" (Maine de Biran, *Influence of Habit*, pp. 57–58).

"We must learn to know it [*la*, i.e., this impression] well," in the first place because it is a matter there of becoming knowledgeable about the condition itself of the knowing. Indeed, an analysis follows, which ascends along the three segments in time of this history of the hand and manual touch, with a view to showing that without a willing motor subject, there is no effort, and without effort, no knowledge. And without the hand, not even an idea for the subject of his [*sic*] own existence, as it were. It goes on:

> Effort necessarily entails the perception of a relation between the being who moves, or who wishes to move, and any obstacle whatsoever which is opposed to its movement; without a *subject* or a will which determines the movement, without a something which resists, there is no *effort* at all, and without effort no knowledge, no perception of any kind.
>
> If the individual did not *will* or was not determined to begin to move, he would know nothing. If nothing resisted him, he likewise would know nothing, he would not suspect any existence; he would not even have an *idea* of his own existence. (ibid., p. 58)

Then comes a counterproof, which examines all that would come about—or rather, all that would not—without manual touch, should the touch die or vanish at the threshold of the first beat, or the second, or the third: what would not happen is perception and knowledge.

At the very place where they have a *hold*, as we noted, where they butt against a "mixed" and a "compound," these analyses and syntheses imply a hierarchy and a teleology. Irreducibly and essentially. At the top are the will to know and the willing subject—the effort. At the top of the senses of effort is this quasi-sense that is touch, the ultrasense. At the top of the organs of touch is the hand, the whole hand, its surface and fingers. A note[21] even enumerates all that would go missing for whoever had at his or her disposal only the tip of an extremely pointy fingernail. We've read it already—the hand, "the foremost instrument of analysis," "opens a feeding ground for intellect" (p. 61).

Now, this hand is the hand of man, the human being as *animal rationale*.[22] Humans are the only beings who have this hand at their disposal; they alone can *touch*, in the strongest and strictest sense. Human beings touch more and touch better. The hand is properly human; touching is properly human: it is the same proposition. Without playing too much, we could call this Maine de Biran's "humanualism" [*humainisme*]—involving the same teleological hierarchy and the same presuppositions about the animal; yielding the same knowledge, the same will, the same will to know, but frequently also the same obscurantism.

Maine de Biran's remark about an elephant's trunk is not disproving this humanualism. On the contrary. The elephant's trunk "fulfills approximately the same functions as the hand of man." Approximately. Kant— within the same anthropo-teleological hierarchy—does not neglect the future of the orangutan or the chimpanzee who could one day develop near-human organs, organs that can be used to handle, touch, palpate, grope and feel objects and speak ("zum befühlen der Gegenstände und zum sprechen").[23] Maine de Biran, for his part, jumps straight to the elephant, and if the latter is placed at the top of the scale of living beings, it is only to the extent that, thanks to what is "approximately" a knowing hand, namely, its trunk, the elephant resembles human beings to a certain extent. A long note once again invokes Buffon's authority. Knowledgeable intelligence and above all *motor activity* and *motility*, which condition it— these are the organizing criteria of this anthropo-zoological comparatism and this teleological hierarchy:

> The elephant's trunk fulfills *approximately* the same functions as the hand of man; *motor activity* and sensible feeling can be found in it equally united to a perfect degree. Therefore, as Buffon remarked, this organ is doubtless the one to which the elephant owes the intelligent features distinguishing it. When comparing the faculties of various species of animals, one may *perhaps* not find it difficult to prove that these faculties are not so much proportional in number or in relation to the refinement of the senses than to the *activity* and the perfection of the *motor* organs; less to the energy and very [*propre*] delicacy of sensible feeling [*la sensibilité*] than to the prompt correspondence, the constant equilibrium that sensible feeling enjoys with regard to *motility*.[24]

"Approximately," "perhaps": these signs of empiricist caution disappear at the top of "all the ranks in the scale"—which goes from man "down to the polyp," from the most "motor" to the most sensible or the most passive —when the "admirable" and "perfection," "human preeminence," and "the foundation or the conditions of human preeminence" are what is admired: "The extreme subdivision of human nerves, the proportion and admirable distribution of sensible and motor organs, the perfection of these organs (especially of the hand and the vocal organ), their correspondence within a unique center built on such a peculiar plane—such are probably the foundation or the conditions of human preeminence."[25]

Several paths are open to whoever may wish to inquire further into this human destination of the hand in such a discourse about the sense of touch. One may ask oneself what the *exemplarity* of this human hand signifies. In Nancy's discourse, in what he says about "my body" as well as the "*technē* of bodies," this seems to me absent, precisely, or implicitly and practically called into question. And what he says is as foreign to the humanistic philosophy of the hand as to this continuistic intuitionism, this cult of natural immediacy, which has inspired so many celebrations of touching. We need to reread "*technē* of bodies," in *Corpus* again and again, since this "question of the hand," which is also a history of the hand, as we know, remains—should remain—impossible to dissociate from the history of technics and its interpretation, as well as from all the problems that link the history of the hand with a hominizing process.[26] It is also the question of the eye and the question of the mouth, of course. But we need what we deemed to be the necessary starting point: for Nancy the question of the mouth (*bucca*) is not to be reduced to the question of orality that speaks (*os*).

There are several paths to interpret the exemplarity of this human hand, and that is because, even with Maine de Biran, it can have a *teleological* and thus irreplaceable (seemingly dominant) sense, as well as a *pedagogical* and secondary one, which is virtually pregnant with every kind of metonymy: manual touching as the *best* example, a convenient and eloquent sample, albeit replaceable and dispensable. The "figure" of the hand could well be the *best* ontoteleological figure, the *best* rhetorical figure, or a trope among others to expose what an "organ of touch" or tactility is in general. Although the teleological sense gives its orientation to the pedagogical sense of the example, although the two senses do not seem to be dissociable in Maine de Biran and so many others, they remain distinct in principle and de jure. This can also be explained by the quasi-"transcendental" paradox evoked earlier. "Transcendentalism" is always guided by a more or less surreptitious "exemplarism." As soon as touch is determined as the master sense or the originary sense by way of a reasoning that turns it into something other and more than a (sensitive and passive) sense, one may include it in the list of the senses or just as well exclude it. And as soon as the tactile is consequently a sense that is at the same time localizable and unlocalizable, its local representation (for example or par excellence, the hand or the fingers of the hand) becomes necessary and just as well contingent and arbitrary.

Where can we find a proof, or at least a sign, of this? Well, for example, in the fact that the same philosophy of effort and motor spontaneity, the same discourse about an essential link between effort and touch, the same praise of their common preeminence in the human "personality" can be displayed without a determining reference, perhaps without even an allusion, to the hand. Félix Ravaisson, as far as I can tell, never mentions the hand in his thesis on habit (*De l'habitude* [1838]). Yet he plainly, and often word for word, derives his axioms from Maine de Biran, whom he moreover often cites—which does not limit the originality of work that leads elsewhere to what I have just for convenience's sake termed his axioms. The ones that matter to us here have to do with motor activity, effort, and touching. If movement presupposes a power exceeding resistance, the relation between power and resistance can be measured by the consciousness of the effort that thus envelops activity and passivity. Effort situates the locus of equilibrium between "action and passion," as between "perception and sensation." Ravaisson then calls on Aristotle (invoking the *Peri psuchēs*, on the subject of force), and on Maine de Biran especially, as he takes the consciousness of effort for the manifestation of personality, under "the eminent form of voluntary activity."[27] In his *La philosophie en France au XIXe siècle* (1868),[28] Ravaisson praises Maine de Biran for having translated "I *think* therefore I am" into "I *will* therefore I am"—and not only, as Merleau-Ponty (quoted earlier) also noted, into "I can." But what difference is there between "I am willing to be able to" [*je veux pouvoir*] and "I am able to be willing to" [*je peux vouloir*]? Now, as effort cannot be dissociated from touch, touch at the same time fulfills it and covers the entire field of experience, every interval and every degree between passivity and activity. Touch [*tact*], the eminent sense of effort, is also the name of all the senses: "Effort is fulfilled in touch [*tact*]. Touch [*tact*] extends from the extremity of passion to the extremity of action. In its development it comprises all their intermediate degrees, and, at every degree, it bears out their law of reciprocity."[29]

And so, touch occupies *two places* in the analyses dedicated to this "development"; this seems to comply with the Biranian legacy.

A. On the one hand, touch, *as such*, occupies a median and *ideal* region of effort poised between passivity and activity. On this score, it is the very best thing about a human being: "It is in the median region of touch, it is in this mysterious middle term of the effort, that one finds, with reflection, the clearest and most assured consciousness of personality."[30]

This attention paid to the "middle term" no doubt confirms a faithful Aristotelianism. It is, however, of interest here from another point of view.

This attention seems inseparable from the *continuism* whose symptoms we have tracked through numerous intuitionistic and spiritualistic haptologies, both classical and modern. By the same token, it is also inseparable—and this aspect is just as decisive—from a postulated *indivisibility.*

(*Continuity and indivisibility*: two traits that could help us to formalize the whole metaphysics of touch, which is often an expressly spiritualistic metaphysics, sometimes a matter of "humanisms." Nancy seems to break away from haptocentrist metaphysics, or at least to distance himself from it. His discourse about touch is neither intuitionistic nor continuistic, homogenistic, or indivisibilistic. What it first recalls is sharing, parting, partitioning, and discontinuity, interruption, caesura—in a word, syncope. In accordance with a "my body" that finds itself involved from the outset with a *technē* as irreducible to "nature" as to "spirit," and in accordance with a sense of touch that Nancy always describes as "local, modal, fractal.")[31]

How does Ravaisson link his overvaluation of the middle term (which is to say of *touch*, as we have just seen) with such an indivisibilistic continuism? He does it by interpreting the concept of *movement* (just as fundamental in his eyes), and by determining it, starting from the necessity of its measure, its fair measure—that is, the best *relation.* One is tempted to say, its *logos.* It is there, in what looks like a magic trick or an effect of miraculous grace, by dint of a "confusion" or the simple explanation that it "implies," that the divisible becomes indivisible and the interval fills up. And it is also there, more or less in secret, in a more or less clandestine fashion, that a figure of touch ("extremes *touch*" [*les extrêmes* se touchent]) grounds this metaphysics of the life of the spirit as a metaphysics of touch. This is a permanent temptation, and any thinking of touch must remain vigilant before it, which is why I am insisting on it. Ravaisson:

> Movement gives intervals a measure. The interval *implies* the—infinitely divisible—*continuity* of the middle. Continuity *implies* an *indivisible middle term* where, throughout the extension of the middle, at any distance from one or the other extreme, extremes *touch* and opposites are *confused.* . . . Extremes *touch* everywhere; the principle and the end are *confused.* This *immediate* intelligence is concrete thought, where the idea is *fused* in Being. This *immediate* will is desire, or rather love, which possesses and desires at the same time.[32]

B. But on the other hand, and simultaneously, touch covers the field of the other four senses, from the most passive and least mobile (taste and smell) to the loftiest [*relevés*], endowed with movement in their function (hearing and sight): "In the four senses placed at intervals between the extreme limits of the development of touch, the same relations prevail, subjected to the same law. . . . A profound law reveals itself outside, in the series of the various senses, from the first to the last form of touch, through the progressive symmetry and independence of the organs, their separation in space, and at the same time their harmony in movement."[33]

In these rather limited references to Ravaisson, I am thus artificially isolating this withdrawal of the hand. To my sole question—namely, why does this interpretation of touch keep silent about the hand, although it has taken over almost everything from Maine de Biran and what I have termed his "humanualism"?—the possible answer is of two types, or rather it is a two-faced answer. If Ravaisson apparently avoids anthropocentrism or anthropologism, if he does not lock himself into a description that would pay much attention to the human hand, it is also because his purpose is to establish a spiritualistic metaphysics of life, a general ontology of the living, which is revealed from one end of his book to the other, and orients his interpretation of touch. "Thus it is in the principle of life that nature as well as Being properly consist."[34] This life aspires to spirit; it tends to become life of the spirit. From the origin to the end, it precedes, traverses, and overflows the humanity of the human without ceasing to *inspire* or *aspire* to it, and therefore to finalize it. It is by reason of this excess of finality or finalism that there is not even any further need to stop at the human hand. Finalism is declared; it defines the freedom of spirit, namely, the principle of life, as the prevalence of final causes over efficient ones. The "necessity" of habit, this "virtue," is not a necessity of constraint but of attraction and desire. "Indeed, it is a law, the *law of members* [Saint Paul], which follows the freedom of spirit. But this law is a *law of grace*. It is the final cause, which increasingly prevails over the efficient cause absorbing it within it."[35]

Life "*implies* the opposition of receptivity and spontaneity,"[36] without which there is neither effort nor touch, that is to say, no consciousness. No spirit. Often influenced by Xavier Bichat's *Recherches physiologiques sur la vie et sur la mort*,[37] further developments abound and are dedicated to the living and its diseases and parasites. They all bring into play an ontoteleology of life, which is also, indissociably, an ontotheology of desire and grace. In order to exit the "circle" and "find the beginning," between the effort that implies resistance and resistance that manifests itself in effort, one must implant will in a desire, "primordial instinct": "*nature* itself."[38] Following a gesture that I believe to be typical, and of which Ravaisson was not the last to offer an example, as we shall see, his invocations of Saint Paul,[39] Saint Augustine,[40] Malebranche, and Fénelon immediately relay, in order to spiritualize and evangelize it, the Aristotelian inspiration that already lies at the core of this philosophy in the very interpretation of desire (*orexis*): "Nature is wholly in desire, and desire in the good which attracts it. And so, these profound words from a profound theologian can strictly be verified: 'Nature is prevenient grace.' It is God in us, God concealed solely by reason of being too far inside, in this innermost intimacy of ourselves that we cannot fathom."[41]

Some might claim, and may even demonstrate (this is the second face of the same answer), that what is hiding, in this withdrawal of the human hand, so as to act in secret, is the hand of God. Is this just another figure? How is one to separate this "prevenient grace" from all the *senses* and ways of the Gospel, from its light or flesh? And Incarnation? And particularly the miraculous touch of Christ?

§ 8 Tangent II

"For example, my hand"—"The hand itself"—
"For example, the finger"—"For example,
'I feel my heart'"

"For example . . . my . . . hand" is Husserl's phrase, and so is "for example, the . . . finger." Sometimes it is *zum Beispiel* that "for example" translates (for example, my hand), and sometimes it is *etwa* (approximately as, like, for example . . . the finger).

Hence, exemplariness. Why have I insisted so much on this ambiguity of *examples*, and the example of the hand, in Maine de Biran and Ravaisson? For numerous reasons, and to pursue more than one motif, running across all the values of exemplariness:

1. The *random* sample: the hand as an *indifferent* example of a tactile organ;

2. *Teleological* value: the hand as the *best* example of what characterizes the *human being*, at the top of an ontological hierarchy—for attaining, taking [*prendre*], comprehending, analyzing, knowing, knowing how to hand out, and so forth;

3. And above all, shall I say, a simulacrum of a sample whose symptom would give away another, hidden teleology: the hand may not be an example among others but the best *metonymy* of some other—or more than one—tactile (or nontactile) bodily locus, and of a "self-touching" or a supplementary "touching-touched," which could go through the hand, or hand itself out, but would not stop at it. I am saying *above all* the symptom of a metonymy, because, as I have remarked, we have always had to treat the question of touch within the ever-open possibility of some figurality, some figural substitute or supplement endlessly running toward its "own proper" abyss: touching figures—and the technical partakes of the game.[1]

Across all these reasons, which are interlaced without excluding one another, I have also tried to prepare to interrogate the "properly" phenomenological moment of this history of touch—hence Husserl's hand and fingers, and the *zum Beispiel* and the *etwa* cited before we started. To interrogate a "properly" phenomenological moment is first and foremost, as well, to ask ourselves whether there is such a moment, before, precisely, presupposing that we trust this motif of properness (about which some doubts earlier arose) and presupposing further that the phenomenological gesture, in what might be "proper" about it, does not reproduce so many traditional patterns. Let us venture some hypotheses on the horizon of this detour, so as little by little to localize the singularity of Nancy's "corpus," as it stands out in the rich trail of Husserlian phenomenology in France. Concerning touch, this trail first and foremost follows the passage, and certain passages, of Husserl's *Ideas Pertaining to a Pure Phenomenology and to a Phenomenological Philosophy*, II (cited as *Ideas II*).[2]

It is more than ever necessary to proceed slowly, prudently, and vigilantly here. Just as we have repeatedly recognized some prephenomenological motifs in Berkeley, Kant, and Maine de Biran among others, we can likewise recognize a very familiar landscape in Husserl's analyses, from the outset, and this even reaches into the places where one might assume that "phenomenological reduction" has deeply modified the pathways. Within one single paragraph where we read "For example . . . my . . . hand," we can see reappearing as a network—often within the same network—each and every organizing concept of the discourse and the attendant logic that we have just evoked, from Maine de Biran to Ravaisson, namely, freedom, spontaneity, the will of an ego, the Ego-subject as will, its can-will [*pouvoir-vouloir*], the motor activity of a *free, spontaneous, immediate,* and so forth, *movement.* And all this, moreover, is to lay down explicitly a "distinctive feature of the Body" (*Leib*) [*corps propre*][3] about which Husserl has just asserted that it becomes body proper only through touch, and more precisely a touch able tactually to feel, grope, palpate, fondle—often by way of the hand (*abtasten*).

"For example . . . my . . . hand" comes forth amid this axiomatic chain, that is, the will, freedom, and spontaneity of an ego auto-affecting itself *immediately* by way of its *own, proper* movement as *body proper,* or "flesh" [*chair*] (as *Leib* has often been translated in France). All these meanings are necessarily involved in the *movement* proper of the body proper (*Leib*), since Husserl, in all his analyses of the body proper and perceptive experience, accords the greatest attention to *kinesthetic* processes and horizons, and even to the effects of empirical habit, or even the *habitus* of the pure Ego, which is still a different thing (*Ideas II*, p. 118). Only on the nonmaterial side is *spontaneity immediate*—the living, animate, spiritual side of the body proper that is my own, and human, and the body of an ego-man (*Ich-Mensch*). The hand is my hand, but first as hand of man; this egological body, this living body proper (*Leib*)

> is an *organ of the will* (*Willensorgan*), the *one and only Object* which, for the will of my pure Ego, is *moveable immediately and spontaneously* and is a means for producing a mediate spontaneous movement in other things, in, for example, things struck by my immediately spontaneously moved hand, grasped by it, lifted, etc. *Sheer material things are only moveable mechanically and only partake of spontaneous movement in a mediate way*. Only Bodies (*Leiber*) are immediately spontaneously ("freely") moveable, and they are so, specifically, by means of the free Ego and its will which belong to them. It is in virtue of these free acts that, as we saw earlier, there can be constituted for this Ego, in manifold series of perceptions, an Object-world (*Objektwelt*), a world of spatial-corporeal things (*raumkörperliche Dinge*) (the Body as thing [*das Ding Leib*] included). The subject . . . has the "faculty" (the "I can") to freely move this Body. (*Ideas II*, pp. 159–60)[4]

Let us leave aside, at least for now, the discussion made necessary, apropos of this concept of freedom, by Nancy's use of the same word, "freedom," to designate an experience that no longer essentially refers to the egological subject [*sujet égologique*], as is the case here. For Nancy, the experience of freedom is not primarily the experience of a subject, a will, or an "I can."

Conversely, I'll stop insisting on this confirmation of my earlier remarks: in Husserl, as in Plato and so many others, the authority of the "eidetic" figure and of optical intuitionism, the implicit philosophy of the gaze—as paradoxical as this may appear—always and necessarily *fulfills itself*, firmly and incessantly strengthens and confirms itself, in an intuition tactually filled-in and in the hyperbole of continuistic haptocenteredness. Hence, in each instance, touching is no longer just one sense among others, since it conditions them all and is coextensive with them. And since it is not a sense like the others, it is designated as *sense*, sensory faculty, by the play of an everlastingly equivocal metonymy. But why then does one keep pretending to treat it as a sense, as one of the senses, throughout the tradition? And furthermore, if in concert we agree to have it designate an in-

sensible or meta-sensible receptivity, the being in the world of a finite existence, the experience of beings in general (and this would already constitute its exceptional excellence), why confer on it—as Husserl does—this
other privilege, namely, *intuitive, immediate, current, and certain plenitude*
in the experience of present being, in the presence of the present? Indeed,
from (1) the axiomatic definition of touch as the experience of presence in
general, to (2) the axiomatic definition of this same experience as full, intuitive, immediate, direct, and so forth, the consequence is not necessary,
and not necessarily good. (This "consequence," this last assurance is what
starts trembling in the interruptive experience of the syncope, and as syncope, at the—interminable—moment when the discourse of the syncope
runs through Nancy's whole work.)

   In the chapter immediately preceding the one containing the afore-
mentioned "For example . . . my . . . hand," Husserl had abundantly illustrated touch, each time describing its digital manipulations—as if the
only way we ever touched were with our hand and as if the fingers were all
our hand were made of. And this unsurprisingly occurs at a point where
the phenomenologist credits touch with an absolute, unparalleled, and
grounding preeminence.
   We are going to identify the signs of this, which is to say the excellence
of touch among the senses, and of the hand among the parts or organs of
the tactile body proper, and of the fingers and their tips in relation to the
hand. But can't we already interpret these signs as so many testimonies to
the primacy conferred upon the thing as "object," first on the external object, and then on what remains as the subjective and phenomenological
experience of the body proper, this other original "object"?
   What Husserl starts from is the objectivity of the material or extended
body, or more precisely the phenomenological experience and subjective
and egological phenomenality of this *objectivity*. From the very beginning
of this chapter (paragraph 37, "Differences Between the Visual and Tactual
Realms"), the external object is at issue, and very soon, the possibility that
one can touch with one's finger lays bare the complication that will make
for a difference between digital touching and seeing: fingers can also touch
each other—"fingers touching fingers," "double apprehension" (*Doppel-
auffassung*), "double sensation" (*Doppelempfindungen*).
   Let us never forget that these fingers are touching fingers and not showing, indicating, signaling, or signifying fingers. The deictic function of the

index or forefinger seems reduced here to the deferred potentiality of a
contact: with my finger I point to and show what I could hope to reach
and to touch, as it were, after moving to approach it. Here Husserl allows
himself to disregard this deictic function of the pointing finger, since what
interests him in this whole chapter is the relation with itself of the body
proper, its constitution, and—that is the title of chapter 3—"The Constitution of Psychic Reality Through the Body." To be sure, in the first place,
or the last, the self-touching of which Husserl speaks here may be under
the control of the auto-deictic dimension of the finger that turns back toward the body proper in order to indicate: "This is me," "myself"—as
much as, and more than, to affect itself with a sensation. Moreover, let us
not forget either that the feeling-itself-touch*ing of* the finger immediately
is a feeling-itself-touch*ed of* the finger, even when my finger does not touch
another one of my fingers: when it touches anything whatsoever external
to my body and my finger, my finger feels itself touched by the thing that
it touches; which at first gives the example of the finger feeling itself
touched by a touching finger only the value of a pedagogical example, gen-
eralizable to any contact in general, even if it can later give rise to a phenomenological analysis of the body proper that is more narrowly specific;
this is especially the "case" (*in dem Fall*) in the *third* of these sentences (I
am numbering them for convenience and clarity in this analysis, where the
stages are subtly interlinked, albeit distinct, and the stakes high):

> [1] In the tactual realm we have *the external Object*, tactually constituted, and
> a second Object, the *Body* [*le corps propre*], likewise tactually constituted, for
> example [modified—Trans.], the touching finger (*etwa den tastenden Finger*),
> and, in addition, there are fingers touching fingers (*Finger, den Finger tastend*).
> [2] So here we have that double apprehension: the same touch-sensation is ap-
> prehended as a feature of the "external" Object and is apprehended as a sen-
> sation of the Body as Object (*des Leib-Objekts*) [*de l'objet-corps propre*]. [3] And
> in the case in which a part of the Body [*du corps propre*] becomes equally an
> external Object of an other part [*pour une autre partie du même corps*], we have
> the double sensation (each part has its own sensations) and the double appre-
> hension as feature of the one or of the other Bodily part as a physical object.
> (Husserl, *Ideas II*, p. 155)

This analysis of touch may tempt us to think that the privilege that it
grants the hand or the finger has to do in the first place with what sentence [3] specifies, that is, the case in which "the one or . . . the other Bod-

ily part as a physical object" can touch one or the other part of the same body—or be touched by it. Yes. And it is also true that this cannot be said about every external part of the body. But why only the hand and the finger? Why not my foot and toes? Can they not touch another part of my body and touch one another? What about the lips, especially? All of the lips on the lips? And the tongue on the lips? And the tongue on the palate and many other parts of "my body"? How could one *speak* without this? (This question merely allows me to point toward some of the most obvious issues at stake in these choices.) And the eyelids in the blink of an eye? And, if we take sexual differences into account, the sides of the anal or genital opening?[5] Some but not all of these questions arise again later, especially when Husserl takes up other *animalia*, primal presence [*l'archi-présence*], and appresentations [*l'apprésentation*], in chapter 4 (paragraphs 43ff.), on "Psychic Reality in Empathy," where the hand and the finger moreover still play a dominant part.

Once more the hand's privilege can be explained, if not necessarily justified. We can explain its title of phenomenological nobility, and of nobility unadorned, by virtue of the primacy of the sub-objectivity just discussed, as well as the strictly anthropological limits of this phenomenology and this phenomenological moment in *Ideas II*. For all its ambition and originality, phenomenological reduction here does not suspend the Ego's human appurtenance or determination, at least not in the passages that interest us here. Things here are subtle and the stakes are serious enough to call for prudence and minute attention to detail, sticking to the text as closely as possible. What introduces the section in which our passage about touch can be found ("The Constitution of Animal Nature") is the definition of a project regarding the "essence of the soul, the human or animal soul" (*der Menschen- oder Tierseele*) (p. 96) in its connection with the body proper, a project Husserl pursued in many other texts. It is thus also a literal resumption of the great project of *Peri psuchēs*, following a phenomenological reduction, and it concerns the living or animate being in general—thus opening onto the abyssal problem of life, phenomenology as thinking of the living, transcendentality of the living present, and so forth.[6] All too soon, Husserl summons up "a rigorous phenomenological method"; immediate, accomplished, and "perfect" intuition (*vollkommene Intuition*) of the psychical; "originary presenting intuition [*intuition donatrice originaire*] (in our case, experience)," the sole founding ground of a theory even if this theory is determined as predicative in mediate thinking

(Husserl, *Ideas II*, p. 96). But very soon, in the very name of this phenomenological intuitionism, there is a need for this general project, which
seemed to concern every living being (human or animal), to restrict itself
to us, since we "phenomenologists" alone can have an immediate, full, and
originary intuition of what we are talking about. And this "we" without
any transition is determined as "we, men." The Ego here is viewed as Ego-
the-man from the moment when one has distinguished the real [*reell*] psychic Ego from the pure (transcendental) Ego—something Husserl does
here explicitly in order to delimit his field—and from the moment when
the said soul is "bound together with Bodily reality or interwoven with it."
At the moment when he is announcing that he will study this link and the
constitution of this body proper that we find "under the heading 'empirical Ego,' which still needs clarification," well, says Husserl (who is not
telling us how or where it can be found and why it can be found precisely
under this name), "we find furthermore also [*finden wir ferner auch*] the
unity 'I as man' [*Ich-Mensch* (*ego-homme*)]." Husserl specifies "the Ego which
not only ascribes to itself its lived experiences as its psychic states and likewise ascribes to itself its cognitions, its properties of character, and similar
permanent qualities manifest in its lived experiences, but which also designates its Bodily qualities as its 'own' and thereby assigns them to the
sphere of the Ego [*Ich-Sphäre*]" (Husserl, *Ideas II*, p. 99).

After discussing this "I as man," Husserl does lead us back to a purely
psychic Ego, the one "Descartes, in his marvelous *Meditations,* grasped
with the insight of genius," this subject who enters the scene and exits it
but is not acquainted with being born and "perishing" (pp. 109–10), this
pure Ego that must be able to accompany all my representations, as Kant
says, on the condition, Husserl adds, that one widen the meaning of this
latter word to include obscure consciousness, and so forth (p. 115). And
even if, in this exploration of the pure Ego, Husserl comes to consider the
moment when it "posits . . . a man" and in him "a human personality [*une
personne humaine*]" (p. 117), it is true that the world itself (the real or fictive world, no matter: "each and every possible and phantasizable world"),
as correlate of this pure Ego, "for this pure Ego," is in fact not necessarily
human. It is also true that the determination of the *"real psychic subject"*
can as well refer to any living being; Husserl says it expressly: "the animal,
man or beast" (p. 128).[7] Nevertheless, it remains that in the chapter dedicated to "Psychic Reality" in general (paragraphs 30 to 34, pp. 128–50), the
human subject had already taken up more and more space and the animal

was named only exceptionally, in allusions and recollections. And above all, it remains that the following chapter (chapter 3, "The Constitution of Psychic Reality Through the Body," the chapter in which lies inscribed the analysis of the tactile realm that interests us, notably in paragraphs 36 to 40), which narrows the field, turns out to be expressly reserved for man, and more precisely "psychic" man, which is to say "man as nature." Husserl had just distinguished the psychic Ego (the object of a pure psychology, paralleling pure transcendental phenomenology, which nonetheless "fits within natural-scientific experience in a broad sense, i.e., within the science of physical nature and of the Bodily-psychic nature founded in the physical") from the personal or spiritual Ego in the world of spirit (object of the spiritual sciences [*sciences de l'esprit*], an object as awkward to delimit as "the difficult distinction between *soul* and *spirit*" [p. 181]).[8] We thus approach the sense of touch in what deals with the constitution of "man as nature" (paragraphs 35ff.). Husserl, of course, when he speaks of "natural reality, man" (*Naturrealität Mensch*), does not forget that natural man pertains to animals, and he adds, in parentheses: "(or animal being [*bzw. animalisches Wesen*])." Indeed, a little farther on, he says even more precisely that the "point of departure for our constitutive analysis, with its entire intuitive content" has to be "related to animal subjects [*animalische Subjekte*]." But not only are there never any serious references to animals or examples drawn from a nonhuman world here, right after these automatic precautions comes the confirmation—which stands to reason—that the sole object of these analyses is "the constitution of the natural Object, 'man.'" This choice can be *explained*, if not always justified, in *three* ways.

1. After all, why not cut out in the animal field in general an original object, a very original one, man, and constitute such a phenomenological anthropology? There is nothing unspeakably shameful or unjustifiable in this—on the contrary.

2. There is no other choice (and then difficulties set in) when the principle of principles, intuitionism, phenomenology itself, commands us to commence with "us," the Ego most *proper, most proximate*, and most *self-proximate*—self-present otherwise than by indirect appresentation (which is a question broached in the following chapter, beginning with paragraph 43, without any more explicit reference to other animals, however, but rather to "the other man"). In any case, the determination as "man" of this

pure Ego that "we" are, as near to us as can be, comes before the most radical phenomenological reduction, the one that suspends the thesis of the world in general.

3. This phenomenology of the psychical, the living, the animate in general (men *and* beasts) never seems to suspend an *evaluation*, a teleological philosophy of life. If Husserl starts with man, be it man as a natural living being, if he only speaks of man here, it is not only by virtue of an order amid phenomenological reasons; it is not only by virtue of a methodological order answering the question: "Where is one to begin if not with what is closest to who asks the question here?"—this necessity had also imposed itself on Heidegger in *Sein und Zeit.* No. If Husserl begins with man, man as a natural living being, if he only speaks of man here, it is also by reason of a teleological hierarchy or an axiological scale. In truth, it will always be difficult to separate phenomenology and teleology at their very roots. If we needed proof of this, in this context, all we would have to do is read the beginning of paragraph 43 on the "givenness of other 'animalia.'" After he has designated the originally given *zōia*, "including men ('rational' living beings)," after he has recalled "the identity of nature for all men and animals" and even admitted "social connections (friendships, marriages, unions)" between men and between animals, this allusion to animals goes hand in hand with a hierarchical evaluation. Social connections are "instituted" (*gestiftet*) between men, says Husserl, and in parentheses he adds: "(on the lowest level, already between animals [*in niederster Stufe schon zwischen Tieren*])." In this second section, on "The Constitution of Animal Nature," he never says more, it seems to me. It stands to reason that "animals" were not at issue in the first section, on "Material Nature," no more, a fortiori, than in the third section, on the "Spiritual World."[9] (Except, precisely, in another parenthesis, as if this inclusion of animals among the living always had to remain "between parentheses," excluded-included, therefore, by parentheses unrelated to the bracketing between parentheses or quotation marks of "phenomenological reduction": "consider again *spiritual living beings*, those beings animated in a special sense, i.e., human beings (but of course all animals are included)" (Husserl, *Ideas II*, p. 251). And then, all that further comes into question explicitly is man, the "apprehension of a man" (*Menschen-Auffassung, die Auffassung dieser Person*, etc.), his flesh "filled with the soul through and through" (ibid., p. 252), and no longer of the said "animals."

The general organization of these *Studies in the Phenomenology of Constitution* corresponds furthermore to an architecture and a teleology that are classical: matter, life, spirit. And concerning life, where the sense of touch is in question (let us come back to it), it is practically man only that comes into question, and especially the fingers of the human hand. The "animal" never seriously comes up, though it is a living being—not even the body proper of animals whose members or organs resemble hands, and even with fingers! And what about opportunities for so many hand-less animals to touch and be touched in countless ways!

Let us now reread this analysis of touch at the point where we interrupted it and planned to situate it in the architecture of the whole work. Here are, again, first of all, the *three* stages of this passage:

[1] In the tactual realm we have *the external Object*, tactually constituted, and a second Object, the *Body* [le corps propre], likewise tactually constituted, for example [modified—Trans.], the touching finger (*etwa den tastenden Finger*), and, in addition, there are fingers touching fingers (*Finger, den Finger tastend*). [2] So here we have that double apprehension: the same touch-sensation is apprehended as a feature of the "external" Object and is apprehended as a sensation of the Body as Object (*des Leib-Objekts*) [*de l'objet-corps propre*]. [3] And in the case in which a part of the Body [*du corps propre*] becomes equally an external Object of an other part [*pour une autre partie du même corps*], we have the double sensation (each part has its own sensations) and the double apprehension as feature of the one or of the other Bodily part as a physical object. (Husserl, *Ideas II*, p. 155)

The privilege of the hand seems all the more difficult to analyze and justify, since two heterogeneous, possibly contradictory, imperatives here seem to command the exception. On the one hand—we have already noted this—as a point of departure for the analysis of the body proper, it is first a matter of the perception of an *external* thing determined as an *object*, an "external object," just as there will be an internal object as well. On the other hand, in this *objectal* structure of apprehension, as we shall verify, Husserl is very much set on describing the *reflexive* specificity (and therefore more immediately ego-phenomenological quality) of the sensation of the *living* body *proper*, and its "self-sensing." And in this regard, what is possible for touch (and the hand does indeed show this *more easily* than the lips, the tongue, the eyelids, or the anal or genital opening) is in no way possible for sight or hearing (whose difference Husserl then examines, without broaching the senses of smell or taste at this point). And almost all the resources of the analysis that comes after the passage just cited are spent in the demonstration of this reflexive, or ego-phenomenological, excellence of touch, the demonstration of the absolute and incomparable unity of touch. This will later lead to a radical and unequivocal conclusion: it is only thanks to touch that there is a body proper; or more precisely the body proper "becomes a *Body* [*zum Leib wird*]" only "by incorporating tactile [*sic*] sensations [*im Abtasten*]," "in short, by the localization of the sensations as sensations" (Husserl, *Ideas II*, pp. 158–59). For after Husserl has described the *double apprehension* proper to touch, he moves on at once, emphasizing, with an energy that marks the whole chapter: "But in the case of an *Object constituted purely visually* we have *nothing* comparable [*Ähnliches haben wir nicht beim rein visuell sich konstituierenden Objekt*]" (ibid., p. 155).

Husserl at once pushes aside a virtual objection. Indeed, some people might let themselves be tempted by a tactilist interpretation of sight. We have encountered many temptations of this type in the Cartesian, pre-Cartesian, and post-Cartesian traditions down to this century and even after Husserl. This is a facile approach, which Husserl challenges outright: according to him, there is nothing in this but a way of speaking, a metaphor, an analogical confusion devoid of phenomenological rigor: "To be sure, sometimes it is said [*man sagt zwar mitunter*] that the eye is, as it were, in touch with the Object [*tastet es gleichsam ab (le touche, pour ainsi dire)*] by casting its glance over it. But we immediately sense [i.e., remark, notice—Trans.] the difference [*aber wir merken sofort den Unterschied*]" (Husserl, *Ideas II*, p. 155).

What difference? Before I repeat this question, let me insist on the reach of this gesture. Dare one say, by way of illustration, that what the question has in view has to do with everything that preoccupies us here? Or that it touches on everything that is at stake and matters to us in this book? Husserl *evidently* knows what touching means *properly* speaking; this he understands and is intent on knowing, and he posits that, in order to be solid and consistent, a serious philosophical discourse must on principle refer to this strict sense, which is also common sense: everyone knows what touching must mean, in the end, and knows that no one has ever touched anything with his or her eyes. A rigorous philosopher, a responsible phenomenologist should resist the figures of everyday language with its *as* and *as ifs* (*gleichsam*); he must resist them and recall us to evidence itself: the eye might act *as if* it touched but we immediately remark the difference: an eye never touches.

Is this difference marked in the language and the linguistic and cultural realm of a traditional semantics? Or, as Husserl seems to imply, is it in the things themselves, in the universalizable intuition of the things themselves, before any discourse and linguistic experience, even before any mark, before any other difference, before any language and culture? Who exactly is this "we" of whom Husserl says, "Aber wir merken sofort den Unterschied," "But we immediately sense [*remarquons*] the difference"? Let this remain an open question since it overdetermines the entire object of this book, as it were. But to come back to Husserl, let us ask ourselves: what difference exactly? What difference would we be led to notice and remark without delay?

It is the difference of a defect, a defect in sight: more than once Husserl designates what is denied us, and thus missing (*es fehlt*), in seeing compared to touching. To wit, the eye is not seen by the eye, not *immediately* seen by the eye; it does not appear visually (das Auge erscheint nicht visuell). In a note both determining and determined, as well as daring, Husserl dismisses any mediation by mirrors, which might yield the perception of the seen eye, to be sure, but in no way "my eye, that which sees *qua* seeing" [mon œil voyant en tant que voyant] (mein Auge, das sehende als sehende) (ibid., p. 155). The narcissistic or specular situation would bring me face to face with something, an eye, that "indirectly," "by way of 'empathy'" and by an inferential judgment, I "judge" to be identical with my eye as a thing (*das Ding-Aug*) [*la chose œil*], which is *mine*, that is to say, for example or approximately (*etwa*, Husserl says again), this thing constituted as mine by touch (etwa durch Tasten sich konstituierenden) "in the same way that I see the eye of an other" (ebenso wie ich das Auge eines Anderen sehe). In other words, whether it is technical or appearing as "natural," this mediation of the mirror, which does not belong to my body proper, becomes technical by reason properly of the indirection it introduces. It places me facing my own eyes as if facing the eyes of another, while appealing to processes of empathy or analogical appresentation deprived of any full, original, and immediate intuition. Let us initially just retain one among the huge problems raised by this note, concerning in the first place —in Husserl's eyes, in this context—the difference between the eyes and the fingers of the hand, between sight and touch. This difference between the two "senses" lies in the self-relation of touch (and therefore its reflexive phenomenological evidence), which is *immediate, spontaneous, direct, intuitive,* and without equivalent in a mirror or mediation (technical or natural—but always technical because always by means foreign to the body proper, by dint of an "intruder," even if, on the outside, it is by way of a natural reflection in the water of a lake). The self-relation of touch, therefore, acts without empathy or analogical appresentation: when I touch myself with my hand or finger there is neither any haptical mirror effect, as it were, nor any insinuation of alterity. In touching myself, since I immediately and simultaneously feel "from the inside," if I may say so, both the touching and the touched, following Husserl, I should not be able to say "in the same way as the skin or the hand or the finger of another," which I could and should do in the case of the eye—my eye, when I look at it in a mirror "in the same way that I see the eye of an other" (ebenso wie ich das Auge eines Anderen sehe).

This fine-tunes a series of propositions all tending to mark how sight at the same time depends on touch and fails with regard to it; and the criterion comes down to an experience of localization. The eye is not seen and color sensations cannot be localized right in [*à même*] the seeing eye, or right in the eye appearing "visually," as would be the case for the touched object perceived right on the touching hand.

[W]e do not have a kind of extended occularity [*sic*] such that, by moving, one eye could rub past the other and produce the phenomenon of double sensation. Neither can we see the seen thing as gliding over the seeing eye, continually in "contact" with it (*"berührend"*), as we can, in the case of a real organ of touch, for example the palm of the hand, glide over the object or have the object slip past the hand. I do not see myself, my Body, the way I touch myself. What I call the seen Body is not something seeing which is seen, the way my Body as touched Body is something touching which is touched (*wie mein Leib als getasteter Leib getastetes Tastendes ist*) [*comme mon corps en tant que corps touché est un touchant touché*]. A visual appearance of an object that sees, i.e., one in which the sensation of light could be intuited just as it is in it (*in dem die Lichtempfindung angeschaut wird als in ihm seiend*)—that is denied us. Thus what we are denied is an analogon to the touch sensation, which is actually grasped along with (*mit*) [*en même temps*] the touching hand. (Husserl, *Ideas II*, pp. 155–56)

What sight is missing, in sum, is the possibility of a "double sensation," and more precisely a double sensation fully intuitive, direct, and synchronous. The French translation introduces "at the same time" [*en même temps*] for *mit*, and it seems justified;[10] it is perfectly faithful to the whole drift of the argument. The local coincidence that is important for Husserl in the touching-touched pair is grounded in a temporal coincidence meant to give it its intuitive plenitude, which is to say its dimension of direct immediacy. (Let us keep in mind this question of time: this passage, where "localization" is the main concern, is not thematizing it but only treating it via paralipsis; we'll get back to this in a moment. For if one questions this absolute *simultaneity* of the touching and the touched—and the active and the passive—for an immediate and direct intuition, this whole argument risks becoming fragile.) Coincidence, intuitive plenitude, direct immediacy—that is, according to Husserl, what characterizes the experience of the touching-touched. The dependence of sight is thus marked, in addition to its failings. If the eye and the visual sensations are "attributed to the Body," "that happens *indirectly by means of* the properly localized sensations" (my emphasis—J. D.), which is to say tactile ones.

> Actually, the eye, *too*, is a field of localization but *only for touch sensations [seulement pour les sensations de contact]*, and, like every organ "freely moved" by the subject, it is a field of localized muscle sensations. It is an Object of touch for the hand; it belongs originally to the merely touched, and not seen, Objects. "Originally" [*originairement*] is not used here in a temporal-causal sense; it has to do with a primal group of Objects constituted directly in intuition (*direkt anschaulich*). The eye can be touched, and it itself provides touch and kinetic sensations; that is why it is necessarily apperceived as belonging to the Body. (Husserl, *Ideas II*, p. 156)

The same applies to *hearing*, Husserl adds thereupon, without concealing the general and programmatic character of these distinctions. The following pages confirm what Husserl himself terms a "privilege" (*Vorzug*) of the localization of tactile sensations: "Each thing that we see is touchable and, as such, points to an immediate relation to the Body, though it does not do so in virtue of its visibility. *A subject whose only sense was the sense of vision could not at all have an appearing Body. . . .* It cannot be said that this subject who only sees sees his Body. . . . The Body as such can be constituted originarily only in tactuality" (Husserl, *Ideas II*, p. 158). The confirmation of this privilege comes forth after the most difficult and—in this passage, at least for me—most obscure moment of this analysis and its indisputable necessity, complexity, and especially friendly open-mindedness toward the more subtly folded pleats of the phenomenological experience. But here we may be in one of the zones where phenomenology itself, without being powerless, disqualified, or simply refuted, meets the strongest resistance vis-à-vis the authority of its intuitionistic "principle of principles." How can we situate this difficulty, and obscurity, and resistance? Well, precisely, it may be in the place where place, localization, and extension are at issue. We have already encountered the assertion that the eye is a field of localization only for contact sensations, as an "object of touch for the hand." Now, at the point where Husserl proposes in a programmatic fashion to secure some "broad distinctions," he draws "in principle" a borderline between two topological experiences, in a way—between the localization of sensings [*impressions sensibles*] and the extension of the material determinations of a thing. Even if in its way a sensible impression or sensing spreads out over spatial surfaces that it covers or runs through, even if it thus occupies a place, its spreading out (*Ausbreitung*) [*déploiement*] and spreading into (*Hinbreitung*) [*propagation*] is something other than, something that differs essentially from the *extension* (*Ausdehnung*) that characterizes the *res extensa*.

We are thus edging into a zone of spatiality—if not extension—of the *psyche*, since *psychic reality* here forms the explicit theme, or the only one, in fact, of this phenomenology of the body proper. And so we literally again find the places from which we may have seemed to have moved away—a certain *psuchē*, Freud's or Nancy's: "Psyche is ausgedehnt, weiss nichts davon." Where does the analogy stop? That is one of our questions.

There are a phenomenological surface and an interiority of the hand, but they are radically heterogeneous with regard to the space and the *real* [*reell*] qualities of the touched thing, and even to the *real* qualities of the hand. Phenomenological reduction, at least implicitly, assures us of this here: "The sensing which spreads over the surface of the hand and extends into it is not a real [*reell*] quality of a thing . . . such as . . . the roughness of the hand, its color, etc." (Husserl, *Ideas II*, p. 157).

Where can we situate the principal criterion for this difference? Real [*reell*] qualities constitute themselves by way of a "sensuous schema" and "manifolds of adumbrations" [*une multiplicité d'esquisses*] whereas tactile sensings, which imply neither adumbrations nor schematizations, "have nothing at all to do with the sensuous schema. The touch-sensing [*l'impression sensible tactile*] is not a *state* of the material thing, hand (Das

Tastempfindnis ist nicht *Zustand* des materiellen Dinges Hand)" (ibid., p. 157).

Husserl is intent on grounding the privilege of the tactile in the constitution of the body proper on the properly phenomenological necessity of this distinction. Now, it is better to remain very close to the letter of the text before we ask the questions seemingly raised by the *reasoning* or the *argument* to which this network of phenomenological evidence gives rise, before we question the demonstrative procedures or the theses that, in truth, seemingly act in advance as parasites or contaminants of the alleged description. Let us first of all quote the consequence that Husserl proposes to draw from this distinction in speaking of "*the* hand itself (*eben die* Hand selbst)," of what comes to pass or what I sense on "this surface of the hand (*auf dieser Handfläche*)," and above all what "I can say," from there, I, the "subject of the Body":

> The touch-sensing is not a *state* of the material thing, hand, but is precisely the *hand itself* (*eben die* Hand selbst), which for us is more than a material thing, and the way in which it is mine entails that I, the "subject of the Body" (*das "Subjekt des Leibes"*), can say that what belongs to the material thing is its, not mine. All sensings pertain to my soul; everything extended to the material thing. *On* this surface of the hand I sense the sensations of touch, etc. And it is precisely thereby that this surface manifests itself immediately as my Body. One can add here as well: if I convince myself that a perceived thing does not exist, that I am subject to an illusion, then, along with (*mit*) [*en même temps*] the thing, everything extended in its extension is stricken out too. But the sensings do not disappear. Only what is *real* [*reell*] vanishes from being.
>   Connected to the privilege of the localization of the touch sensations are differences in the complexion of the visual-tactual apprehensions. Each thing that we see is touchable. (Husserl, *Ideas II*, pp. 157–58)[11]

We could then orient a certain number of questions in different directions, and such questions—all preliminary ones—will here organize themselves in the determined perspective that is ours: between the modern tradition of haptology and the thinking or pondering of touch according to Nancy, we shall begin to discern the places and modes in which the latter's thinking pertains to the former but also breaks away from it.

There was a good reason for the choice of the "example" of the hand, as there was for the starting point of the analysis in "the external Object, tactually constituted." To wit, a certain *exteriority* is heterogeneous with regard to the sensing or sensible impression, be it real [*reell*] (be it, as Husserl recalls, "a real optical property of the hand"); and it *partakes*—that is, it (the exteriority perceived *as* real) *must* even partake of the experience of the touching-touched, and of the "double apprehension," even if it is in a hylomorphic or noetico-noematic fashion, even in the case of illusions. Without an outside and its "real quality of a thing" announcing itself in the sensible impression or sensing, already within its hyletic content, the duplicity of this apprehension would not be possible. This exteriority is needed; this foreign outside is needed—foreign to the "touching" and the "touched" sides of the phenomenological impression at the same time, there where the latter does not offer itself in sketchy adumbrations. (Moreover—let us pause at this last point for a moment—if in immanent and phenomenological perception there is never any sketchy adumbration, as for the material and transcendent thing, no more sketches for what offers itself to sight than to touch, then the criterion for the prevalence of one over the other seems more problematic than ever, at least in this zone of the body (*Leib*) proper's immanent properness, of which Husserl is studying the constitution and analyzing first the "solipsistic" moment.) This detour by way of the foreign outside, no matter how subtle, furtive, and elusive, is at the same time what allows us to speak of a "double" apprehension (otherwise there would be one thing only: only some touching or only some touched) and what allows me to undergo the test of this singular experience and distinguish between the I and the non-I, and to say "this is my body," or, quoting Husserl himself, to draw the consequence that "I, the 'subject of the Body,' can say that what belongs to the material thing is its, not mine." For that, it is necessary that the space of the material thing—like a difference, like the heterogeneity of a spacing—slip between the touching and the touched, since the two neither must nor can coincide if indeed there is to be a double apprehension. No doubt, in the sensible impression or sensing, I—still I—am the touching and the touched, but if some not-I (material thing, real [*reell*] space, extension, as opposed to phenomenological "spreading out and spreading into," and so forth) did not come to insinuate itself between the touching and the touched, I would not be able to posit myself as I, and "say" (as Husserl says), This is not I, this is I, I am I. And it is there, precisely because of *extensio*, because of visibility and the possibility at least for the hand to be seen, even if it is not seen (a possibility involved in the phenomenological content of the sensible impression), that manual touching—even just touching my other hand—cannot be re-

duced to a pure experience of the purely proper body. This would hypothetically be the case for the heart touching, however (but even that is not
so certain), and Husserl speaks of it in the following chapter. What he says
about this then is important for us, for *two* sets of reasons at least:

A. The first reasons are architectonical, in a way. In chapter 4, Husserl
broaches the great question of empathy in the constitution of the reality
"I as Man." To that end, as in the previous chapter to which I have just referred, he takes up his starting point again in what he terms "solipsistic experience," the one where "we do not attain the givenness of our self as a
spatial thing like all others (a givenness which certainly is manifest in our
factual experience) nor that of the natural Object, 'man' (animal being),
which we came to know as correlate of the 'naturalistic attitude,' a material thing upon which the higher strata of what is specifically animal are
built and into which they are, in a certain way, inserted, 'introjected' (*'in-
trojiziert' sind*)" (Husserl, *Ideas II*, p. 169).[12]

I quote this long passage because I would later like to suggest that we
already have to presuppose this introjection in the experience termed
"solipsistic" of the manual touching-touched, where it is already at work.
(Husserl situates the introjection as a late and upper layer of experience,
as an exiting moment out of solipsism.) How could the duplicity of the
double apprehension appear without the beginning of such an "introjection"? All this should lead to the reproblematization of what Husserl asserts in such a striking and enigmatic way at the end of paragraph 45, about
the "grammar" that would befit the expression of pure, purely proper,
purely "solipsistic," psychic life, before any "introjection"; and thus about
"an objectivity which is precisely double and unitary [*doppeleinheitliche Ge-
genständlichkeit*]: the man—without 'introjection.'"

Hence the question: where does introjection begin? What is one speaking of, and how can one speak of it, when there isn't any introjection yet at
all? Can there be a random, pure, immediate, not-spaced-out-in-itself phenomenological intuition, of this "thing" that seems to defy any grammar?
If there is some introjection and thus some analogical appresentation starting at the threshold of the touching-touched, then the touching-touched
cannot be accessible for an originary, immediate, and full intuition, any
more than the alter ego. We are here within the zone of the immense problem of phenomenological intersubjectivity (of the other and of time), and
I shall not re-unfurl it once again. Let me merely revive the question here:
shouldn't a certain introjective empathy, a certain "intersubjectivity," al-

ready have introduced an other and an analogical appresentation into the touching-touched for the touching-touched to give rise to an experience of the body proper allowing one to say, "it is I," "this is my body"?

B. Let us not forget that it is in the said "solipsistic" sphere of the experience of the body proper that Husserl first proposes all these analyses (of manual touching as well as of *Herzgefühl*, the "heart sensation"; of the "for example, 'I feel my heart'": "z. B. ich 'empfinde mein Herz'"). Now, let us even suppose, as Husserl seems to do, that one may retain an "I feel my heart" within this sphere of appurtenance or solipsistic properness; let us suppose that this "I feel my heart" is possible even before I can say it, since saying it already presupposes the grammar of a break in the solipsistic sphere, a break as grammar, even if it is only to myself that I say it. (But isn't grammar, which is also a *technē*, like rhethoric, to be found there already—already irreducibly announced—in the possibility of this "localization," this phenomenological distinction of places, that Husserl recalls? He does so all the time to speak of touch and discern this "touched, and not seen" phenomenological localization, which is distinct from the spatial, objective determinations of *extensio*.) Well, even within this hypothesis of an immediate "I feel my heart," a purely, properly "solipsistic" heart sensation, Husserl never dares speak—it stands to reason—of this "double apprehension" of the touching-touched, which he analyzed earlier on and profitably drew from so as to assert the "privilege" of touch. And so, there is a certain embarrassment when it is further a matter of connecting with touch an example ("I feel my heart") that illustrates better than the hand the feeling, which is first solipsistic, of a body proper. *First stage*: "In the case of the solipsistic subject we have the distinctive field of touch in co-presence with the appearing Bodily surface and, in union with that, the field of warmth; in second place we have the indeterminate localization of the common feelings (*Gemeingefühle*) [*affects communs*] (the spiritual ones as well) and, further, the localization of the interior of the Body, *mediated* (*vermittelt*) [*médiatisée*] [my emphasis—J. D.] by the localization of the field of touch" (Husserl, *Ideas II*, pp. 173–74).

I emphasized "mediated" (*vermittelt*): here again it implies that this localization is mediated *by means of* a tactile localization, which would be immediate. This purported immediacy of touch comes into question, immediately afterward, in the following sentence—the *second stage*—with the example of the heart: "For example, I 'feel my heart.' When I press the sur-

face of the Body 'around the heart,' I discover, so to say, this 'heart sensation,' and it may become stronger and somewhat modified. It does not itself belong to the touched surface, but it is connected with it" (ibid., p. 174).

For reasons that are now evident (he attempts to find again the internal
property of the body proper, and the most solipsistic possible), Husserl is
already keen on connecting this heart sensation with the experience of
touch, even if the sensation "does not itself belong to the touched surface
[*surface tactile*]." But since there is no "double apprehension" there (precisely because the touching-touched then seems—*seems*, indeed—absolutely to be "in union with that" [ne faisant qu'un avec lui] and then seems
to pertain to some incredible touching without any tactile surface), Husserl
has to find a phase or an intermediate stratum of touch in order to uphold
his demonstration, and there, *with my hand*, I touch the inside of my body
by "feeling *through*" a surface. There begins, in this place, to be some surface, and therefore some touching, in a stricter sense, but also, with surface,
some visibility, even if the visible in fact eludes actual sight. "Likewise, if
I not only simply contact the surface of my Body but press on it more
strongly, press into the flesh (*das Fleisch eindrücke*), i.e., with my touching
finger 'feel through' to my bones or inner organs (just as, similarly, with
other bodies [*Körper*] I feel through to their inner parts)" (ibid.).[13]

But—*third stage*—after the immediate "heart sensation" (internal "touch"
without any visible corporeal surface), after the half-visible manual touch
that "feels through" a surface, here is the touch of the hand visible from
both sides, the touching and the touched:

> Besides, solipsistically there belongs to every position of my eyes an "image"-
> aspect (*ein "Bild"-Aspekt*) of the seen object and thus an image of the oriented
> environment. But also in the case of touching an object, there belongs to every
> position of my hand and finger a corresponding touch-aspect (*ein Tast-Aspekt*)
> of the object, just as, on the other side, there is a touch-sensation in the finger,
> etc., and obviously there is visually a certain image of my touching hand and
> its touching movements. All this is given to me myself as belonging together in
> co-presence (*für mich selbst in Kompräsenz zusammengehörig gegeben*) and is
> then transferred over in empathy: the other's touching hand, which I see, app-
> resents to me his solipsistic view of this hand and then also everything that
> must belong to it in presentified co-presence (*in vergegenwärtiger Kompräsenz*).
>
> Yet to the appearance of the other person there also belongs, in addition to
> what has been mentioned, the interiority of psychic acts [*l'intériorité psychique
> de l'acte*]. (ibid.)

This last example (the visible hand touching a visible object) defines the typical situation upon which Husserl establishes the privilege of touch in the strong sense—as the possibility of "double apprehension": touching-touched. And this possibility, which depends on the hand or in any case a visible part of my body, presupposes a surface, the visibility of it, and ("then," *dann,* says Husserl: but we may wonder what justifies this succession) the possibility of moving toward empathy and the indirect appresentation of the other man's *solus ipse.* Let me quote this passage again: " . . . and is then transferred over in empathy: the other's touching hand, which I see, appresents to me his solipsistic view of this hand and then also everything that must belong to it in presentified co-presence (. . . *und geht dann in die Einfühlung über: die tastende Hand des Anderen, die ich sehe, appräsentiert mir die solipsistische Ansicht dieser Hand und dann alles, was in vergegenwärtiger Kompräsenz dazugehören muss*)." (ibid.)

Hence our question: if this *possibility* of appresentative empathy, of indirect or analogical access, already partakes of the solipsistic "moment"—be it as a virtuality but thus also as an *essential* possibility—how can it be said that it comes "then," afterward, finding itself grounded in an intuitive and pure presence or co-immediacy? And thus if we assume the "interiority of psychic acts," isn't it necessary, from the outset, that visibility, being exposed to the outside, the appresentative detour, the intrusion of the other, and so forth, be *already* at work? And would this not condition, or at least co-condition, that on which it seems to depend and that it seems to follow, moreover in the very inside of the touching-touched as "double apprehension"? Mustn't the intruder already be inside the place? Isn't it necessary that this spacing thus open up the place for a replacing, and that it make room for the substitute, the metonymical supplement, and the technical?

Let me be more precise about the meaning or orientation of our question. Denying the possibility of a tactile experience of the touching-touched is not the point; but in acknowledging what its manual or digital example implies (as *best* and paradigmatic example, or "guiding thread" of the analysis), I ask whether there is any pure auto-affection of the touching or the touched, and therefore any pure, immediate experience of the purely proper body, the body proper that is living, purely living. Or if, on the contrary, this experience is at least not already *haunted,* but *constitutively* haunted, by some hetero-affection related to spacing and then to visible spatiality—where an intruder may come through, a host, wished or unwished for, a spare and auxiliary other, or a parasite to be rejected, a *pharmakon* that already having at its disposal a dwelling in this place inhabits one's heart of hearts [*tout for intérieur*] as a ghost.

When Husserl seems to draw a line between, on the one hand, pure auto-affection of the body proper in the "double apprehension" of the touching-touched, and, on the other hand, the hetero-affection of sight or the eye (which, it will be recalled, can be seen as seeing only in an *indirect* fashion, by means of a mirror that is comparable in its effects to the appresentation of the eyes of an other), shouldn't one rather distinguish between several types of auto-hetero-affection without any pure, properly pure, immediate, intuitive, living, and psychical auto-affection at all? No doubt, there would be some auto-affection "effects," but their analysis cannot escape from the hetero-affection that makes them possible and keeps haunting them, even there where this hetero-affection *in general* (the one coming from the transcendental thing or the living other) seems to vanish, irresistibly coming back to impose itself in the analysis and the expounding of its results. This, at least, is what I have attempted to demonstrate, while reconnecting in other ways with the thread of ancient preoccupations.

According or restoring a privilege or priority to any sense—sight, touch, hearing, taste, smell—would thus no longer come into question. "There is no 'the' sense of touch," Nancy says, and he could likewise say, I believe, "There is no 'the' sense of sight," and so forth. It would then rather be a question of reorganizing in another way this whole field of the said sense or sens*es*. No longer would the general haptology one constructed with this depend on a particular sense named touch. The constitution of the body proper thus described would already presuppose a passage outside and through the other, as well as through absence, death, and mourning, as well as through "ecotechnics" and the "*technē* of bodies." This would presuppose interruption in general, and a *spacing* from before any distinction between several spaces, between psychical "spreading out" or "spreading into" (*Ausbreitung, Hinbreitung*) and *extensio* of the real [*reell*] thing. We should then reintroduce the outside itself, the other, the inanimate, "material nature," as well as death, the nonliving, the nonpsychical in general, language, rhetoric, technics, and so forth—all that this phenomenological reduction to the sphere of pure appurtenance of the "solipsistic" body proper tries to keep out. Life of the living present and life as "transcendental life" are, as always, the great question, to which we shall not yet again return here.

This type of question concerns the whole problematic of phenomenological reduction, pure intuition, and so forth, and it obviously even invades it, wherever this problematic meets with the themes of passive genesis, time, and the other. This dehiscence of the outside and the other comes to inscribe an irreparable disorganization, a spacing that dislocates, a noncoincidence (which also yields the chance *effects* of full intuition, the fortune of immediacy effects), wherever Husserl speaks of "overlapping" and "coincidence" (*Deckung*)[14] in the texts just invoked, wherever this alleged coincidence becomes determining for the fulfilling of an intuition or identification. And although there is no mention of this in the passages that we have perused (at least no more than furtively and cursorily), this occurs from the movement of temporalization and its hyletic layers onward, which these analyses of tactile sensation must presuppose in this way, whether it is a matter of "immanent" perception (the kind to which Husserl ceaselessly wants to lead us back here) or perception said to be "transcendent," thus regularly reintroduced—already by the hand—within immanence itself. The noncoincidence of which I speak here is, first of all, the kind that works at, worries, and renders the "living present" *effects* both possible and impossible. Let us say that these "effects" are constituted; they reintroduce a priori what is constituted into what is constituting. Since I have often taken up the consequences or implications of this in other places, I shall content myself here with situating these regular reminders around the question of touch and the texts by Husserl that are expressly dedicated to this. And we begin to glimpse where the thinking of touch, which Nancy is making us meditate, "touches" without touching, and detaches itself from, this phenomenology, wherever an interruption, or let us say a syncope, a *technē* of bodies, and first of all and everywhere an irreducible *spacing* (the first word of any deconstruction, valid for space as well as time) constitute the more insistent motif in this thinking.

Why have I, in turn, paid so much attention to Husserl's privileging in practice of the hand in order to show the "privilege" of touch? By reason of the following paradox: more than any other part of the body proper, the hand has imposed a detour leading through visibility and exposition to a surface, precisely when it was meant better to illustrate the pure, psychic auto-affection of the touching-touched. Through this outlet, the hand has finally imposed the possibility of empathic appresentation, that is, exappropriation, the interminable appropriation of an irreducible nonproper, which conditions, constitutes, and limits every and any appropriation process at the same time. It has been an early threat to what it was meant to make possible. It has reintroduced into sense the other sense and the other of sense, in all the senses and ways of the word *sense* [*sens*].[15]

And so we at our own pace approach the place of a resemblance that we can already guess at: a hand and especially a hand of "flesh," a *hand of man*, has always begun to resemble a *man's hand*, and thus a fatherly hand, and sometimes, more "originarily," the hand of the merciful Father, which is to say his Son—the hand that the Son is, according to the Logos or Word of Incarnation. As we shall see, all these values touch one another by virtue of a "spiritual touch," which is *infinite, mutual, and immediate*. The last of our five *Tangents* (five, like the five fingers of one hand, like the five senses) will perhaps unfurl the indisputable consequence of this.

§ 9 Tangent III

*The Exorbitant, 2, "Crystallization
of the impossible": "Flesh," and,
again, "For example, my hand"*

Singularity of Nancy's "corpus." It would be fair also to *approach* in another way what, in him, weighs, ponders, and thinks in the vicinity of touching. One would approach this from the places where this singularity is *set off* [*s'enlève*], in a way, in and against what we might too easily and empirically—*approximately*, as it were—term a certain French *proximity*. We suggested this earlier: within a certain philosophical history of touch for the past two centuries, there have been regular passages across European borderlines, as well shiftings of these borders. And the way in which these occur may be ostensible, legitimate, or bordering on the clandestine— smuggling, even, particularly between France and Germany. The passages much exceed the market of "imports" and "exports"—and "debts." What is only too obvious in Heidegger's case was already so in Husserl's—to wit, two Franco-German histories that are moreover indissociably linked, each profoundly overdetermining the other. If, well beyond imports, one spoke the language of inheritance and filiation, one would still have to let it do justice to all the aporias that make them as inconceivable as the very conception of concepts. There is not and there could not be and there must not be any inheritance or filiation worthy of these appellations without transformation, re-beginning, re-invention, diverting, resistance, rebellion, and sometimes also betrayal—and especially without an interbreeding of genealogies. We have read Husserl, a Husserl who wants to be such a radical Cartesian—more Cartesian than Descartes himself—so as to do justice to all these genealogical crossbreedings. Beforehand, I already gave reminders of a certain French tradition that follows the intertwined threads of a haptology passing through idioms and arguments as different, certainly, as those of Maine de Biran, Ravaisson, Bergson, Merleau-Ponty, Deleuze, and so forth. Without even speaking of Husserlian phenomenology in general (a topic rather too large for the dimensions of the present essay), but limiting myself to the most explicit analyses that Husserl left us about *tactile* sensation and perception (the ones in *Ideas II* referred to in the preceding chapter), how am I to set afoot a modest analysis of what, today, partly resembles such a French "heritage," what I earlier termed a French trail [*sillage*], in a vaguer way and with another, even less justifiable figure? I shall have to limit myself to merely pointing to some paths, pending a more ambitious and less incomplete exploration, or in any case a fairer one. In first scouting this terrain, the principle is simple. It might be justified with regard to the following question: aside from the light shed on it by Levinas's exploratory work (i.e., his discourse on the caress and his references to *Ideas II*,[1] which I have already touched on), we may ask ourselves who in France has worked out an interpretation of touch while *accommodating* explicitly —briefly, cursorily, or elliptically, at times; somewhat more analytically and insistently, at other times—Husserl's analysis of touch, precisely within the pages of *Ideas II* that I have just in turn located or interpreted. Strictly within the scope of the sense experience of "touch," how is it that what was thus accepted, accommodated, read, and received could each time give rise to a displacement, a reinscription, and an original reconfiguration, which is to say another crossbreeding that other traditions would come to pollinate in their turn?

Let me provisionally—albeit again too quickly, and conscious of limitations, incomprehensions, and unjustifiable exclusions—summon up the different paths of three thinkers, Maurice Merleau-Ponty, of course (who has already come up more than once), Didier Franck, and Jean-Louis Chrétien.

Merleau-Ponty: Nancy does not cite him often, but their implicit affinities seem undeniable although sometimes difficult to outline or formalize. Still less deniable are certain gestures of moving away, which also signify that some distancing took place with regard to this French "phenomenology of the flesh" that we are now coming to. The only reference to Merleau-Ponty that I found in Nancy (within the limits of my reading him) is at once brief and allusive, but it goes quite far, and it should be kept in mind in everything that I am henceforth going to say about Merleau-Ponty or the discourse on "flesh" in general. Let us retain at least *three traits* of this reference (I should quote its whole context), namely, the chapter titled "Black Hole," in *Corpus*.[2]

1. Indeed, although the word "hand" is not uttered, it is about what I termed "humanualism" [*humainisme*]:

> The body signifies *itself* as body (of) sensible-interiority: we just have to see all that we have the human body say, and its upright posture, its opposable thumb, its eyes where flesh turns into soul (Marcel Proust). And so the body presents the sign's being-itself, which is to say the accomplished community of the signifier and the signified, the end of exteriority, the sense right at [*à même*] the sensible—"Hoc est enim. . . . " (Jean-Luc Nancy, *Corpus*, pp. 64–65)

2. Thus at the principle of what "we have the human body say," there is, according to Nancy, who names the most decisive theme of this phenomenology, a certain phenomenon, a phenomenology of "self-touching":

> But the body is not this Living Temple—Life as Temple and the Temple as Life, self-touching as a sacred mystery—except on the condition that the circularity grounding it be completely finished. (ibid., p. 65)

3. And here, especially, is the connection between this "human body," the "self-touching" of this flesh, and the body of a Christian ontotheology, in its eucharistic ecstasy par excellence—or in this "communion," mentioned earlier,[3] apropos of *Phenomenology of Perception*. At this point Nancy quotes Merleau-Ponty, and he then emphasizes the definite article ("*le* corps") several times in this chapter, for it is what is thus signified by it that he is after:

> *The* body, therefore, is nothing other than the *auto-symbolization of the absolute organ*. It is unnamable like God, it exposes nothing to the outside of an extension, it is the organ of self-organization, unnamable like the rot of its self-digestion (Death in Person)—unnamable, as well, as this self-texture toward which strains a philosophy of the "body proper" ("What we are calling flesh, this interiorly worked-over mass, has no name in any philosophy," says Merleau-Ponty).[4] God, Death, Flesh—the triple name of the body in all of ontotheology. The body is the exhaustive combination and common assumption of these three impossible names, where all meaning wears itself out. (ibid., pp. 65–66)[5]

Merleau-Ponty, therefore. One of the first texts in which he takes into account the "haptological" moment in Husserl's *Ideas II*, in an explicit and insistent fashion, is probably "The Philosopher and His Shadow," in *Signs*.[6] The movement, "a network [*lacis*] of implications," is already complex, and Merleau-Ponty tries to unravel it in such passages in Husserl's analysis in which, he says, "we no longer sense the pulsation of constituting consciousness" (Merleau-Ponty, *Signs*, p. 166). It is true that Merleau-Ponty *chooses* his pathway, with the "preferences" and "partialities" mentioned earlier. He then chooses very quickly to bring himself to the site of this defeat, to these limits of the "constituting consciousness," and he does it with as much energy and determination as Husserl conversely manifests in delaying coming to such a term. The case of the sense of touch is just one example in the trajectory of this article. Although Merleau-Ponty seems to follow *Ideas II* and begin with touch, all too soon, he associates with it, on the same plane, the example of sight, in a way that Husserl would never have deemed legitimate, and further frames this with considerations of seeing. No sooner has he mentioned *Ideas II* than he summons up an "I am able to" (a Biranian as much as Husserlian one, I may fairly say) and at once connects it with visibility: "The relation between my body's movements and the thing's 'properties' which they reveal is that of the 'I am able to' to the marvels it is within its power to give rise to. And yet my body must itself be meshed into the visible world; its power depends precisely on the fact that it has a place *from which* it sees. Thus it is a thing, but a thing I dwell in" (ibid.).

What counts here, before the multiplicity of senses and sensible things, is the originary *here*, and that it should be included in the world, like a thing, even while it remains the origin of the world as well as of my "I am able to." Nonetheless, the first example remains that of the *visible* and not the *tangible* world. Immediately afterward comes the example of touch—and again it is the hand, the hand itself, the hand alone, the two hands alone, or the metonymic hand: "the touched hand becomes the touching hand."

The example of the hand, certainly, is at hand, yet at the same time it is not. It imposes itself for two reasons: because Merleau-Ponty is in the process of discussing *Ideas II*, where the hand finds itself at home, so to speak (though it has trouble, there, finding itself on its own), and because the law of the sensible-*here* [l'*ici* sensible] demands this, there where for Merleau-Ponty it is such a dear topic, in this text and elsewhere. Yet the *here* does not seem to be able to refer to itself except in an experience that is at the same time tactile and deictic and resembles a "reflection" of the body. When describing the "relation of my body to itself which makes it the *vinculum* of the self and things," Merleau-Ponty follows Husserl's hand, but he also begins to lead it where it does not always seem, simply enough, to go on its own. The movement of this leading remains rather subtle, however, and it is so respectful of certain possibilities and virtualities, which are literally attested in Husserl's text, that it is difficult to sort out Merleau-Ponty's actively interpreting share. Everything—almost everything—seems to play itself out in the differential between one insistent locus and another, and on the keyboard of varying thematic emphases and metaphorical displacements. And since Merleau-Ponty's writing hand both follows and inflects Husserl's hand, the one that writes and that *Ideas II* describes, let us in turn follow these hands.

In this place, Merleau-Ponty shows less of an interest in "touching," that is, in what might come before sight, or condition it, in the constitution of the body proper (*Leib*), than in a "sort of reflection"[7] of the "touching-touched," the "extraordinary event" of this sensible reflexivity:

> There is a relation of my body to itself which makes it the *vinculum* of the self and things. When my right hand touches my left, I am aware of it as a "physical thing." But at the same moment, if I wish, an extraordinary event takes place: here is my left hand as well starting to perceive my right, *es wird Leib, es empfindet* [it becomes Body, it senses (Husserl, *Ideas II*, p. 152)]. The physical thing becomes animate. Or, more precisely, it remains what it was (the event does not enrich it), but an exploratory power comes to rest upon or dwell in it. Thus I touch myself touching; my body accomplishes "a sort of reflection." In it, through it, there is not just the unidirectional relationship of the one who perceives to what he perceives. The relationship is reversed, the touched hand becomes the touching hand, and I am obliged to say that the sense of touch here is diffused into the body—that the body is a "perceiving thing" [*empfindendes Ding*], a "subject-object" [*das subjektive Objekt*].
>
> It is imperative that we recognize that this description also overturns our idea of the thing and the world, and that it results in an ontological rehabilitation of the sensible. (ibid., pp. 166–67)

With respect to this passage, as to so many others, it is necessary to localize the instant when the accompaniment of the commentary and the pedagogical restoration, which involve a simple rhetorical shift, begin discreetly to bend the other's intentions, without betraying them outright, and to drive them elsewhere. Indeed, sometimes the caution that consists in giving a precise reference and seeking shelter behind a literal citation in German comes to betray the betrayal—and not only in Merleau-Ponty. What the latter is keen on showing is that he remains as close as possible to Husserl at the moment when he is announcing an "ontological rehabilitation of the sensible": yet Husserl would never have spoken of it in such terms, it seems to me, and this would not have interested him for a single second, supposing that he even sought to lend an ear to it—no more than to a "description" that "overturns our idea of the thing and the world" (Merleau-Ponty, *Signs*, p. 166). Similarly, Husserl would not admit to being "obliged to say" whatever it might be, and "obliged to say that the sense of touch here is diffused into the body [*répandu dans le corps*]," given the stratified reasons that we have already examined. Husserl speaks about a sense of touch that is not diffused throughout the body. I imagine that Husserl would have also asked what "comes to rest upon or dwell in it," rigorously and not metaphorically, means to say (the two terms are hardly compatible, as a matter of fact) when used to describe the manner in which "an exploratory power" relates to a "physical thing" when it "becomes animate." All this shifting is preparing and blazing the way for a discourse carried out in advance, the discourse of flesh and incarnation, which will increasingly and in a complex and refined way become the path of Merleau-Ponty's thinking—and we have already seen how Nancy veers from it.

Starting with the next page we pass from the translation of *leibhaft* as "in person" or "in the flesh" to *incarnation,* to "my own incarnation" as "carnal subject," and this in the name of what has be to "taken literally," precisely where Husserl would never have concluded from the fact that a thing can be present or "perceived '*leibhaftig,*'" that the thing—any thing —has flesh (in the sense, this time, of the living, animate, and incarnate "body proper"), or that there is a "flesh" of the world. It is in this rather non-Husserlian passage, this audacious translation, always proposed in the name of Husserl—and even the letter of Husserl's text, thus "translated"— that Merleau-Ponty gets involved: "When we say that the perceived thing is grasped 'in person' or 'in the flesh' [*leibhaft*], this is to be taken literally: the flesh of what is perceived, this compact particle which stops exploration, and this optimum which terminates it all reflect my own incarnation and are its counterpart. Here we have a type of being" (Merleau-Ponty, *Signs*, p. 167).

We can imagine Husserl's spontaneous resistance—justified or not—to this "translation," to this discourse, at every step and every turn. But this literal displacement of the letter, in which, however, "literally" is still said, signs Merleau-Ponty's whole design in *Signs* and *The Visible and the Invisible.* Both the violence of interpretation and the necessity of philosophical writing that is given over to the figure are accepted, claimed, and signed. This is even the conclusion of "The Philosopher and His Shadow." The others are there, already, with their gestures, spoken words, "to which our own respond . . . to the point that we sometimes turn their words back upon them even before they have reached us, as surely as, more surely than, if we had understood . . . for although meaning is everywhere figurative, it is meaning [*sens*] which is at issue everywhere" (ibid., p. 181).

Objecting to these statements themselves is not the issue for us here. In a moment we'll follow their consequences as far as the figural relation between the senses of touch and sight are concerned, but it is fitting first to recall two interpretative preliminaries.

1. We can never sufficiently emphasize that Husserl's resistance is precisely to a metaphorical slant on the subject of the becoming-touch of sight or the becoming-seeing or becoming-visible of touch. The principle of this resistance, in the name of the proper and the sense said to be proper, which is also common sense, is an axiom of phenomenology in its Husserlian discourse. Even if translating or metaphorizing Husserl's language is unavoidable, does one have the right to disregard its axiomatics on the subject of what language should be or should not do? Who says what is right, here? Let us leave this question hanging and proceed toward a second reminder on the subject of reading Husserl.

2. Merleau-Ponty's major concern is not only the "reflexive" access to the "incarnation" of "my body," in this first allusion to the touching-touched of the hand; it is also and immediately to involve the other, and my experience of the other's body or the "other man's"—the other as other human being—in the being touched of my own proper hand that is touching. And here again, we are not objecting to the interest or necessity inherent in this movement (which mobilizes the immense, fearsome problematic of *Einfühlung* and the appresentation of the alter ego or the other man in Husserl, and the destiny of this problematic in France). But shouldn't we mark—in a limited, pointed, but acute fashion—where Merleau-Ponty gives in to a rather ambiguous—and problematic—gesture in his reading of *Ideas II* (a reading aiming to be as literal and faithful as possible, supported by notes and German terms)? This gesture is important for us, not so much for reasons of integrity or philological discipline (though I am keen on those as well), but because of some of its paradoxical and typical consequences. What are they? Before stating them formally, let me again quote from "The Philosopher and His Shadow" and emphasize some passages:

My right hand *was present* [*assistait*] at the advent of my left hand's active sense of touch. *It is in no different fashion* that the other's body becomes animate before me when I shake another man's hand or just look at him [Husserl, *Ideas II*, pp. 173–74]. In learning that my body is a "perceiving thing," that is able to be stimulated [*reizbar*]—it, and not just my "consciousness"—I prepared myself for understanding that there are other *animalia* and possibly other men.

 It is imperative to recognize that we have here neither comparison, nor analogy, nor projection or "introjection" [ohne Introjektion (ibid., p. 175)]. The reason why I have evidence of the other man's being-there when I shake his hand is that his hand is substituted for my left hand. . . . (Merleau-Ponty, *Signs*, p. 168)[8]

The Husserlian references and citations must not delude us. At the very same time when Merleau-Ponty claims that he is making a comment on Husserl or seeking inspiration in him, he puts the shoe on the wrong foot, literally, turning upside down, short of completely misreading, the sense of Husserl's text, which I have, for this very reason, already sought to situate. The page in question clearly says that I can *never* have access to the body (*Leib*) of the other *except* in an indirect fashion, through appresentation, comparison, analogy, projection, and introjection. That is a motif to which Husserl remains particularly and fiercely faithful. And when he says "without introjection," indeed, this is not to qualify our access to the other's living body, but the access that others have—that they have, just as I have—to their own proper bodies ("without introjection"). But this access that others have without introjection to their bodies, I can have—to their own proper bodies—only by introjection or appresentation. Husserl would never have subscribed to this "It is in no different fashion . . . [ce n'est pas autrement . . .]" ("*It is in no different fashion* that the other's body becomes animate before me when I shake another man's hand or just look at him" [*Signs*, p. 168]), which assimilates the touching-the-touching [*le touchant-toucher*] of my own proper body or my two hands with the contact of the other's hand. Let us again reread this passage in Husserl. He has been speaking of the appearance of the other person (Erscheinung des fremden Menschen), "understanding of the other's psychic life," and especially of the "system of signs 'expressing' psychic events" in the language that is "actually spoken" and its "grammar": "Since here this manifold expression appresents psychic *existence* in [carnal] Corporeality, thus there is constituted with all that an objectivity which is precisely double and unitary: the man —without 'introjection'" (Husserl, *Ideas II*, p. 175).

 "Without introjection": these words do not describe my relation to the other's carnal "corporeality" (*Leiblichkeit*), which, as Husserl always says unambiguously, is present for me only indirectly and by way of analogical "introjection," which is to say appresented, as this passage clearly puts it. However, what this appresentation delivers to me is another man, and what for him is inscribed—in *his* phenomenon, which *he* has, *for his part, and which will never be mine*—is an originary relation, "without introjection," to his own proper body, which is the relation I have with my body but will never have with his. There we can find the appresentative analogy between two *here*s. Husserl had continually insisted—be it only in the two preceding pages—on indirect appresentation and even on the fact that the other's hand, such as I see it while it is touching, "appresents to me his solipsistic view of this hand." (Let us be quite clear that without this unbridgeable abyss, there would be no handshake, nor blow or caress, nor, in general, any experience of the other's body as such.)

I thus call the consequences of this active "interpretation" on the part of Merleau-Ponty, and the liberties he takes with regard to what Husserl seems to hold to most keenly, "paradoxical and typical." They are typical because they have often given rise to similar gestures, in France notably, and they are paradoxical: at the moment when it is a matter of orienting Husserl and making him take the other into account in a more audacious way (the other who is originarily in me, or for me, and so forth)—at the expense of a Husserl who is more classical, more ego-centered, and so forth—there is a risk of the exact opposite resulting. One runs the risk of reconstituting an intuitionism of immediate access to the other, as originary as my access to my own most properly proper—and in one blow, doing without appresentation, indirection, *Einfühlung*, one also runs the risk of *reappropriating* the alterity of the other more surely, more blindly, or even more violently than ever. In this respect Husserl's cautious approach will always remain *before us* as a model of vigilance. It is necessary to watch over the other's alterity: it will always remain inaccessible to an originally presentive intuition, an immediate and direct presentation of the *here*. It is necessary to watch over this, even if, for a phenomenology that is faithful to its intuitionistic "principle of principles," it is difficult to assimilate—the very principle that governs haptocenteredness in *Ideas II*. I do know or feel that there is *another* here, and since this is our theme, the other here of a touching-touched (which is to say others who themselves are also put at a distance from themselves, up to and including in the presentation of their present, by the timing of their experience and the simple gap, the syncopated noncoincidence in their self-relation), but this other "here" presents itself as that which will never be mine: this non-mine-ness is part of the sense of this presentation, which, like my own, itself suffers already from the "same" expropriation. No substitution is possible; and the more surprising logic of the substitution, wherever it is necessarily at work, presupposes the substitution of nonsubstitutables, of unique and other ones, of uniquely others. *Being singular plural,* Nancy might say at this point.

If I have often spoken of pre-originary mourning on this subject, and tied this motif to that of exappropriation, it has been in order to mark that interiorization, in this mourning before death, and even introjection, which we often take for granted in normal mourning, cannot and must not be achieved. Mourning as im-possible mourning—and moreover, ahuman, more than human, prehuman, different from the human "in" the human of humanualism. Well, despite all the differences separating the discursive way in which I am holding forth at this moment from a discourse in Husserl's style, and probably as well from the great massifs of phenomenology, I do find this way to have more affinities with the discourse that Husserl obstinately upholds on the subject of appresentation (which I am tempted to extend and radicalize, while paying the price of the necessary displacements—but this is not the place to insist on this) than with the one of a *certain* Merleau-Ponty, that is, the one, at least, whose *typical* gesture we are following here—typical because he repeats it often, as do others, even if (hence my respectful caution) the gesture is far from exhausting or even dominating his thinking throughout. His thinking also, simultaneously, exposes itself to an antagonistic necessity, to the other law—we'll come to this. Husserl, on the other hand, in the name of phenomenology, and phenomenological faithfulness, prefers to betray phenomenology (the intuitionism of his principle of principles) rather than transform indirect appresentation into direct presentation, which it may never be—which would reappropriate the alterity of the alter ego within "my Ego's" own properness. Husserl obstinately persists in this, at the risk of running into all the well-known difficulties (upon which we have focused elsewhere), notably there where the principle of principles, the principle of intuition, finds itself threatened—as it happens to be, once again, by the experience of temporalization that is indissociable from this. Of course, even if there are still so many uneasy questions to ask about the constitution of the alter ego, I was earlier tempted to extend rather than reduce the field of appresentation and to recognize its irreducible gap even in the said touching-touched of my "own proper" hand, my own body proper as a human ego, and so forth. And this would strictly be neither Husserlian nor Merleau-Pontyian. Even between me and me, if I may put it this way, between my body and my body, there is no such "original" contemporaneity, this "confusion" between the other's body and mine, that Merleau-Ponty believes he can recognize there, while pretending he is following Husserl—for example, when he follows the thread of the same analysis and writes: "The constitution of others does not come after that of the body [with which Husserl could agree, but without inferring what follows.—J. D.]; others and my body are *born together from the original ecstasy*. The corporeality to which the *primordial thing* belongs is more *corporeality in general*; as the child's egocentricity, the 'solipsist layer' is both transitivity and *confusion* of self and other" (Merleau-Ponty, *Signs*, p. 174; my emphasis—J. D.).

This "confusion" would be as originary as the "primordial thing" and would make possible the substitutions (that we have noted are impossible) between the other and me, between our two bodies, in what Merleau-Ponty unhesitatingly terms "the absolute presence of origins." In another example, he writes:

> The reason why I am able to understand the other person's body and existence "beginning with" the body proper, the reason why the compresence of my "consciousness" and my "body" is prolonged into the compresence of my self and the other person, is that the "I am able to" and the "the other person exists" belong here and now to the same world, that the body proper is a premonition of the other person, the *Einfühlung* an echo of my incarnation, and that a flash of meaning makes them substitutable in the absolute presence of origins. (Merleau-Ponty, *Signs*, p. 175)

And so, must we not think, and think otherwise (without objecting to it frontally and integrally), that the said "same world" (if there is some such world, and if it is indeed necessary to account for it, and account for its "effect," as "sense of the world") is not and will never be the "same world"? The fact that this proposition is intelligible and even convincing for "every man," throughout more than one possible world, does not contradict its content. When I take into account a whole history, from hominization to socialization connected to verbal language and its pragmatic conditions, and so forth, I can convey to "every man's" ear that the world of each person is untranslatable and that finally there will never be any "same world." These two possibilities are not incompatible; they even condition, and call for, one another, as paradoxical as this may sound.

Digression or anticipation: the chosen expression ("sense of the world") also makes a sign, of course, in the direction of Nancy's book *The Sense of the World*. We shall come back to it, notably to its chapter on "Touching" (written—and therefore, unfortunately, read by me—after the completion of the first version of this book). At this point, let us simply note that after "Touching," Nancy, for his part, in the chapter on "Painting," insists on the limits of vision, a *limit that it touches*, touching itself "intact," a limit "always attained and always withdrawn."[9] And the "logic" of all these oppositions, hierarchies, and orderings [*ordonnancements*] (between vision and touch, the touchable and the untouchable, and so forth) finds itself routed, displaced, upset, "touched" and tampered with [*"touchée"*]— not through any confusion, but on the contrary by reason of the plural singularities that once more inspire one of Nancy's numerous and regular statements to the effect that "there is no 'the' . . . "; here "there is no 'Art' in general."[10] He has just said, once again, what touches the limit, reaching but also displacing it, and setting it in motion:

> So that vision should touch the limit, that it should touch its limit, that it should touch itself intact. Painting is always on the threshold. It makes up the threshold between intactness and touching—between the intactness and touching *of* light and shadow. . . . Access is no longer of the order of vision, but of touch. . . .
>
> . . . there is no "Art" in general: each one indicates the threshold by being itself also the threshold of another art. Each one touches the other without passing into it, and there is properly speaking no art of touching (not even a "minor" art such as those for taste and smell), for touching is sense as threshold, the sensing/sensed apportioning of the aesthetic entelechy. Touching is the light/darkness of all the senses, and of sense, absolutely. In touching, in all the touches of touching that do not touch each other—touches of color, traced, melodic, harmonic, gestural, rhythmic, spatial, significative touches, and so on—the two sides of the one sense do not cease to come each toward the other, acceding without access, touching on the untouchable, intact, spacing of sense.
>
> Barely to touch: to skim the surface. Sense levels off. . . . There is sense only on the (flowering) surface of sense [*il n'y a de sens qu'à fleur de sens*]. Never any fruit to be harvested—but the *painting* of fruits as their coming ceaselessly resumed, ceaselessly re-brought into the world, superficially, as on the rosy surface of the skin [*à fleur de peau*].[11]

When Nancy speaks of "painting" here, painting itself, of course, but of what in it "touches" the other arts; when he speaks of fruit that is not for picking, which we can barely touch, at least three discriminating traits are noticeable:

1. He takes into account the threshold of all the figuralities and the figurality of the threshold, as the threshold of touch.

2. Indeed, he designates the world, the bringing forth into the world [*mise au monde*] and birth, as a "re-bringing" [*re-mise*] into the world; and the (sense of the) world as at the same time a place of birth and of a gift thus repeated, given or "rendered" by art—but I don't believe that Nancy would ever say, like Merleau-Ponty, that "others and my body are born together from the original ecstasy."

3. Above all, Nancy says "the sensing/sensed *apportioning*" [*partage*], and not the sensed-sensing or touched-touching confusion or reflection. As always with Nancy, *partage*—apportioning, sharing out, parting, partaking —signifies participation as much as irreducible partition, which is to say the "spacing of sense." Syncope is this parting and sharing out of spacing: the syncope separates and interrupts at the heart of contact. It breathes or marks the breathing, and gives it a threatened chance, its threatening possibility, to the same beat—the other's beat, the other's heartbeat. It is a sharing out without fusion, a community without community, a language without communication, a being-with without confusion.

We shall stick as close as possible to our theme and focus on marking that this "confusion," Merleau-Ponty's confusion, as well as the confusion of which he speaks ("confusion of self and other"), among other connections, cannot be separated from what makes him purposely confuse the senses of seeing and touching and put them on the same plane and allocate them the same "carnal" "reflexivity"—precisely there where Husserl was set on dissociating them radically. There are a thousand possible illustrations of this. Here is first of all his passing to sight, a passage that immediately follows the allusion to touch in *Ideas II*, together with the hurried or improvised interpretation of the words "without introjection." One can distinguish two beats and a shifting between the two; the first beat is essentially faithful to the Husserl of appresentation and *Einfühlung*, but, for good reasons, this does not yet deal with the seeing, the sight or the visibility of others, *sensu stricto*.

First beat, therefore. At this time Merleau-Ponty is intent on responding to an "objection," saying that he does so in Husserl's name, in a language, I believe, that could never have been Husserl's, for the reasons already mentioned—in any case, when Merleau-Ponty invokes a "singular eloquence of the visible body." It is in any case a question of refuting a possible "objection," which:

> would ignore the very thing that Husserl wanted to say; that is, *that there is no constituting of a mind for a mind, but of a man for a man.* By the effect of a singular eloquence of the visible body, *Einfühlung* goes from body to mind. When a different behavior or exploring body appears to me through a first "intentional encroachment" [*intentionale Überschreitungen*, a term used in Husserl's *Cartesian Meditations*], it is the man as a whole who is given to me with all the possibilities (whatever they may be) that I have in my presence to myself in my incarnate being, the unimpeachable attestation. I shall never in all strictness be able to think the other person's thought. I can think *that* he thinks; I can construct, behind this mannequin, a presence to self modeled on my own; but it is still my self that I put in it, and it is then that there really is "introjection." (Merleau-Ponty, *Signs*, p. 169)

Indeed, there is nothing very Husserlian up to now, except precisely for this "singular eloquence of the visible body," already announcing the shift, which appears as early as in the sentence that follows.

Second beat. This is the beginning of a long development: it is not only going to contradict the Husserlian privilege of touch, and the ensuing logic, but also break apart any symmetry to the benefit of sight. Nothing of what follows can be sustained, it seems to me—I mean particularly from the Husserlian viewpoint from which Merleau-Ponty pretends to seek his inspiration:

> On the other hand, I know unquestionably that that man over there *sees*, that my sensible world is also his, because *I am present at his seeing*, it *is visible* [*se voit*] in his eyes' grasp of the scene. And when I say I see *that* he sees, there is no longer here (as there is in "I think that he thinks") the interlocking of two propositions but the mutual unfocusing of a "main" and a "subordinate" viewing. (ibid.)

If one supposes that all the words he has chosen (particularly his "I know" and "I think," not to mention his *se voit* ["is visible," "sees itself"]) are only ambiguous with regard to a Husserlian phenomenology implemented here, it seems impossible—both in general and from Husserl's viewpoint—to uphold the conclusion to which these premises firmly lead, that is, the "as" which makes symmetrical, compares, and analogizes seeing *and* touching—notably, on the one hand, seeing-a-man-seeing, *and,* on the other, touching-my-left-hand-touching-my-right-hand. We may wonder in fact what (identical, neighboring, and different) meanings Merleau-Ponty here gives to the words "perception" and "esthesiological" when he explains how a "riddle of *Einfühlung*" which would only be "initial," and "esthesiological," would then be "solved" "because it is a perception." (This already rouses our uneasiness: who could pretend that the riddle of *Einfühlung* remains "initial" only, and is "solved" without some mystifying sleight-of-hand? Husserl himself has doubtless never been able or willing to "solve" this "riddle," and this will keep tormenting phenomenology.) Indeed, Merleau-Ponty writes:

> The whole riddle of *Einfühlung* lies in its initial, "esthesiological" phase; and it is solved there because it is a perception. He who "posits" the other man is a perceiving subject, the other person's body is a perceived thing, and the other person himself is "posited" as "perceiving." It is never a matter of anything but co-perception. I see that this man over there sees, *as* I touch my left hand while it is touching my right. (ibid., p. 170; I have emphasized "as"—J. D.)

By way of a problematic "as," the logic of this argumentation has quickly become indispensable for an "ontology of the sensible" and of "incarnation" ("my own," as well as the incarnation of the flesh of the world),[12] as the continuation of this text and so many others indicate, and this seems doubly unfaithful to Husserl. This in itself certainly does not constitute an offense, and the least we can say is that we are not here to assert the rights of some kind of Husserlian orthodoxy. Moreover, in this instance, such a reminder of Husserl's intentions is not so shocking, since Merleau-Ponty pretends—in this passage especially—that he is answering an objection that ignores "the very thing that Husserl wanted to say." As he then speaks in the name of "the very thing that Husserl wanted to say," we may by all means have some questions on this subject here. But beyond this problem of reading Husserl, the important thing for us here is to formalize the logic that— *from the point of view of touch,* as it were, and since this is our concern here —compels the most original movement in Merleau-Ponty's thinking, which starting in *Phenomenology of Perception* goes on to *Signs* and *The Visible and the Invisible.* The double unfaithfulness to what Husserl wanted to say in the name of what "Husserl wanted to say" has to do with this purported "co-perception." Thus interpreted, it reduces, on the one hand, the irreducible difference between the originary, direct intuition of my own body proper touching itself (without *Einfühlung*, as Husserl, at least, puts it) and the indirect appresentation that, by way of sight (and *Einfühlung*, this time), gives me access to this man there, *insofar as he sees—to this seeing man*. On the other hand, the "co-perception" reduces the irreducible difference between sight and touch, according to Husserl—we have insisted on this enough. Concerning the "as" in "I see that this man over there sees, *as* I touch my left hand while it is touching my right" (Merleau-Ponty, *Signs*, p. 170), everything leads us to think that Husserl not only would have objected to its phenomenological legitimacy; he would have seen in it one of those facile rhetorical turns about which his misgivings—precisely on this point—were great, as noted earlier.

Henceforth there is a logic compelling Merleau-Ponty's thinking, and it will lead him simultaneously or in succession, as it were, to alternate between two intuitionisms of the "flesh": first, one that requires a certain privilege for the gaze, for originary immediacy, sensible presentation, coincidence, "confusion," "co-perception," and so forth; and second, one that is just as intuitionistic and will reinscribe within the same values an experience of apartness, inadequacy, distance, indirection, noncoincidence, and so forth. To signal this, I earlier quoted [Merleau-Ponty's observation] that "it is a non-coincidence I coincide with here," which could serve as a motto for the unity of this double movement.[13] It is a formula that I may by all means reverse ad infinitum without harming any formal discursive logic: if I coincide *with* a noncoincidence, I do not coincide *with* my own coincidence, and so forth. Coincidence and noncoincidence coincide *with* each other in not coinciding; coincidence and noncoincidence coincide without coinciding, and so forth. All that remains is to think the *cum* and the "with" otherwise.

With—the one and the other of the *with*. Having reached this point—and before we go any further in the company of Merleau-Ponty—I would like to make another anticipatory digression toward Nancy. What his book *Être singulier pluriel* (*Being Singular Plural*) sets out to do is to think the *cum* and the "with" in other ways—precisely in the chapter titled "The Measure of the *With*." I refer the reader to the progress of its analysis, and merely retain here what comes down, again, to our question of touch (and confirms the need for this "deconstruction of Christianity," Nancy's new project that we keep bringing up), of "distance [*écart*] and contact," the parting into "on the one hand" and "on the other hand," one part and the other of a sharing out of the *with*:

> With regard to this constitution, then, and at the heart of Judeo-Christianity and its exact reverse side [always "exact," to be sure: even at the "heart" and "reverse side" he still dares to say "exact"—J. D.], it is a matter of understanding how the dimension of the *with* both appears and disappears all at once. On the one hand, the proximity of the next, of the fellow [*du prochain*], points to the "next to" of the "with" (the *apud hoc* of the etymology of *avec* in French). . . . [Nancy then develops this semantic logic until its internal and ineluctable reversal.—J. D.] On the other hand, this is why . . . the simultaneity of distance [*écart*] and contact, that is, the most proper constitution of the *cum*-, is exposed as indeterminateness and as a problem. In this logic, there is no proper measure of the *with*: the *other* draws it away from it, within the alternative or dialectic of the incommensurable and of common intimacy. In an extreme paradox, the other turns out to be *the other of the with*. (Nancy, *Being Singular Plural*, pp. 80–81)

It is always the law of *parting and sharing* at the heart of touching and con-tact, presentation, appearance, and co-appearance: sharing out as participation *and* partition, as continuity and interruption, as syncopated beat. An ethics, politics or law, and a thinking of an "inoperative community," also come out, through the test of this incommensurable, the "other of the with"—and not even in the reassuring "simultaneity of distance and contact," but what, in it, thus remains an "indeterminateness" and "a problem." At the moment when Nancy's thinking is thus decided (and, as has been noted, it often is), and always sets itself to think while measuring *exactly* the "incommensurable" and measuring itself *with* [à] the "incommensurable," his thinking is "with" Merleau-Ponty, as near and far as possible in relation to the Merleau-Ponty who claims, it will be recalled, to coincide *with* a noncoincidence ("it is a non-coincidence I coincide with here"), which in fact does resemble Nancy's "simultaneity of distance and contact." However, at this point ("problem," "indeterminateness"), "the other of the with" interrupts all contemporaneity, co-appearance, and commensurability.

Earlier in *Being Singular Plural* (p. 56ff.), moreover, in the section "Co-appearing," Nancy analyzes what he terms the "chiasmus" between two thoughts, Husserl's and Heidegger's, as two "styles of the essentiality of the with." And he does this precisely by first quoting Husserl: "The *together-ness* of monads, their mere *co*-existence" necessarily signifies a "*temporal* co-existence." It is a matter of conveying that "It is undoubtedly here [in the *Cartesian Meditations*—J. D.],[14] more than anywhere else, that Husserl shows how phenomenology itself *touches* its own limit and exceeds it [emphasis added]."[15] We can recognize the recurrent syntagma in Nancy—a phrasing as regular as it is disorganizing and disturbing: *touching the limit*, thus touching the untouchable, or touching without touching, or touching in passing the touchable or touched, touching while doing without it [*en se passant de toucher*], touching and traversing what one is touching toward its beyond, and so forth. Now—he goes on—this simultaneity of co-existence "needs time" and "needs space," that is, what is needed is "time to space itself" out, and a space of temporal "dis-tension," "space of the passage that parts."[16]

Let us return to Merleau-Ponty. I have just drawn a hypothetical sketch of an alternation: in what way is it held to this question of touch? In the way of a paradox: the very thing that neutralizes or reverses the primordiality that Husserl acknowledges in touch in order to reappropriate appresentation in originary presentation (immediate perception, "confusion," "coincidence," and so on) will enter a much richer problematic of the eye, seeing and visibility; this very thing is precisely that which, conversely, is going to make it compelling, in optical space, to take into account apartness, distance, tele-vision, and even the invisible, the invisible right in [*à même*] the visible. Let us clarify this formal schema somewhat.

First, we established this symmetrization of touching and seeing (which is both a drifting away and a deviation with respect to *Ideas II*), and especially of touching-oneself and seeing-oneself (" . . . we could not possibly touch or see without being capable of touching or seeing ourselves" [Merleau-Ponty, *Signs*, p. 16]). Françoise Dastur (see n. 7 above) has justly highlighted a "conception of vision" that "leads Merleau-Ponty to restore the parallelism between seeing and touching that Husserl contested."[17] Earlier—and we can agree that this is something altogether different and even more serious than a "parallelism"—she even mentions the "exorbitant privilege" that Merleau-Ponty "grants to vision." This "exorbitance" of the privilege thus, in a reversal, comes as a substitute for the "astonishing" of another privilege, the "astonishing ontological privilege" that Husserl bestows on the sense of touch. It may be "astonishing" "if we connect it not only to the theme of *Wesensschau* [intuition of essences] but also to the general importance that falls to sight in Husserlian phenomenology."[18] In this respect at least, Merleau-Ponty belongs to the "Western tradition from Parmenides to Husserl" that, according to *Sein und Zeit*, "has privileged seeing as the unique 'mode of access to beings *and to being*.'"[19] Dastur observes that

the privilege[20] given to pure intuition on the noetic plane corresponds to that given to objectively present being on the ontological plane. Heidegger specifies, moreover, in explicit reference to Husserlian phenomenology, that "The thesis that all cognition aims at 'intuition' has the temporal meaning that all cognition is a making present";[21] defining thereby the meaning of Being as *making present* for these philosophers of *consciousness*, Kant and Husserl. Merleau-Ponty, with regard to the *exorbitant privilege* [my emphasis—J. D.] that he grants to vision, hardly seems to have distanced himself in relation to this long tradition, which seems on the contrary to find its culmination in the unique question that the author of *Eye and Mind* continues to ask from his first to his last book: what is vision? Is it not possible, nevertheless, while remaining the inheritor of the tradition, to put into question *from within* the nonexplicit presuppositions on which the tradition is founded?[22]

A few remarks, now, to lie in wait, at the crossroads of some thoughts in progress about "Heidegger's hand," and the animal world that is purportedly "world-poor" (*weltarm*) where one is to suppose that human beings (being *weltbildend*) would therefore be world-rich (or -richer—a little richer? Much richer? To what point? Regarding *all* humans, as opposed to *all* animals? And so on.).[23] Some things are of first importance for us in this context (a certain history of touching and sight, the hand and the eye, hominization or humanualization processes, and "living bodies," and "animals" who may not have the "hand of man" at their disposal and yet would not be simply armless, and so on), and in this matter let us acknowledge the *place* of these considerations by Heidegger on the connection between the priority or privilege (*Vorrang*), which is supposedly traditional and continuous (throughout Western ontology!), of seeing "taken in its broadest sense," intuition (*Anschauung*), and this "making present" (*Gegenwärtigung*), more particularly in its temporal dimension. The chapter in question deals with an analysis concerning, first of all, what presents itself in various manners *to the hand, by the hand, at hand,* or *handily*. To be sure, Heidegger mentions neither the hand as such, the hand alone, nor the sense of touch (only "seeing": *Sehen, Umsicht, Übersehen,* and not expressly as a sense, or as the sensible that might be dependent on a sense organ), but rather hand gestures, the hand in motion, the hand in action, and manual labor. Indeed, everything here leads back to an analysis of the temporality of being-in-the-world starting from *Zuhandenheit* and *Vorhandenheit*. There where ontological questions come into play on the subject of scientific objectivation and especially useful things (*Zeug*), while Heidegger does not name the hand, in several instances, he designates *handling, manipulation* (*Hantieren, Hantierung*), as well as the effects of the interpretation of beings as *Vorhandenheit,* or, here especially, as "handiness," *Zuhandenheit*. Let us not forget that the remark at issue here, about the "priority" or "privilege" of seeing, begins with an allusion to "manipulation" (*Hantierung*) in the sciences, of which it is said that it is *in the service of* "pure observation," that is, finally, in the service of seeing and the intuition of the "things themselves." Leading to the conclusion by Heidegger that "The idea of the *intuitus* has guided all interpretation of knowledge ever since the beginnings of Greek ontology up to today, whether that intuition is actually attainable or not,"[24] Kant's sentence then quoted by Heidegger is worth recalling—not only literally but also in the words that Heidegger emphasizes, including the remark he makes to draw attention to his emphasis. The term "means" weighs heavily here. It is when—and insofar as—thinking is thought as a *means* that *intuition* is dominant —and with it, therefore, *seeing,* and more precisely still, an optical intuitionism of the *immediate*. Kant thus writes, with Heidegger's emphasis: "'To whatever kind of objects one's knowledge may relate itself and by whatever means (*durch welche Mittel*) it may do so, still that through which it relates itself to them immediately (*unmittelbar*), *and which all thinking as a means has as its goal* [Heidegger's italics] *is intuition* (*und worauf alles Denken als Mittel abzweckt* [v. Vf. gesp.], *die Anschauung*).'"[25]

After which Heidegger goes on with a fundamental analysis of the consequences and questions made necessary by what thus links seeing (inspection, perspective, circumspection, *Umsicht*) with "practical" taking care (*das "praktische" Besorgen*). At the outset of this development, Heidegger had recalled the complexity of the relation between *praxis* and theoretical investigation that pretends to be independent. From the crudest to the most refined, from pencils to microscopes, these manipulations properly pertaining to scientific investigation are never "ontologically" insignificant or indifferent, no more than the boundary between the theoretical and atheoretical appears in the light of day.[26] Before we interrupt this digression, let us again emphasize that the terms "sense" or "sensibility" do not appear in this argument. We further know that Heidegger regularly says that it is not because we have ears that we hear but, inversely, we have ears because we hear. He would likewise say that seeing does not depend on any ocular organ, and so forth.

Let us come back to Merleau-Ponty once again. It is, no doubt, hardly disputable that he has in fact tended to "restore the parallelism between seeing and touching that Husserl contested" (perhaps especially in his article in *Signs*), and that he has also conferred on vision an "exorbitant privilege," which is a different thing. Dastur then sets afoot a reading that is even more accurate, asking herself whether it is possible, "while remaining an inheritor to the tradition, to put into question *from within* the nonexplicit presuppositions on which the tradition is founded"; it is more accurate, which is to say generous, with regard to the Merleau-Ponty who is more attentive to distancing and noncoincidence, to the invisible and the untouchable, to a hiatus not absent even in the *Urerlebnis* of which Husserl speaks—and this even in a living present that has to be interpreted differently from coincidence and fusion, and start instead from a retention, a "past-present simultaneity" for which a "philosophy of consciousness" "cannot account." And even if the "specularity of Being is Merleau-Ponty's last word, as it is the culmination of the metaphysics of vision in the Hegelian dialectic," he has carried out a "displacement at once both infinitesimal and radical" in this philosophical tradition of absolute reflection.[27]

Between touch and sight, the question of "privilege" or "parallelism" certainly takes on the greatest importance, with all that still seems to be at stake in what it commands, with the evaluations it involves, the hierarchical orders, and the more or less subtle and stabilizable reversals to which these "senses" can give rise. (If they still are sensible senses! As I have just remarked, Heidegger's pondering about the said traditional privilege of "seeing" is not, from the outset, a reflection on sensibility as such.) What remains, as I suggested earlier—*against* Heidegger, in a way—is that one might have to go in for a structure of experience in which this "privilege" or "priority" (*Vorrang*) of sight or touch (whether "exorbitant" or not) no longer means much, if the said "tradition" ("since the beginnings of Greek ontology"!) never shows any privilege for the gaze (no optical theoretism) without an invincible intuitionism that is accomplished, fulfilled, fully effectuated, starting from a haptical origin or *telos*; if there is no optical intuitionism without haptocentrism; and if furthermore (in regard to this intuitionism, which is finally homogeneous, undifferentiating, absolute, stubborn, absurd, and in the final account insensible or "smooth"—i.e., deaf, blind, and impassive) the fate of this intersensibility (henceforth irreducibly tropological, figural, and metonymic) allows one to see and hear and feel and taste a bit of touching everywhere: indeed, who would deny that we can touch with our voice—close or far away, naturally or technically, if we could still rely on this distinction, in the open air or on the phone—and thus, even touch to the heart? Whether they are maintained or subverted, these "parallelisms" are no longer determining—nor, finally, are they determined or even determinable.

And these battles for the hegemony or equality, for the aristocracy of one sense, or the democracy of all the senses—don't they then become trifling, no matter how virulent, how *fiercely embroiled, tooth and nail* [*acharnées*]? In their polemical duels, these battles are possible only insofar as there is no longer any sense proper, strict and circumscribable, to each of these senses, but only tropological displacements and substitutions, that is, prosthetic possibilities. If there were any possible accord about a sense proper—strict and circumscribable, stabilizable, irreplaceable, not reducible to prosthetic substitution—you can bet that no discord could have lastingly arisen, whether about "parallelism" or "exorbitant" "privilege." This is not because it would be necessary to start from an undifferentiated sensibility or a body without organs—quite the contrary—but from another organization (natural *and* technical, originary *inasmuch as* prosthetical) of what is termed sensibility, the "body proper," or the "flesh"; and in the final account, without too much faith either in common sense or in a historical culture that withholds its name and passes itself off as natural, or in the common sense of a culture that still forces us to count the senses on the fingers of a single hand, the hand of man—man always. There is not one sense—nor one, two, three, four, five, or six. We are to feel and count otherwise, and besides, we are doing it—that is how it goes. And that is why the technical, that is to say, prosthetics, never waits. In the end, this is what Nancy, to me, seems to mean when he speaks of a "*technē* of bodies" — we'll talk about this again—and what these days comes under the somewhat religious appellation "flesh" or "body," as the "flattest" and "least trendily 'connected'" of "themes and terms—in a terminal coma," a body all at once common and exceptional, "substitutable with any other *inasmuch as it is unsubstitutable*" (Nancy, *Corpus*, pp. 80–81); and especially when he says "there is no 'the' sense of touch" (ibid., p. 104). I suppose he could just as well have said, "There is no 'the' sense of vision," and so on. And there his problematic of sense and the senses, of the sense of the world, and so on, opens up.

Now, how can we explain, without prosthetic and tropological play, and without the originary supplementarity just designated, that Merleau-Ponty could make so much room for antagonistic motifs (or that he had to, later or at the same time)—namely, for touching, distancing, noncoincidence that dissociates within *both* seeing *and* touching, for the imminence of an ever-concealed access, for interruption, the invisible and the untouchable —while having "parallelized" the senses of sight and touch, or, as a first oddity, additionally conferred an "exorbitant privilege" on the former and remained so eloquent about confusion, coincidence, reflection, originarity, primordial presence, and so on? For *The Visible and the Invisible* is, in this respect, as rich a text as it is heterogeneous, and all the more profuse since it stays on the move and undecided with respect to all these alternatives and their logical consistency. It is impossible here to do justice to this great work "in progress," and especially to detect in it in a very rigorous fashion what serves as further development to *The Structure of Behavior*[28] and *Phenomenology of Perception*. However, let us recall, for example—though too hastily—the attention given to "replacement" [*suppléance*] and "substitution," in *Phenomenology of Perception*, thus to a certain spontaneous, quasi-pretechnical prosthetics, in the course of Merleau-Ponty's famous analyses of the "phantom limb,"[29] the "unsound" or pathological sense of touch, or "potential [*virtuel*]" touch (ibid., pp. 109, 118). Let us also think of the difference that he explores between the "alleged 'purely tactile' which I try to extract by investigating blindness" and "integrated" touch, of the nonjuxtaposition between "tactile and visual data" in normal subjects (according to [Dr. Kurt] Goldstein); and especially of the *synaesthetic* unity of the senses, "intersensory unity of the thing," man as *sensorium commune* (Herder): "Synaesthetic perception is the rule" (Merleau-Ponty, *Phenomenology of Perception*, pp. 229, 235, 239). "For the senses communicate with each other. Music is not in visible space, but it besieges, undermines [it]" (p. 225). This language, which Husserl would have often judged too metaphorical, makes it permissible to speak of synaesthetic analogy finally grounded in a spatiality that is common to the visible and the tangible, as well as a touching "by the eyes," for example: "The very fact that the way is paved to true vision through a phase of transition and through a sort of touch effected by the eyes would be incomprehensible unless there were a quasi-spatial tactile field, into which the first visual perceptions may be inserted" (ibid., p. 223).

It is insofar as vision that is properly spatial already "prepares" for this ("the way is paved") and secures a "phase of transition" through "a sort of touch effected by the eyes" that the "tactile field," which is only "quasi-spatial," seems to come beforehand—so that the visible comes already before what comes before it. Vision properly speaking is ahead of what nonetheless seems to condition it. Such a presentation of things is rather significant—and quasi-teleological, let us add. This presentation will persist in *The Visible and the Invisible*, in terms that are close to this (seeing "is being premeditated . . . the visible body provides for the hollow whence a vision will come, inaugurates the long maturation at whose term suddenly it will see, that is, will be visible for itself" [Merleau-Ponty, *Visible and the Invisible*, p. 147]). Indeed, although Merleau-Ponty gives the greatest weight to this synaesthesia, he never excludes a hierarchical order from it, and then confers on vision a heavy primacy, accompanied by an "it seems to me" as serious as it is authoritarian. For example, "the senses should not be put on the same basis, as if they were all equally capable of objectivity and accessible to intentionality. Experience does not present them to us as equivalent: it seems to me that *visual experience is truer than tactile experience*, that it garners within itself its own *truth* and adds to it, because its richer structure offers me modalities of being unsuspected by touch" (Merleau-Ponty, *Phenomenology of Perception*, p. 234n1; my emphasis—J. D. [slightly modified—Trans.]).

This did not prevent him a little earlier from associating on the same basis or plane—of "primordial contact with being"—"touch or sight," "see or touch," and to state: "Thus the unity and the diversity of the senses are *truths* of the same order" (ibid., p. 221; my emphasis—J. D.)—an ambiguous formulation that does not allow us to set things straight. Are the "truths of the same order" for diverse meanings that still become united, or for a diversity that is equivalent to a unity? In any case, if "our own body" proper is "as the heart," it is also a heart that sees or gives life to the living: "Our own body is in the world as the heart is in the organism: it keeps the visible spectacle constantly alive, it breathes life into it and sustains it inwardly, and with it forms a system" (ibid., p. 203).

Let us at last note that this same book very often (too often for an exhaustive survey) deals with the "example of the hand," the pair "eye and hand" (ibid., p. 216) or the "set of *manipulanda*" (ibid., p. 105).[30] (This confirms to what extent this phenomenology of perception is an anthropology; it overshadows the problems of both animality and hominization.) In order to map things out at first, we can at least try to follow the dotted outline of a few of his lines when—without any betrayal or denial—their tracings scramble the statics of borderlines that would stabilize a "parallelism" or establish a "privilege."

In *The Visible and the Invisible*, the matter of the looking eye will later, and everywhere, remain an overflowing theme, to be sure: at the origin of the world and the very notion of world, it knows no border, in a way—no external border. Still, this theme that spills overboard is visibly overrun at once by knowing as well as by saying, first of all—even before the internal fold of a running border, which cannot be distinguished from it and is called the invisible, overruns it. Knowing and saying, on the other hand, can neither see nor be seen: "It is at the same time true that the world is *what we see* and that, nonetheless, we must learn to see it—first in the sense that we must match this vision with knowledge, take possession of it, *say* what *we* and what *seeing* are, act therefore as if we knew nothing about it" (Merleau-Ponty, *Visible and the Invisible*, p. 4).

By the same token, the eye's authority is questioned, or called into question, in the eye of the world, precisely: "But am I *kosmotheoros*? More exactly: is being *kosmotheoros* my ultimate reality?" (ibid., p. 113).

Likewise, we must take into account the original way in which he treats the invisible, an invisible that is not intelligible or ideal, but an invisible that would not—though *right* at the visible—be "the invisible as an *other visible* 'possible,' or a 'possible' visible for an other" (p. 229). That is why we must "raise the question: the invisible life, the invisible community, the invisible other, the invisible culture. [¶] Elaborate a phenomenology of the 'other world,' as the limit of a phenomenology of the imaginary and the 'hidden'" (ibid., p. 229).[31]

The singular motif of the invisible-visible invades everything; it is all at once overflowing and overrun, exceeding its bounds or lost on its borders, internally coiled over a running border that puts its outside in—unless it lets everything affect it, in particular everything that was up to then kept circumspectly and respectfully at bay, that is, beginning with "noncoincidence," with which it seems henceforth that "I" no longer coincides so easily. And more hospitably now, it is the threshold of the sense of touch that is openly greeting noncoincidence, interruption, all that makes reversibility or reflexivity always inaccessible, and only imminent—the threshold of touch, certainly, but a sense of touch (in this instance deprived of any given reversibility between touching and touched) always conspicuously put on an equal footing—which should be an equal hand —with all the other "senses" or other organs of my body, sight or eye, hearing, ear or voice. This seems particularly obvious (or gripping, or better grasped by the ear) in "The Intertwining—the Chiasm." Here, in the course of one of the most explicit definitions of "the flesh we are speaking of," the example of the hand comes pedagogically to drive the discourse, even there where this discourse is intent on demonstrating that feeling is somewhat "dispersed." The argument is balanced and stretches between two poles, as if it wanted to say: there is some dispersion, but nevertheless . . . ! "There is no 'the' sense of vision," but nevertheless . . . there is "that central vision"! "There is no 'the' sense of touch," but nevertheless . . . there is "that unique touch"! Which moreover is like an "I think" that finally is nothing but my flesh. Among the remarkable traits of the passage quoted below, a continuous transition seems to proceed—as if on its own, as if this went without saying—from an infrastructural exemplarity of vision ("my visible is confirmed as an exemplar of a universal visibility . . . [thought] must be brought to appear directly in the infrastructure of vision") to the dispersion without dispersion of a "unique" way of touching of which the first example is "my hand." Let us quote this argument, therefore, from the moment when Merleau-Ponty makes use of the word "[we] touch" in a figurative sense to say "a second or figurative meaning of vision"; and let us once more underscore the work of the example, the "exemplar," or the "for example":

> At the frontier of the mute or solipsist world where, in the presence of other seers, my visible is confirmed as an *exemplar* of a universal visibility, we touch a second or figurative meaning of vision, which will be the *intuitus mentis* or idea, a sublimation of the flesh, which will be mind or thought. . . . Thought is a relationship with oneself and with the world as well as a relationship with the other; hence it is established in the three dimensions at the same time. And it must be brought to appear directly in the infrastructure of vision.

(Merleau-Ponty, *Visible and the Invisible*, p. 145; slightly modified—Trans.) (I have emphasized *exemplar*.—J. D.)

"Infrastructure": the word may come as a surprise. Does "infrastructure of vision" mean that vision *is* the infrastructure *of* "thought" or that "thought" is already in the infrastructure—there, as infrastructure *of* "vision"? What follows is all the more equivocal in this respect. On the one hand, Merleau-Ponty deliberately leaves "in suspense" the question of what is *implicated*, and, on the other hand, the example of the hand comes forth without any delay, immediately afterward, in order to illustrate what, a moment ago, was termed dispersion without dispersion of feeling and touching. In order to illustrate this or perhaps—but there is no telling—in order to approach the "infrastructure" thus "implicated":

> And it [thought] must be brought to appear directly in the infrastructure of vision. Brought to appear, we say, and not brought to birth: for we are leaving in suspense for the moment the question whether it would not be already implicated there. Manifest as it is that feeling is dispersed in my body, that for example my hand touches, and that consequently we may not in advance ascribe feeling to a thought of which it would be but a mode—it yet would be absurd to conceive the touch as a colony of assembled tactile experiences. We are not here proposing any empiricist genesis of thought: we are asking precisely what is that central vision that joins the scattered visions, that unique touch that governs the whole tactile life of my body as a unit, that *I think* that must be able to accompany all our experiences. (ibid., p. 145)

Let us note in passing that this figure of feeling "dispersed" in "my body" already imposes itself in *Phenomenology of Perception*, in the course of the rich, complex chapter titled "Sense Experience," just at the point where Merleau-Ponty asserts that "sensation is *literally* a form of communion" (as quoted earlier): "Because I know that the light strikes my eyes, that contact is made by the skin, that my shoe hurts my foot, I disperse through my body perceptions which really belong to my soul, and put perception into the thing perceived" (Merleau-Ponty, *Phenomenology of Perception*, pp. 212–13).

One of the conclusions we can unambiguously draw from this analysis, in *The Visible and the Invisible*, of his "example" (the hand, "my hand" as the hand of a man) as well as of the definition of "flesh," which will not be long in coming, is that these can only refer this thought about an "infrastructure of vision" to a "we" meaning "we, men." What then follows,

announcing and naming the concept of flesh, could not be said about any
other living being, nor in any other way except in the first person of a *human* plural:

> that unique touch that governs the whole tactile life of my body as a unit, that
> *I think* that must be able to accompany all our experiences. We are proceed-
> ing toward the center, we are seeking to comprehend how there is a center,
> what the unity consists of, we are not saying that it is a sum or a result; and if
> we make the thought appear upon an infrastructure of vision, this is only in
> virtue of the uncontested evidence that one must see or feel [why "see," at
> first? Why "see or feel"? What is the value of this "or"?—J. D.] in some way in
> order to think, that every thought known to us occurs to a flesh. (Merleau-
> Ponty, *Visible and the Invisible*, pp. 145–46)

It is fairly obvious that this "we," this "us," this "every thought known
to us occurs to a flesh," can imply nothing but a "we, men"; and that this
concept of flesh, of the "infrastructure of vision," and finally and correlatively of "world," and "flesh of the world," can in no way refer to other
"animals," other living beings. This would be less obvious if the precautions Merleau-Ponty takes to withdraw his project from some anthropology were more convincing, and if a discourse about the status and the
rights of this "we"—as well as nonhuman or supposedly handless "animals"—were sufficiently developed at this point. My hypothesis, that is,
that this "we" is a "we, men," does not seem to be contradicted by the
very last "working note," which announces the "plan" of the book and
purports to reject "any compromise with *humanism*," and any beginning
"*ab homine* as Descartes" did. The projected blueprint would hardly have
avoided such a "compromise," I think; and we could probably say the
same of the architecture of *Phenomenology of Perception*. While the second
part he announces (Nature) is a "description of the man-animality *intertwining*" (resembling Husserl's *Ideas II*, precisely in its middle section), the
third part is "neither logic, nor teleology of consciousness," but "a study
of the language that has man." A privilege for man, therefore—man who
is thus called, and, from this point on, called upon to answer for the *logos*
that he does not have, to be sure, but *that has him*; and above all, which "is
realized" solely "through man" and "in man." In truth, this *logos* is nothing but the visible: "*The visible* has to be described as something that is realized through man, but which is nowise [*nullement*] anthropology (hence
against Feuerbach-Marx 1844)" (ibid., p. 274).

Is it enough to assert it? Doesn't this "nowise" [*nullement*] have the energy of a denial? How can something "be described" that "is realized through man" without or beyond an "anthropo-logy"? An anthropo-*logy*? Especially if what is thus *realized* "through man" and "in man" is precisely Logos, the Word? Using another "nowise," Merleau-Ponty further speaks of "Logos also as what is realized in man, but nowise [*nullement*] as his *property*" (ibid., p. 274).[32]

It is therefore always in the form of a denial—a fairly unconvincing denial—that Merleau-Ponty protests against an anthropological interpretation of his design. For example, when he undertakes to demonstrate that "[w]hen we speak of the flesh of the visible, we do not mean to do anthropology, to describe a world covered over with all our own projections" and "it is indeed the paradox of Being, not a paradox of man, that we are dealing with here" (ibid., p. 136), one of his arguments leads to hands, *our* hands: "Yes or no: do we have a body—that is, not a permanent object of thought, but a flesh that suffers when it is wounded, hands that touch? We know: hands do not suffice for touch—but to decide for this reason alone that our hands do not touch, and to relegate them to the world of objects or of instruments, would be, in acquiescing to the bifurcation of subject and object, to forego in advance the understanding of the sensible and to deprive ourselves of its lights" (ibid., p. 137).

What makes reading Merleau-Ponty so troublesome (for me)? What makes the interpretation of his mode of philosophical writing a thing at once passionately exciting and difficult, yet also irritating or disappointing at times? It may be this, in a word: we reencounter the movement that we had evoked—this experience of coincidence *with* noncoincidence, the coincidence of coincidence *with* noncoincidence—transferred to the order of (inconsequential) consequence or (interrupted) continuity in philosophical discourses, and in a way that is not always diachronic—following the evolution or mutation of a way of thinking—but synchronous at times. Shall we give the philosopher credit for this, as I am often tempted to do, or, on the contrary, regret that he was unable to carry out a more powerful reformalization of his discourse in order to thematize and think the law under which he was thus placing himself—always, *in fact*, and all things considered, *preferring* "coincidence" (of coincidence with noncoincidence) to "noncoincidence" (of coincidence with noncoincidence)? Let us remain with our favored subjects, as they are treated in *The Visible and the Invisible*, and give a few examples of this.

Partly, on the one hand, we can recognize an increasing insistence on self-inadequation, dehiscences, fissions, interruptions, incompletion, and the visible body openly gaping, as well as hiatuses, eclipses, the inaccessibility of this plenitude or this reversibility, this pure, sensible reflexivity, which always remains *imminent* (and then the question will always remain: what counts more: is it imminence, always in suspense, or that after which imminence is chasing, driving it and keeping it ever disappointed and breathless? From where is one to depart? With what is one to part? What is imminence? What counts most in it? What the imminence expects, or the fact that it is doomed forever to wait, to wait in vain?). We can even recognize his admission that he had once spoken "summarily of a reversibility of the seeing and the visible, of the touching and the touched"—and the two are now put on the same plane, apparently. And this is the very definition of flesh by way of the recurring figures of *coiling* and *encroaching*:

> Once again, the flesh we are speaking of is not matter. It is the coiling over of the visible upon the seeing body, of the tangible upon the touching body, which is attested in particular when the body sees itself, touches itself seeing and touching the things, such that, simultaneously, *as* tangible it descends among them, *as* touching it dominates them all and draws this relationship and even this double relationship from itself, by dehiscence or fission of its own mass . . . as though the visible body remained incomplete, gaping open. . . . To begin with, we spoke summarily of a reversibility of the seeing and the visible, of the touching and the touched. It is time to emphasize that it is a reversibility always imminent and never realized in fact. My left hand is always on the verge of touching my right hand touching the things, but I never reach coincidence; the coincidence eclipses at the moment of realization, and one of two things always occurs: either my right hand really passes over to the rank of touched, but then its hold on the world is interrupted; or it retains its hold on the world, but then I do not really touch *it*—my right hand touching, I palpate with my left hand only its outer covering. Likewise, I do not hear myself as I hear the others . . . I am always on the same side of my body . . . this incessant escaping [*dérobade*], this impotency to superpose exactly upon one another the touching of the things by my right hand and the touching of this same right hand by my left hand, or to superpose, in the exploratory movements of the hand, the tactile experience of a point and that of the "same" point a moment later, or the auditory experience of my own voice and that of other voices—that is not a failure . . . this hiatus between my right hand touched and my right hand touching, between my voice heard and my voice uttered, between one moment of my tactile life and the following one, is not an onto-

logical void, a non-being: it is spanned [*enjambé*] by the total being of my body. (ibid., pp. 146–48)[33]

We should thus be thinking *at the same time, simultaneously,* this spanning [*enjambement*] "by the total being of my body," and the whole interruption of what, precisely, lets itself be neither "spanned" nor totalized, completed, or reflected. This *at the same time* belongs to the very experience—itself disjoined and synthetic—of *imminence* and *presentiment.* For, just as Merleau-Ponty notes of this imminent reversibility that never happens that it always miscarries, he likewise nonetheless maintains the possibility or virtuality of a synthesis on the score of a "presentiment" or feeling of imminence.[34] This noncoincidence as ever-imminent coincidence, this irreversibility that is always on the verge of becoming reflexive reversibility, is what Merleau-Ponty describes at work in vision *as well as* in touch, and he sometimes puts the two on exactly the same plane, just as he proposes that the situation of the untouchable is rigorously and literally analogous to the situation of the invisible. The untouchable is not a possible (or only "*in fact* inaccessible") tangible, not any more than the invisible, as we recall, is "an *other visible* 'possible,' or a 'possible' visible for an other":

> To touch and to touch oneself (to touch oneself = touched-touching). They do not coincide in the body: the touching is never exactly the touched. This does not mean that they coincide "in the mind" or at the level of "consciousness." Something else than the body is needed for the junction to be made: it takes place in the *untouchable.* That of the other which I will never touch. But what I will never touch, he does not touch either, no privilege of oneself over the other here, it is therefore not the *consciousness* that is the untouchable— "The consciousness" would be something positive, and with regard to it there would recommence, does recommence, the duality of the reflecting and the reflected, like that of the touching and the touched. The untouchable is not a touchable in fact inaccessible—the unconscious is not a representation in fact inaccessible. . . . The untouchable (and also the invisible: for the same analysis can be repeated for vision . . . (ibid., p. 254)

Merleau-Ponty never closed the parenthesis, as Claude Lefort noted when he edited this text, which is so remarkable, so far removed from all those with which we began. The parenthesis remains unclosed, upon an analysis that goes on, on the subject of the visible, and that I should have quoted and closely analyzed *in extenso.*

What does Merleau-Ponty designate by "something else than the body," that is not the mind or consciousness? We shall never be closer to what Nancy—the Nancy who wrote *Corpus*—here shares with Merleau-Ponty; nor closer to the beginning outline of other sharings, proximities, and partitions.

For, *partly*, on the other hand, Merleau-Ponty—in the same passage—intends to retain the "junction"; and in what immediately follows within the parenthesis left open, as in so many other places of this planned book, the "contact . . . with *self* " reappears, as well as "indivision," and a specularity that, through "fission," produces "only a more profound adhesion to Self." The schema of the "corporeal schema" is as unifying and synthetic as a Kantian schema:

> this movement is entirely woven out of contacts with me. . . . The corporeal schema would not be a *schema* if it were not this contact of *self* with *self* (which is rather *non-difference*) (common presentation to . . . *x*)
> The flesh of the world (the "quale") is indivision of this sensible Being that I am and all the rest which feels itself [*se sent*] in me, pleasure-reality indivision—
> The flesh *is a mirror phenomenon*. . . . To touch oneself, to see oneself, is to obtain such a specular extract of oneself. I.e. fission of appearance and Being—a fission that already takes place in the touch (duality of the touching and the touched) and which, with the mirror (Narcissus) is only a more profound adhesion to Self. (ibid., pp. 255–56)

And above all, the logic of this "extract" leads back—reasserting it—to this exemplarity of the hand and the finger, importing with it, in the thinking of flesh, the whole discursive machine that we are questioning here under the heading humanualism.

For example (one month earlier), adjustment and reciprocity govern everything:

> One would here have to study in what sense the other's sensoriality is implicated in my own: to feel my eyes is to feel that they are threatened with being seen—But the correlation is not always thus of the seeing with the seen, or of speaking with hearing: my hands, my face are also of the visible. The case of reciprocity (seeing seen), (touching touched in the handshake) is the major and perfect case, where there is *quasi-reflection (Einfühlung)*, *Ineinander*; the general case is the adjustment of a visible for me to a tangible for me

and of this visible for me to a visible for the other—(for example, my hand). (ibid., p. 245)

Or again, a few months later, this point of the chiasmus where nothing seems to count but reciprocity: "So also the touched-touching. This structure exists in one sole organ—The flesh of my fingers = each of them is phenomenal finger and objective finger, outside and inside of the finger in reciprocity, in chiasm, activity and passivity coupled. The one encroaches upon the other, they are in a relation of real opposition (Kant)—Local *self* of the finger: its space is felt-feeling" (ibid., p. 261).

It would be unfair and violent to reach a conclusion here and close the argument upon the reservations that this exemplarity of the hand, with all that it implies, inspires. Such a closing would be unworthy of what remains open and at work in pages so strong, so alive, which have contributed so much to open a pathway for the thinking of its time, and our time. We shall proceed by questioning (always following Nancy's tracks), this time, this "other's sensoriality . . . implicated in my own" and this "crystallization of the impossible" that seems to sign the very last notes in *The Visible and the Invisible* (March 1961):

> The definition of the *intuitus mentis*, founded on analogy with vision. . . . This analysis of vision is to be completely reconsidered (it presupposes what is in question: the thing itself)—It does not see that the vision is tele-vision, transcendence, crystallization of the impossible.
>
> Consequently, the analysis of the *intuitus mentis* also has to be done over: there is no indivisible by thought, no simple nature . . . all these are "figures" of thought and the "ground" or "horizon" has not been taken into account. (ibid., p. 273)

§ 10 Tangent IV

*Tangency and Contingency, 1: The "question
of technics" and the "aporias" of Flesh,
"(contact, at bottom)"*

Before outlining a new tangential trajectory, it may be appropriate forcefully to recall a primary concern, if not the only one. Because it seems out
of reach to me and moreover of little interest, I am not preparing the arguments of a critical debate, even less a polemical one, between all the "contemporary" ways of thinking about the sense of touch that I am simply, in
gratitude, trying to identify. It is rather a question of beginning timidly
to orient myself inside a kind of movement—or rather *trend* [*mouvance*].
When the ground shifts, it tends to produce solidarities, affinities, filiations,
attractions, mirages, at least, of magnetic fields; together with its divergences,
its lines of fracture, which may be virtual, its fissures or its dislocations.

A "trend" and not a path or line of thinking—for this latter figure also
comes with neo-Heideggerian or pretechnical *connotations*, now, at the very
point where somehow taking into account technics, the *technē of bodies*, or
ecotechnics may deliver to us a criterion for certain discrepancies between
the different motifs of this trend. And it is furthermore a "trend" of thinking and not a "field" or "context," so as to avoid the risk of adding to the
connotations that I have just recalled a hypothesis I hold to be question-
able: it is the hypothesis of a historical space with a strictly determinable,
objectivizable contour; a space with its unity, the self-contact of some self-
identity, an inside and outside; in a word, the whole objective set of a configuration, a "paradigm" or an *epistēmē*, a set that would not be structurally
open—as I believe it remains forever—and that from then on, crouching
on the front lines, could occasionally become a battlefield (*Kampfplatz*) and
a field of appropriation in the good or bad tradition with which I would
like to break here.

The movement of an open trend, therefore: in a mobile itself composed of multiple, no doubt countless, motives, I am trying to isolate a few motifs—just a few—and to stabilize them provisionally: what are called "working hypotheses," arrived at here using the artifice of an abstraction for which I must confess that I have no impeccable justification, and for which I cannot answer in an absolutely responsible fashion. My responsibility, if there I have any, merits the following feeble explanation: such are the markers that are helping to orient me, myself, for the time being, in an ultimately contingent way. These, in short, are the signals with which, swept along by this trend, in a very specific place, which is not a mere observation post, I am somewhat familiar.

Certain writings, as it happens. Which? Well, they are the ones I am going to cite, no less than the ones I have already cited, and that I was led to read, always passionately, profitably, and with admiration (those are my first criteria). Nevertheless, what would I do if I also had to try to justify my *choice* of these texts in a more convinced and convincing way? What if I also had to legitimize my way of organizing my reading of them, and their co-appearance or configuration, within the inevitable and unfair selection process that the setting up of a particular perspective doesn't—ever —fail to impose on the setup of a particular interpretation? I might invoke the rule assigned by an implicit "contract," which is to say, the law of this book, *On Touching—Jean-Luc Nancy*.

Therefore, in this place along the trajectory, I shall try to orient myself toward certain books, in keeping with what has been announced. Once again, which are they? They are some of those on the French and "contemporary" side of the said trend that concern the sense of touch "today," or are partially or totally occupied by this *theme as such*. I shall cull this theme in them myself—in keeping with the artifice that I have just admitted to, if not justified—there where these works themselves have it out with the legacies that have come into question until now, precisely about this privileged motif of touching, at least to the somewhat uncertain extent, no doubt (and this is the heart of the question), that one may identify this motif, and dissociate and measure it, in the very place where Nancy reminds us that "there is no 'the' sense of touch."

In a space itself open and insaturable, these "legacies" would stretch— to cite the departed—from Plato, Aristotle, Plotinus, and the Gospels to Kant and Husserl, and so on; from Descartes, Berkeley, Diderot or Maine de Biran to Ravaisson, Bergson, Levinas, Merleau-Ponty and Deleuze, and so on. This list of names is far from being final or enclosable, and we shall have the opportunity to specify this. Later, Aquinas or John of the Cross, for example, will appear in it.

One can hardly isolate Husserlian phenomenology in the trend of these legacies or filiations, to be sure. By the few signs that we have gathered up to this point, however, we can recognize that it retains a particularly strong and often hegemonic hold on the French zone of the said trend today. That is one of the reasons why I have laid such stress precisely on the Merleau-Pontyian interpretation or transformation, which has just detained us, of this phenomenology of touching. By following these lines of force on the French slope of this trend (let us repeat this in order to remove any possible misunderstanding), I am trying to understand how Nancy *shares* things *out*, and does this at least *virtually*. For as has been said, he almost never cites Merleau-Ponty, even where there is enough room for us to assume that he is familiar with Merleau-Ponty's thinking. Likewise, Nancy does not, I think, cite either of the two books that we are about to tackle (at first simply following the thread that links them to Husserl's *Ideas II*, our main guideline here): neither Didier Franck's nor—with one belated exception, to be specified subsequently—Jean-Louis Chrétien's.

As always in our Nancean use of these words, "sharing out" first of all means participation, indisputable proximity, affinities, crossings, crossovers and crossbreedings—a sort of community or contemporaneity of thinking, language, and discourse. I summarize this under the heading "tangency." But they also mean something else—as always in the Nancean sense of these words—that is, a partitioning that imparts the parts, an *other departure* ("other departure" is a quotation from Nancy that I shall shortly clarify), another way of proceeding, another writing, as well as the uneasy turbulence of another determination (which is often concealed and barely decipherable under the shelter of utterances seemingly stemming from the same *koinē*), another experiencing of decision making, another gesture of thought, which is also another experiencing of the body, that is, another body and another *corpus*. Let me put this bluntly, with just a few words whose meaning remains largely undecided: this difference, this partitioning, this alterity of bodies follows the line (a line that is often barely visible and still quite enigmatic) partly of the *technical* and partly of a *beyond Christianity*. The self-seeking body, seeking to touch itself without touching itself, like any other, throughout Nancy's corpus, is *partly* a body that is originarily and essentially friendly and open to the *technē* (transplantation, prosthetic devices, substitutions, metonymies, tele-sensible expropriations, and so on) that he gives us to ponder and weigh (since we are not yet sure what to think under the heading of this word): without this *technē* this body is not even born to itself as "human" body, caught up in a hominization process exceeding the human as its past and future. And *partly*, on the other hand, this body is involved in a "deconstruction of Christianity," of the Christian body, a *deconstruction of Christian "flesh,"* a deconstruction that—even if it seems impossible and unending—already leaves its signature right on the singularity of the corpus in question—giving us the said "Christian body" to ponder and weigh (since we are not yet sure what to think under the heading of this word). Here, then, is my hypothesis once again, and I proffer it shyly and a little uneasily: there is some sharing out as parting, in the sense of partition or separation, or new departure, in this taking into account of *technē*, there where (in the same gesture) it reaches beyond the Christian body. As such, we cannot read this gesture (a gesture all at once double and one) in the other texts about touching that have come into question up to this point, no more than in the ones that I shall now still hail as forceful, necessary, rich, and new: a couple of books by Didier Franck and Jean-Louis Chrétien respectively.

The idiomatic singularity of the gesture is never pure or purely reappropriable, and it cannot be separated from a scene, at times, a mise-en-scène, a strategy, or a discursive *tactics*. We know that "tactics" does not point toward anything tactile but toward order, arrangement, a more or less calculated disposition. More than a style, or a *manner* (things having to do with fingers or hands), it is here a moving of the body, a syntax that reckons without reckoning, with its whole body, "in the flesh" [*en chair et en os*], to tackle things, be in the world, and be in touch with it without touching or tampering with it.

Before recommencing, in order to convey the keynote of Nancy's sharing out (in the double sense of the term), let us read two long passages from *Corpus* to stand in for the book as a whole.

1. I am culling the first one from two chapters, titled "Glorious Body" and "Incarnation"—in a book that continuously has it out with the history of the Christian body, and thus with what we term "flesh." While here and there I have questioned the translation of *Leib* as "flesh" [*chair*] (and we shall come back to this) and wondered about the extraordinary way in which this word and concept, "flesh" [*la* chair], has stretched across the

French philosophical landscape; while on several occasions, I have taken note of Christian accentuations and figures in Merleau-Ponty's thinking about "the" flesh [*la* chair] (*the* flesh of my own body proper; "my incarnation"; or "*the* flesh of the world" in *The Visible and the Invisible*), and at the time of *Phenomenology of Perception* already, in allusions to an "operation of Grace," the Eucharist, and "sensation [that] is literally a form of communion" (a rhetoric that no pedagogical intention can quite neutralize), I have not done this in order to denounce, or criticize, or even suspect any— latent or open—*Christianity*. Just as it is neither enough to present oneself as a Christian nor to "believe" or "believe oneself to be a Christian" in order to hold forth in a language that is "authentically" Christian, likewise it is not enough *not* to "believe" or believe oneself and declare oneself *non*-Christian in order to utter a discourse, speak a language, and even inhabit one's body while remaining safely sheltered from all Christianity. This is not about being free of harm, safe, and saved, seeking one's salvation or immunity outside of Christianity. These values would still be Christian ones. That is why, as I have suggested on several occasions, even if there were any sense to or necessity for it, the "deconstruction of Christianity" that Nancy has announced seems such a difficult, paradoxical, almost impossible task, always in danger of being exposed as mere Christian hyperbole. This is not to say that one should give up beforehand and not show any interest in the singular limitations of such hyperbole in order to think it. Georges Bataille protested against those who saw a shameful Christian in him by shielding himself behind the hyperbole of an ultimate mask (was it a mask?): what he sometimes referred to as his "hyper-Christianity."

Here, then, is the announced passage to give the right note; as always, it is violently excerpted, despite the length of the quotation: one should re-read everything before and after it. Here in any case, Nancy himself sets forth this double *sharing out*, which is necessary and impossible. But what I would emphasize here, above all, so as to measure the split with regard to modern French discourses on *the* "flesh" and incarnate touching, the discourses that we are in the process or still on the verge of studying, is his taking into account of *plasticity* and *technicity*. Opening onto the history of animalities and hominization, the latter reach, at a stroke, beyond the anthropological, anthropotheological, or even ontotheological limits within which phenomenology stands, in spite of so many reductions and denials (and we have just seen an example of this with Merleau-Ponty)—not to mention other philosophies that do not even pretend to carry out this reduction of an anthropology or a "wordliness" in general. What seems to prescribe this necessary taking into account of plasticity and technicity "at the heart" of the "body proper" is an irreducible *spacing*, that is, what spaces out touching itself, namely con-tact. In thus opening up a gap and making room for the hiatus of noncontact at the heart of contact, this spacing makes for the trial of noncontact as the *very* condition or experience *itself* of contact, the *selfsame* experience itself of the *same* open forever —and spaced out by the other. Such an experience is always affected by the singularity of that which—by reason of this spacing—*takes place*, which is to say, by the event of a coming. *Taking place* and *taking the place of*, I would add, in order to inscribe the possibility of metonymy and substitution, that is, of technical prosthetics, right onto the very singularity itself of the event.

Taking place and taking the place of: taking place while taking the place of, taking place in lieu of *taking the place of—by virtue of taking the place of and in view of taking the place of: held (in place) to taking the place of: taking the place of taking place.*[1] (If I wonder how any translator could take this on and translate the idiomatic phrases I am suggesting and emphasizing in this way, it is also because they say something about the operation of every translation, in its im-possible essence, there where it is a *mano a mano* struggle between idioms, which will never be spared its metonymies, substitutions, and technical prostheses. Translation, where it is a considerable event in thinking,[2] is *held to (the place of) taking the place of . . .*)

As far as this taking-place is concerned, Nancy always pairs "touching one another" and "distancing oneself," coupling and placing them side by side and putting them in contact or contiguity. And this, I think, also opens onto organic articulation, *technē*, substitution, prosthetics, the *place of taking the place, what is held to taking the place of* something—from before man, before humans, well before and thus well beyond the humanualism of the-hand-of-man. I have quoted other examples of this. Here, Nancy says, as he does fairly regularly: "touching one another, distancing themselves," or "they are touching and pushing one another away." He further says, "God had made himself into a body; he had stretched out . . . " —yet another version of extended Psyche . . . :

Glorious Body

In truth, God's body was the body of man himself: man's flesh was the body that God had given himself. (Man is—absolutely—body, or he is not: he is the body of God, or the world of bodies, but nothing else. That is why, destined to signify, oversignify, and insignify his body, man, the "man" of "humanism," has slowly dissolved this body and himself all at once.) God had made himself into a body; he had stretched out. . . . This ambivalence of the truth of the body, as *glorious body*, works its way through all of ontotheology. . . . And if the *body* is, par excellence, what is *created*, if "created body" is a tautology—or rather "created bodies," for (*the*) Body *is* always in the plural—then *the body is the plastic matter of a spacing out* without form or Idea. The body is the very plasticity of expansion, of extension, in accordance with which existences *take place*. . . . But the body is a *coming into presence*, in the way and manner of images that come to a television screen, or movie screen, coming not *of* and *from* the depths of the screen, but rather *being* this screen, this screen spaced out, and existing as the screen's extension . . . but *on* [*à même*] my eyes themselves (my body), as their areality: the eyes themselves come to this coming, they are spaced out, spacing out, themselves a screen, and are less a "vision" than a *video*. (Not "video" = "I see," but *video* as a generic appellation for the *technē* of coming into presence. *Technē*: "technics," "art," "modalization," "creation."). . . . Its coming, thus, will never be finished; it *goes* as it comes; it is coming-and-going; it is the rhythm of bodies born, bodies dying, bodies that are open, closed, bodies in pleasure, bodies in pain, bodies touching one another, distancing themselves. Glory is the rhythm, or the plastic expression, of this presence—which is local, bound to be local.

Incarnation

But all along this tradition, there is the other version of a coming into presence and its *technē*. The other, the same—they are indiscernible yet distinct, paired as in lovemaking. "The" body will always have been on the limit of these two versions, there where, at the same time, they are touching and pushing one another away. The body—its truth—will always have been the in-between of two *senses* and *ways*—and among those, the in-between of left and right, up and down, front and back, phallic and cephalic, male and female, inside and outside, sensible sense and intelligible sense, do nothing but interact expressibly.

Incarnation is the name of the other version of the *coming*. When I say *verbum caro factum est (logos sarx egeneto)*, I am saying in a sense that it is *caro* that makes for the glory and the genuine coming of *verbum*. But all at once I say—in another meaning altogether—that *verbum* (*logos*) makes for the genuine presence and sense of *caro* (*sarx*). And though, *in a sense and in a way* (once more), these two versions are part and parcel of one another, and though "incarnation" names them both together, yet, *in another sense and another way*, they exclude one another. (Nancy, *Corpus*, pp. 54–58)

2. We can dissociate none of these motifs: the project of a "deconstruction of Christianity," long announced or prepared; the attention paid to the *"technē* of bodies" and ecotechnics that "deconstruct the system of ends," there where we are in "the *technē* of the *next* one," the "fellow man" (Nancy, *Corpus*, p. 79); a certain decentering of the hand and the fingers; the connection between the interrupting spacing out of con-tact and the question of the technical, and so forth. When I take them together, they seem to draw the shared-out *dividing line* [*la ligne de partage*], about the problem of touch, between Nancy's *corpus* (to which, for all too obvious reasons, I have been feeling so close for so long) and other problematics of touch, all remarkable, neighboring, yet dissimilar, ones, including the ones already evoked (especially Merleau-Ponty's), or the ones that I shall try to identify with Didier Franck and Jean-Louis Chrétien. These thinkers have spawned original works, while sooner or later referring to Husserl's *Ideas II* —and let me repeat that it is on this score, first of all, that I am privileging the reading of these works. They also, albeit differently, according to their separate trajectories, but with equal intensity, take some account of the irreducibility of the *other* and of the *untouchable* in the experience of touching; and they sometimes pay a certain attention to a spacing out or interruption as the paradoxical and intervallic "medium" of con-tact.

But of them, who from the beginning would have associated with that the plastic and substitutive structure of prosthetics or the *technical* supplement? Who takes it into account, as it has always seemed to me that one should do, and as Nancy has never failed to do, with an increasingly legible insistence, a powerful conceptual consistency that has always remained indissociable from his forceful writing (or exscription)? Apart from him, in dealing with touch at least, who has recognized the locus of this *technical* supplementarity of the body and acknowledged its essential and necessary originarity, as it seems to me that one should always do (and that of course is what is orienting me here)? It goes without saying that "essential originarity" is conveniently translating this "law" into a classical language that precisely meets its limit here. For this supplementarity of technical prosthetics originarily spaces out, defers, or expropriates all originary properness: there is no "the" sense of touch, there is no "originary" or essentially originary touching before it, before its necessary possibility—for any living being in general, and well before "the hand of man" and all its imaginable substitutes. A technique, a mechanical technique (always—but how much more manifestly so, henceforth, in present and future machines) is what can discriminate or "perceive" by functioning with the simulacrum of something "sensible" (with light, "digital" contact and odorous compounds, for example) but is not "feeling," does not give in to the distribution or hierarchization of the "five senses," and above all does not feel itself feel—and thus remains anesthetic in the very place where a machine supplies, and stands in for, sense. And there where the self-relation of a "self-touching" is missing, for example, be it in what we term our "body proper," the place opens up for some machine, some prosthesis, some metonymic substitute, and some sense replacing some other sense. That is where the dividing lines are going to run, I believe.

To limit the risks of an appropriating interpretation and literally better to display the way in which Nancy does what he says he will, and *writes*, and *incorporates* what he thinks into *exscribing*, here is a second passage from *Corpus* here. We could find others as well in the same book whose scope is virtually analogous. But this one exhibits more manifestly and densely than ever this indissociability of "touch" (of "the" sense of touch that "isn't") and technical supplementarity. Nancy is no doubt also doing this in a deliberately philosophical fashion, which is also demonstrative, performative, and actual, but in an act that is neither active nor performative throughout nor just a speech act or simply a discursive act. (Let me say in passing that what I try to think here is that which—by way of the event, by way of what happens singularly, the event, the arriving of the newcomer—routs and exceeds any performative power.) In this text, Nancy also says that he lets the other come, and lets the other body co-appear, and this does not necessarily mean to say "come into presence," it seems to me, but come, yes—at least if the host [*l'hôte*] does not shut the door upon the guest arriving [*l'arrivance de l'hôte*]. This text, the beginning of the chapter titled "Corpus: Other Departure," it seems to me, is precisely the touchstone most surely allowing us to recognize all the parts shared out that we are attempting or will attempt to think. Here again, what seems most distinctive and determining is what links a dissemination of haptics with the body's technical character. Note that this passage is *here*, in this very place, under the command of a conditional commitment (*il faudrait* [would be needed]), an "almost without waiting," which displaces or spaces out the very here-and-now and (strange speech act, indeed) presents itself as an untenable promise, certainly, yet one that exists and insists *here* in the untenable of what "deals" (and is dealt with) here—or writes, or exscribes. And let us be attentive to the "touching" of such *hands* (in parentheses) of which it is said that "something diverts and defers" it "infinitely—machines":

Corpus: Another Departure

A *corpus* is not a discourse, and it is not a narrative. A *corpus* is what is needed [*qu'il faudrait*] here, then. *Here*—there is something like a promise that this has to *deal* with the body, that it is *going* to deal with it—there, almost without waiting [*délai*]. It is a kind of promise that will be neither the object of a treatise nor the topic of citations and recitations, nor the character or set of a story. To put it in so many words, there is a sort of promise tacitly to *hush* [*se taire*]—a promise less to hush up "on the subject" of the body than *hush off the body* [*se taire du corps*], materially to draw away the body from the printing of meaningful impressions, that is, to do this *here, right on the selfsame writing and reading page.* Bodies are in touch on this page, whether we want it or not; or else, the page itself is the touching and toying [*attouchement*] (by my writing hand and your hands holding the book). Something diverts and defers this touching infinitely—machines, conveyances, photocopies, eyes, and other hands have interfered—but what remains is the infinitesimally small, stubborn, and tenuous grain, the minute dust of contact, a contact that is interrupted and pursued in all parts. In the end, your gaze touches upon the same character tracings that mine are touching now, and you are reading me, and I am writing you. In some place, in *some parts*, that is what takes place. Sudden transmittal, as facsimile-copying machines exemplify it, is not a feature of these parts. Rather than fax-similitude here, this is about diversion and dissimilarity, transposing and reencoding, which is to say that "some parts" distribute themselves over very long technical circuits; "some parts" *is* the technical—our discrete, powerful, and disseminated *contact*. And in a silent flash, a suspending of the circuits, the touch of the promise: we'll be silent about the body, leave the field to it, and only write, only read to abandon to bodies the places of their contacts.

Because of this untenable promise, which no one can keep or has ever made—despite its insistence, there, in some parts—a *corpus* is needed, that is, a catalogue instead of a logos. (Nancy, *Corpus*, pp. 46–47)

If one reads on (as one *needs* to do), one will perhaps see, in the place of a certain "here lies" (although Nancy does not want any individual here), a persona making a comeback after twelve years, namely, Psyche, "ausgedehnt, weiss nichts davon," the mask or ghost of the reclining, extended one, who knows nothing about this: "A *corpus* is needed, which is to say a writing of the dead that has nothing to do with the discourse of Death—

and everything to do with this: the space of bodies is not acquainted with Death (fantasizing space abolished) but knows each body as a dead one, as *this* dead one who shares out for us the extension of his or her 'here lies' [*ci-gît*]. It is not the discourse of being-*toward*-Death, but the writing of the dead ones' horizontality as the birth of the extension of all our bodies, all our *more than* living bodies" (ibid., p. 49).

To keep "giving the key" and inscribe what follows to resonate with it or rather serve as counterpoint, let us recall finally that Nancy is also very sensitive to the strange—*aporetic*—relation that Husserl's phenomenology, like everything that trails it, has with its own limit. It is a limit that it "touches" and "transgresses," too, by the same token. The aporia here consists in touching, attaining, reaching, and meeting a limit that bars any passage, to be sure; but also, by the same token, in getting embroiled in the contradiction that consists in passing the limit that one should not cross at the moment one touches it. In a passage evoked earlier, Nancy refers to Husserl's *Cartesian Meditations* and specifies: "It is undoubtedly here, more than anywhere else, that Husserl shows how phenomenology itself touches its own limit and exceeds it: it is no longer the egoical core, but the world 'as a constituted sense' that shows itself to be constitutive [*Cartesian Meditations*, p. 137].[3] The constitution is itself constituted."[4]

I refer to this as an aporia because, first of all, concerning touch, everything started in this book with what Aristotle's *Peri psuchēs* already calls aporias. But it is also because the force of the remarkable book by Didier Franck, *Chair et corps: Sur la phénoménologie de Husserl* (where we are about to follow certain pathways) particularly stems from its own tireless debate with certain aporias of phenomenology.[5] It is greatly to his credit that in naming them and analyzing them as such, he never seeks a pretext in them that would lead him to a conclusive verdict of paralysis, or to criticize, discredit, disqualify, and even less to abandon or simply interrupt phenomenological work—even when this work works against the principles it puts forward as its own.

The first of these aporias seems to prohibit any access to what defined the very perspective of the book, and its problematic and program, that is, an "analytics of incarnation,"[6] which is simultaneously invited and prohibited by the need, indicated above all in the *Cartesian Meditations*, to take into account a "splitting of the ego" and the "pregiving [*pré-donation*] of the alter ego."[7]

Although Franck mentions Merleau-Ponty only infrequently,[8] we can imagine the virtual presence of the latter's way of treating flesh—and precisely in his relationship with Husserl. But we can also imagine a charged silence discreetly filled with implicit, virtual reservations about Merleau-Ponty's reading of Husserl, somehow surveying him from above, precisely on the subject of *Einfühlung* and the alter ego. The first aporia would thus have to do with the closing of an egology, the reduction to the *eidos* ego in which intuition—like the variation that leads there—cannot fail to presuppose the giving of other egos. The alternative would then be between, on the one hand, a breaking away from solipsism "without phenomenological justification," and, on the other, the "skeptical absurdity" of a "transcendental empiricism." Noting that this "aporia" "has not escaped Husserl's vigilance," Franck immediately announces that the "solution" might come by way of an analysis of the immanent temporality of the ego, which would bring out either a doubling of the flux, and thus the involvement of the alter ego in the *eidos* ego, or the taking into account of an "archefacticity" [*Urfaktizität*] of the ego—two things that Husserl seems moreover to recognize in a text from 1931 that Franck cites (*Chair et corps*, p. 67): "Teleology. Implication of the *eidos* transcendental intersubjectivity in the *eidos* transcendental ego. Fact and *eidos*."[9]

Instead of going along with *all* the consequences that Franck draws from this, step by step (it would be necessary to do this but is impossible here), I limit myself, as always, to what touches on touching, and more precisely contact as "contact from oneself to oneself." Now, after he has taken into account the famous passages about touching in *Ideas II*, after he has answered "perhaps" to the question seeking to find out whether "touching, as contact from oneself to oneself first of all," constitutes, inasmuch as it is fleshly, the support of localized sensations,[10] Franck takes on the theme (which he views as essential) of a sort of priority of flesh over immanent time. He then comes to name contact ("which is to say contact, at bottom," he notes in parentheses) as the very thing itself ("flesh," in truth, "touching, as contact from oneself to oneself first of all") that is presupposed by immanent temporality itself and is therefore what would *precede* time itself, by reason of this presupposition. Without flesh (that is, without contact), there is no pure temporalization. Far from being first and being only (as absolute proximity) the self-presence of a spatial *here*, contact is what makes possible the temporalization of time. Contact gives time—a formula that comes back more than once in these pages. But it is from an "absolute movement," not temporal and yet the origin of time, that this contact makes temporalization possible. Contact, at the origin of time, is *not yet* temporal.

What is important for Franck, as it were, is that "flesh" (here, contact itself, "(which is to say contact, at bottom)," "contact from oneself to oneself") "precedes" time in a way, and thus it is from an untemporal locus that contact gives time. Before we recognize the programmatic consequence that Franck draws from this (beyond Husserl and Heidegger, if one may say so, and he does say it), let us focus on the decisive moment in the sequence of his argument where "contact" is renamed and defined, in sum, as "untemporal," to which I refer the reader: "flesh must always be given in the flux of time; otherwise the now-moment of the tone could never be 'incarnate,' as the 'Lectures on Time'[11] put it. In addition, flesh must 'precede' temporality if temporality is constituted in a hyletic flux" (Franck, *Chair et corps*, p. 190).

In putting the word "precede" in quotes, Franck thus designates this untemporal anteriority (which is of course inconceivable and unsayable: how is one to "precede" time? What is this temporal "not yet"?). He does hold to this untemporal anteriority, and this explains the meaning of his "in addition," that is, of this problematic overbid making it permissible to go from a "flesh" "always" "given in the flux of time" to a flesh supposed to "precede" time: "In addition, flesh must 'precede' temporality if temporality is constituted in a hyletic flux." Why should that which is always given in time "precede" time?

This question is of interest to us here—in itself as well as beyond the interpretative discussion in which I shall briefly indulge. It is of interest to us where it "touches" on an experience of tactility and touching of the other —in the caress, for example. (But it will have become noticeable that I always worry a little about certain connotations of the word, I mean the "word" "caress" and not all the "things" that it purports to name, as much as I worry about those too, the same, for the same reasons, at bottom, of the word "flesh" and the carnal, which is to say the cherishing and dear [*carus*] charity [*caritas*] in the caress of the former, and the incarnation [*caro, carnis*] of the latter.) What is the time of touching? Does touching—does the tactility of con-tact, in the syncopated interruption that allows its advent—give time or retract it? Does it give it, all the while retracting it, retracing it? Does it retract it in giving it? What about this retraction or withdrawal of a gift? What relation is there with syncopes and the sharing out and parting of time? What relation with spacing and metonymies, plasticity, prosthetics, and technics, which are important for us here in the ecotechnics and *technē* of bodies? And so forth.

I would invoke the double motif, which is classical in Husserl, of *epochē* and the nonreal [*non-réelle*] inclusion of noemata in the phenomenological life (*Erlebnis*) of consciousness here, if I had to bring forth arguments from a point of view that would be neither Nancy's nor Franck's (and yet would not oppose them) about what *phenomenologically suspends* contact *in* contact and divides it right within tactile experience in general, thus inscribing an anesthetic interruption into the heart of aesthesic phenomenality. *On the one hand*, from the threshold of its possibility onward, epochal reduction suspends the reality of contact in order to deliver its intentional or phenomenal sense: this interruption or suspensive conversion gives me the *sense* of contact, as such. I therefore cannot fully have *both* contact *and* the sense of contact. For *on the other hand*—another interruption, another conversion, another unpertaining [*désappartenance*]—the noematic content (corresponding to the includedness, which is then real, of a hylomorphic noesis or correlation) can only appear and can only be phenomenalized, by *really* pertaining *neither* to the touched thing (whatever it is, transcendent or immanent thing, my skin or the other's) *nor* to the stuff of my *Erlebnis*. Such is the law of *phainesthai*. This double possibility (*epochē* and *real* nonpertaining of the intentional sense content) would open up the spacing of a distance, a disadhering [*désadhérance*], a *différance* in the very "inside" of haptics—and *aisthēsis* in general. Without this *différance*, there would be no contact *as such*; contact would not appear; but with this *différance*, contact never appears in its full purity, never in any immediate plenitude, either. In both cases, the phenomenality, or the phenomenology, of contact is interrupted or diverted; it is suspended *in view of contact*. Such haptical (or aesthesic in general) *différance*, which is interruption, interposition, detour of the between *in the middle* of contact, could analogically open onto what Nancy calls a "syncope" or what Chrétien terms *interval*, the "intervallic character of touch itself," in a book to which we shall soon refer.[12] But whatever concrete, "technical," or "prosthetic" form it wears to determine itself between a skin and something, or between two skins (instruments, veils, clothing, gloves, condoms, and so on), this *différance* of the *between*, this elementary *différance* of inter-position or intervals between two surfaces is at the same time the condition of contact and the originarily spaced opening that calls for technical prosthetics and makes it possible, without any delay. What calls for "technics," then, is phenomenological necessity itself. It is not even a moment; it is an *anesthetic* instance, a unpertaining that maintains its hold on aesthesic appertaining or participation, and pertains to it—that is to say insensibility in, and as, sensibility; anesthetics as the very ecstasy at the heart of pleasure. Phenomenologies must bow before the truth of this ecstasy—not give up in front of pleasure, but ply it and pray. Faced with pleasure as *différance.* Ply, plait, pray, and invent substitutes, prostheses, fetishes, culture, technics—that is, all of "history," as it were, before and beyond "the hand of man."

Let us now come back to the passage in which Franck puts the word "precede" in quotation marks ("flesh must 'precede' temporality"). The question comes down to the one raised by the conversion of omnitemporality into untemporality in the next paragraph. The nerve of the argument seems at the same time powerful and troubling, in accordance with a necessity that is logical yet arbitrary: for what "gives time," what makes time possible, or even what is coextensive with time, that is, omnitemporal, would *not* be *temporal,* at least not *in time.* This argument interests us here to the very extent that what is thus designated, what is supposedly "preceding" time—with all the consequences that Franck wants to draw from this—is a hyletic sensuality of flesh as *contact,* contact as self-contact:

> However strange this priority of flesh over immanent time may appear, stranger still is that this has not escaped Husserl. The latter had already implied this priority in the text where he criticized his own analysis of internal time-consciousness and asked himself whether he should not presume a universal intentionality of impulses that would constitute all originary present and ensure the unity of the flux;[13] and he expressly acknowledges and recognizes this priority in a 1930 manuscript:
>
>> In the flux of primordial presence, we have a bodily perception, always already (*immer schon*) and immutably (*unabänderlich*); and thus in the temporalization of immanent time, my bodily perception continually goes through this whole time, omnitemporally constituting this body synthetically, identically.[14]
>
> (Franck, *Chair et corps,* p. 190)

It will have been noted that Husserl here in no way speaks of any "priority" of flesh over time, though Franck gives him credit for not having disregarded this "priority." Husserl speaks of omnitemporality, and con-

tinually going through—and this is something different. Nor does he say
that this continual movement—even if it is indissociable from temporalization—is the "origin" of time. To be sure, the translation of *omnitemporality* by *untemporality*, and temporalization movement or "absolute movement" by "origin" of time is not purely arbitrary. Even if it may seem
rather violent here, it could find its justification in some long detours inside and outside Husserl's text. However, beyond a rigorous reading of this
Husserlian manuscript, what comes to light here is the aim of this interesting forced interpretation in Franck's strategy precisely where it is a question
of *contact*, "contact from oneself to oneself"—for this is our sole thematic
focus here—and a certain connection between *contact* and *con-tingency*.
Let us read what follows before being more specific about this aim. The
passage presents itself as a commentary or rather the consequence drawn
from the manuscript that was just cited:

> If the perception of the flesh of my body proper, which can here only mean
> the perception of my flesh by itself (which is to say contact, at bottom), con-
> tinually and integrally traverses time, it is because it is the very "movement" of
> temporalization, an absolute movement, which moreover is not temporal be-
> cause time finds its origin in it. Flesh constitutes time, but since every flesh
> bears upon another flesh, one can say that carnal difference and carnal rela-
> tionships are temporalizing time. (ibid., pp. 190–91)

Abutting on time, on the temporalization of time, at the origin of the
synthesis of time as relation and linking from oneself to oneself, from one
now to another, there is contact, flesh, "contact from oneself to oneself,"
"(. . . contact, at bottom)"—the time to give and be given time, the time
to touch and be touched, as well. The aim of this audacious interpretation
is at least double. Let us quickly—too quickly—mention the two gestures
positing the need, first, to overrun the bounds of a certain intentional analytics toward an existential analytics (from a certain Husserl toward a certain Heidegger), then, second, to overrun such an existential analytics,
which would only be "oriented and dominated by temporality" (*Sein und
Zeit*, as it were). The two movements would be made necessary by what
links contact (flesh, at bottom, "contact from oneself to oneself") with
archefacticity as con-tingency, and on the other hand, as we just saw, by
what, in the contact of flesh, in flesh as contact, *precedes* time.[15]

Let us rather tend to this connection between contact and contingency.
Latin affords us this chance—a chance that Franck invests, and in which

he invests in a very active fashion. It allows him to articulate between the two the haptocenteredness of *Ideas II* (about the constitution of the *Leib* and its self-relation by way of touch only) and the theme of an archefacticity of the "flesh" or rather "carnal difference," which resists a certain phenomenology, that is, both its eidetics and the "variation" that it implies, and a kind of contract between phenomenality and intentionality. If a single word—the best word, in a word—named the connection between archefacticity and touching, it would be "contingency." The word "contingent" retains all the resources obtained from its philosophical filiation, while also emancipating itself from it, becoming younger in one blow, and it thus reappears at the end of the book, with a hyphen that recalls and underscores its etymological contact with touching.[16] But in an earlier chapter, "The Caress and the Shock" ["La caresse et le choc"],[17] it was already a strongly vested word. For several reasons—strategic and semantic ones, in a way—this chapter is particularly important for us here.

1. On the one hand, this chapter steps forward, so to speak, to meet what is termed "aporia" on several occasions (and since the first mention of Aristotle at the beginning of this book, I have said why this word seems necessary to us, and why we might find it enlightening if we accompany it throughout this whole history of philosophy as the aporetic history of a haptology and an (over)interpretation of touch). 2. Then, on the other hand, this chapter fastens upon a reference to the passage in *Ideas II* dealing with the privilege of touch in the constitution of the body proper. Franck puts the word or concept of *contingence* [contingency] in charge of a difficult, or even impossible, mission: take on the phenomenological filiation and drive it where it seems not to have been able to go. He does this by finally proposing a series of "performative" decisions, and coming up with names or nicknames—the word "con-tingency," among them, is not alone, as we shall see in a moment.

Let us come back to this configuration. Just before the opening of the chapter "The Caress and the Shock," Franck recalls the "aporias" that he has followed in their development (ibid., p. 155) and concentrates this reminder around the notion of *Verflechtung*, interlacing [*entrelacement*] (now, at least since Merleau-Ponty, commonly translated into French by *entrelacs* and into English by "intertwining")—here, first of all, the intertwining between originary *presentation* and (indirect, analogical, empathic) *appresen-*

tation. The intertwining between present and nonpresent is what ensures "the presence of the alter ego at the very heart of the ego" and by the same token, by not leaving phenomenology powerless before the problem of the other, provides it with a threatening resource: it can no longer retreat toward an egological sphere that is absolutely proper, by way of transcendental reduction. And so, in the next chapter, "The Caress and the Shock," the word "aporia" reappears, and then it is a matter of following the efforts of an intentional analysis to "resolve the aporia" of a "presentation" that is "at the same time" (*zugleich*) "appresentation" (ibid., pp. 160–61).

The reader of these two pages may judge how rich and necessary they are. I shall do no more than retain from them two powerful initiatives, which have in common that they are partial to writing and naming and entail considerably important stakes in each instance. At issue, *on the one hand* (A), is what the words "flesh," "fleshly," "incarnate," and "incarnation" are in charge of *translating*, and, *on the other hand* (B), the three values that the word "con-tingency" has as its mission to *condense*. Therefore: *translation* and *condensation*.

A. *Translation.* I have already evoked this delicate passage across the border between German and French. Since Merleau-Ponty, the more or less systematic translation of *Leib* by "flesh" [*chair*] may, strictly speaking, be justified. We could substitute "flesh" for "body proper" for the good reasons that Franck gives for doing so (ibid., p. 99),[18] despite the risk of some unerasable connotations that "flesh" may risk importing, be it noted, where the question of the "Christian body" keeps reopening. To be sure, not everything in the word "flesh" comes down to Christian semantics; asserting such a thing would be absurd or imprudent. However, it would be equally imprudent to ignore the filing and scraping action of this semantics, even where the ones using this word may be anything except "Christians" and would not for a single moment dream of putting their discourse about flesh at the service of a Christian cause intentionally. Likewise, we could justify—strictly, *but only in certain cases or contexts*—the translation of *Leibhaftigkeit* by "incarnation."

But don't things become less certain with regard to the translation of the *use* that Husserl and Heidegger, for example, make of the adverb or adjective *leibhaftig*? Or *Leibhaftigkeit*—when all this word does is constitute a noun based on the common use of the adjective? May one legitimately see in it a more or less thematic and deliberate reference to some flesh or in-

carnation, or, as Franck suggests, one that is denied, avoided, and repressed? Besides, common sense itself stops us from believing that the reference to flesh and incarnation—beneath the word *leibhaftig*—is *at the
same time* explicit or thematic (thus lending Franck the authority to translate it steadily by "incarnate" or "carnally") *and* denied, avoided, repressed,
in any case unacknowledged (which is also something Franck says: his thesis comes down to maintaining that, despite the frequent use of this word
in some texts, in Heidegger as well as Husserl, "the question of the sense of
flesh does not arise" [ibid., p. 21];[19] hence, the translation of *leibhaftig* by
"incarnate"—which is certainly not illegitimate—but also giving "incarnate" a powerfully vested meaning, which is an altogether different matter). Neither in Husserl nor in Heidegger does this everyday expression
(*leibhaftig*), in the quoted texts, necessarily refer to some living flesh, it
seems to me, but only to what relates to the ipseity (*Selbstheit*) of the thing
itself, to the experience of it that is given, without re-presentative or substitutive detour, whether this thing is present to intuition in general (in
Husserl) or *perceptive* intuition (in Heidegger, about Husserlian phenomenology, that is, in the text that Franck cites: we'll come back to it).[20] This
is so, even when this thing is not essentially *living*—no more than the experience that relates to it—and has neither *flesh* nor "bone" [n'a *chair* ou
os], nor *anyone*, or any *person*, allowing one to say, as one says all too often
and easily in French, that it then presents itself in the "flesh and bone" [*en
chair et en os*], *in the flesh, in person*, which is to say, for example, an essence
aimed at by an intuition of an essence [*Wesensschau*] or a transcendent material thing aimed at by a perceptive intuition, such as this bridge about
which Heidegger speaks in the text[21] that is quoted at the beginning of a
discussion deserving all the more to be closely followed in that it conditions the problematic, the strategy, and the fundamental lexicon of Franck's
original book. I suppose that the latter would be the first to know that he
is carrying out an active displacement here—too violent, some might say;
I would say, powerful in its interpretation—of the everyday use and our
ear's traditional reception of the word *leibhaftig*. When he, in two instances,
modifies Ricœur's translation of *Ideen I*[22] and substitutes "incarnate" for
"bodily"—already an equivocal risk, indeed—the result is not less ambiguous, or less chancy, where it is only a question of the intuition of an
essence in its *ipseity*.[23] For the essence in question may be the essence of
anything whatsoever and even of that which, though appearing to be *leibhaftig* (an everyday expression, therefore, here to express the thing itself,

the thing appearing in a presentive intuition [*intuition donatrice*], and most often in a perception, but always without representative substitute), does not necessarily have a "body proper" or a "flesh"—any more than (necessarily, essentially, structurally) does the intuition that tends to it. This equivocality started in France, as we know, where it was all too often thought necessary to translate *leibhaftig* (the everyday, figurative term, as I would like to insist—and risk a banality) by "in person" or "in the flesh" [*en chair et en os*] (alas, the Italian translation of Husserl also says *in carne ed ossa*). But still—one could have understood the phrases "in person" or "in the flesh" in a weakly figurative fashion, as one can in German, I think, in the original text, without turning *everything* that appears before intuition or perception (and therefore the world itself, if we follow Merleau-Ponty) into a *flesh* in the proper sense, an *incarnation*, or a carnal thing.

Franck must therefore reject both the everyday use of the word (which is vaguely and conventionally metaphorical) and the reading of this use (which is also common, and vaguely and conventionally metaphorical) in order to justify his intervention and the systematic recourse to the lexicon of literal incarnation (if I may put it this way) in translating *leibhaftig*. He does this in a complex passage; in it, I believe I can read an uneasy awareness, right after the sentence modified in Ricœur's translation of *Ideen I* to which I have just alluded:

> One must not mistake incarnate givenness, which defines evidence in general (before any criticism and thus any problem concerning what is apodictic, for example), for a metaphor, a manner of speaking, a trait proper to Husserl's style. There would be in this a double presupposition, possibly sharing the same root: first, the one concerning the trivial concepts of metaphor, utterance, and style, which is rather ignorant about the part played by flesh in Husserl's analysis of language; second, the one concerning a phenomenological state-of-things in itself, which is juridically unconnected to any relation with flesh. Now, if one keeps to the second one, all of Husserl's analyses assert that flesh accompanies each perception—incarnate givenness in which flesh is all at once given and giving. (Franck, *Chair et corps*, p. 19)

But can't we take Husserl's frequent use of the word *leibhaftig* to be conventional and metaphorical (indeed, "a manner of speaking, a trait proper to Husserl's style") without giving in to a trivial concept of metaphor (that, on the other hand, we can deconstruct)? Can't we legitimately dissociate it from the part that Husserl—*on the other hand, elsewhere,* within specific and thematic analyses—does indeed attribute to flesh (*Leib, Leiblichkeit*) in his analysis of language?[24] May we not take seriously Husserl's propositions on the subject of the fact that "flesh (*Leib, Leiblichkeit*) accompanies each perception," without drawing the conclusion that, each time he writes "leibhaftig" to designate the modality of the thing or essence given to intuitive experience, he designates the flesh of the said thing or the "carnal" character of the said intuitive experience? The same type of question is raised by Franck's long quotation (*Chair et corps*, pp. 20–21) from Heidegger's *History of the Concept of Time*. In it, Heidegger makes an important distinction between what is "bodily-given," or "given in the flesh" (Franck's translation of *Leibhaft-gegeben*), and what is "self-given" [*Selbstgegeben*]. In the first case, a bridge, for example, I can "envisage" or "represent" it to myself [*vergegenwärtigen*] when I set myself before the bridge itself [*ich versetze mich vor die Brücke*]. There, the bridge can be given to me, *itself*, in this envisaging or re-presentation [*in dieser Vergegenwärtigung*] that is not a perception, outside of any "image" or "fantasy," without for that matter being given to me leibhaftig [*leibhaftig gegeben*]. But does this mean that for Heidegger, in the perception, the bridge itself would be "incarnate," made of "flesh" or given to "flesh" as such? I hardly think so.

For if the "question of the sense of flesh does not arise" (which is not a self-evident hypothesis, incidentally), neither for Husserl nor for Heidegger, it is perhaps precisely because—well, yes, they wish to say nothing that one could translate by literally and thematically investing it with flesh, incarnation and carnal values, when in these contexts they write *Leibhaftigkeit, leibhaft*, or *leibhaftig*—even in the case of perception. Moreover, isn't this what Franck himself is saying when he establishes that the two do not bring up the question of "flesh" where Franck, for his part, reintroduces the word in his translations in such an active fashion?

The stakes of this decision overrun the ones of a translation that is simply "linguistic"; and it is because, beyond the virtually Christian connotations of the word "flesh," one also (though the two things may go hand in hand—more than ever) runs the risk of a sort of "globalization" [*mondialisation*] of flesh, bestowing a flesh upon "things," "essences," and modes of experience that are fleshless (without *Leib*) by essence, and without self-relation or self-contact. Or one would further run the risk of multiplying obscurities when it is necessary to translate *Fleisch* (I gave an example of this earlier) and more especially the becoming-body or being-body (*Kör-*

per) of the *Leib*, the *Leibkörper* that Husserl also discusses. Doesn't Franck himself note this?[25] And doesn't he specify it elsewhere, precisely on the subject of appresentative pairing and the constitution of the other's body?

> If one firmly maintains the difference in meaning of bodily flesh and body, and if one holds to the very letter of this description [by Husserl in paragraph 54 of the *Cartesian Meditations*—Trans.], one can hardly see from where the sense bodily flesh might come ["the sense animate organism," in Dorion Cairns's translation of the *Cartesian Meditations*—Trans.]; it can evidently not derive its origin from my body. What emerges from this is that the other body cannot take on any sense that my own body proper does not possess, and that the constitution of the other cannot take place. Husserl's use of the words *Körper* and *Leib* makes complete sense; he initially assigns them opposed meanings but then uses them indiscriminately later on. In addition, when a body takes on the sense of bodily flesh and consequently the sense of bodily flesh in a world, bodily flesh belonging to another world, this signifies that it is by way of the incarnation of a body and the incorporation of a flesh that there is some world. When we have determined the conditions making this incarnation and this incorporation possible, we shall have attained the origin of the world. (Franck, *Chair et corps*, pp. 150–51)

Shouldn't this be the place to speak about machine-bodies [*corps-machine*], that is to say, technical prostheses (something neither Merleau-Ponty nor Franck mentions as a possibility, or, in any case, takes into account in an essential way)? Shouldn't this be the time to speak of this *Körper* right on or in the *Leib*—right on or in the said "flesh" from which it becomes indissociable? Shouldn't this be the place where one needs to take into account the possibility of transplantation, from which the body proper or bodily flesh—in their possibility, precisely—have always been indissociable, always undecidably indissociable? And isn't this intertwining itself (*Verflechtung*)? This technical supplement, which is both *Körper* and *Leib*, would thus force us to reconsider this distinction from the locus of an alterity or heterogeneity that is no longer necessarily and from the outset the locus of an alter ego, especially in the figure of other human beings or God. And it will have become clear, in keeping with our hypothesis, that the dividing line we seek to recognize no doubt runs there.

The whole problem of "flesh" itself is its corporeity before and beyond any incorporation, precisely (and even in the psychoanalytical meaning of this latter word—in what is called the work of mourning), for "flesh" is also a body: it is even on this very subject that Franck introduces his "aporia"

(*Chair et corps*, pp. 159–60). About the constitution of flesh as physical flesh, that is, as "physical thing," there again Franck precisely speaks, already, of a "fundamental aporia" (ibid., pp. 98–99).

Though perplexed by these problems, I do not have at my disposal a satisfying linguistic solution for a regular, unequivocal translation of *Leib* —and especially *leibhaftig* or *Leibhaftigkeit*. I am not acquainted with any translation of these words that might fit within one word, and so I merely underscore the dangers that lurk in translating in a unique, regular, and *systematic* fashion, without any further precaution, the word *Leib* by "flesh," and especially *leibhaftig* by "in the flesh" [*en chair*], "carnally" [*charnellement*], or in an "incarnate" way [*de façon "incarnée"*]. When one organizes an entire problematic and rests an entire interpretative handiwork and a program ("analytics of incarnation") upon such an "active" translation, doesn't one run the risk of *effacing* or *cutting out* the body, there where there is some remaining (some "body," proper or improper—or just body); and conversely, of adding some—when *leibhaftig* does not necessarily refer to "body" or "flesh" (proper or improper)? When Husserl speaks of *Leib*—but much less, perhaps not at all, when he employs the word *leibhaftig*—it is life that he implies (life, in phenomenology, is already an enormous problem—it has kept a fair number among us, including Franck, at work for quite some time), *yet very often the mind as well*. Husserl often insists on the *Geistigkeit* of *Leib* or on *geistige Leiblichkeit*. By making flesh ubiquitous, one runs the risk of vitalizing, psychologizing, spiritualizing, interiorizing, or even reappropriating everything, in the very places where one might still speak of the nonproperness or alterity of flesh.[26]

B. *Condensation.* Let us now come to the deliberate accumulation of three semantic powers that a single naming act gathers in the word *con-tingency*:

(1) Touching (and therefore the reference here, both implicit and explicit, to the famous passage about touch in the constitution of the *Leib* in *Ideas II*).

(2) Con-tact with the body proper or with flesh—more precisely "the contact from oneself to oneself as contact from oneself to the other" (contact with the body proper, with "flesh," or con-tact from oneself to oneself as con-tact with the other's *Leib*, and so forth).

(3) The contingency of this "flesh" as essential facticity (let us recall that *contingere* is touching, attaining, but also happening to come, befalling,

falling to one's lot or part): the essential facticity of this aleatoric event-fo-calization would set up a locus of resistance to eidetic variation.

I would like to emphasize in this happy, lucky, and seductive condensa-tion that it is accompanied by a series of terminological and program-matic decisions and performative naming acts (declared or not), the justi-fication of which remains elliptical or suspended at times. Here, now, is the first interpretation of the tactile, of contact with oneself as contact with the other, "pure auto-affection as pure hetero-affection":

> Originarily proper, flesh, the origin of the proper, is originarily unproper and is the origin of the unproper.
>
> More precisely: if my flesh is originarily constituted tactilely, that is, in the first stratum in the order of constitution [an implicit reference to *Ideas II*, thus essentially giving credit to Husserl's text—J. D.], this is a fortiori valid for the flesh of the other [why "a fortiori"?—J. D.]. And carnal relations, the refer-ence of one flesh to another, are thus *first of all* a con-tact [why "first of all"? What if, by reason of the indirect *appresentation* of the other's body—over there, of the other here—one had all at once to go through sight, and mirrors, or hearing, or smell? Or through an altogether different synaesthetic, or anes-thetic, or already mechanical, organization?—J. D.]. Where does my flesh end if not where the other flesh makes itself felt to it [*à elle se fait sentir*]? "Where ends" further means "where begins." My flesh is at its limit, on the verge of being exceeded, altogether on its own border, which is the border of the other —that is, mine. Husserl has grasped this co-belonging of flesh: "The apper-ception of one's own bodily flesh [*Leib*; *chair*] and the apperception of the other bodily flesh [*Leib*; *chair*] essentially belong together."[27] The contact of oneself with oneself as contact of oneself with the other (pure auto-affection as pure hetero-affection) is the contact of one flesh with the other. (Franck, *Chair et corps*, pp. 167–68)[28]

Several imperative or performative *naming* acts ("caress," "shock," "con-tingency") follow thereupon. Earlier, on the preceding page, another ini-tiative in naming, which is just as abrupt if not arbitrary, has moreover led the way for or prepared these two decisions or decrees, these two instances of "let's call": "One can call this limit—or reference of my flesh to another —sexual difference" (p. 167).[29] Therefore, "let's call" twice:

> Let's call this touch in which no incorporation intervenes "caress." But incor-poration necessarily derives from merely relating one flesh to another, which is a "caress." Then let's call the encounter of bodies "shock." The caress is also a shock. What this yields is the account one may thus give of all that is am-

biguous in and about phenomenology, and of the phenomenal duplicity that it describes and tirelessly tries to master and reduce.

All flesh is constituted from one contact to the other; in other words, flesh is essentially *con-tingent*, and this contingency rebounds onto the upper constitutions of intersubjectivity, of objectivity. (ibid., p. 168)

This double naming not only presupposes that the definition of carnal difference be *originarily sexual*—provided that a caress is always sexed (see the previous note and the questions that it raises). It immediately associates the caress (of one flesh by another) with the shock (between two bodies). Now, the caress is a shock; it is "also" a shock, says Franck: this presupposes that, while the caress cannot be reduced to "shock," it always implies some shock, just as flesh (*Leib*) always implies some body (*Körper*). Further on, this is reiterated: "Originarily, intentionality is a carnal pairing; sexual difference, the caress and the shock determine its most general structure. . . . The origin of transcendence is the caress, but, immediately turning into shock, it is also its reduction" (ibid., pp. 169–70).

Why two nouns, then—caress and shock? And where is one to locate any *blow* that, like a shock, also involves the flesh and not only the body (and yet the body as well)—if one is to keep this distinction and this translation of it? What if there were some blow struck within the caress? Where would one situate it, in this network of distinctions that all have to do with haptics? What does "immediately turn into" mean here? Does it imply some originarity of the caress, some anteriority, be it subtle and instantaneous, of the caress and therefore of flesh before the body? Would the caress come before the shock, as the flesh before the body? And before the blow? The answers to these questions are suspended here, but we can quickly perceive what is classically at stake in them—that is, whether or not the everyday appellation "body" (*Körper*) [*corps*] refers to something secondary or not.

There is yet another consequence following this condensating and over-determined use of the word "contingency," a consequence that commands the motif of the archefacticity of the *eidos* ego as "flesh." Franck immediately goes on:

This, no doubt, is the determining motif that leads Husserl back toward this archefacticity about which we have already spoken in the context of the reduction to the *eidos* ego. If flesh is contingent, if facticity is its essence (and as such invariable and resisting variation), it will no doubt thwart the eidetic pretensions of any constitutive analysis, to the extent that it intervenes in any constitution of transcendence (and let us keep in reserve the problem of temporality). No doubt, phenomenology thus demands an interpretation of this archefacticity to which Heidegger first dedicated himself. (ibid., pp. 168–69)

If we were to develop our questions about these programmatic naming performatives here (but it is not our direct concern), one of them would have to do with the tasks of a "transcendental deduction" of "flesh" [*transzendentale Deduktion des Leibes*] (a Husserlian expression).[30] Franck is specific about these tasks, comparing them to the ones of a Kantian deduction that analyzes an object's conditions of possibility. As far as this deduction is concerned, Franck further states that "Husserl has never set it up and put it to work [*mise en chantier*]" (ibid., p. 171).

There are two "directions" at least among these tasks: (1) the "deduction of sexual difference as the reference of one flesh to another" (I have mentioned the difficulty of this "deduction": can one "flesh" only be referred to another in accordance with sexuality, and more especially "a" or "the" sexual difference?); (2) the "deduction of the 'body politic' as the reference of one flesh to the community of all others" (ibid., p. 171). What could "politic" mean here? Does being "politic" pertain to the essence of every community? We may doubt it. If one went beyond the program or site of the "setup" [*chantier*] still to come (not only for Husserl), the determination—and naming—of "community" as body "politic" would presuppose a history that is so overdetermined and a stratification so thickly layered with phenomenological strata that one would run the risk of putting off the said deduction forever; it may even become impracticable in principle, as a transcendental phenomenological deduction—a completely different story (and history), we might say, and then make it our turn to set up this thing and leave it under construction.

Let us gather schematically what seems to set apart, from the outset and virtually at least, this book by Didier Franck from Nancy's "corpus" as far as the themes that are important to us are concerned, without in any way disputing or diminishing the originality of Franck's book and the need for it. No doubt, there hardly seems to be anything more necessary and convincing than to take into account the nonproper (the *other*, in a word) in the sphere of the proper or my "flesh," with all the consequences that Franck is right to draw from this. But doesn't this reckoning contend in the first place in a kind of flesh-on-flesh in which the techno-prosthetic substitute (the intertwining of *Körper* and *Leib*—the *technē* of bodies or *ecotechnics*, in Nancy's language) is not given any status, or any essential thematic organization, it seems to me? Hence the risk of marginalizing or leaving in shadow the *partes extra partes* structure (which is nonliving, anorganic, and essentially divisible, as it were) of a body (*Körper*) that is no longer essentially alien or external with regard to "flesh" (*Leib*)—or rather that pertains or "belongs" to it, if one could still say this, but as something foreign, that is, as supplementary transplanted graft. It pertains to it without pertaining to it. Isn't there a *risk* of marginalizing the margin there? (For I am merely speaking of a virtual risk here, of a potential discursive concatenation tied to a certain degree of thematic insistence, and not of an accepted philosophical thesis.) This would also, simultaneously, paradoxically be the risk of a (carnal, spiritual, vital or vivifying, and interiorizing) *reappropriation*, the risk of a return to the proper on the part of the very thing that is *ichfremd*, not the ego's properly, but rebecoming or still remaining egological. By the same token, and despite the obligatory phenomenological vigilance on this subject (once the world has been "reduced" and, with it, every thesis properly anthropological), it is the human ego that remains the measure of all things phenomenological—as I suggested it earlier about Merleau-Ponty.[31]

In order to make myself better understood, I here refer to two fragments by Husserl, cited in Franck's notes, that take the measure of the task at hand, as well as its difficulty. Franck merely points them out and does not find any frightening limit there. The first note quotes a long and fascinating passage from Husserl's *Krisis* having to do with "animals" in addition to the "insane" and "children" (Franck, *Chair et corps*, p. 130n2).[32] The second note (ibid., p. 131n5) has to do with the temptation, which Husserl feels, but in fact wards off at once, to "think a world without any bodily flesh [*leiblose Welt*]." Franck then quotes Husserl in a context in which the "intersubjective world" and intersubjectivity seem to belong to, to be part and parcel of, the order of the human. Husserl then excludes any nonhuman "flesh" and deems nature without human beings "unthinkable": he says, at this point, "without *Leiber*, therefore without human beings." And this thing seems clear to him: "Clearly, a nature without bodies, therefore without human beings, is unthinkable."[33]

This closing is not illegitimate in itself, to be sure; and about "we, men," "we, humans," oh yes, there are certainly enough things to say that are not simple!

But, first, this anthropocentric privilege (sometimes unavowed), be it transcendental, is not always consequent in relation to the most ambitious transcendental reduction, the one that should suspend every thesis involving the existence of the world or in the world, including that of human beings. Second, this same privilege sometimes drives one to neglect what is not "human flesh," outside of the human world and sometimes even in the human world (the *Körper*-body), technical prostheses, animals in the human world and outside of it. Third, at the very point where a certain historicity of transcendental archefacticity is taken seriously (as Franck says and does), this selfsame anthropological privilege tends to overshadow the historicity that *produces-human-beings-and-technics*, always in a prosthetical way—what I have more than once, using common words, termed hominization or the emergence of "the hand of man."[34] Fourth, and finally, when this privileging of the human imparts itself too readily, it frees the path more easily—unless it has already entered it—toward this anthropotheological, or even Christian, thinking of flesh, tactility, the caress, in a word, the Christian body, which I am not trying to denounce or reject here, but to "think"—"to ponder," "to weigh."

§ 11 Tangent V

*Tangency and Contingency, 2: "The 'merciful
hand of the Father,' with which he thus
touches us, is the Son. . . . the Word that is
'the touch that touches the Soul' (toque de
la Divinidad . . . el toque que toca al alma)"*

[T]he heart of Christology is the doctrine of the incarnation,
and . . . the heart of the doctrine of the incarnation is the
doctrine of *homoousia*, of consubstantiality, of the identity or
the community of being and substance between the Father and
the Son. This is what is completely new [*inédit*] with Christianity.
—Jean-Luc Nancy, "The Deconstruction of Christianity"[1]

Let us start over again. Let us come more directly to the *double motif* that
we have been grazing against since the beginning—no doubt obliquely and
virtually, but insistently—while always tending to touch with tact.

1. Jean-Luc Nancy's stated project of a "deconstruction of Christianity,"
a project more specifically described, albeit with some reservations and
concerns about the possibility of this hyperbolic thing, as a deconstruction of the *body*, of *corpus*, and therefore of Christian "touching," itself entailing "humanualist" or anthropotheological touching.

2. The notion of "flesh," and its connotation or overdetermination, and
Christian "touch," whether or not it translates the German *Leib*.

For this more direct approach, and in order to "touch" more explicitly,
thematically and pertinently, I hope, on this question of Christian "touching," let us place ourselves at the point where the originary involvement
of the other (of the alter ego), for example in Franck, seemed to disorga-
nize or uncenter in advance a certain phenomen-egological, but nonhuman, approach toward tactility, self-contact, and "touching oneself."

Touching, touching oneself: to be sure, Nancy has put in words this
strange reflexivity, *as* have others before him, but he has also said it *otherwise*, differently, for example from Maurice Merleau-Ponty, or Henri
Maldiney.

Reminder: Merleau-Ponty: "To touch is to touch oneself."[2]

Maldiney: "In touching things, we touch ourselves to them, as it were; we are simultaneously touching and touched."[3]

Jean-Louis Chrétien has also wished to hear these discourses of reflection *otherwise*. He cites them at the very beginning of the magnificent last chapter of his book *L'appel et la réponse* [The Call and the Response], which I discovered when it was published in 1992, and then quoted,[4] all too briefly, at the proof stage, in the first, minimal version in English of this text.[5]

Today, I would like to come back to it more patiently, be it only to pay a tribute to it, in all fairness. This book, and its chapter on "body and touch" more particularly, may have had one flaw, that is, it ignored or lacked all knowledge of Nancy's immense work, even if sharing this serious ignorance with too many of our contemporaries, alas, was its excuse. Let us bet that this ignorance will not last.

I do not know any thinking that is more forceful and coherent, more prepared to give to the concept of *flesh*—to flesh touching and touched— the Christian vocation to which I have frequently alluded before. One is no longer dealing with connotation or overdetermination, or a "touch" more or less accepted or denied, but with deliberate declarations. Chrétien puts in perspective again nearly every avenue of thought that we have situated up to this point, from Aristotle to Husserl's phenomenology. He accommodates the other and inscribes an essential dwelling to accommodate the other—the other exceeding the I (as does Franck—whom Chrétien never mentions, however, I think)—at the carnal heart of the ego and egological properness.[6] In this way, he, too, dissymmetrizes the reflexivity of touching, as well as *self-touching*, and reverses its origin. But he does this in a text that one can read this time as a powerful, modern Aristotelian-Thomist haptology. In fact, its claim is to take Aristotle's thinking as a "guiding thread" (Chrétien, *L'appel et la réponse*, p. 102),[7] though the quasi-last word, or at least the decisive argument, that calls into question a reflexive "self-touch," is that of Thomas Aquinas, Aristotle's interpreter's. The transitivity of touch always wins over reflexivity. Chrétien says "transitivity" rather than "intentionality," although his discourse shows many marks of the phenomenological tradition and precise references to Husserl and Merleau-Ponty. Concerning the *who* and the *what* of this irreducible *transitivity*, Chrétien wants to remind us of some decisive moments: to touch is to touch someone or something, touch *something else*, touch *something other, some other*—or it is nothing, it is not touching. Even when we are in (*self-*)touch, or when the touching ones touch *themselves*, they are in touch with something other than themselves and are touched by something other than the same self that touches: the touching cannot be the same as the touched even when the touching touches *itself.* Then some other is in itself. One does not *touch* when one touches *nothing,* when one touches *on nothing* and tampers with it.

There is nothing more logical, more logico-grammatical, nothing that makes more sense than this axiom. Hence the difficulty (let us not say the impossibility) conferring on the untouchable the legitimacy, dignity, necessity, and the very signification, that we recognized for it in other discourses and in different senses, from Levinas to Merleau-Ponty, for example. Transivity does not let itself be reduced, even in the presumed reflexivity of *self-touching* (to which, incidentally, Chrétien is a party from the very beginning [*L'appel et la réponse,* p. 102]). The difficulty lies not so much in reflexivity or reversibility, which Chrétien acknowledges and takes into account (between me and me, i.e., Merleau-Ponty: "To touch is to touch oneself"—or between things and myself, i.e., Maldiney: "In touching things, we touch ourselves to them, as it were; we are simultaneously touching and touched."), but has to do with *symmetry.* There may be some reversibility or reflexive folding but it is in the exposed incurvation of a disymmetry. Chrétien's initial statement ("This reversibility does not yield any symmetry" [p. 104]) fulfills itself in his modern repetition of Aquinas, relayed by some assertions of affirmation, assertive instances of "yes" and "yes to," in a fair number of thinkers and poets—for example, Rilke. To be sensitive to touch, feel contact, and to sense, is to *consent.* The sense of touch is first of all, like the sense of every sensation, a sense of consent; it is and has this sense: *yes, to consent,* which always, and in advance, implies transitivity (*yes to, to consent to*):

> Every sensation first consents to the world, and only thereby can it come back to itself. The joy of being is of an altogether different order from any sensation and any self-pleasure. All joy burns with a pure yes and rises like a flame without leaning back onto itself. It is not to oneself that one says yes, and that is why it is only within the yes that one is truly oneself.
> Transivity is thus foremost and it is radical; to live, indeed, is to be outside—*draussensein,* as Rilke puts it in his last poem. (Chrétien, *L'appel et la réponse,* p. 145)[8]

For the moment let us allow this *yes* to burn and its flame to rise; we'll see a need for it later.

Why, and how, can the "transitivity" be "foremost" and "radical"? Here
is where the reference to Aquinas becomes necessary; it christianizes this
haptologics. Aquinas comments on and relaunches Aristotelian theology
dealing with intellectual contact and the intellect's touching the intelligible
(we spoke of this earlier), and he thereby simultaneously asserts the *immediacy* of intellectual touching and the *primacy* of the intelligible. Spiritual
touching[9] as pure act knows neither any intervallic medium nor any distance; it even transcends the value of affect. Being a touching without affection, an active and actual touching, it is no longer mediatized as "carnal
touching" would be. But for all its immediacy, it nonetheless remains
"transitive." It is no longer simply flesh, but spirit already; it is no longer
temporal or potential, but eternal—like the pure act or Aristotle's first
mover. Transitivity that is maintained is a transition from self to self—pure
reflection as pure transitivity. Hence a break from the phenomenology of
carnal auto-affection, that is to say, from a sensible haptology. What this
says is that the sense of touching may not come from the senses; the proper
sense of touch is foreign to sensibility. Such is this story, this history extra-
ordinaire—the ordinary story and history of Christian language: far from
taking spiritual or intellectual touching for a metaphor of sensible touching, we on the contrary have to convert (it is a *conversion*, indeed) the interpretation of sensible touching so as to decipher in it the incarnate trope
and the carnal figure of a purely spiritual touch. This conversion is not a
rhetorical operation; it is a conversion of the body, its becoming-flesh. "By
actually touching the intelligible that it is itself, spirit eternally accedes to
itself and transits from itself to itself. It becomes what it touches and as it
touches. The primacy of the intelligible is always clearly asserted. There is
thus a radical difference from the 'my absolute contact with myself' of
which Merleau-Ponty speaks and from auto-affection" (ibid., p. 151).[10]

By the same stroke (and this indissociability, this rigorous consequence
may be what gives this text its originality and impressive, imperturbable
force), the Christian body of this conversion presents itself as a *historic*
body marked in its very essence by the historical event of revelation, Incarnation, the Eucharist, by the giving, the announcing, the promising,
and the memory of "Hoc est meum corpus." There is no longer any denial
whatsoever of the body's historicity, no assertion of an abstract historicity
without a history of touch, as in some phenomenologies of essential archefacticity, or some (Heideggerian) thinking of *Offenbarkeit* (revealability) as
more originary than *Offenbarung* (revelation). It is as a Christian body that

the Christian body presents itself here and signs itself, which is to say as the post-sin, post-Incarnation historical body—as what it is, which is to say as what it aspires to be, in spirit, in its truth. It is up to others to demonstrate, if they can bring proof, that they have nothing to do, see, make, and touch with the history and story of this truth.

By the same stroke (and this *stroke* will not be long in converting itself into a fiery *caress*), the notion of *contingency* takes on a fully historical meaning, from its etymological contact with touching. Chapter 10 analyzed the remarkable condensation to which the word "contingency" gives rise in Franck's writing. Here, in a gesture that is analogous yet radically different (partially explaining the lack of a reference to Franck, no doubt), Chrétien in his turn determines and emphasizes the word "contingency"—through the (originary and etymological) contact between touching (the self-touching of the divine spirit that goes up in flames by itself) and the historical contingency of the creature that "comes after it" and lets itself be touched by it. Only since the history of creation, and then incarnation, does contingency have any sense. The creature is contingent. Contingency touches on touch as the experience of created humanity—in historical time, forever and eternally. After he has quoted Aquinas about touching the "first intelligible," Chrétien thus produces, re-produces, or motivates the word "contingency": "It is from contact with itself as intelligible that the divine spirit is inflamed and sets itself on fire eternally, and it is by letting itself be touched that it sets on fire what comes after it. What is most necessary is *contingency* itself, in the etymological sense of the term—the very contact from where the eternal flash of light [*éclair*] springs forth, from which all is suspended and all depends" (ibid., p. 151).

Why this flame? A flame that sets on fire, no doubt (transitively), but because it first sets *itself* on fire ("the divine spirit is inflamed and sets itself on fire eternally, and it is by letting itself be touched that it sets on fire what comes after it")? The flame is not only a figure for desire and love, which will soon inspire, aspire, and spiritualize this hapto-onto-theo-teleology of Christian flesh (the Christian "repetition" of "desire" according to Aristotle, which we had already followed in Ravaisson);[11] and as early as the next sentence: "Only the thought of love, however, gives flesh all its spiritual charge, and leads touch to its highest possibility" (ibid., p. 151).

The flame is the becoming-love of Aristotelian desire (*orexis*), because it touches and affects, and it signifies first of all the spontaneity of a *causa sui*: a flame is inflamed and sets *itself* on fire; in any case, it seems to catch fire without any outside cause, and in this way, it is divine—like the First Mover or Pure Act, the thinking of thought,[12] the desirable God who moves by himself and inspires desire. But here Aristotle's God is infinitized. He was already discontinuous and transcendent in the scope of the sublunary world, and he now becomes infinitely distant or discontinuous without any possible analogy with the world of creatures (though mediation by the Son, and Incarnation, as we shall see, may extend its hand to this analogy, or even shake hands with it). By burning as if by itself (reflexively), the flame touches and inflames (transitively). It is as if one had to start from fire to think the touching of *self*-touching, and not the opposite.

It would not only be from fire but from flames, since light is the joint meaning of what is thus more than a figure—a light that self-touches, therefore, and touches itself and us, and that we can touch. But this haptical light of self-consuming flames eludes worship; it does not dwell, as an image to be adored. It is the truth of a light without idols and icons, an iconoclastic light—and its flame spontaneously burns down effigies. That is why we said it is "more than a figure," rather a transfiguration of figurality itself. Touching, this luminous touching, becomes naturally more iconoclastic than vision. "Presence without image and without representation," Chrétien calls this luminosity (ibid., p. 152). No wonder that this *haptologetics* of the flame—if one can put it that way—intersects, sometimes literally, with Levinas's discourse about the *caress* ("intimate proximity" that "never becomes possession," "naked exposition to the ungraspable," and so on).[13]

This is, indeed, what immediately follows the passage just quoted. Here is the flesh, then, the flesh itself, what is called the flesh, that which calls for the Christian *caress*, and Christian *love*, and Christian *charity*; and we had turned toward this flesh for such a long time, even while reading discourses on the flesh whose intentions were evidently not Christian (with Merleau-Ponty or Franck at the top of the list)—"flesh" to which "only the thought of love . . . gives . . . all its spiritual charge":

> What is most necessary is *contingency* itself, in the etymological sense of the term—the very contact from where the eternal flash of light [*éclair*] springs forth, from which all is suspended and all depends.
>
> Only the thought of love, however, gives flesh all its spiritual charge, and leads touch to its highest possibility. Indeed, from the finite to the infinite, all continuity breaks up, yielding to an increasingly forceful discontinuity, and all resemblance flourishes in an even more luminous dissimilarity. Contact with

the infinite is necessarily of an order that is different from contact with the finite. (ibid., pp. 151–52)

Despite this discontinuity, and despite this transcendence of the infinite, and despite this abyssal difference between finite and infinite touching, the latter announces itself *already* in the former. And this theo-teleological *already* opens up at the same time the experience of a *critical* touch, the one reaching beyond idolized images, and the experience of a *stroking* touch, which exposes itself to what already exceeds it. In both cases, there is an experience of *presence*, but a presence without representation. Touching unrepresentable presence: isn't this ultimately the best definition of touching in general? But I wonder if we can say this (as I am tempted to believe) and abstract this definition from the "theo-teleological already" that I just mentioned to describe Chrétien's gesture. "But touch," Chrétien goes on to say, "in and of its own finiteness, is precisely already open to a presence without image and without representation, as well as to an intimate proximity that never becomes possession, and to an exposure naked to the ungraspable. Of what I touch and what touches me, the excess over me is endlessly attested in the caress. Aquinas . . . " (ibid., p. 152).

To the distinction between *mediate* and *immediate* (it is always mediate carnal touching, always immediate spiritual touching), then between *reflexive* or *reversible* and *transitive* (touching is always transitive, whether or not it is a reflexive self-touching), we still need to add a third distinction, that between *reciprocity* and *nonreciprocity*. Aquinas no doubt accepts that physical touching can be reciprocal or nonreciprocal between creatures, between created things or persons. But contact between God and the soul or mind of humans can only be mutual (*mutuus contactus*), at least in the gracious tactility of love. And such, moreover, is the very essence of this Christian loving [*aimance*]: immediate transitivity, dissymmetry—and reciprocity. Aquinas says: "Now God . . . touches the soul (*tangit animam*), causing grace in it. . . . But the human soul in some sense touches God (*tangit Deum*) by knowing Him or loving Him."[14] "In a way," Chrétien concludes, "there is indeed a *mutuus contactus*" (ibid., p. 152).

Even if it does not in any way signify symmetry, this particular reciprocity would no doubt, this time, be unacceptable in a discourse such as Levinas's, if not in Judaism in general, because of the touching and because of this mutuality as experience of the divine.

Is one dealing here with a mystical or ecstatic tactility? Chrétien disputes that such might be the "direct orientation" of this passage in Aquinas's

Disputed Questions on Truth. But he concludes—and we can feel that he does not mind doing it—with reminders of some admirable texts by Saint Bonaventure or especially Saint John of the Cross, "the greatest Christian mystic speaking of the sense of touch." For the latter, God's touch (*toque de la Divinidad*) is "a substantial touch; that is, of the substance of God in the substance of the soul."[15]

The mystical ecstasy that *The Living Flame of Love* describes thus justifies the nonfigure of the flame, the fierily inflamed transfiguration just mentioned. It gathers the very heart of the matter in the last pages of Chrétien's book *L'appel et la réponse*, first, because it again leads to the hand, the hand of man *responding* or *corresponding* to the "hand of God" to which reference was risked in concluding our reading of Maine de Biran and Ravaisson; and second, because, by identifying this hand of God with his Son and the Word, by handing over speech to this hand, as it were—giving it a given word, a donating and ordaining word—it summons both the ear and the eye, that is, the "totality of flesh," to the same "hearing." Flesh, touching and touched, to the heart, gives ear and listens. It is a haptology of the heart, of an openhanded heart, open-hearted hand, the touch of divine, *heartfelt mercy*: the eye listens, the ear listens, flesh listens—and burns up all but dying to listen, docilely. It responds to this word of excess with a song. This *Logos* dictates the last words in *L'appel et la réponse*:

> The "merciful hand of the Father," with which he thus touches us, is the Son. Therefore it is the Word that is "the touch that touches the soul" (*el toque que toca al alma*).[16] To be thus touched by the Word, in one's very substance, beyond any image, is properly to listen, to listen with one's whole being, body and soul, without anything in us that might elude this hearing and stay outside of it, by way of the gracious transfiguration that this very touch achieves. Ears are not alone in listening; eyes do it too, and they respond. But it is lastly by taking root in the totality of flesh that they are able to do it. Flesh listens, and listening in this way makes it respond. Saint John of the Cross, who rediscovered the vigor of biblical language, does describe how this supernatural touch can shine and glorify the body—glorify the body in its entirety: " . . . David says, *All my bones will say: God, who [is] like You? (Ps. 34:10)."[17] When the whole body shines and burns from this divine contact, it turns into song and Word, but what it sings—from its whole self, which the Other has gathered and collected—is what it cannot say, what exceeds it infinitely, and this excess, to which touch itself is destined, has been open for us forever here, in the humblest of sensations and the slightest contact. (ibid., pp. 153–54)

(The hand of the Father, then, the hand with which he touches us, is the Logos and is the Son. This passage follows a discourse on the *caress*: Chrétien cannot be certain that Aquinas gave it a mystical sense. Moreover the word "caress," as Chrétien pens it, comes to translate and interpret Aquinas's *contactus mutuus* (and although Chrétien's use of the word is legitimate, it would be difficult to neutralize it). This movement, from the caress to the Son, is also something that we have followed with curiosity and up to a point in Levinas. It is not the same Son, to be sure, although each time, in his ascent, in both Levinas and Chrétien, he bears the initial capital letter of a proper name in the singular—the Son, the line to follow, in the direction indicated earlier.)[18]

I purposely started at the end, which is to say, with the "spiritual touch," the one that "no longer presents any medium or distance" and is no more "of the order of affection" than "auto-affection"; but that is also the one to which "only the thought of love" gives "all its spiritual charge." When the hand of man corresponds with the hand of God in this "divine contact" whereby "flesh listens," when the "merciful hand of the Father" is the Logos (of) his Son, then in return one better understands both the general economy of the book (titled *L'appel et la réponse*) and the logic proper to its last chapter, "Le corps et le toucher" (The Body and Touch). Indeed, it opens with the experience of ecstasy and excess. Where looking and hearing intersect, this experience is attested and delivers "the sense of the senses," the carnal nature of the voice that itself presupposes the flesh of "our whole body." Chrétien proposes many things that Husserl, as we recall, would have deemed equally frivolous and metaphorical or heretical for phenomenology as a rigorous science. And in fact, as we shall see, it is a certain phenomenology that Chrétien disputes with, even while calling upon it respectfully. "Eyes listen and voices look on, ecstatically. The sense of the senses is the excess of sense, giving itself only through the word and within it. Now, there is no voice except a carnal voice, and our whole body is what it presupposes in order to be what it is, and what, in return, the voice makes into its mouthpiece and thus into the highest manifestation of spirit" (ibid., p. 101).

How can self-feeling, which through suffering or pleasure characterizes the "tactile body, in the widest acception of the word," open transitively onto excess or ecstasy? This is the place for the needed return to Aristotle and the common place for all the aporias wanting a solution, on the subject of a sense, the sense of touch, which has regularly been characterized, with the help of a great number of references and authorities, as "the most fundamental and universal" (ibid., pp. 103–4, 112, 127–29, 133), "the commonest one" (pp. 104–11), and thus also the most "unfindable" (p. 108), the "hyperbolic sense" (p. 119). The final chapter's program and problematic are in fact already clearly announced in the book's introduction.[19]

At this point, rather than reconstituting the linear path of this chapter's rich complexity (although the reader is invited to do so, and more than once), let me try to define a few edges instead—the ones seeming at the same time to call for some questioning and to situate some partitions and dividing lines, from our point of view. As always, they are the parting lines that bring one close to Nancy's *corpus* and depart from it all at once, at least in the reading proposed here.

1. The end of an *immediate* spiritual touch, full, and therefore intuitive, without "medium or distance," and without affection or auto-affection, is indeed what appears to orient everything (*more theologico et teleologico*). This plenitude of haptical immediacy has more than once been identified as the pole of all metaphysical intuitionism, be it from the outset an optical intuitionism. This immediate plenitude of haptical fulfillment is of the order of the *infinite* (the Christianization of Aristotle's pure act). Yet in other parts, and consistently before reaching this conclusion, Chrétien on the contrary insists on mediacy, intervals, veils, and all the spacings of interposition, and so forth, and therefore we have to assume that he is then speaking of the finite touching of creatures in touch with finite beings. Let me cite a few examples of this. From the beginning, in following Aristotle, Chrétien puts the accent on a "veiling," proper to the sense of touch, which conceals its own conditions of exercise and produces every theoretical prejudice concerning it. Since there is no touching without an interval (a film, a membrane "that keeps the skin apart from things, and that we are not feeling" [ibid., p. 106]) and since this interposition slips away —well, mediation meets with oblivion and produces an *illusory* belief in immediacy of contact. This illusion is also the illusion of phenomenology casting a shadow, in this case, instead of showing off. "The theoretical error of those who hold the sense of touch to be immediate relies on its own phenomenological occultation. . . . Prejudices about touch are ordered in keeping with its own veiling [*les préjugés sur le toucher s'ordonnent à son propre voilement*]" (ibid.). "The sense of touch works by way of something [the interposed veil—J. D.] that remains untouchable. In phenomena,

therefore, there is an internal veiling" (ibid., p. 108).[20] This spontaneous veiling lets touch slip from standard phenomenology; it is about a mediatized sense of touch that can be nothing but human, sensitive, and finite, as we have seen, and not divine and spiritual. For an access to spiritual and immediate touch, it is necessary all at once to overcome Aristotle's aporias and learn how to see or think and attain another phenomenology of ecstasy and mystical love. That is the task Chrétien assigns himself before this first development about the veiling of touch or its first "phenomenological occultation." We must learn again how to see—against this occultation: "Are these just internal quandaries in Aristotle's thinking, partaking of a bad positioning of the questions—or do these difficulties have a foundation in the things themselves? Does touch itself slip away from itself by itself in regard to thinking, or is it just we who do not know how to see, which would only tell about ourselves [*ce qui n'apprendrait que sur nous-mêmes*]?" (ibid., p. 105).

In other words: believing that human touching (or that finite touching in general) is immediate is a prejudice, a theoretical error, credulity—and elsewhere Chrétien also mentions "the illusion of its immediacy" (ibid., p. 147). The genesis of this credulity may be the most widespread philosophical naïveté, and we could account for it by analyzing the very structure of veiling in its properness and intervallic interposition, which are part of tactile experience. By contrast, this immediacy no longer corresponds to a theoretical prejudice, credulity, or philosophical naïveté—it is no longer an "illusion"—as soon as infinite touching, *mutuus contactus* with God, is at issue. There, intervallic interposition is no more. Essentially, excellently, it is this *immediate*, infinite, spiritual touch that would teach us to *think* what *touching* means to say, in truth, and call on us to do so. Isn't it solely *by analogy* with this *mutuus contactus* that we interpret human or finite touching, and then forget the interval and give in to illusion? Immediacy is the absolute truth of divine touching, "the hand of God," his Incarnation in Logos or the Son's flesh—and therefore of *creation* and the act of creating; but it is a "theoretical error," an "illusion" born from "phenomenological occultation" in the case of human or finite touching in general—and therefore in the case of the *creature*.

2. According to its standard interpretation, phenomenology of perception would therefore be ignorant about *both* the veiling *and* the prejudices that it generates on the subject of the sense of touch's alleged immediacy.

The finiteness of human living circumscribes it, as a phenomenology of *affection* and *auto-affection* (what true touching, spiritual or divine touching, which is proper, infinite, absolutely transitive, is not). As a phenomenology of the creature, or more precisely the fallen creature, locked upon itself, it should be disputed, or at the very least saved from itself, overcome, transcended toward the authentic *immediacy* of spiritual touching (without "medium" or "distance"), that is, toward its infinite, excessive surplus. But once more, precisely by reason of the *mutuus contactus*, we must not take the Incarnate Word or Infinite Logos ("the hand of God"—or "the Son"), to which this spiritual and infinite touch corresponds (without "medium" or "distance"), to be, in its excess or infinite transcendence, simply *separated* from human finiteness and its veiled or mediatized touching. Logos gives us a sign of the hand. Logos (which Chrétien always translates as the Word [*le Verbe*]—and I wonder why: there is much to say about this here), which is to say, the hand of the merciful Father, which is to say, the Son. Incarnation is this sign of the hand. This sign of the hand of the Father-and-the-Son is announced in the excellence of the hand of man— precisely where he touches or lets himself be touched by what makes One here, that is, Logos-the-Hand-of-the-Merciful-Father-the-Son. And this sign of the giving hand comes again from the heart—the forgiving, merciful heart, the sacred heart.

The element of this discourse ("call" and "response") is indeed the Logos's, an anthropo-theo-*logical* Logos's. Incarnation into the flesh of a God making himself into Man. Logos—also known as the Son—calls on man, on man's response and responsibility, even if man is neither the Logos's origin nor its owner.[21] Logos makes itself known to Man, as does God's Hand to man's hand. It follows that, in spite of Chrétien's insistence on veiling, mediacy, and the prejudices making one take for granted the immediacy of human touching, the tireless and all too classical praise of the hand of man and the excellence of human tactility, which we can then read, will come as no surprise. Chrétien invokes numerous texts from the tradition in order to bear witness at the same time to this superiority of human tactility and to what puts it right with the hand itself. Most of these pronouncements about the excellence of human touching are expressly inscribed within the Aristotelian tradition—more precisely, within Aristotelian teleology here and there relayed by its heirs, more or less direct or declared. "The sense of touch is the only one pertaining to all animate living beings, but at the same time Aristotle proclaims its excellence and its superiority in humans: man is a tactile being; his very humanity depends on it" (ibid., p. 113).[22]

What is properly man's, namely, the hand, once again corresponds to this excellence of the human sense of touch: "How is one to describe and specify this excellence of human touching? The hand, proper to man, naturally comes to mind because of its extreme tactile sensitivity and its power to discriminate and explore, to such a degree that some thinkers make it the privileged organ of touch" (ibid., p. 113).

Although things *manual* and *human(ual)* are on a par here, as they so often are; although this teleological excellence of human touching is most often embodied in the hand; although the "hand" is the very thing itself that most often extends between human touching and divine touching (between the hand of man and, on the other side, the "merciful hand of the Father": Logos and the Son, the Word that "is" the Son), Chrétien has to account for a fact that he deems "surprising and disconcerting": though Aristotle has, "in unforgettable pages," "meditated on the essence of the human hand," he seems not to "give any particular role to the hand" in the excellence of the sense of touch. "It behooves us to note," Chrétien writes, "that Aristotle does not put the perfection of the human hand directly and expressly in relation with the perfection of human touching" (ibid., pp. 113–14).

(We established something analogous in Ravaisson: the Aristotelian ascendant upon his philosophy perhaps spared him this connection between the excellence of human touching and the hand's power, while bypassing Maine de Biran's competing influence, at least on this point. But we also established that this discursive economy remained superficial and in no way jeopardized his call to the "law of grace" and the "prevenient grace" of a divine hand.)[23]

Around this "disconcerting" silence on the part of Aristotle, a rather interesting and subtle discussion feeds on numerous hypotheses heedfully giving ear to Galen or Kant. It starts out during an inventory of the *three* ways in which the sense of touch is *universal*. (First, the way of touching is "common to all animate living beings"; second, this way "extends nearly to the whole body, or in any case to all flesh"—two sufficient reasons for Aristotle not to insist so much on hands; third, the way of the touched or the tangible covers the whole field of the sensible: We seek the principles of the sensible body, that is, of the tangible, says Aristotle.) But what will detain us here in the first place is that, as in Ravaisson's logic, just recalled, this (relative) silence about the hand finds itself invested with an even greater spiritual or teleological power at the service of an end that is placed even higher—an overbid for the hand. Aristotle keeps silent about the tactile hand (or about the digital touch [*doigté*]), and this is because he puts it even higher; it may be that the hand is an "organ of organs" that "can become anything because it is nothing, and in that way is like the soul" (ibid., p. 114).[24] When he then wonders what to make of this silence about the feeling of fingers [*doigté*] and whether it is necessary to "speak up in Aristotle's place," as Galen did, Chrétien also seems ready to "acknowledge this silence as heavily loaded with a strong philosophical meaning that invites thoughts of a sense of touch without organs, in a sense still to be determined" (ibid., p. 115).

(Here, this "without organs" openly serves a thinking of Christian flesh. It reminds us of a tradition following [Antonin] Artaud—and complicated relays after him—that we should not too hastily and simply judge to be foreign to the Christian body, no matter how hostile it pretends to be. But let us leave this aside for the time being.)

The interest, the "strong philosophical meaning" that Chrétien seems to expect from this "silence" in Aristotle (not about the hand's privilege, of which Aristotle speaks eloquently, but about the hand *as* the organ of touch), is that this apparent avoidance this time in fact opens onto a thinking of the universality of flesh. For if human touching only found its representation in an organ, the hand, or in the "fineness" and tactile excellence of the hand, and the "feeling in the fingers," then one would have to give up one of the three "universalities" of the sense of touch, the one that makes it coextensive with flesh in general by extending it to the whole body.[25] One would thus miss *the question of flesh*, or at least remain unacquainted with its immense dimension. And it is at this precise point—on the same page, I think—that Chrétien's whole problematic lays itself out. From a historical point of view, it answers a rather complex strategy, which some might call devious. *On the one hand*, it deals with "changing," yet keeping, Aristotle, and with christianizing—I won't say converting—and "modernizing" him, too, in order to orient him, by way of Aquinas, as we have seen, toward a "modern" Christian thinking of flesh, the Merciful Father, and his Hand which touches us, that is, Incarnation, or the Word his Son, and so forth. But simultaneously, and *on the other hand*, it is necessary to rely upon *this* Aristotle, and Aquinas, and then John of the Cross, and first of all on their *transitivism*, in order to go against or beyond another "modern" thinking of flesh that is phenomenological in kind. The latter thinking is deemed too reflexive, narcissistic, self-centered, or too centered on its finiteness; hence the question that Chrétien asks himself after wondering about Aristotle's "silence": "Does touching, which constitutes animal life, deliver up flesh, leaving it on its own to feel itself? Does any continuity exist between the Aristotelian concept of flesh and its contemporary concept, which insists on its quasi-reflexivity—or on the contrary, should one separate them radically? Touching is the place of this decisive question" (ibid., p. 115).

The thinking of flesh wants a hand, and first of all God's hand, but one also has to know how to do without the hand of man, or aim beyond it in any case. Then one has to come back from it all—and this is Incarnation, this is flesh—in order to receive the hand of man from God. The question then comes back, but perhaps lacks the time to dwell as a question in this dwelling, and it comes to ask itself, and comes down to asking oneself whether the question is properly formulated, that is, formed in a fitting *manner*: what is a hand? What are hands? What gives the hand its being a hand? More precisely: *who* gives the hand its being a hand? Who offers a hand?

3. Fundamentally, this question has followed us relentlessly since the beginning. Chrétien does not put it, or at least *articulate it, as such*, but this silence is not necessarily unjustified. To whoever might be tempted to say to him: "Finally, the only hand that we know, see, and touch, and about which we can come to an understanding by pooling our fund of common sense—literally, without any metaphor—is the hand of man, man's sensible, finite hand; and as for you, you are using a *substitutive figure* when you speak of 'the hand of God' and when you readily accept that a discourse about (intuitive, absolute, immediate, full, without 'medium' or 'distance') touching is ruled according to God's hand and not man's, and so forth," Chrétien might respond in two manners at least, following two typical arguments. First, he could refer (expressly, in a way that he does not) to the Aristotelian discourse (about the proper, the actual, and potency, but especially about analogy) that gradually makes the hand of man

approximate—and be virtually *analogous* with—the hand properly speaking, God's hand, a hand that is truly touching and touched, this time, as well as knowing, actually all-powerful, as well as intelligent and intelligible —the hand we remember in the absolute touching of pure actuality, putting *nous* in immediate contact (without "medium or distance") with the *noēton*.[26] And the *logos* of this analogy could also have, as it often does, the meaning of *proportional relation*. Second, Chrétien could also refer (expressly, in a way that he does not) to the immense exegetical tradition dealing with figures, so as to turn common sense around and handily demonstrate that there is a trope there because the hand of man is, for its part, nothing but a figure of God's hand, and the latter's proper sense is given, forgiving, and giving in Incarnation, Transubstantiation, Passion, and especially, perhaps, in Crucifixion.

But Chrétien has no need to unfurl these arguments with their detours, which would be long and laborious, because—I think—they are folded and involved in an apparently more economical form: there is no "hand *in general*," before man's or God's hand. The question from which we seemed to start (What are hands? What is a hand? What does "hand" mean to say?) could be badly formulated, not only—as we could put forward each time we speak of metonymies and substitutions—because hands, fingers, and sexes have deputies and replacements in so many figures, but because —as Chrétien would rather put it—our preunderstanding of this word, the hand, involves at least the *transitive* ability to touch and know, and therefore to present, make present, give, and give an actual intuition of the present (always of something else or other to someone else or other, even if this presentation also presents itself to itself, and so forth). Of the series of questions I proposed and listed earlier, only the question "who?" (*Who* gives his or her hand? *To whom?*) would be legitimate and meaningful, that is, pertinent, in the last analysis. For it is solely in spiritual touching as divine touching that all these predicates find themselves actually gathered, in an infinite, and thus full and immediate form, without spacing (without "medium or distance").

Two translations, then, are sufficiently satisfying. This does not mean self-satisfied, facile sufficiency, nor a manner of manipulation, but rather the highest, most elevated exigency—the most respectable one, I would say, and mark that, before it, the same respect also demands some vigilance.

A. *First translation.* It is sufficient at first to translate Aristotle into Aquinas. Between our two earlier quotations, Chrétien ensured the medi-

ation, which is to say the mediation between the mediate and the immediate—what an incarnation always is: "While this spiritual touch no longer
presents any medium or distance; while, as pure act, it is no longer of the
order of affection; while unlike carnal touching, which is always mediate,
it is totally immediate, it is nevertheless unfailingly transitive. By actually
touching the intelligible that it is itself, spirit eternally accedes to itself and
transits from itself to itself. It becomes what it touches and as it touches"
(ibid., p. 151).

B. *Second translation.* It is then sufficient to translate Aquinas into John
of the Cross: "'This touch [divine touch, *toque de la Divinidad*]' is a 'substantial touch; that is, of the substance of God in the substance of the
soul.' It takes place 'without any intellectual or imaginative shape or figure.' The 'merciful hand of the Father,' with which he thus touches us, is
the Son. Therefore it is the Word that is 'the touch that touches the soul'
(*el toque que toca al alma*) . . . The flesh listens" (ibid., p. 153).

"Without any shape or figure," then. The figuration of the figure vanishes, as does the image from the imaginary. God's hand is no longer a figuration. One hands the hand of man in passing, one comes to pass through
it—the accepting and listening hand—but one immediately passes it and
does without it. In the very passage itself. The hand of God is the hand in
the proper sense, beyond any icon, idol, or human tropologics. Moreover,
human touching, in its very finiteness, in its mediacy, could already accede
to this—to this "presence without image." Let's read it again: "But touch,
in and of its own finiteness, is precisely already open to a presence without
image and without representation, as well as to an intimate proximity that
never becomes possession, and to an exposure naked to the ungraspable.
Of what I touch and what touches me, the excess over me is endlessly attested in the caress" (ibid., p. 152).

The stroking hand that caresses no longer is a prehensile hand, then, or
a knowing one, but rather a hand that is exposed, giving, and accepting;
it is the hand of salvation, the God-ward goodbye hand.[27]

How can one go about the passage from the unfigurable, which is to say,
the hand of God in its proper sense, to the figure of its figurative sense,
which is to say, the hand of man? How about the passage from spiritual
touching, which is infinite and immediate, without "medium" or "distance," form or figure, to "carnal touching, which is always mediate"? How
about the passage from the immediate to the mediate, and thus to flesh?

To all these questions, which come down to the same thing and which are all questions of *passage*, and therefore of transition and transitivity, and figural transfer, there is but one answer, it seems to me: passage, like Passion, Incarnation, Transubstantiation, "Hoc est enim corpus meum," and so forth, and the mediation between the infinite immediate and the finite mediate, just as between infinite and singular finite in general, between God and Man: it is Logos fashioned into flesh, the Son, the Hand of the Merciful Father.

Although this is doubtless also verifiable, I won't repeat here—to conclude for the time being, as in the preceding chapters—that this anthropotheo*logical* thinking of flesh does not leave any spare room for a questioning of technics (ecotechnics or the *technē of bodies*, to put it in Nancy's terms), nor of the animal, or rather animals, nor of the hominization process that produces what is termed the hand in "everyday" language, nor of the possibility of prosthetics onto which spacing in general opens, and so forth. (Transplantation of the heart, and even the Sacred Heart, is the locus here of a notable example, but I shall do no more than mention it.) I won't put it that way, although I believe it is just so. Indeed, it does seem as if everything in Nancy's thinking about exscription and the syncope leads back toward this spacing (irreducible even in temporalization itself), which Chrétien would reduce to this phenomenon of finitude, and finite flesh that touching assigns to the interval, to mediatizing interposition, and to the "medium" and "distance" that spiritual touching (which is infinite, immediate, etc.) will have first of all *elevated*, and *uplifted* and *relieved*. Indeed, Chrétien makes room for spacing, as well as for everything that depends on it, but it is a finite place, which can be relieved, in the elevation of Logos and Incarnation. He also makes room for substitution, that is, the figuration of the unfigurable, the hand of man, the heart of man, and so forth. And one could think of *substitution* as does Levinas (though he does not use this term in the same way), or in a more literally Christian way, as does the tradition that leads to [Louis] Massignon. The Passion of the Son, Incarnation, Logos, Transubstantiation, Passion are substitutions calling for Substitution or Imitation; and in a certain manner, here, too, there is a *hominization* process, but it is finally and always already the hominization of God, the gift of a God who makes himself into Man, through the mediation of the Son or the Word, and the Hand of the Merciful Father. This hominization is a humanization *after the fashion* of God, according to the Face and the Hand of God; it goes through this very Christian "death of God" of which we spoke earlier. And so forth. But Chrétien will never translate this substitution into any prosthetics, transplanting, or *technē*—and especially not into a heart transplantation. And though there may be some spacing in it, Incarnation will never be the phenomenon of an irreducible finitude; it would never lend itself to thought in what Nancy terms "a finite thinking" for "the sense of the world."

Two ways of thinking substitution, therefore, but two tangential ways —though no doubt incompatible. It is a rather troubling, even dizzying, duality, and may lead to the temptation—Temptation itself—to substitute one for the other.

I can imagine, desire, and dread as well, as a "mortal sin," the least venial, perhaps the most serious and least expiable Temptation (because it is the lightest), that is, attempting, and letting oneself be tempted, to think substitution without sacrifice.

What there would remain to think is the place, the placing of this replacing, or the neutral spacing (*chōra*, I might say), that would still extend its hospitality to this virtual substitution of substitution, unless it should detain it forever as a hostage.

PART III

Punctuations: "And you."

§ 12 "To self-touch you"

Touching—Language and the Heart

A guiding thread is twisting along. It is more or less visible in the course of this last part of my trajectory. It is contained in three letters, sometimes less than a word, and is guiding me continually. It will go through everything like the tenuous thread of a point, a stitched point, the dot of a punctuation, the punctuation of "you," after "you."

Another way of asking oneself: how about the passage from "touching *him*" to "touching *you*"? You?[1]

As for her, she remains—ever extended in her deep sleep.

Flesh and body all at once, a corpse "in her coffin" already, Psyche will have had enough time—let me not say patience—to wait for us along these detours and "tangents." She has all the time in the world; this time she will have had it, and she keeps it—before her and behind her.

Let us remember that her resemblance to more than one Mary—two at least—flustered us, and the question of touch that she put to us, seducing us already, from the flesh of her body or the body of her flesh, from her deadly sleep, was always or nearly always the same question: am I Christian?

—What about you? From where does this body come to us?

The answer is pending, and desire suspended.

Why would the question of touch still be without an answer—unheard of, perhaps? Unheard of—like this other "possibility" [*ressource*], "at the heart of Christianity a root [*provenance*] more original than Christianity itself"?[2]

The question is one and multiple, traditional yet still virginal, as if untouched, in spite of the plowing of philosophers and theologians. I knew, I thought I had known for a long time, that if there is a work of thinking today that measures up to this, to this question, and actually measures itself against it as the incommensurable, in acts of language and reflection, then it is Nancy's work, even when it doesn't acknowledge all the references that I have just evoked, beginning with Aristotle and the Gospels.[3] I thought I had known this for a long time. To be sure, a search (which may have been too hasty) through a number of Nancy's early works—roughly until the middle of the 1980s, and strangely including, therefore, *The Experience of Freedom*—had shown us that neither the *theme* nor the *figure* of touch lays siege to his discourse, invests in it, or above all invades it, as will be the case—we can establish it today—in all his recent publications.

Let me insist that this is an issue of the *theme* and the *figure*—and this is more than just one difficulty among others. Because if there is "the" sense of touch, which is to say this motif of which Nancy speaks and that he now thematizes increasingly, while saying "there is no 'the' sense of touch," there are also—before or beyond this *object* of thought or discourse, beyond what is called *touch* [*le toucher*], which he is henceforth dealing with—all these figural and apparently nonthematic operators with which he is continually playing (as I am doing here), through which and thanks to which Nancy has long since put touching into words, and *said* it and touched it.

But insisting is not nothing. Even if it did nothing but bring to the light of day what was sleeping in the shadow, even if it exhibited *literally*, and *as such* (thus painfully baring its body) what had until then been a used-up metaphor, a familiar trope we use without paying much attention to it—well, this intensification of insistence is no longer a simple rhetorical movement. It comes down to thinking and to the thinking body of thought.

Two examples: I am choosing them almost randomly in my index; for, on the score of "Touching," in Nancy's corpus, I have prepared for myself an index at the end of each book. An index is a certain order—a taxonomic and deictic order, and also a way of obeying orders, under the thumb of the finger and the eye. From this index I would like to tackle a small number of entries. Why would such an index not be exhaustive even after one has reread the whole work, more than once, from beginning to end? This may be what I hope to begin to demonstrate thanks to these *two examples*.

1. The *first example* touches upon a *figural* manner of making use of the tactile schema. It is an example of "touch" in Nancy's language, or more precisely, an example of the manner in which Nancy touches on or tampers with language and what touches on language, in language, and for language. The heart is never far away, *his* heart, first of all, which I do not want to avoid mentioning. The heart is one of those interior surfaces of the body that, in principle (unless one performs the unimaginable, at least for now, operation of open-heart surgery on oneself), no "self-touching" can ever reach—what might be termed the heart's hide.[4] A thinking of touch must at least go through a theory of skin. Now, what is skin, the pellicular, *peau*, peel, pelt, fell, or hide? In *Corpus*, Nancy has invented *expeausition*, a great and necessary word.[5]

The heart: absolute intimacy of the limitless secret, no external border, absolute inside, crypt for oneself of an untouchable self-interiority, place of the "act of faith" (about which we read in "The Deconstruction of Christianity"),[6] inmost core of that which symbolizes the origin of life, within the body, by its displacement of it (*metabolē* of the blood). And yet nothing appears at least to be more auto-affective than the heart. But so many of Nancy's texts have touched upon the heart over the past few years (this deserves another study intersecting with the present one).[7] Here, then, is one of the first examples I noted when I referred in a seminar a few years ago to his "L'insacrifiable" ("The Unsacrificeable"),[8] in which he analyzes the remarkable denial whereby Western sacrifice is constituted, from Plato's *Phaedo* to Hegel and to Bataille. A "deconstruction of Christianity" is thus already announced. According to this analysis, it is a matter of the spiritualization, which is also a dialectization, of sacrifice, its *sublation* in auto-sacrifice or in the sacrifice of sacrifice. By denying itself, by denying in itself an ancient sacrifice, it covers over an infinite process of negativity with the name of sacrifice, which is sacred or sacralizing. In doing so, it installs in its heart—"at the heart," says Nancy, at the "heart" of this process—the sacrificial destruction that it claims to go beyond or abandon. It repeats, one could say, the "ancient" sacrifice. The heart is not only the insensitive figure of the center or of secret interiority; it is the sensible heart, the rhythm, respiration, and beating of the blood, the bloody heart or the bleeding heart, an uncircumcised heart (and further on Nancy evokes the "circumcision" of the heart):[9] "At its center, this double operation simultaneously combines, in an onerous ambiguity, the infinite efficacy of dialectical negativity and the bloody heart of sacrifice."[10]

There then follow, in the next sentence, two instances of the word "touch." They deserve an *infinite* analysis, on the scale of that upon which they touch, namely, precisely, a process of infinitization, the very same one that was questioned in the preceding chapter: "To *touch* upon this denial, or, to put it succinctly, this manipulation, is to *touch* upon this simultaneity; it is to be obliged to wonder whether dialectical negativity washed away the blood, or whether the blood must, on the contrary, inevitably hemorrhage from it. In order to prevent the dialectical process from remaining a comedy, Bataille wants the blood to flow" (my emphases—J. D.).[11]

In this case, one may easily say that it is a question of a manner of speaking, of some kind of trope. Just try to find someone who has ever literally "touched" a denial. At times Nancy seems to be drawing on the fund of an old rhetoric that says "to touch" for "to concern," "to aim," "to think," "to refer to," "to speak of," "to take as its object," "to thematize" precisely, in a precisely *pertinent* fashion, and so forth. But because, in the same sentence, one sees first the hands of "manipulation" (another figure but more strictly determinate), next the "blood" rise up or take shape, the literality of "touch" thereby becomes more sensitive, nearer, less conventional. One begins to ask oneself: whence comes and what comes as the authorizing instance of this figure of "touch"? Why does one say "to touch" for "to speak of," "to concern," "to aim," "to refer to" in general, and so forth? Is it because touch, as Aristotle said, is not a "unique sense"? More and more, Nancy plays this game—the most serious game there is—which consists in using, as if there were not the slightest problem, this common and ancestral figure of tactile language in order to draw our attention to "'the' sense of touch" itself—that there is not. He invests this very invasion that, little by little, prevents us from distinguishing between thematic sense and operating function, between the proper or literal sense of this sense and all its tropological turns of phrase. When this nondistinction becomes troubling, one can no longer avoid eyeing this double writing. Is it touching upon something or is it touching upon touching itself, there where, having more or less surreptitiously drawn our attention to the irreducible figure of touching, this writing makes us put our finger on language, touching itself by touching us and getting to us while making us notice what is going on with touching, to be sure in a manner that is as obscure as it is aporetic, but above all in a *touching* manner to the point where all affect, all desire, all fascination, all experience of the other seems to be involved, in an unavoidably sensitive, or sentimental, fashion?

Unfailingly, the quasi-compulsory obligation to make everything converge toward the tactile has destructive effects. Abusive spending puts the lexicon of touch at risk of ruin, in one of those postwar, eschatological inflations, which excoriate themselves in the desperate call for a new era, as well as a new "provenance." It is there, perhaps, that the "deconstruction of Christianity" finds one of its apocalyptical symptoms: all we speak is "touching"; now, there is no "the" sense of touch—something else would have to come, something absolutely new, but still more ancient. Another body, another thinking body.

2. One would find the *second example* a little earlier in the same text. One must recall that *pertinence* is, literally, etymologically, the quality of that which touches, of what is important, of what counts ([Latin] *pertinet*). One says that a gesture is pertinent when it *touches*, touches *rightly*, concerns, refers to, or stands as it has to in relation to what has to be, and thus adjusts itself to the contact. It is said, figuratively, about discourse itself or thought that inscribes itself in it. Now, here is what one may read *in parentheses*, when Nancy seems to be dreaming (he is right to dream and I want to dream along with him), about a pertinent kiss, about being pertinent at last with regard to kisses or sex.

For Nancy's stubborn impertinence, the impertinence I like and admire the most, is that, at the heart of ecstasy, of offering, of ravishment, of the abandon of self to the other, even of sacrifice, he resolutely recalls—he is the most resolute man I know; he recalls exactly: he is the most exact or punctual person I know; he never misses an appointment—that one must not renounce pertinence, one must not renounce knowing and saying pertinently what is necessary on this subject to "safeguard reason": a whole politics of the Enlightenment to come, never renounce either philosophy, or knowledge, or thought, and take the time to add, even if *in parentheses*: "(All the same, something else needs to be added here. . . . But I can't dwell on this question here)": "(All the same, something else needs to be added here: confronted with non-Western practices of sacrifice, the non-pertinent character of our idea of sacrifice is doubtless not entirely distinct from many other sorts of impertinence, indeed, from impertinence in general. In a sense, we don't really know what "eating," "kissing," "having sex," or "commanding" mean outside of the West. . . . But I can't dwell on this question here.)"[12]

The impertinence, here, would consist in not touching, in not knowing how to touch, *attain,* accede (for example) to those experiences of touching called eating,[13] kissing, or having sex (and no doubt as well, although less directly, commanding) outside one's own home, here outside our West (presuming that one can speak calmly of *our* West and say *we* without touching it). Here again, the operating schema crosses the network of thematic figures. This crossing is troubling, it causes one to think, more precisely to reflect on touch. And this is confirmed when, along the way, one takes or holds the mouth,[14] eating, and kissing to be privileged places of an auto-affection for which "self-touching" seems to deliver up the transcendental model. This auto-affection (beginning with the suction of the nursling who presses his or her own lips together when the breast is taken away) goes from the mouth and the tongue to the hearing-oneself-speak of voice. But the voice divides, multiplies, and hetero-affects itself already in "sharing voices" [*le "partage des voix"*].

Here then, first of all, is a deduction of the kiss and of a "self-touching" whose grammatical reflexity I shall allow, as, I assume, he does, to oscillate from one to the other (touching *oneself* or touching *each other?* Is that really something else? How to say it? Is it the object of a possible knowledge?). The kiss, "the imperative . . . of kissing," is deduced, if one can believe the author of *The Categorical Imperative,*[15] from a law of sex or from "sex as law." (I tend to think that this is a manner of speaking, a pedagogy, a rhetoric meant for those who think of nothing else; as for me, I would just as well deduce "sex as law" from the aporias of the "self-touching," but this matters little; besides, he will indeed go on to say that the "libido" does not suffice to account for it, nor does some zoo-anthropology): "[F]inally, sex as law, this imperative of touching, kissing, which neither the drive of the species nor even the 'libido' can account for. For this imperative doesn't aim at any object, either large or small, either self or child, but only the pleasure/pain of a '*self*-touching' [d'un *se*- toucher]" (Nancy, *Corpus,* p. 36).

I provisionally interrupt the quotation here, at the point where an important parenthesis commences—concerning precisely an interruption that is important to me, which is to say interruption itself, the *punctuated* passage from self to you at the heart of self, a certain "and not 'oneself.'" Before I approach Nancy's prosthetical parenthesis about his "and not 'oneself'" or his "*without* returning to self," allow me to leave things suspended for a while.

The law of "self-touching," therefore: this fatal imperative produces *and* interrupts—it punctuates by the same token all the syntaxes of narcissism. Let us reread what could have been the most economic point of departure, namely, a certain page from *Une pensée finie* [A Finite Thinking] that brings together the most explicit and formalizing of Nancy's remarks—on, let us say, *touch*. His discourse extends to all the registers (*operating* or *thematic*, if, for convenience, we are still distinguishing there where the dissociation between these two modes is no longer strictly *pertinent*), it touches on all the senses, it integrates the infinite dimension of the "self-touching" that touches on everything, on the tangent, the tangible, *and* the intangible. Nancy transcendentalizes or ontologizes everything that comes down to "touching," and like a madman he goes on a ruinous spree, spending the resources, the credit, the capital, and the interest of the transcendental-ontological. He reduces them to monetary simulacra, it seems to me. And he even names, anticipating thereby my dream about eyes, the kiss of the eyes, the scene of eyes touching themselves and each other, eye to eye.

Yes, talking about us, in fact, he names the place "where touching and vision touch," as well as "orbital touch," and touching the "eye" itself. Let us scan a page:

> To touch language: to touch the trace, and to touch its effacement. To touch what moves and vibrates in the "open mouth, the hidden [*dérobé*] center, the elliptical return." To touch the ellipsis itself—and to touch ellipsis inasmuch as it touches, as an orbit touches the edges of a system, whether cosmological or ocular. A strange, orbital touch: touching the eye, the tongue, language, and the world. At the center, and in the belly.
> . . . *to discern* is to see and to trace. . . . Discerning is where touching and vision touch. It is the limit of vision—and the limit of touch. To discern is to see what differs in touching. To see the center differing (from itself): the ellipsis.[16]

From the first pages of the original book, *Une pensée finie*, from the general presentation of its logic and major concepts, notably the *ex-scribed*, as they will later be put to work, Nancy had laid out this drama of *contact at the limit*, which is to say an act without act, the affected act of touching, like this thinking that touches onto the limit. But it is a limit that also becomes *its own limit,* in a frighteningly enigmatic sense. It is a limit that the said thinking touches, therefore, without appropriating it for itself, however. Such would be the sense of the word "finite," in "a finite thinking." It is there that the infinitism that I have questioned in the Christian thinking of flesh finds itself altogether and at the same time proved and disproved, in a way—disproved at the heart of attested proof itself. We have no access to it except from this way of referring touch to the limit. For example, "a finite thinking: a thinking that, without renouncing truth or universality, without renouncing *sense,* is only ever able to think to the extent that it also touches on its own limit and its own singularity."[17]

It is all too obvious that there remains some uneasiness, a concern, and the confession of it is signed in passing: by all means, we should not renounce! Above all, we shouldn't even think of renouncing. Renouncing what? Truth, universality, sense! No less! Whether this is a confession, a concession, or a warning, matters little. Indeed, it is a reminder that the privilege of touch, like the privilege of singularity (privilege itself!) entails the risk of jeopardizing what has imposed itself *against* touch throughout history, for example, in this battle between the haptical and the optical, and in all the places where the value of the visible (*eidos,* revelation, unveiling, intuition, and so forth)[18] has so powerfully brought into accordance truth (and the universality one attaches to it) with the sense of sight and all the figurality that this sense organizes. There has been too much plowing through the field of this problematic (we have verified this often enough) for there to be any time, room, taste, or patience here, to come back to this once again. However, let us note that the first condition of a reexamination would consist in dissociating (just to see, or touch) the value of "sense" from the values of truth and universality, which Nancy here so quickly gathers in the same series. Is sense necessarily ordered within the aim at truth? This, too, is a terrain much stirred up in the past decades. (There is room here, for example, for a kind of Husserlian distinction between pure grammar and *logical* pure grammar.) Furthermore, in the very experience of the exscribed, Nancy must also take into account a tearing away from this finiteness and an opening toward the excess of the infinite, and there, no doubt, the truthful moment is produced, if not the moment of truth. For example: "This is why we call this thought 'writing,' that is, the inscription of this violence and of the fact that, through it, all sense is *exscribed,* ceaselessly refuses to come back to itself, and that all thinking is the finite thinking of these infinite excesses."[19]

The introductory chapter of *Une pensée finie* lets the word "touching"[20] recur and ends in the surroundings of one Rimbaud:

How to act, O stolen heart?[21]

Stop at the point of the question mark. Sigh, cry, or protest, the question is just a quotation, a reminder. It is isolated and insular on a line making up a paragraph by itself. Nothing explicitly announces (or follows up with) a commentary about it. This may be because all that is said here, before and after this question, *actually acknowledges*: it acknowledges this certainty that touching, in any case, touches the heart and on the heart, but inasmuch as it is *always* the heart of the other.

Even *self*-touching touches upon the heart of the other. Hearts never belong, at least there where they can be touched. No one should ever be able to say "my heart," my own heart, except when he or she might say it to someone else and call him or her this way—and that is love. There would be nothing and there would no longer be any question without this originary exappropriation and without a certain "stolen heart." This book, *Une pensée finie*, with the quotation "How to act, O stolen heart?" first came out in 1990, which is to say shortly after a certain surgical "operation," the heart transplantation, which I have already mentioned—but ten years before Nancy's *L'intrus* (The Intruder).[22] These dates do and do not count. What makes these texts strongly necessary does pertain to *finite thinking*, that is, a thinking both linked to contingency and foreign to it.

In *L'intrus*, from its association, this time, with the "*technē* of bodies," the "history of techniques" and "technical possibilities," the word "contingency" takes on a value that we can no longer reduce to the two remarkable and different uses of the same word "contingency" as analyzed earlier with regard to Franck's and Chrétien's texts. There again, it seems to me, through the question of transplant, grafting, and technical prosthetics, runs the dividing line that concerns us, inscribing and imposing itself in its most literal form:

. . . my own heart, therefore, was no longer of any use, for a reason that was never clarified. [The last I heard about this came from a doctor who told me: "Your heart was programmed to last fifty years."] And so, in order to live, it was necessary to receive someone else's heart, the heart of another.

(But what other program was my own physiological program coming across then? Less than twenty years earlier there were no transplants, and above all not with recourse to cyclosporine, which protects against one's rejection of the transplanted organ. Twenty years from now we shall certainly be dealing with another kind of transplantation, using other means. Personal *contingencies* are crossing *contingencies in the history of techniques*. Earlier, I'd have been dead; later, I would survive some other way. But "I" always finds itself squeezed into the narrow slot of *technical possibilities*. That is why it is in vain that those who wanted it to be a metaphysical adventure take on those who held it to be a *technical accomplishment* [performance technique]: it is a question of both—one within the other.)[23]

But right after the "limit of touch," upon or next to which he would still like to be touching, here comes nonlimitation itself, the transcendental quasi-ontologization of this sense: touch as *self-touching*. To be sure, touch, as *self-touching*, is touch, but also touch *plus* every other sense (whence the dizziness of the rhetorical turns of phrase). Touch, as *self-touching*, is the being of every sense in general, the being-sense of sense, the condition of possibility of sensibility in general, the very form of space and time, and so forth. But first of all, the will, the essence of the will, and therefore every metaphysics of the will (perhaps from Descartes to Kant or even to Nietzsche) will have been brought back to touch. Perhaps reduced to touch: haptico-transcendental reduction.

A strange tautology, therefore, which includes touch in the will, an analytic definition of the will that uncovers in it touch through simple explication. To will is to will touch, to want is to want to touch (it). To will is to want to touch, thus to bend [*plier*] activity to fall back into the fold [*repli*] of the passive-active auto-affection that is, in any will-to-touch, the let-oneself-be-touched by that which, the other, one touches at will. A "dangerous supplement" (Rousseau), a vicarious surplus of masturbatory pleasure does in no way reduce the alterity of the other who comes to inhabit the self-touching, or at least to haunt it, at least as much as it spectralizes any experience of "touching the other." For this affect, what here inflects or conjugates the *passive* activity of the will, goes equally no doubt by the name *desire*. Like the ontological and the transcendental, the will affects itself with its other from the first contact, as soon as it touches or one touches on touch, as soon as one wants *touch, wants to touch it, itself* [dès qu'on veut *le toucher, lui, lui-même*]:

It is the system again. It is the will to system. (But what is will? Who knows, or thinks he knows? Doesn't will differ in its essence?) [We can hear him mur-

muring, as usual, "there is no 'the' will."—J. D.] It is the will to touch: the wish that the hands touch, across the book, and through the book; that its hands touch, reaching just as far as its skin, its parchment; that our hands touch, always through the intermediary of skin, but touch nonetheless. To touch oneself, to be touched right at oneself, outside oneself, without anything being appropriated. That is writing, love, and sense.

Sense *is* touching.[24]

How is one to decipher this *is* in italics? Neutralized, in cautious suspension, it is also at the same time firmly insistent: sense itself, the sense of the senses, is the *very* sense of touch *proper*; the essence of touching is sense—and the essence of sense is touching. One could also understand this *is* as a sort of *transitive* whose active, haptical movement touches already, itself to itself: *to be* means *to touch* and *to touch touch*: sense (is), that is, touches touch, touch *is* (touches) touch: thus will or desire (see the preceding paragraphs). Touch touches on everything—altogether like philosophy, some people might say, and like philosophers, those meddlers who can't keep their hands off anything, in their insatiable polymorphous perversity or imperious encyclopedism.

Once more our subject slips off. Touch is no longer a category among others, whence its *quasi*-transcendental-ontologization—*quasi*, because the touchable of this touch gives itself over as untouchable. If it were a category, it would also be that which carries it off beyond itself, just as writing [*l'écrit*] exports itself into exscription, that other conceptual invention of Nancy's. "Sense *is* touching. The 'transcendental' of sense (or what is 'ontological' in it) is touch: obscure, impure, untouchable touch."[25]

If touch is the sense of all the senses, that is, of all sensitive or sensible presentation, of all that makes sense by presenting itself thus, one only writes *to touch on it* (in view of it, on it, in its favor, and so forth) by inscribing that limit on which, as we have just begun to sense, stands (but also overflows itself) the self-touching of any contact. Therefore this writing is never appropriate or appropriated, no more than it appropriates anything to itself: "To touch oneself, to be touched right at oneself, outside oneself, without anything being appropriated. That is writing, love, and sense."[26]

Nancy calls this the "exscribed"—and the call for a "deconstruction of Christianity." His recent works have laid out the consequent elaboration of the concept of ex-scription.

Absent reconstruction here of all the developments that tell of the ex-scription of writing, of the trace as self-effacement, let us just read the lines that are closest to this analytics of touch—there where it overflows itself, at once figuring or fictionalizing itself, in a *quasi*-transcendental-ontological hyper-analytics. This analytics calls into question "all material or spiritual modalities of a presence full of sense, charged with sense," all the philosophemes or theologemes that we have examined within the problematics of "flesh":

> As soon as writing touches the body [i.e., a certain body "lost," headlong, *à corps perdu*—J. D.], writing loses touch itself. Writing has only to trace it or efface it. But the body is not lost in the simple exteriority of a "physical" or "concrete" presence. Rather, it is lost to all material or spiritual modalities of a presence full of sense, charged with sense. And if writing loses the body, loses its own body, *à corps perdu*, this occurs to the extent to which it inscribes its presence beyond all recognized modalities of presence. To inscribe presence is not to (re)present it or to signify it, but to let come to one and over one what merely presents itself at the limit where inscription itself withdraws (or ex-scribes itself, writes itself outside itself). . . .
>
> . . . The experience named "writing" *is* this violent exhaustion of the dis-course in which "all sense" is altered, not into another sense or the other way, but in this exscribed body.[27]

Touching with tact upon the thinking of touch, but also hugging it, body and soul, in one's arms [*à bras-le-corps*], such thinking must at the same time offer itself and expose itself—to letting itself be touched. For to touch, so one believes, is, touching what one touches, to let oneself be touched by the touched, by the touch of the thing, whether objective or not, or by the "flesh" that one touches and that then becomes touching as well as touched.

This is not true of all the other senses: one may, to be sure, let oneself be "touched" as well by what one hears or sees, but not necessarily heard or seen by what one hears or sees, whence the initial privilege of what is called touch (this at least is Husserl's argument, discussed earlier).

To touch, so one believes, amounts therefore to letting oneself be touched by what one touches and is thus to touch, with pertinence, upon touch, in a manner that is at once touching and touched. Now, Nancy says and thus thinks this *as* did others before him, to be sure, but *otherwise*. In what way does he also say something other than the tradition up until Merleau-

Ponty or Maldiney, for example? That is where one now needs to start or start over again.

Make believe I'm starting over again, since I obviously and avowedly have the feeling I can never get to it, to the truth, and I can never touch the point of departure, not to mention the end. I dare to content myself with telling, out of order, the story of what I would have liked to write in order to reach him, precisely, in an appropriate, fitting [*apte*] way. No, not even the story, then, but certain stories that are more or less anecdotal, of what touched me while I was trying to write "On Touching."

Thus, for example, this scene of friendship, of meetings, and contretemps; the contretemps at the rendezvous, in 1992, probably. I remember one of our meetings, that of a missed rendezvous one evening at the Strasbourg airport, on the eve of one of those innumerable colloquiums on the geophilosophy of Europe. Impossible to get in touch on the telephone. Jean-Luc is punctual and comes to join me after having missed me at the airport, and after I had already gotten to town; he is accompanied by our friend Jacqueline Risset, to whom I had just written to say (on the eve of that day), rather belatedly, how much I liked and admired, once again, *L'amour de loin* [Love from a Distance].[28]

The title of one poem there[29] was already echoing, without my realizing it, the title chosen much earlier for the "text-on-touch-that-I-dreamed-of-writing-for-Jean-Luc-Nancy . . . "

No punctuation whatsoever in this poem, no punctuation mark, not even at the end, except after the question to "you" ("sinon toi?" [if not you?]). Is the punctuation of the *you* the least of the beauty of this poem in which all the modalities are inflected between *if, not,* and the point of the question mark?

Le toucher

. . . .

mais qui

pourrait me toucher à présent
sinon toi?

. . . .

[. . . but who/could touch me at present/if not you? . . .]

In what way does Nancy also say something other than the tradition up to Merleau-Ponty and Maldiney? Is it only in that he says something *other,* precisely the *other*, the other who anticipates and inter-venes [*pré-vient . . . inter-vient*] at the heart of the presence-to-self of the self-touching? Is it only in that he says the other at the heart of the most hyperbolic reflexivity or the most narcissistic specularity when it comes to "self-touch"? This would keep him in close, tangential proximity to Franck's and Chrétien's intent, if the question of technical contingency did not come to complicate things.

But there isn't just the potential difference [*différend*] regarding technical contingencies; there is also all that gives itself to *think* in the different gestures of the body, the different scene and staging, "style," or writing pragmatics.

At this point, on this stage, this other is neither enunciated nor designated, neither written nor even *exscribed* by Nancy in the third person of a constative. The signatory of this thought addresses himself to "you," and punctuating otherwise, he apostrophizes you in the second person at the heart of a philosophical discourse on the heart. He thus writes you in his *Corpus*, and I pick up the preceding quotation where I interrupted it:

> For this imperative doesn't aim at any object, neither large nor small, neither self nor child, but only the pleasure/pain of a "*self*-touching" [d'un *se*- toucher]. (Or yet again: of a remaining-self, or a becoming-self *without* returning to self. To take pleasure [*jouir*] is at the *heart* of the dialectic a diastole without systole: this heart is the body.)
>
> *To self-touch* you (and not "oneself") [*Se toucher* toi (et non "soi")]—or again, identically, *to self-touch skin* (and not "oneself"): such is the thinking that the body always forces to go further, always too far. In truth, it is thought itself which forces itself in this way and dislocates itself: for all the weight, all the gravity of thought—itself a *weighing*—in the end goes toward nothing except *consenting to the body and bodies*. (Exasperated consent.) (Nancy, *Corpus*, p. 36)[30]

How is one to gauge the full consequence of this "toi," of "toi," yours, when the "self-touching" offers its reflexivity to *your* effraction without all the same renouncing it, without yielding or giving in in its relation to self?

If (in an absurd hypothesis) I had to choose the most decisive word in these last sentences, it would no doubt be "exasperated": "*exasperated* consent." I would then try to justify my choice with the appropriate analysis: exasperation neither contradicts nor negates consent; it sharpens it, stretches and challenges it; it turns it over to its contrary so that it suffers itself to be what it is—consenting. But there again—the word "consenting" may call for it—this would in a way draw a tangent to Chrétien's thinking ("Every sensation first consents to the world"),[31] if so many other contextual features did not keep them distinct: first, the irreducible plurality of bodies to which it is a question of consenting ("consenting to the body and bodies"), a plurality that cannot be gathered in a divine, Christic body that would in some way be one and common; and second, therefore, this experience of the technical at the heart of the heart, a timed experience that bears witness, at one stroke, from an indisputable event, to an "exasperated consent" as foreign to revolt as to acceptance. Each thus deals with a different "yes" or an altogether different provenance of the same "yes"—by essence always addressed to a "you," a *toi*.

L'intrus describes this consenting and exasperated experience that leads beyond "revolt" and "acceptance," but also beyond all metaphysics of the *proper* and *salvation*, and therefore Christian flesh. What is just as remarkable is this evidence: a certain description here has recourse to schemas and to a lexicon dating from before the "operation"; we have verified that it puts to work a "logic" that had long been formalized.

Thus, the multiple stranger who intrudes upon my life (my feeble, winded life, which at times slides into a malaise that verges on a simply astonished abandonment) is none other than death—or rather, life/death: a suspension of the continuum of being, a scansion wherein "I" has/have little to do. *Revolt and acceptance are equally foreign to the situation.* But there is nothing that is not foreign. The means of survival themselves, these, first of all, are completely strange: what can it mean to replace a heart? The thing exceeds my capacity to represent it. (Opening the entire thorax, maintaining the organ to be grafted in the proper state, circulating the blood outside of the body, suturing the vessels. . . . I fully understand why surgeons proclaim the insignificance of this last point: the vessels involved in the bridging grafts are much smaller. . . . But it matters little: organ transplant imposes the image of a passage through nothingness, of an entry into a space emptied of all property, all intimacy— or, on the contrary, the image of this space intruding in me: of tubes, clamps, sutures, and probes.)

What is this life "proper" that it is a matter of "saving"? At the very least, it turns out that it in no way resides in *"my" body;* it is not situated anywhere, not even in this organ whose symbolic renown has long been established.

(One might say: still, there's the brain. And of course, from time to time the idea of a brain transplant enlivens the news. Humanity will one day doubtless speak of this again. For the moment, it is accepted that the brain cannot survive without the rest of the body. On the other hand, and to leave the matter here, the brain would perhaps survive with an entire system of transplanted body parts . . .).[32]

Shouldn't the "self-touching you" henceforth accommodate the *possibility*, at least, of this event (of this "operation," for example) and of the thinking discourse that it thus calls for? Isn't the *effective* thinking of this possibility in itself (at least if it is *effective*) already an indisputable, unforgettable event, which is always unexampled and always ready to deprive us of a "for example"? An event from which one should thus always start and de-part again—at least prepare oneself for "another departure"? For another thinking of the event, of the *effectivity* of what arrives and happens, and what happens—to you.

§ 13 "And to you." The Incalculable

Exactitude, Punctuality, Punctuation

Thinking of "self-touching you": one will have had to prepare this now; some precaution or protocol will have had to forestall its grammar.

1. One must first of all speak of *reflexivity* and not *specularity*, since the contact (the *self-touching* and the *self-touching you* of the two borders) does not submit to the paradigm of sight or the mirror, of the speculum, or something like: "the eye can hear," no more than to the system of phenomenological (at least Husserlian) prescriptions discussed earlier. Here, on the contrary, and this is the ontological transcendentality of the haptical, sight is a touching. The question remains: what happens when our eyes touch? And do they not touch as soon as our looks intersect, hesitating infinitely between two Orients, between the visible eye (which it is therefore possible to touch) and the seeing eye (which is finally, essentially, absolutely untouchable)?

2. The *self-touching-you* remains incalculable. It weighs, but thinking it exceeds its calculation. It is neither *one* (monadic), a single one, a unique self-touching-oneself, nor the *double*, symmetrical, and above all immediate relation of a reciprocal self-touching-one-another whose impersonal law could be uttered in the third person. The dissymmetry (and the fact that it is double does not at all make it symmetrical) opens onto the inaccessible transcendence of a *you*, of you, who do(es) not let it(your)self, is (are) obliged, owe(s) it first of all to desire, not to let itself ever be reappropriated in the mastering reflexivity of the self, of the relation to self of whatever touches itself and accedes to self in the self-touching. This latter

"you" will never let itself be inflected in a first or third person (singular or plural); it must remain the touchable (that is, untouchable) pole of a vocative or an apostrophizing address. This is not *said*, or not said *in this way* (in disrespect of grammar out of respect for the other), in all the utterances about self-touching that we have encountered up to this point. But the fact that it is not said in this way does not mean that it remains unthought. It should not prevent us from reading it there while putting something of our own into it.

3. This effraction of the other, of what cannot return to self, is the condition of desire; it is the heart, this "organ whose symbolic renown has long been established."[1] The thinker of the syncope is also a thinker of the diastole, of the gap or dilation without return, of this *other heart*, at the heart of which the diastolic difference or diastema does not let itself be gathered up or contracted in the relation to self, in the *syn-* of any systole. This thinking of dilation without return to self, without exchange, of a heart without circulation is the thinking of an absolute generosity, of a generosity more generous than generosity itself, which as its name indicates, would still be genial and too natural.

Reread—from the perspective of Descartes's and Nancy's respective concepts of the circulation of blood and of generosity—Nancy's *Ego sum*, and *L'expérience de la liberté* (*The Experience of Freedom*), two great books, in what they give one to think about the gift, that is to say, a generosity of nonsubjective freedom, *a surprising generosity of being*. This generosity is announced from the vantage point of a death that is as inappropriable as birth, "in an 'immortality' of freedom which is not a supernatural life, but which frees in death itself the unprecedented offering of existence."[2]

Once again, this "generosity of being" orients us toward what is beyond being, beings, or essence (*epekeina tēs ousias*). It may seem "surprising" in that it lets one think of a gift beyond being, and connects genesis or generation with this movement of abandon that lets be—without it, without itself, and without its origin—the very thing itself to which it gives rise. In this connection, Plotinus cites the observation of "the ancients" [i.e., Plato *Republic* 6.509B9] that the One is beyond the essence He generates, and is a slave neither to essence nor to himself. He who made the essence "left it outside himself, because he has no need of being."[3] Earlier, Plotinus describes this same necessity-freedom of the One, by drawing—so to speak—the place of the One, with the help of striking haptical figures: here is contact or tangency, there where the difference between the inside and the outside is no longer a pertinent distinction or opposition. Plotinus makes a drawing, then, as it were, with the help of circles, of lines or letters—of rays (*grammai*). And he does this, as always in these texts, while apostrophizing the other; he likewise punctiliously addresses himself to you:

> And you when you seek, seek nothing outside him, but seek within all things which come after him; but leave him himself alone. For he himself is the outside, the encompassment and measure of all things. Or within in depth, but what is outside him, touching him in a kind of circle [*tangent à Lui comme en cercle*] and depending on him, is all which is rational principle and intellect; but, rather, it would be Intellect, in so far as it touches him and in the way that it depends on him, in that it has from him its being Intellect.[4]

The heart of this other heart cannot be touched, does not touch *itself*: it *self*-touches *you*. It can only touch itself/be touched by your eyes. And this other heart, mine, is not an organ that can be cut out of my body ("this heart is the body," he says). But it is also not something else; it is not a figure inherited (from the Bible, for example) that means the center, life, *psuchē*, *pneuma*, spirit, interiority, feeling, love. It is the body, it is the heart insofar as it is yours belonging to me [*m'appartient à toi*], the other heart, the heart of the other, there where the "spiritual" figure, the inherited metonymy, touches this heart, my body, in my body, and can no longer be dissociated from it.

In order for there to be this heart, this good heart, the possibility of the bad heart must remain forever *open*—which is to say to itself as altogether (any) other. A heart would not be good unless it could be other, bad, radically, *unforgivably* bad, ready for any infidelity, any treachery and perjury (which we have precisely linked with an inevitable-impossible vow of abstinence and thus with the structure of the untouchable's and the tactile's fate)—and therefore unless one could have a change of heart.

We have to know, when the time comes, how to have a change of heart.

This may be how one can translate the analysis in *The Experience of Freedom* of malignancy, diabolical wickedness, and radical evil, in short, what Kant terms the "evil heart."[5] This may be a way of orienting the reading of the richly complex, fundamental chapter titled "Evil: Decision." Consid-

ering what has been said here about the carnal, or "flesh" [*chair*], such a
reading would especially dwell on the passage linking the motif of "unpar-
donable" evil with a note about the "[concentration] camps"—carnality
that is fiercely tenacious [*acharnement*], wasting away [*décharnement*], and
heaped in a mass grave [char*nier*].[6]

4. At stake is the pleasure taken in pleasure [*jouir de la jouissance*].What
pleases us when our eyes touch? That is what I was finally asking you.

Nancy's response: "To take pleasure [*jouir*] is at the *heart* of the dialectic a diastole without systole." The heart *of* this other dialectic (diastole
without systole), namely, the pleasure of taking pleasure, is the heart itself,
namely, this other heart that self-touches you, that belongs to you, that
gives pleasure only there where pleasure is made all the more intense by
not returning to me, by returning to me without returning to me, there
where I self-touch you.

The ecstatic and haptical *without* of the "*without* returning to self*" is
what interrupts the circulation in this heart, this other heart, which is to say
also what makes it beat with a beating that is no longer, has never been the
regular alternation of systole and diastole. What interrupts circulation is
what makes the heartbeat and it's you, the *you* of self-touching-you. He emphasizes the word "heart": "only the pleasure/pain of a '*self*-touching' [d'un
se-toucher]. (Or yet again: of a remaining-self, or a becoming-self *without*
returning to self. To take pleasure [*jouir*] is at the *heart* of the dialectic a diastole without systole: this heart is the body)" (Nancy, *Corpus*, p. 36).

"And you," *et toi*: these are, be it noted, the last words of his *Corpus*.
"Corpus" is within *Corpus* the *mise en abyme* of the title at the head of the
last two pages. In it, we can pick out precisely that which cannot be picked
up or sublated (*aufheben*), that is to say, the dissemination of essence, of the
One, and of what confers Oneness on the Being of whatever it may be. But
this dissemination is not tied to anything like the body, "the" very body *itself*, the being-body of the body, the being-properly the body proper: *the*
"flesh." First of all, dissemination pluralizes any singularity that allows one
to say "the" ["*le*" ou "*la*"], to utilize an article that is definite or defining for
whatever it may be whose very being itself, universal essence, or individual
substance could thus be designated properly as *it self* [*cela même*], for example "the body," "the" sense of touch, *the* [la] "flesh," and so forth. Now,
he terms *corpus* this sublating dissemination that does not come upon the
body by way of the body. He gathers, without gathering, around the word

corpus, which can above all not be translated merely as "body" [*corps*], all the ways of speaking that come to "tell" of this dissemination. This is the passage that opens rather than closes with "and you" at the final end of *Corpus*. We might say that this final and endless passage is a *response* and corresponds to the programmatic announcement at the beginning of the book: "Let There Be Writing the Body," "Let there be writing, not *about* the body, but the body itself" (ibid., p. 12). This "program of modernity" multiplied its haptical injunctions to the point where it made them shoulder, all at once, the entire resolution and the entire responsibility of a self-dissolution. On two pages, for example (but we would have to pursue this throughout the book):

> Writing: to touch on extremity. And how is one to touch upon the body instead of signifying it or making it signify? . . . how is one to touch upon the body? . . . touching on the body, touching the body, *touching* at last—happens all the time in writing. . . . touching the body (or rather touching this or that singular body) *with the incorporeal* of "sense," and consequently, *making the incorporeal touching*, or turning *sense* into a touch [*une touche*].
> . . . By essence, writing touches upon the body. . . . Writing touches on bodies *in accordance with the absolute limit* that separates the sense of the former from the skin and the nerve endings of the latter. Nothing comes to *pass*, and that is where it touches. (ibid., pp. 12–13)

But at the very moment when he seems about to give in to a haptical inflation, Nancy knows, better than anyone, not to credit "the" sense of touch with any semantic capital. None of the senses is *assured*, even if it can be quoted in the stock market. Nancy often repeats this. I choose this passage because in it he associates a critique of the presupposed *immediacy* of carnal or spiritual touching (which concerned us in the preceding chapters) and a critique of the ideologies of the "body" (as for me, I would more bluntly say the "philosophies of the body"):

> As we have already said, the "touch" of this thinking—the scales of this "nerve-meter" [*pèse-nerfs*] that it must be or it is nothing—does not belong to an immediacy that is anterior and exterior to sense. It is, on the contrary, the very limit of sense—and the limit of sense is to be taken in all senses, each of which breaks into the other. . . .
> But one must not therefore extend to "touch" too simple a *credit*, and, most important, one must not believe that one could touch *the* sense of "touch," insofar as it sets a limit on sense(s). This is a rather common tendency of the

most robust ideologies of the "body," that is, the crudest ones (of the type
"muscle-bound thinking" or "sacred-heart thinking," vitalo-spiritualist fascism
—with, no doubt, its real and secret horror of bodies). (ibid., pp. 40–41)

The continuation of the same chapter describes a certain "mobile . . . caress," the "touches" of pleasure taking pleasure in [*d'une jouissance qui jouit*]
the "yes" ("the 'yes' [*oui*] that *jouit*"), and this "consenting" that not only
says *yes* to sense, to the senses, to the "touches" among them by way of
which they touch, divide, and share themselves, but also to the commitment of who senses in what he or she senses, to his or her consenting and
co-appearance. And there—both through this consenting and the example
of the "visible"—the tangency with Merleau-Ponty or Chrétien is all too
obvious (for example: "Complicity, consenting: the one who sees *co-appears*
with what he or she sees" [ibid., p. 43]). But here, too much *local* evidence
risks concealing the *distance* that sets him apart and that we are continually
measuring. His writing implements this discrepancy, a writing that is en-
gaging in its "form" (its tone, connotations, setup, mise-en-scène of the
scene, indeed in ob-scene: for this discrepancy also turns into strong language [*écarts de langage*] and inventive language), beyond the external surface, the surroundings and wrappings of thought. This writing *engages* the
body of thought and thought as body, precisely, for what is at issue is a self-
seeking body, a body to think or promise, a body to come.

It may be time to make a point, which is more than a mere technicality,
about this discrepancy and the distance between Nancy's corpus and the
work of all the others we have hitherto touched on. So far, in order to
mark out this difference and to pretend that it could be assembled, in order to insist, I have often invoked a "technical" dimension (prostheses,
transplants, metonymic substitutes, and so forth). Nancy's constant attention to it distinguishes his thinking on "touching" (and therefore about
the rest as well), it seems to me. But most often, not always, instead of
"the technical," of *technē*, and "technology" or even "the question of technics," I have preferred to quote Nancy and say "*technē* of the body" or
"ecotechnics," and this was in order to follow him and warn against the
general-singular ("the" technical) and against a modern *doxa* always prone
to misusing this conceptual bent or alibi. First of all let me refer to what
Nancy himself says about this in "A Finite Thinking." Again, he calls for
vigilance as regards "technology" as a "fetish-word." And to pinpoint just
one word in this rich, necessary, and complex analysis (which should be

examined more closely), I shall merely quote the following sentence in which we can recognize one of Nancy's typical gestures, of which we already found a good number of examples. The sentence conforms itself to the typical syntagma "There is no 'the' . . . "; here: "And this is why there is no 'the' technical, merely a multiplicity of technologies."[7] Earlier, he has marked his analysis with these two other propositions: "'The' technical is nothing other than the 'technique' *of* compensating for the nonimmanence of existence in the given"; or: "'The' technical—understood this time as the 'essential' technicity that is *also* the irreducible multiplicity *of* technologies—compensates for the absence of *nothing*; it fills in for and supplements *nothing*."[8]

As regards this example—an exemplary example, precisely more than an example—I am tempted to up the ante a little more. The "there is no 'the' technical" isn't just another "there is no 'the' . . . " among others, or just a sample in a homogeneous series. Rather, under this name or another, it would give us a privileged access to all the "there is no 'the' . . . "'s, and thus to something like the "essence" of the technical that precisely "there is not." Hence a quasi-transcendental dizziness. For this is the process opening onto the possibility of a supplementary substitution, onto a metonymy that compromises the unity or oneness proper of essences. It is because there is *some* [*de* la] technical (which there is not) that there isn't this or that, and so forth, and that one can infinitely repeat or multiply examples and gestures that deconstruct the *very* unity or the properness *itself* of all essences or even all "beings."

Nancy's deconstructing gesture thus often inscribes itself within the form of the "there is no 'the' . . . ," and we can perceive its necessity. But Nancy himself knows that one has to use cunning, make deals, and negotiate with it. This necessity could deprive him of any conceptual determination and virtually any discourse—or hand over discourse to the most irresponsible empiricism. Socrates has been teaching us this for thousands of years. He would say: I'm not asking you for an enumeration of techniques, but for what you mean to say when you term them techniques in the plural. In what way are they techniques? And so forth. The definite or defining article is already engaged or required by the discourse that disputes it. It is with this limit that Nancy grapples, within this transaction, in this wrestling match of thinking. And deconstruction, too. No, deconstruction*s*, because neither is there, in the first place, any "the" deconstruction. Writing this, I perceive that the syntagma that has imposed itself on me these past few years (or decades), even as I insisted on the multiplicity of deconstructions, hasn't been "there is no 'the' . . . " but "if there is any" [*s'il y en a*] (the pure and unconditional in so many forms: event, invention, gift, forgiving, witnessing, hospitality, and so on—"if there is any"). Each time, it was necessary to point to the possible (the condition of possibility) *as* to the impossible itself. And "if there is any" doesn't say "there is none," but rather, there isn't anything that could make room for any proof, knowledge, constative or theoretical determination, judgment—especially not any determining judgment. It is another way of inflecting the "there is no 'the.'" It isn't the same, precisely, for here are two irreducibly different "deconstructive" gestures. The fact remains that this multiplicity announces itself as "deconstructive." It is necessary to account for this analogy or affinity, to say deconstruction in the singular again, in order to say it in the plural, in the "singular plural"—and explain at least why in the two syntagmas, the "there is" turns *to a conditional* ("if there is any") in one instance and to a *negative modality* ("there is no . . . ") in the other. The "any [of something]" [*en*] ("if there is any") precisely refers to what there is not, commanded by the defining article ("there is no 'the' . . . "). Surely not, not surely. One could draw many additional consequences from this discussion thus sketched—for example, if one said, for all those reasons: "Yes, but there is no *the* deconstruction of [*the*] Christianity [*'le' christianisme*]," because there isn't and never has been either a "the" deconstruction or a "the" Christianity.

And Nancy has written, moreover: "There is that there is: creation of the world" (*Corpus*, p. 104).

Let's come back to "you." To "and you." To its punctuation—which counts and *effectively* determines the tone, the gesture, and the address, cut short only by the ruling that comes from the other: from you.

How does the "and you." [*sic*] arise ("you" followed by a period)? How does this apostrophizing come to close and suspend at the same time—suspending without suspending, suspending and stopping short? How does it come to decide, to turn toward *you* the last chapter, which is precisely titled "Corpus," in a *mise en abyme*? By interrupting a series, a kind of "etc."; by interrupting the suspension points, which no longer appear as they did in our earlier questioning of the "tactile corpus"?[9] "And you." [*sic*] closes a chapter that started with the reminder that: "There is no 'the' body; there is no 'the' sense of touch; there is no 'the' *res extensa*" (Nancy, *Corpus*, p. 104). "A body is an image offered to other bodies, a whole corpus of images stretched from body to body; colors, local shadows, fragments, moles, areolas, half-moons [*lunules*], fingernails, body hair, tendons, skulls, ribs, pelvises, bellies, meatuses, froths, tears, teeth, foams, clefts, blocks, tongues, sweats, liquids [*liqueurs*], veins, pains, and joys, and me, and you" (*Corpus*, p. 105).

End of book. This multiplicity resists the infinite; it finitely resists the infinite and infinitely challenges every presupposed unity of whatever it may be—self, body proper, and flesh. And of the hand, I would add. But the decidedly finite series doesn't spread out in a purely random way, for that matter; it is *written*, it writes itself symphonically (sharing voices) toward a "joy" that at once recalls the "yes" of pleasure, the *"oui* that *jouit."* The final syllables open up the voice [*voix*], leave open the passage but part the way [*voie*] thus opened; they part the lips of a mouth full of joy and pleasure, toward me, no doubt—but in the end from me to you: " . . . and joys, and me, and you." Words—but a mouth before orality: kissing. Then singing or speaking. These offerings, anything and everything whatsoever being offered, bodies, pieces of a body not in pieces or shards, this world, these shared-out worlds do nothing but feign empirical accumulation. Apparently, it is a headlong contagious abandoned thrust, a general contamination,[10] and yet everything remains exactly calculated.

First of all, in this generous profusion, among all the glorified gifts, there is the "limit" and the "border," which are nothing, but make possible any gift whatsoever—if there is any.

And *then* all the words—so well chosen, in a list that is bound to stop (border and limit of the "etc.")—are in the *plural*, except *moi* and *toi*, "and me, and you." I *and* you—that is even more singular than I or you. Singular plural singular.

5. Of course, none of this takes place, and first of all this interruption (diastole *without* systole), except by risking death at every moment. This other heart self-touches you only to be exposed to death. We are here at the heart of *a finite thinking*. The heart is always of a finite thinking. It thinks, for the heart is the place of thinking and not only the place of feeling, love, desire; in it a finite thinking is thought. You are/is also my death. You, you keep it for me, you keep me from it always a little, from death. Keep me from it still a little longer, if you please, just a little longer, keep me from it as much as possible, as well as possible, as long as possible.

Finally, isn't what the "heart" names the ultimate place of absolute mourning, the sanctuary of what one keeps when one can no longer keep anything—keep inside oneself, as one often says, to name what infinitely exceeds the inside? The sensible but invisible and untouchable place for what one not only keeps committed to memory, not only in oneself, but in yourself in myself, when you are greater still, a heart in me greater than my heart, more alive than I, more singular and more other than what I can anticipate, know, imagine, represent, and remember? When "my" heart is first of all the heart of the other, and therefore, yes, greater than my heart in my heart?

I renounce speaking all of Nancy's heart, all of Nancy's hearts ("cor tuum mondum est totum tuum"), and ask readers to go beyond [Rimbaud's] "O stolen heart" on their own, at least to [Nancy's] "The Heart of Things,"[11] to "Shattered Love," which comprises a section on "The Heart: Broken."[12] In passing, they will come across an overabundance of haptical figures there.

6. One has to understand what is being thought about finitude in this extraordinary invention of a grammar or a syntactic anomaly: *se toucher toi* and not *se toucher soi* or even *se toucher lui, elle ou l'autre*, that is, "to self-touch you" and not "to touch oneself" or even "to touch him, her, or the other": this invention exscribes, it finds a way of making writing come out of itself by marking that you, here, will never be a simple mediation in a reappropriating movement of self-presence. You, metronome of my heteronomy, you will always resist that which, in my "self-touching," could dream of the reflexive or specular autonomy of self-presence (be it that of the *Dasein*) or of self-consciousness, absolute knowledge. The interruption of the dialectic (which does not exclude the dialectic, no more than Kierkegaard ever did at the height of his altercation with Hegel: and "taking pleasure" is at the heart of the dialectic, says Nancy) is you, when I self-touch you. That is why I love you, and sometimes so painfully, at the heart of pleasure itself. And if I insist here on this interruption of the reflexivity that is an absolute specularity at the heart of the "self-touching," it is because only touch (contact, caress, kiss) can, as "self-touching-you," interrupt the mirror reflection in its visual—ocular or optical, or haptical —dimension.

That is why we began with the kiss of the eyes: the meeting of looks, eyes that see themselves in the eyes of the other should be an example of the "self-touching-you" and be part of tactile experience; in short, they should involve skin—a caress or a kiss, eyes kissed by eyes—if desire or love passed through them. But when we say *love*, we must never exclude from it, of course, that modality called hate, jealousy, death dealt to the other, to you, at the very moment in which I ask, "Keep me a little from death."

If one followed through all the consequences of this hyper-transcendental-ontologization of *tact* (rather than *touching*), one would have to say of speech in general what has just been said of sight: only the *"self-touching-you"* (and not "oneself") can interrupt the reappropriation or the absolute reflection of self-presence (pure life or pure death: it is always, infinitely, the same thing). When I speak to you, I touch you, and you touch me when I hear you, from however far off it comes to me, and even if it is by telephone, the recollection of a voice's inflection on the phone, or by letter or e-mail, too. But of course, in order for me to be touched in this way by you, I have to be able to touch *myself*. In the "self-touching-you," the "self" is as indispensable as you. A being incapable of touching itself could not bend itself to that which absolutely unfolds it, to the totally other who, as totally other/like all others [*comme tout autre*], inhabits my heart as a stranger. There isn't any anthropological limit here, and this should be valid, *on the one hand*, for all "animal" or "divine" *life*; and *consequently, on the other hand*, make the life of the living in general a derivative concept with regard to this possibility of self-touching-you. (I don't know whether Nancy would still grant me this much here.)

It is necessary to love *oneself, each other* [*il faut s'aimer*], says every "I love you," and without this (impossible) auto-affection, without the reflected experience of impossible auto-affection, without the ordeal of the possibility of this impossibility, there would be no love.[13] It is necessary for us to love ourselves—each—other: "il faut *s'aimer*"—yet another piece of good fortune in French grammar, which puts transitivity in reflexivity, right at the reflexive form, and indissociates them forever—at least if it is necessary, and wanting.

Whence the all-powerful logic of narcissism: not as experience of the gaze, but as the painfully ironic discourse of the confession that mimics the appropriation of the unappropriable, you, my Echo, when you ruse, as I do, with the divine interdiction, when you deceive it in order to speak in your own name and to declare untranslatably *your* love while pretending to repeat the end of my sentences. As I have done at length elsewhere, I could invoke Ovid or Novalis here, but I choose the latter because my

theme is the kiss from you/of you: "One ought never to confess one's love. The secret of this confession is the vivifying principle of the only true and eternal love. The first kiss in this comprehension is the principle of philosophy—the origin of a new world—the beginning of an absolute era—the act that accomplishes an alliance with self [*Selbstbund*] that grows endless. Who would not like a philosophy whose kernel is a first kiss?"[14]
    After which, one must hasten to specify:

A. The principle of philosophy is not philosophy. The latter, which comes after its principle, might therefore consist in no more than a frenzied forgetting of the first kiss. I, the philosopher, hypothetically, run to catch the recollection of the first kiss. Would I have taken it? Was it given to me? And I no longer know the difference between kissing (on the mouth, forehead, eyes, and so forth) and blessing—for example, the recollection of a kiss before the kiss.

B. This latter, as auto-hetero-affection, inaugurates all experience, in particular speech and the declaration of love; it does not bring closer only lips, my two lips to the two lips and to the tongue of the other, but everything of the body that lets itself be touched in this way by auto-hetero-affection: for example, our eyes.

C. Novalis says elsewhere: "The authentic philosophical act [*echte philosophische Akt*] is suicide [*Selbsttötung*]; that is the real beginning of all philosophy—where every need of the philosophical disciple [*des philosophischen Jüngers*] will lead him—and only this act corresponds to all the conditions and characteristics of transcendent action [or transcendental: *der transcendenten Handlung*]."[15]

What remains to be thought *together* is the first kiss *and* suicide, the principle *and* the act of authentic philosophy, their youth *and* their discipline, the act *and* the action. The impossible task of a general haptology.

7. This *quasi*-hyper-transcendental-ontologization of tact (and not of touch) must remain paradoxical: it *exscribes* itself instead of inscribing or writing itself. For that which touches on it or that about which one speaks in speaking of touch is also the *intangible*. To touch with tact is to touch without touching that which does not let itself be touched: to embrace

eyes, in a word (or in several words, and the word always brings to your ear the modest reserve of a kiss on the mouth). To touch as tact is, thanks to you, because of you, to break with immediacy, with the immediate given wrongly associated with touch and on which all bets are always placed, as on self-presence, by transcendental idealism (Kantian or Husserlian intuitionism) or by ontology, the thinking of the presence of beings or of being-*there as such* in its Being, the thinking of the body proper or of flesh.

   8. I have just gone too quickly. In order to demonstrate that the great thinker of touch is interested, as is finally only right, in nothing but the intangible—and this is not something else—one would have to think, once again, to weigh here, to weigh *exactly* what he says about the relation between *thinking* and *weighing.* One would have to read and meditate here step by step *Le poids d'une pensée* [The Weight of a Thought] and in particular its opening, where Nancy tells us what to think about the fact that: "Etymology relates thinking [*pensée*] to weighing [*pesée*]."[16]

   Exactly: one cannot overemphasize the concern that Nancy, the man and the thinker, has for *exactitude.* One has to know him well. Even when he oversteps the bounds, as he must, and opens himself up to excess, to exaggeration, ecstasy, ex-scription, he is *set* on giving himself over to it— he stands by it—not only with the probity (*Redlichkeit*) that he has spoken of so precisely,[17] but with a singular exactitude that is not necessarily opposed to rigor, as others have maintained. Husserl or Heidegger, for example, limit the exact to the objective and calculable form of quantitative measure (of a "what"), forgetting that exactitude can also be a virtue (the relation of a "who" to a "whom").
   Nancy says both—the exactitude of measure and that of the person (to Georges [a man photographs of whom appear in *Le poids d'une pensée*— Trans.]: "You are exact"—utmost praise).
   Exactitude here describes exactly (*exact*: in a correct manner; *apte*) an acute, incisive, precise punctuality, as at the driving pen point of the drawing (*exact*, from *exigo, ex-ago*: to push, finish, require [*exiger*], measure, rule), the faithful punctuality of one who commits himself to be at the rendezvous *on time* and thus respects, for that which concerns [*regarde*] the other when I look at him and he looks at me, all the determinations, limits, contours: the most exigent respect for *that which is in question when*

it is a question of acting [ce dont il s'agit quand il s'agit d'agir]—and acting *on time*, which has never meant all at once or immediately.

Those who are interested in Nancy's exactitude will find confirmation of what I am saying at the exact tip of his pen, exactly acute like the beam of a scale that is as just as justice, for example in *Le poids d'une pensée*, beginning with the end, on the back cover of the original book: "Thought weighs exactly the weight of sense," a sentence that says exactly its *disturbance*, between *transitivity* and *intransitivity* or even *reflexivity*, for thinking weighs *itself* in weighing what it is weighing: does thought weigh . . . the weight of sense, having therefore the same weight? Or does it weigh . . . the weight of sense, having therefore not the same weight since it weighs it, that is, evaluates it, measures it? The answer: exactly! Within the same book, the photographs of *Georges* are exactitude itself: it is exactly him and it is the exact image of exactitude that is the law. (Within ten pages: "The photo was taken just before, exactly"; "The photo shows how exact you are. You look exactly into the lens, you know exactly what it's all about: your image"; "Once again, you look so exactly into the lens that one has the feeling of being, not looked at, but measured with great precision"; "You are one of the most exactly real persons that I have ever known"; "You are playing your role exactly, Georges.")[18]

As for his most extraordinary recourse, that is, very exactly superlative, exactly exaggerated, to the excess, exactly, that enters into the exigency of exactitude, here is another example: "*The weight of a thought* is very exactly the inappropriability of appropriation, or the impropriety of the proper (proper to the proper itself, absolutely)."[19]

How can anyone say *exactly* (which does not mean *properly*)—how could anyone say the improper and inappropriable, *exactly*? How can anyone say that *exactly*? Well, like him, just as he does.

He, Nancy—who also knows how to affect this "exactly" with some negation, which is just as exact: "it isn't exactly . . . ," "there isn't exactly any more. . . . " The two examples I have just quoted come from a 1996 text that strangely announces *L'intrus*, and makes a heart appear, or disappear, under the breast. Of course, it is also a philosophical poem about touch, tact, or the caress. Thus, a paragraph in *La naissance des seins* [The Birth of Breasts; or, Where Breasts Begin; or, Where Breasts Are Born—Trans.],[20] years after his "heart transplant," seriously plays at playing off the breast against the heart, under the pretext, as one says, that the latter can be transplanted and the former not:

Something rises—it is sinuous without insinuation. Suddenly something is gripping, something ungraspable moves the chest, something other than the heart. Hearts are nothing but elastic muscle beating in time precisely. Hearts have no emotion whatsoever. We can change hearts, for that matter, graft a new one in place, a denervated heart, ready to function. But we can't transplant breasts: we can repair a breast, suture its wounds, remodel it, but it's still the same breast and its modulation extends to the scar.

"Heart" is a nauseating word, "breast" a failing one. We cannot—we can only—say it badly.[21]

Then, in the very next paragraph, I find my first example, that is, the negative grammar of another "exactly": "It isn't exactly an anatomical or descriptive term—it goes beyond already . . . it touches on modesty, yet without sliding to the embarrassed proximity of the thighs or buttocks. It doesn't touch obscenity, or shame. It is the word for modesty without shame, yet it is not immodest."[22]

The second example has met or confirmed (how lucky I am!) all that I tried to formulate before I came across it, since the beginning of this book, about an originary perjury as inevitable as it is unforgivable. Here he terms it "transgression," a "transgression" that "isn't *exactly*" any longer:

Here, there is no longer transgression. There isn't *exactly* transgression, if this term designates the violation of a prohibition, and the crossing of an uncrossable limit, and penetration into a sacred space. . . . This [the violation—J. D.] is what posits the prohibition while ridiculing and breaking it. A priori the structure here is of sacred separation and transgressive offense—whether this offense is subject to condemnation or is a sacrificial impurity whose own workings make for its redemption. (Heavy, twisted, morbid thoughts.)[23]

Thought weight, therefore. Let us first recall that this effect of etymology cannot be presented, therefore touched [*ne peut . . . se toucher*] except on the tip of the tongue of certain tongues and risks becoming unintelligible, in truth, intangible in translation. But that is what is in question here, as we shall see, in other words, the loss of the idiom and the expropriation of the proper. I propose to define as weight that which, in touch, is marked as tangible by the opposed resistance (as the brilliant Berkeley had already seen): the place of alterity or absolute inappropriability (limit, weight, thus finitude, and so forth). Unable to follow this great text here step by step and word by word, as one nevertheless should, I shall go quickly to the place of confession, that place of a thinking of touch as thinking of the untouchable or intangible, the very place of what happens, as we were saying at the beginning, when one *touches on, tampers with the limit*: there the untouchable becomes tangible, it presents itself as inaccessible to the tactile, in tact—unfit, inapt for the haptical. In a word, impossible. It is in this place, this locus of untouchables, that a vow of abstinence (even before one keeps or betrays it) owns to transgression, perjury, sacrilege, and unforgivable profanation—in faithfulness itself, right at faithfulness itself. Exactly.

In contact with the intangible, this contradictory experience of tact (touch without contact) vows itself to the confession. But this experience can only be recognized in the form of a paradoxical confession, the avowal of an impossible confession. In it, one recognizes that one cannot do or say or think what one should, there where nevertheless, recognizing it, one transgresses not only the fault but the confession. The confession does not confess or tell the fault; it *says* it, *declares* it, *takes it on*. But it also commits it by the fact of saying it; the confession is the fault, it commits the transgression that does not take place before it and that it merely feigns to tell in the past. Confession is perjurious, as is the vow of abstinence that we pronounce, denouncing it. Unforgivably. Before confessing the inexpiable, the confession *is* inexpiable, the inexpiable fault, its crime of itself to which it owns, fated to remain inexpiable. Torment of an ever-revolving revolution. Hence the dizziness of the comedy that absorbs every confession. Tragedy of lies in good faith, incredible heartfelt lies. Who—which unconscious—could ever without laughing think up a lie in good faith?

"Let us confess": he dares to tell us this and give himself the right (or recognize it for himself) to drive or rather recall us toward this fate: with him—as he—we have to confess, we even have already—let's confess—confessed. What? What transaction? What further compromise?

Let us confess, instead, what everyone knows full well: thinking can never grasp weighing; it can offer a measure for it [doesn't it then "grasp" it and thus touch it, test it? How is one to measure a weighing otherwise than by weighing, feeling the weight, thus by letting weigh? And what difference is there between weighing and thinking once thought is not limited to subjective representation (Hegelian argument)?—J. D.], but it cannot itself weigh up [*soupeser*] the weight. Nor can weighing touch thinking; it may indicate a few ounces of muscles and neuron, but it cannot register the infinite leap of which they would supposedly be the place, support, or inscription. (And what is a leap, if thought is indeed a leap? What sort of escape from gravity? What counterweight?) Against these obvious truths, the etymologist's desire would be to give us access, at least as a trace inscribed in language, to a weighty/weighing property of thought, which would be identical to a thinking property of the weighty thing.[24]

Before coming back to the extraordinary density of this paragraph (but is density of the order of the thinkable or the weighable?), let me say a word about what I would have liked to do but shall not do: to find the law of the relation between the semantics of *Denken-Danken-Gedächtnis* (thinking-thanking-remembering, and so on) and that of *penser-peser-repenser,* and so forth. Not as that of a double, heterogeneous filiation, with the infinite complications that they would import into what touches on language and thought, but there where what we are talking about here involves *both semantics at the same time* (to touch, weigh, think, give, thank, generosity, gratitude, grace, gravity-and-grace, recalling, memory without memory, gift without debt, and so forth—but let us leave off here with this immense task, however necessary it may be). The infinite leap that separates thinking from weighing, at the very place where they remain inseparable (at least insofar as thought is not limited to representation nor the body to the objectivity of neurons), is but the leap, in the very experience of touching, between the touchable and the touchable, at the limit, therefore, between the touchable and itself as untouchable limit. It is touching that touches on the limit, its own "proper-improper" limit, that is to say on the untouchable whose border it touches. To touch on the limit is not, for contact, just any experience among others or a particular figure: one never touches except by touching a limit *at the limit.* This is a truism that one finds at work in any profound thinking of the limit (Aristotle, Kant, Hegel) as well as in locutions of the *doxa* (such as the one that Nancy cites, for example, on the subject of the lexicon of finitude when it enters "current," everyday usage: "One understands by this that humanity seems to touch on, to come up against, some limits. . . . "[25] To touch is to touch a border, however deeply one may penetrate,[26] and it is thus to touch by approaching indefinitely the inaccessible of whatever remains beyond the border, on the other side.

To underscore this impossible but inevitable inclusion of the outside in the inside, of the untouchable in the touchable, and to recall that a consistent thinking about touch can only be a thinking of the intangible (thus of tact), I could find support in what Nancy himself says about experience and limit on the same page. In the next paragraph, he in fact writes: "But this experience remains a *limit-experience*, like any experience worthy of the name. It does take place, but not as the appropriation of what it represents; this is why I also have no access to the weight of thought, nor to the thought of weight."[27]

Just as, he says, "Sense *is* touching. The 'transcendental' of sense (or what is 'ontological' in it) is touch . . . ,"[28] so, and for the same reasons, experience is touch, there where it touches its limits. Touch is finitude, period. One could conclude from this—at the risk of going against the reading that many have done of Nancy's work, beginning with Nancy himself—that what we have here is an irreducible thinking of transcendence. When one touches on the limit of *self-touching-you*, is there still any reason to decide between transcendence and immanence? Come now, show some tact. Let's leave it be.

Where it divides and ex-appropriates touch into tact, this (internal/external) limit therefore inscribes (ex-scribes) the untouchable-intangible in contact. What one does not touch is that which one touches, and it *is part* of what is called touch: what parts touching and divides it makes it be a *part* greater than the whole that it designates, and so forth. A part of oneself. Undecidable play of the metonymy. To touch, to touch him/it, is possible only by not touching. Experience of the impossible. One thus touches either upon the *intangible* or on the *untouchable*, depending on whether one accentuates the *cannot*-touch or the *must*-not-touch.

Between the intangible and the untouchable, the *différance* of tact. One might also call it modesty or decency [*pudeur*]. Clever, renouncing without renouncing, it/she [*elle*, that is, *pudeur*; grammatically feminine] spreads out its/her veils infinitely, it/she confesses and betrays in an infinite renunciation: from one law to the other (cannot/must not, must not because it's impossible, must not because it's possible, must not must not because it is impossible not to have to (impossible to renounce: what is called the unconscious) and because a "must" worthy of the name must remain foreign to an economy of the debt).

The law marks in this way the *without* [*sans*] in sense or in existence ("insofar as it *is* the without-essence" or insofar as it "*is* the appropriation of the inappropriable").[29] It thus inscribes the uninscribable in inscription itself, it *exscribes*. The law of exscribing, of exscription as "the ultimate truth of inscription,"[30] finds at least one of its essential demonstrations here. Nancy has just spoken of "the most proper sense." He immediately adds the following, which touches on *exscribing* itself, there where one cannot say "itself" without making it go out of itself: " . . . the most proper sense, but proper on the condition of remaining inappropriable, and of remaining inappropriable *in* its appropriation. Of being both eventful and disruptive even as it inscribes itself in the register of sense. Of *ex-scribing* this inscription—such that the ex-scription be the Being-inscribed, or rather the true Being-inscribing of inscription itself. Of having *weight* at the heart of thought and in spite of thought."[31]

In spite of thought: thought thinks only in spite of itself, or, I would say, *à son corps défendant* [i.e., reluctantly, notwithstanding itself]; it thinks only there where the counterweight of the other weighs enough so that it begins to think, that is, *in spite of* itself, when it touches or lets itself be touched *against its will.* That is why it will never think, it will never have begun to think *by itself.* That is what it is necessary to think of thought, to ponder and weigh of weight. *What is necessary*, in other words, what must pass by the test of the *in spite of,* in the inappropriable, thus the untouchable of the tangible itself. In what we are calling tact here. This is "quite exactly" the superlative exactitude we were speaking of earlier: "*The weight of a thought* is quite exactly the inappropriability of appropriation, or the impropriety of the proper (proper to the proper itself, absolutely)."[32] Another way of saying that "existence," "*is*," "Being," "is quite exactly," are all names of the impossible and of self-incompatibility. Compassion itself, if there is any, is not possible, except in a test, as the test of this impossible compatibility.

At the internal/external limit of touch, such a compassionate exscription of tact, let us note in passing, accounts for all the paradoxical chiasmuses that have affected the evaluation of touch. In order to explore systematically all its combinations, one would have to display this *logic* of the limit: what lets itself be touched does so on its border and thus does not let itself be reached or attained even as it exposes the untouchable itself, the other border of the border, to touch. But one would also have to integrate the *rhetoric*, which would be more than a rhetoric, when, with each figure, it crosses the limits between the sensible and the intelligible, the material and the spiritual—the carnal of the "body proper" finding itself by definition on both sides of the limit.

Salve

Untimely Postscript, for Want of a Final Retouch

A supplementary touch or past retouch left stalled long ago, almost seven years ago, on my computer, that is, a place where the relation between thought, weight, language, and digital touch will have undergone an essential mutation of ex-scribing over the past ten years. A description is needed of the surfaces, the volumes, and the limits of this new magic writing pad, which exscription touches in another way, with another kind of "exactitude" or "punctuality," precisely, from the keyboard to the memory of a disk said to be "hard." All I have written, then, is—see Chapter 13 n. 26—on *die Härte*, about the hard, hardness, hardship—obduracy of duration or enduring, resistance, as it were.

It is a pretext to bring up another challenge, a supplementary one, of the *technical supplement* challenging the discreet, discrete, and calculable multiplicity of the senses—and the assurance that touch is on the side of the *act* or the actual, whereas the *virtual* partakes more of the visual, with the appearing of *phainesthai*, that is, with the phantasm, the spectral, and the revenant. One spontaneously has the tendency to *believe* that touching resists virtualization. And if (continuous and continuistic) haptocentric intuitionism is indeed a dominant tradition, which I have taken as my theme here, then philosophy, as such and constitutively, may be subjected to this very belief. To this credulity. How is one to believe that touch cannot be virtualized? And how can one fail to see that there is something like an "origin of technics" there? Let's note that in California, a haptical museum does exist (it's not a proof of anything, just a sign): the Integrated Media Systems Center at the University of Southern California, Los Angeles, makes available for its visitors a web site [http://imsc.usc.edu/ (accessed February 25,

2005)] on which they can experience "remote touching," "realistic" sensations in "touching" works of art. The description of the setup uses many quotation marks, of course. We can thus feel the weight, form, and structure of the surface of a Chinese vase while "holding" a three-dimensional digital model. The user may put questions to the tactile image of the virtual object: "Why is this side so rough and this one so soft to the touch?" Beyond the museum, haptical technologies are developing software in scientific visualization, medical simulations, and so forth, which is useful in many areas. The researchers of the Integrated Media Systems Center set up experiments that produce tactile sensations, for example, PHANTOM, an instrument in the shape of a pen that gives a powerful sensation to the tip of the fingers when its user outlines the contour of an object; or CyberGrasp, a glove that endows users with a "realistic" sensation of strength or resistance on their entire hand when they grasp, push, or move objects around a screen. Their research areas have to do with algorithms of "immediate contact," of detection and collision in virtual objects; and also with the exact determination of the hand's position during its manipulations in the haptical exhibits; and further, with algorithms having to do with force feedback in the experiments with virtual objects; and especially, with acquiring, exhibiting, and exploring interactive processes between hearing, seeing, and touching in the exhibits of objects at the museum. All this leads to the archiving of data that are increasingly differentiated and overdetermined in their coding. Tomorrow's Sigmund Freud will have to refine his magic writing pad and the topography of bodies during psychoanalytical sessions, not to mention erogenous "distance touching" and amorous bodies wrestling in the sheets of the Internet's web. No doubt, this possibility hasn't waited for our century, but let's put these things under the heading "facts of the day" [*questions d'actualité*], or artefactuality, for all the reasons just put forth. The artefactual haunts and works through both technics and desire. And work in general. It's the same labor, the same pleasure, the same torture—*tripalium*, the suffering during the Sabbath.

Let's rush toward the ending and recapitulate. I'm now sincerely asking that this book be forgotten or effaced, and I'm asking this as I wouldn't have done—with as much sincerity—for any of my other books. Wipe it all away, and start or start again to read him—Nancy—in his *corpus*.

For my part, what to give him? A kiss? On the eyes? It should remain invisible to any third party.

A secret offering, as it were, I promised myself. How can one promise *oneself* to give? An offering that would touch on the multiple question of touch in a mode at once *necessary* and *contingent*: what is touching? What does "touching" mean? Is there an essence of touching? Is it sayable, intelligible, sensible, *tangible*, or not? Who or what touches what or whom? How can one remove it from its vast tradition even as the latter is never forgotten?

One day—I've never told this to him himself, but I told Hélène Nancy during a phone call—I dreamed that I kissed him on the mouth; it was not long after the transplant of his new heart when I had just seen him and did kiss him, in fact, on the cheeks, for the first time. As after a resurrection— and not only his. For I remember, and this still touches me, that at our first meeting after he had received into himself the living heart of another, we embraced, spontaneously, in an apparently spontaneous double movement, apparently of an instant (why?), which we had never done before, because of that invincible reserve or modesty [*pudeur*] of old friends. (My real friends always intimidate me, as do my sons.) What's the relation? What am I going to do with that? Draw attention to myself once again, of course, they will say, and blame me for it. No, I want rather to hide something and to make a secret offering to him. Yes, the truth is I would have liked to be capable of recounting what was and remains, for my heart, striking it itself, the ordeal of this other heart that Jean-Luc Nancy was nevertheless alone in undergoing and "knowing" at the bottom of his heart, his, yours, the only one, the same, another man's or woman's.

So my offering would touch my friend, I said to myself, even as it touched on this thematics, this onto-logic, this rhetoric or poetics of touch in a manner that is at once necessary and contingent.

Necessary, that is to say pertinent, but then pertinence itself, the [Latin] *pertinere* of pertinence is already a figure of the tactile. We have already accounted for this borrowing, and its usurious wear and tear. Is pertinent ([Latin] *pertinet*) whatever attains its end by touching it in a necessary and appropriate fashion? A pertinence does not fail to touch or to hit the object, which is both risky and cocky ("I know what I'm talking about!"), arrogant, impolite, impertinent.

Contingent as well because I, myself, a finite being, would like to touch him, Jean-Luc Nancy, himself and no other, in his singularity, in the singularity, *hic et nunc*, of his body. For this, I have had to call upon two original reinventions of the word "contingent" while distinguishing them from a third one, which is his.

While the figure of *contingency* is also a figure of contact, of tangency or the tangible; while *L'intrus* gives it another future or recalls it to it, one still has the impression that we are always going to be at a loss for a meta-language with which to say anything whatever about touch, touching, or the touchable that is not in advance accommodated by the skin, exscribed right on the skin. Without even being watched over or pointed out, each word speaks in tongues to the skin, each word has a word on the tongue with the skin. Before a deictic is showing, before an auto-deictic shows itself, by pointing its finger toward itself, before and in view of narcissistic speculation, *it touches.*

As for this strange couple of the two tactilities, that of appropriate necessity (*pertinent*) and of aleatoric, random singularity (*contingent*), I shall mention very quickly, without being able to explain myself here, that [Nancy's] powerful, untimely, and still unrecognized book *The Experience of Freedom* helps us better than any other to think it, there where Nancy draws the entire consequence from this fact: "If philosophy has *touched the limit* [my emphasis—J. D.] of the ontology of subjectivity, it is because it has been brought to this limit."[1]

Therefore: how to touch him in speaking of touch—"'the' sense of touch" that isn't—and hope to reach there, in a way that is at once pertinent, but not without tact, and contingent, but not arbitrary, and first of all, in the way he himself does so, namely, in the way he touches on touch, without all the same imitating him or following him? Beyond imitation or commentary, beyond simple repetition, what form of baroque contagion or imperceptible contamination should I have imagined? And how to do it in the right fashion, by touching it without touching it too much, while observing the limits of decency, of duty, of politeness—of friendship?

Le toucher: I see that I have oriented myself, once again, more or less blindly, in the direction of the untranslatable of a text that I knew would appear in English in its first version. Like any good blind man, I have oriented myself by touch. A long time ago, well before the publication of *Corpus*, I recognized in Nancy's work a certain trail that I thought I was the only, at least perhaps the first, well, yes, to identify: it was, let's say, a certain thematics of touch (oblique, constrained, but discreet, insistent, but oddly kept back or kept waiting, suspended). I could specify a few of these early markers.

One of the first concerned precisely the offering, and I wanted to note it before any other because it is an offering that is in question here. I had been intrigued, upon reading the more than sublime "The Sublime Offering,"[2] by the quotation marks within which he took up the word "touch," as if he were keen on it, on this word, in a compulsive, irresistible fashion, giving in thereby to a barely avowable temptation, even if he did not touch on it, discreetly and silently approaching the word as if it were contaminated in advance, touching it with the quotation marks as if they were tweezers, confessing in this way his interest in something that it was too early to declare, perhaps because the said thing did not answer generally or *properly* to its common name and because it was necessary to change the whole language, rewrite, ex-scribe, everything before one could *properly* speak and think of touching it. But note that the proper is also what escapes from contact, from the contagious, and from contamination. At that point of the text, it was a matter of explaining why, on the very limit of the sublime, a thinking of the offering defies the distinction between the aesthetic and the ethical. A note at the bottom of the page, probably added from one edition to the next of the same essay: "It defies it because it implies, along with moral determinations (good/bad), the ethical as *presentation* of the fact that there is moral praxis. Freedom is given and gives one to see or to 'touch.'"[3]

To see freedom itself (he says: "Freedom is given and gives one to see"), to let it present itself to sensible sight is already improbable, and here Kant remains, it seems to me, indisputable. But to touch freedom! ("Freedom is given and gives one to see or to 'touch' . . . "). Nancy has felt the hyperbole, the exact exaggeration, the overbid in the impossible: not only to see but to "touch" freedom! To "give" it or rather to have it give and given to see and touch! Is this "given" a free gift or a "given" (*Gegebenheit*) of experience, a presentation or self-presentation? And to want it to present itself in flesh and blood, is that not to suppress it on the pretext of having its hide? To touch freedom, is that not to touch on, that is, to tamper with freedom? Is it not to assail it under the pretext of attaining it? What, then, about morality, and politics? For this double reason, the quotation marks were necessary, yes, or italics ("*Freedom* is given and gives one to see or to 'touch' . . . "). For in *The Experience of Freedom*, a book far too complex and novel for me even to dare touch on it here, he also writes *touched* in italics: "the danger of having surreptitiously 'understood' freedom—somehow even before it has *touched*."[4]

And yet the surreptitious thinking of the surreptitious will have oriented this great chapter of the book, "The Free Thinking of Freedom," notably during the powerful moment represented by the discussion of a certain Heideggerian gesture (as he withdraws freedom from the "theoretical" in order to turn it over to "philosophizing" and later to "thinking")—about which Nancy warily says, before problematizing it: "Such 'philosophizing' can actually be presented as the deconstructive penetration that *touches* [my emphasis—J. D.] the core of metaphysical idealism at the point where the Idea binds [*enchaîne*] freedom."[5]

There, touching seems to presuppose a "penetration" (and Nancy terms this deconstructive) that goes through the surface or passes the limit. To touch upon "touch" in quotation marks or italics means perhaps that one must correct, complete, specify what would have been insufficiently seen —more precisely, insufficiently thought—about freedom *because only seen.* In order to think, weigh, to put freedom to the test, Nancy wants to go back before sight; he is intent on exploring that which, at the heart of the body proper, exscribes itself in absolute invisibility—and it is the heart, the selfsame heart itself. What can this "selfsame itself" mean to say about the heart's heart? The heart proper, the essence of the heart, of the sovereign heart, of the heart by itself, of the heart with itself nearest to itself (*ipse, ipsemet, metipse, meisme, même*)? Nancy knows that the *selfsame* heart *itself,* in every possible sense of the self and the same, is the place where the selfsame itself exappropriates itself, at the same instant when I am invisibly touched by the other, without any possible reappropriation, which is what I earlier termed absolute mourning—but also the locus of possible transplants, possibly from another "sex." It is quite possible, as I have heard it said, that women's hearts lend themselves better to transplantations and have a better survival rate.

If we have to go by Nancy's schooling, it isn't when he leads us beyond or before sight, or when he suggests that we think out of sight, farther than the eye can reach—others had preceded him on this path, and no one recognizes this more than he does—nor, for that matter, is it when he leads us back to touch; but it is at the point where he recalls us to the untouchable of touch, it seems to me, in order to delimit the latter, in order to avoid extending it "too simple a credit."

This is not getting me very far. What to do? Go on keeping quiet? I decide not to give up. At least I would offer him some proof, in this way, of both my courage and my humility by trying to touch him/it, touch, to touch him/it there where, knowing that he is expecting it and that we are already waiting for ourselves/each other [qu'il s'y attend et que nous nous attendons déjà] and that he has nothing more to take, or take in, or up, or learn from me; I could still please him by repeating to him, in other words, what he has already said very well himself—without me: "Thought self-touches, without being itself, without returning to itself" (Nancy, *Corpus*, p. 102).

I'll speak to him so as to touch him, about what a "kiss on the eyes" might be, I said to myself so long ago already ("Freedom . . . given . . . to see or to 'touch,'" perhaps.) Not a kiss planted, as one says, by the lips on the eyes of the other—love, death, benediction. No. A kiss on the eyes as one says a kiss on the lips, a kiss of the eyes on the eyes of the other. Is that possible? Which figure does this yield, if it is a figure still?

With the exception of Novalis, there has rarely been, to my knowledge, an attempt at *thinking*, what is called thinking, the kiss. It is already very difficult to think what happens—and just to think, no doubt, but this may be where "thinking" begins—when a mouth comes in contact with another mouth and when lips, and sometimes tongue and teeth, get mixed up in it.

Not the kiss on the mouth, but the kiss on the eyes, and without being satisfied with insipid figures, however interesting or necessary they may be ("to embrace in a glance," "to devour with one's eyes," and so forth).

When eyes meet—intensely, infinitely, up to the point of the abyss, plunging Narcissus into the chasm—when nothing in the world, not even the light, not even the third source of a sun, can interpose itself, when I see the beloved gaze that looks at me beyond all reflexivity, for I love it only inasmuch as it comes to me from the other, is it day or is it night? Is there or is there not contact? Is it a caress, and can I say so otherwise than by means of a figure?

If, as I believe and accept, as if to save time (if there were time for us still, time as quickly annulled as objective space in such a kiss), there is no day or night possible, except from the possibility of the gaze and thus of the ex-changed look of eyes that meet, as one says, in the abstinence and perjury of tact, since one cannot see anything in the world (this is the origin and the possibility of the world that only a world can also give) without the possibility, at least, of a reflecting surface that makes visible, be it to Nar-cissus, other eyes, be they his own, still; if all that, then in the instant of this kiss of the eyes, one can ask oneself whether there is already day or night.

Then the haptical begins.

Touch, which was already onstage, enters the scene. With Psyche.

For one can also ask oneself—yet another question—whether this was only an *announcement* of the pure and simple possibility of a world, a possibility, then, that couldn't see the light of day except by the annulment of its possibility, that is to say, by becoming the impossible or what will have stopped being simply possible after having become present, or rather effective.

In the kiss of the eyes, it isn't day yet, it isn't night yet. A nightless, dayless point, still. But day and night themselves are promising each other. One says to the other point-blank: I'm going to give you some. To the point, the break of dawn.

Philosophy hasn't spoken much about kisses: must we do it, then, and how? Now, [Nancy's] *Corpus* does it, as I discovered (in Nice, during the night of August 19, 1992). I who planned years ago, well before *Corpus*, to constitute an index of the concepts and lexicon of "touch" in the work of Jean-Luc Nancy, here I find *Corpus* has said it all, anticipating me without warning me. It has said everything about the kiss (p. 36), the caress (p. 42), tact, the tactile, and the intact.[6]

One has to admire the strategic assurance of the thinker—his political sense as well. He mistrusts himself. And precisely he mistrusts the perverse effects of a generalized haptics, even of some super-haptics. He knows that his great transcendental-ontologization of touch can be (in advance it will have been) reappropriated by all sorts of onto-theo-ideologies of immediacy—*except*, except if the movement in "hyper," if the leap of an infinite upping-the-ante cuts off contact and amounts to taking this weapon away from all suspect manipulations; even so, one must read and read carefully Nancy's overbid, his exact exaggeration—and to judge by the newspapers, the battle has not yet been won. It is not a matter just of those sons of the earth, the literalist philistines, and thus (the Gospel truth) sensualists-materialists; it is not a matter just of Thomas, nor even of those odd Christians who would like to remember that Christ offers his wounds to the touch; but so many others as well, as you're going to see. Do not touch, Nancy warns in addressing the onto-theo-ideologues. Do not touch touch—which moreover cannot be touched, does not touch itself. One would have to reread the whole chapter titled "Mystery?" of which here are the first lines (our meditation of them will never be enough):

As we have already said, the "touch" of this thinking—the scales of this nerve-meter [*pèse-nerfs*] that it must be or it is nothing—does not belong to an immediacy that is anterior and exterior to sense. It is, on the contrary, the very limit of sense—and the limit of sense is to be taken in all senses, each of which breaks into the other. . . .

But one must not therefore extend to "touch" too simple a *credit*, and, most important, one must not *believe* that one could touch *the* sense of "touch," insofar as it sets a limit on sense(s). This is a rather common tendency of the most robust ideologies of the "body," that is, the crudest ones (of the type "muscle-bound thinking" or "sacred-heart thinking," vitalo-spiritualist fascism—with, no doubt, its real and secret horror of bodies). (Nancy, *Corpus*, pp. 40–41) [My emphasis—of this appeal to unbelief.—J. D.]

The following page, which I suggest be read closely in its extreme density, calls for another touch, beyond the Platonic *epopteia*, the Vision of the Mysteries, or the consummation of the Mystery of Sense Certainty ("see here, from out of Cybele's basket, the phallic and cephalic, 'Hoc est enim corpus meum'" [p. 41]). To "mysteric *epopteia*" that "knows only one face and one vision," Nancy opposes the concept of *areality* (elaborated elsewhere):

Epopteia, sight accomplished: this is sight where initiation is overtaken (all it does is "understand"), sight that accedes to "contemplation," to a "super-seeing," which is a "devouring with one's eyes" (the eye itself eats itself), which is a *grasping* and finally a *touching*, that is, the very absolute of touching, touching the other as self-touching, one within the other absorbed and devoured. Throughout the tradition, this is the *consummation* of the Mystery of Sense Certainty: see here, from out of Cybele's basket, the phallic and cephalic, "Hoc est enim corpus meum."

But areality cannot come out of a basket, be it that of the Mysteries. Areality cannot be seen—not as the term *epopteia* would have it. It is in no way to be seen: neither as extension or pure ex-tensivity of the body, the outside-self that as such does not make (itself/anything) visible (and that the logic of the Mystery poses as "unpresentable" *in order to* present it to its super-optic), *nor* insofar as it is also, and identically, the presentable itself: the determined configuration, the *trait* of this body *here*. . . .

. . . To see *a body* is not precisely to grasp it by *a* vision: sight itself becomes distended there, spaced out. . . .

Mysteric *epopteia*, on the other hand, knows only one face and one vision. . . .

. . . it is properly and absolutely vision of death. . . . Medusa. . . . (Nancy, *Corpus*, pp. 41–42)

Distinguished from this petrifying "masturbation of the eye" is the stroking movement of the caress: we already heard the "yes," the *oui* that *jouit.*" Once there is no "the" (this or that, *the* body or *the* sense of touch, for example) in language or discourse, then, to tell the truth, one risks no longer knowing what one is saying (or to whom), and this risk will never be excluded, herein in this very place itself, in what you have just read— if you have at least even got this far.

No assurance worth a thing. There against, no certainty (yours) *holding* its own.

When I say "holding"—that is, *tenir* and not just *tiens* ["take this!"]— as I did above, am I still grappling with touch? Without knowing who is holding out, *perhaps* one has to try—this is the singularity of the singular. But the singular is not, nor should it be, any more assured. It must be *taken* and *run*—like chances or risks. Nancy doesn't say much about "betting," it seems to me (but I may be wrong in this), yet I perceive him as a thinker of the bet and a player—or rather like a bettor, a desperate bettor, that is: he never stops staking, committing, committing himself, and doing anything to calculate some *hyperbolic* odds with *exactitude* as well as exaggeration. He does this without any expectations, counting neither on the gains of some Pascalian "wager" nor on any salvation. It may also be this perdition frenzy, this impossibility—his "deconstruction of Christianity." If I were to imitate him in this, there would still remain the way in which a Christian remnant or style still resisting any deconstruction could be seen to differ from one to the other, and how this signs our respective histories and stories in such mutually untranslatable fashions. We are not "Christian" or "non-Christian" in quotation marks, in the same fashion—but no doubt it matters little here.

The greatest risk is run at the very moment when one does have to try to *know*. Know what? Not what, but whom; not about what one speaks, but first of all to whom one says, "and me, and you."

Never trust any tongue for that—nor the grammar of sexual differences.

—On touching, you said—whose touching? Touching whom?

—That's why I dreamed of a kiss on the eyes—that there be some, if there should be any. There is no "the" kiss, there is a kiss, this or that one,

one day or one night, carrying off vision, anyway, and the voice, too. A caress—and one no longer knows if it bodes well or ill, hitting like a phone
call to the heart.

   And let it be—blessed, like a benediction still unthinkable, an exasperated benediction, a benediction *accorded* to his "exasperated consent" and
in accordance with it, a benediction without any hope of salvation, an ex-
hoped-for *salve*,[7] an incalculable, unpresentable salutation in advance renouncing Salvation (as should any salute worthy of the name).

   Just *salut*, greeting without salvation; just a *salut* on the way.[8]

Χαῖρε

Salut to you, *salut* to the blind we become

Jean-Luc Nancy

Salut! How could I refrain from bidding you *salut*, now you have gone? How could I fail to respond to the *salut* that you bade us, a *"salut* without salvation, an unpresentable *salut,"* as you put it? How could I fail to do this, and what else is there to do? As always, the time of mourning is not a time for analysis or discussion. All the same, it doesn't have to be a time for slick tributes. It can be—it has to be—a time to hail you: *salut!* Goodbye! In quitting us, you leave us facing the obscurity into which you vanish. And so: *salut*, obscurity! *Salut* to this erasure of figures and schemas! And *salut* to the blind whom we become. The blind were a theme that you favored: *salut* to the vision that did not cling to forms or ideas but that let itself be touched by forces.

You practiced being blind all the better to greet the clarity that only obscurity possesses, which is out of sight and envelops the secret—a secret not concealed but evident, the manifest secret of being, of life/death. And so, *salut!* to the secret that you safeguard.

And *salut* to you! *Salve*, be safe! Be safe in the impossible health or sickness you have entered. Be safe in death—not from it. Or, if you'll allow me, be safe as death, immortal like death, having dwelt in her since birth.

~

On p. 311, Χαῖρε [*Claire*] = Greetings! Farewell! *Salut!*

This tribute by Jean-Luc Nancy, titled "Salut à toi, salut aux aveugles que nous devenons," appeared in *Libération* on October 11, 2004 (http://www.liberation.fr/page.php?Article=245193&AG [accessed February 25, 2005]).

Salut! May this greeting be a benediction to you (you said this to us too). "To speak well" and "say the good": to speak well of the good, the good or the impossible, the unpresentable that slips away from all presence and hangs entirely on a gesture, a kindness, a hand lifted or laid on a shoulder or forehead—a welcome, a goodbye that says *salut*.

Salut to you, Jacques . . .

Reference Matter

Notes

Foreword

1. *On the Work of Jean-Luc Nancy*, ed. Peggy Kamuf, *Paragraph* 16, 2 (July 1993).

2. See Jean-Luc Nancy, *Corpus* (Paris: Métailié, 1992) [there is also a later, expanded edition of *Corpus* (Paris: Métailié, 2000), but all quotations here are translated from the 1992 French edition.—Trans.]; Nancy, *Le sens du monde* (Paris: Galilée, 1992), and its English-language version, *The Sense of the World*, trans. Jeffrey S. Librett (Minneapolis: University of Minnesota Press, 1993); Nancy, *Les muses* (Paris: Galilée, 1994), and its English-language version, *The Muses*, trans. Peggy Kamuf (Stanford: Stanford University Press, 1995); Nancy, *Être singulier pluriel* (Paris: Galilée, 1996), and its English-language version, *Being Singular Plural*, trans. Richard Richardson and Anne O'Byrne (Stanford: Stanford University Press, 2000).

"When Our Eyes Touch"

Note: The pronominal form of the verb in the French chapter title, "Quand nos yeux se touchent," is lost in translation. In a note accompanying her translation of Jacques Derrida's *"Le toucher*: Touch / To Touch Him," in *On the Work of Jean-Luc Nancy*, special issue of *Paragraph*, ed. Peggy Kamuf, *Paragraph* 16, 2 (July 1993): 122–57, Kamuf writes: "*Caveat lector.* . . . The reader should also be aware, and here and there reminders will be inserted, that the verb *toucher* has an idiomatic extension in French which can only be approximated in another language. For example, *toucher à* can mean both to touch on, but also to tamper with, even to violate (cf. Mallarmé's famous exclamation: 'On a touché au vers.' . . . Finally, however, the most recalcitrant syntactic formation is the pronominal form, *se toucher*, which can be either reflexive or reciprocal in the third person or the infinitive, but may also have the value of a passive voice (*cela se touche*, i.e., it is touched)" (p. 152).—Trans.

1. Aristotle *Peri psuchēs* 2.11.422b–424a. I cite the French-Greek Budé edition, *De l'âme*, ed. A. Jannone, trans. E. Barbotin (Paris: Les Belles Lettres, 1966). [Quotations in English are from *De anima*, trans. J. A. Smith, in *The Basic Works of Aristotle*, ed. Richard McKeon (New York: Random House, 1941), pp. 535–603.—Trans.] To my knowledge, Nancy refers only once to *Peri psuchēs*, and it is on another subject, not touch. See Jean-Luc Nancy, *Ego sum* (Paris: Aubier-Flammarion, 1979), p. 161. However, it is true that Nancy recalls Aristotle in two powerfully elliptical texts, respectively titled "Psyche" (Jean-Luc Nancy, "Psyche," *Première livraison* no. 16 [1978])—which is discussed in the next chapter and thereafter—and "De l'âme" ["On the Soul"] (in *Le poids du corps* [Le Mans: École régionale des beaux-arts, 1995]). Only after completing this book did I become aware of the latter text—the transcription of a remarkable, more or less improvised conference, and I may say that I found it retrospectively encouraging. Readers will understand this if they refer to it, as I urge them to do, and they may share the emotion I felt upon discovering in the first pages Jean-Luc Nancy's young mother stretched out, "extended" (*ausgedehnt*, like the Psyche who lies in wait for us, but so much more alive) on a beach.

2. On this "etc.," see "et cetera," in *Deconstructions: A User's Guide*, ed. Nicholas Royle (Basingstoke, Hants, U.K.: Macmillan, 2000).

1. Psyche

1. Jean-Luc Nancy, "Psyche," *Première livraison*, no. 16 (1978).

2. Jean-Luc Nancy, *Le poids d'une pensée* (Sainte-Foy, Québec: Le Griffon d'argile, 1991), pp. 14, 110, and passim. [*The Gravity of Thought*, trans. François Raffoul and Gregory Recco (Atlantic Highlands, N.J.: Humanities Press, 1997), includes parts of *Le poids d'une pensée* in translation; see esp. "The Weight of a Thought."—Trans.]

3. Nancy, *Corpus*, pp. 22, 83–84, 93, and passim. A year later a reminder of the latter citation appears in a note in Nancy's "Différance," in *Le sens du monde*, p. 58 ("Différance," in *The Sense of the World*, trans. Librett, p. 35n30 [p. 178]). Nancy even declares this to be the "sole theme" of *Corpus*.

4. Nancy, *Corpus*, p. 22.

5. Sigmund Freud, *The Complete Psychological Works*, vol. 23 (New York: Norton, 2000), p. 300; id., *Schriften aus dem Nachlass: 1941*, in *Gesammelte Werke*, vol. 17 (Frankfurt a/M: S. Fischer, 1993), p. 152.

6. Jean-Luc Nancy, "Psyche," trans. Emily McVarish, in *The Birth to Presence*, trans. Brian Holmes and others (Stanford: Stanford University Press, 1993), p. 393 [modified—Trans.].

7. The words "rests" and "lies" are in English in the original.—Trans.
8. See Jean-Luc Nancy, *L'intrus* (Paris: Galilée, 2000).—Trans.

2. Spacings

1. Jean-Luc Nancy, "Unum quid," in *Ego sum*, p. 161. [Nancy is referring to Aristotle *Peri psuchēs* 412a–412b10.—Trans.]
2. Nancy, "Unum quid," in *Ego sum*, p. 162n46. [Further references to this text, cited as "Unum quid," appear parenthetically in the text. Quotations in English of Aristotle's *Peri psuchēs* are from *De anima*, trans. Smith, in *Basic Works of Aristotle*, ed. McKeon.—Trans.]
3. In this silencing, this bracketing of touch, in the context of eating, one can recognize a gesture of thought that is both Aristotelian and non-Aristotelian. This would thus be a good "introduction" (through the mouth) to our problem, as well as to the subtle yet necessary distinctions or implications between eating and touching, eating and taking nourishment. Aristotle does concede that the nutritive power (*to threptikon*) can be separated from touch (*haphē*), theoretically and abstractly, just as touch can be separated from all the other senses. But that is a theoretical abstraction, for all animals have the sense of touch. Above all, for all animals, touch remains the primary sensory function. Without it, no other sense exists. Furthermore, Aristotle points out, the qualities of food can only be appreciated through touch: "Touch is the sense for food" (*Peri psuchēs* 414b7). In addition, it is true that, for animals at least, unlike plants, the other powers cannot be isolated from this power of nutrition (ibid., 413a–414b).
4. Martin Heidegger, "L'art et l'espace," in *Questions IV*, trans. Jean Beaufret, François Fédier, Jean Lauxerois, and Claude Roëls (Paris: Gallimard, 1976), p. 101.
5. The French text is: "Espacer, cela apporte le libre, l'ouvert, le spacieux, pour un établissement et une demeure de l'homme": Nancy's quotation is from *Questions IV*, which, with the addition of the words "le spacieux," reprints the translation by Jean Beaufret published in the German-French bilingual original: Heidegger, *Die Kunst und der Raum* (St. Gallen: Erker-Verlag, 1969), pp. 20–21. Here is the German text: "Das Räumen erbringt das Freie, das Offene für ein Siedeln und Wohnen des Menschen" (p. 8).—Trans.
6. Jean-Luc Nancy, *L'expérience de la liberté* (Paris: Galilée, 1988), and its English-language version, *The Experience of Freedom*, trans. Bridget McDonald (Stanford: Stanford University Press, 1993). [Citations of *Experience of Freedom* appear parenthetically in the text.—Trans.].
7. Obviously, there is something regularly compelling for Nancy in the need to do justice to this "there is no 'the' decision," and further to any "there is no 'the' [masculine or feminine] *x*," with a definite article in French, marking the general identity of a concept or essence beyond any singularities that resist nam-

ing. Later we'll even read "there is no 'the' sense of touch; there is no 'the' *res extensa*" (Nancy, *Corpus*, p. 104). And, furthermore, "there is no 'the' language . . . " (Nancy, *Being Singular Plural*, p. 85 [modified.—Trans.]).

8. See Jacques Derrida, *Politics of Friendship*, trans. George Collins (London: Verso, 1997), esp. p. 304, and other, more recent texts. Nancy returns to these questions in *Being Singular Plural*, p. 198n28, and p. 80.

9. I try to shore up these arguments in *Donner le temps* (Paris: Galilée, 1991), pp. 26ff. and passim, and its English-language version, *Given Time: I. Counterfeit Money*, trans. Peggy Kamuf (Chicago: University of Chicago Press, 1992), pp. 13ff. and passim.

10. The word "hole" [*trou*] appears earlier, on p. 157, between "touch" and "mouth," in a passage that is quoted later.

11. Nancy's analysis ("Unum quid," p. 137) separates feigning and the subject's being-feint from the "feint in the structure of the most proper 'feeling.'" The structure of the feint has "nothing to do with the feeling and sensing subject's fictitious nature—the intellectual or corporeal, or intellectual and corporeal subject" (ibid.).

12. See René Descartes, *Meditations on First Philosophy in Focus*, trans. Elizabeth S. Haldane and George R. T. Ross, ed. Stanley Tweyman (London: Routledge, 1993). This is a translation of the French, rather than the Latin, *Méditations.*—Trans.

13. This is the famous passage in the Sixth Meditation in Latin (emphasis added): "me non tantum adesse meo corpori ut nauta adest navigio, sed illi arctissime esse conjunctum et *quasi permixtum*, adeo ut *unum quid* cum illo componam"; and its translation by the duc de Luynes (emphasis added): "[La nature m'enseigne aussi par ces sentiments de douleur, de faim, de soif, etc.,] que je ne suis pas seulement logé dans mon corps, ainsi qu'un pilote en son navire, mais, outre cela, que je lui suis conjoint très étroitement, et tellement confondu et *mêlé* que je compose *comme un seul tout* avec lui" (quoted in Nancy, "Unum quid," p. 132).—Trans.

14. "The world *must* reject and be rejected as a festering immundity" [*le monde* doit *se rejeter im-monde*]; see Nancy, *Corpus*, p. 93 and passim. We'll come back to this later, more particularly in Chapter 3. [Another possible translation comes to mind: "What the world must again throw off is itself, soiled world." —Trans.]

15. Paul Valéry, "Bouche," in *Œuvres I* (Paris: Gallimard, 1957), p. 323.

16. In a note on the following page, Nancy recalls his first reference, in the previous year, to this "posthumous" note by Freud, in *Première livraison*, no. 16 (1978). We shall later note other uses he makes of the word "exorbitant."

17. Descartes, "Second Meditation," trans. Haldane and Ross. Here is the Latin text of this passage: "*At certe videre videor, audire, calescere. Hoc falsum esse non*

---

potest; hoc est proprie quod in me sentire appellatur; *at*que hoc praecise sic sumptum nihil aliud est quam cogitare." Emphasis (*At . . . at*) added.—Trans.

18. Jean-Luc Nancy, *Le discours de la syncope: I. Logodaedalus* (Paris: Aubier-Flammarion, 1976).

19. Here are the translations of this passage in Descartes's Second Meditation, (1) by Nancy: "enfin il faut statuer, établir, décider, ériger en statue et fonder en statut que ce prononcement, ce prononcé, cet énoncé, *Je suis, j'existe,* toutes les fois que je le profère, le propose, le prononce, ou que je le conçois dans mon esprit, ou qu'il se conçoit dans mon esprit, ou par mon esprit, est nécessairement vrai" (Nancy, *Ego sum,* p. [5]); (2) by the duc de Luynes: "Enfin il faut conclure, et tenir pour constant, que cette proposition, *Je suis, j'existe,* est nécessairement vraie, toutes les fois que je la prononce, ou que je la conçois dans mon esprit" (Descartes, *Meditationes de prima philosophia. Méditations métaphysiques,* trans. de Luynes [Paris: Vrin, 1978], p. 25); (3) by Haldane and Ross: "we must come to the definite conclusion that this proposition: *I am, I exist,* is necessarily true each time that I pronounce it, or that I mentally conceive it."—Trans.

20. "Ça se touche, un Je" = "an I can be touched"; "an I—it touches itself"; "you can touch it, this I . . . ," etc.—Trans.

21. Edmund Husserl, *Studies in the Phenomenology of Constitution,* trans. Richard Rojcewicz and André Schuwer (Dordrecht: Kluwer, 1989), *Ideas Pertaining to a Pure Phenomenology and to a Phenomenological Philosophy,* vol. 2. [Cited as *Ideas II.*—Trans.]

22. Shouldn't one make this *spacing* (which I've defined as *différance* or the very trace itself), which is as spatial as it is temporal "before" the opposition space/time, agree with the *tension* in distancing (*Gespanntheit*) of which Heidegger speaks (in relation to time and datability, often recalling Aristotle), rather than with Descartes's *extensio* or even Freud's *Ausdehnung* [extension, outstretching]? No doubt, *Ego sum* was oriented toward the "locus" of this "spacing," especially in its "distending itself." But it seems to me that Nancy takes this on much later in an explicit way—in the four pages of "Spanne" (Nancy, *Sense of the World,* trans. Librett, pp. 64–67). He also speaks of "replacement" there.

3. This Is My Body

1. See "Unum quid," in *Ego sum.* Cited parenthetically in the text.—Trans.

2. Nancy, *Le discours de la syncope: I. Logodaedalus.* Cited below and parenthetically in the text as Nancy, *Logodaedalus.*—Trans.

3. Before and after Husserl in *Ideas II,* from Pierre Maine de Biran and Félix Ravaisson or Henri Bergson to Maurice Merleau-Ponty, Emmanuel Levinas, Henri Maldiney, Luce Irigaray, Gilles Deleuze, Didier Franck, and Jean-Louis Chrétien.

4. "Let's not forget that for Kant, in the *Anthropology*, woman is 'an object of study for the philosopher much more than man [is]'* [Kant, *Anthropology from a Pragmatic Point of View*, trans. Victor Lyle Dowden (Carbondale: Southern Illinois University Press, 1996), p. 216]," Nancy says in a footnote (n. 105), and then asks, "[W]hat about 'the philosopher'? Isn't he *virile?*"

5. Georg Groddeck, *Der Mensch und sein Es: Briefe, Aufsätze, Biografisches* (Wiesbaden: Limes, 1970), p. 56.

6. Immanuel Kant, *Kant's Critique of Judgement*, trans. J. H. Bernard (London: Macmillan, 1931), p. 226.

7. Immanuel Kant, Reflexion 4959, in *Kant's handschriftlicher Nachlass: Band V: Metaphysik* (Berlin: De Gruyter, 1928), pt. 2, pp. 41–42, quoted by Nancy, *Logodaedalus*, pp. 144–46, from Gérard Lebrun, *Kant et la fin de la métaphysique: Essai sur la Critique de la faculté de juger* (Paris: A. Colin, 1970), p. 34. —Trans.

8. Playfully, one could juxtapose—in order to oppose them—a formula by Maurice Merleau-Ponty about Descartes and Nancy's phrase about Kant. Whereas Nancy says that all in all, unlike Descartes, "Kant the philosopher, in truth, has *nothing* to say" about a connection between the body and thought, Merleau-Ponty asserts that, for Descartes, "There is nothing to say on this point." This formula can be found in a 1947–48 lecture: "Thus, nowhere does Descartes claim that we can conceive of the union. There is nothing to say on this point. The concepts he introduces in this regard are mythical in the Platonic sense of the word: designed to remind the listener that philosophical analysis does not exhaust experience. The union can only be known through the union: '[I]t is the ordinary course of life and conversation, and abstention from meditation and from the study of the things which exercise the imagination, that teaches us how to conceive the union of the soul and the body' [letter to Princess Elizabeth, June 28, 1643]. A new question then arises: no longer 'how to reconcile the experienced union and the distinction of essences' but 'how does it happen that there exists a realm of experience which we cannot conceive'?" (Merleau-Ponty, *The Incarnate Subject: Malebranche, Biran, and Bergson on the Union of Body and Soul*, trans. Paul B. Milan [Amherst, N.Y.: Humanity Books, 2001], p. 35). One could and should follow the rich indications of these lectures and the insistence of their concern, as well as their logic, reaching into the analyses of *Signes* (Maurice Merleau-Ponty, *Signs*, trans. Richard C. McCleary [Evanston, Ill.: Northwestern University Press, 1964]) and *Le visible et l'invisible* (Maurice Merleau-Ponty, *The Visible and the Invisible: Followed by Working Notes*, trans. Alphonso Lingis [Evanston, Ill.: Northwestern University Press, 1968]), in particular. We'll come to this later in connection with the notions of the touched-touching and self-touching.

9. We'll later deal with the *example of the hand* in Chapter 3 of *Ideas II*, and more particularly in ¶¶ 35–40, around the passage that attaches itself to the dif-

ference, as far as the hand is concerned, between visual and tactile phenomena. See Husserl, *Ideas II*, pp. 151ff.; *Husserliana* (The Hague: Nijhoff, 1973), 4: 144.

10. I deal with this problem from another point of view in "*Geschlecht* II: La main de Heidegger," in *Psyché: Inventions de l'autre* (Paris: Galilée, 1987) (see "Geschlecht II: Heidegger's Hand," trans. John P. Leavey Jr., in *Deconstruction and Philosophy: The Texts of Jacques Derrida*, ed. John Sallis [Chicago: University of Chicago Press, 1987], and in *Mémoires d'aveugle: L'autoportrait et autres ruines* (Paris: Réunion des musées nationaux, 1990) (see *Memoirs of the Blind: The Self-Portrait and Other Ruins*, trans. Pascale-Anne Brault and Michael Naas [Chicago: University of Chicago Press, 1993]).

11. Traveling with Kant: his cosmopolitanism dispenses with travel or travel narratives. Observing one's fellow citizens and compatriots is enough—especially, Kant notes in the preface to his *Anthropology from a Pragmatic Point of View*, if one inhabits a large city as exemplary as Königsberg, at the center of a state, with parliamentary assemblies, a university, sea traffic, inland commerce on its rivers, neighbors speaking foreign languages, and so forth. One can thus come to know the world and write one's anthropology "ohne zu reisen," without traveling—not even within Europe, like a lowly Descartes.

12. Kant, *Anthropology from a Pragmatic Point of View*, trans. Dowden, p. 3 [slightly modified. Further citations of Kant's *Anthropology* appear parenthetically in the text.—Trans.].

13. I am merely quoting and situating these passages here. Elsewhere, it is necessary to interpret their limits and anthropologizing naïveté, whether it is a matter of other organizations termed animal or of the said insects themselves, but that is not the aim here.

14. Of course, Nancy is the one emphasizing *touches*, which is one of the things that make this sentence interesting. On "fraternal" union and "incest," see Nancy, *Logodaedalus*, p. 107.

15. [Freud, *Complete Psychological Works*, 23: 300.—Trans.] The German reads: "Räumlichkeit mag die Projektion der Ausdehnung des psychischen Apparats sein. Keine andere Ableitung wahrscheinlich" (Freud, *Gesammelte Werke*, 17: 152).

16. "Anstatt Kants *a priori* Bedingungen unseres psychischen Apparats. Psyche ist ausgedehnt, weiss nichts davon" (ibid.).

17. Immanuel Kant, "The Transcendental Aesthetic," in *Critique of Pure Reason*, trans. Norman Kemp Smith (New York: St. Martin's Press, 1965), p. 68.

18. Ibid., p. 70.

19. Ibid., p. 66.

20. See Jean-Luc Nancy, *Une pensée finie* (Paris: Galilée, 1990), and *A Finite Thinking*, ed. Simon Sparks (Stanford: Stanford University Press, 2003), the contents of which overlap partially with *Une pensée finie*.—Trans.

21. This had already been written when I received a copy of Nancy's *La ville*

au loin (Paris: Mille et une nuits, 1999), which had just been published (in the series La ville entière), only to discover in it, at once, a series of sentences once again amplifying the thematics of touch while marking it with the same inhibiting restriction, the one that maintains the touchable within the untouchable, the tangible within the intact, contact within tact, and so forth. The insistence on "contiguity" (p. 53) does aim at *partes extra partes*—one of his favorite terms—and the quasi-contact of proximate bodies that are not truly touching. The city "cannot be captured under one identity. . . . lets itself be touched by coursing, tracing, drawing. . . . " (p. 54), but nevertheless, within it "one goes side by side, passing by narrowly, touching and stepping back: the pace is the same" (p. 56); and one "touches without touching, one is touched" (p. 58) by everything that appears in the city. Any contagion by contact "is the contagion of remote places, disseminated communication" (p. 61).

But of course one will still be far from having exhausted the strength and beauty of this text—one of the fairest that I have had the chance to read about cities in general, and singularly about Los Angeles—after analyzing this obsession of touch, which is also an obsession *of* the city, obsessive by essence and beyond essence, namely, of the place where, before being, one is being *besieged* ("The city hardly allows one to utter 'I am' but rather 'I am in it.' There, folded and unfolded, space precedes being" [p. 59].)

22. Kant, *Critique of Pure Reason*, trans. Smith, p. 77.

23. See Martin Heidegger, *Kant and the Problem of Metaphysics*, trans. Richard Taft (Bloomington: Indiana University Press, 1997).

24. See the introductory chapter, "When Our Eyes Touch." To repeat, sense, the *faculty* of sensation—the tactile faculty, for example—is only *potential* and not *actual* (Aristotle *Peri psuchēs* 417a). Feeling or sensing *in general*, even before its tactile specification, already lends itself to being taken in two senses, potentially and actually, and always to different degrees. Touch was already an exception in the definition of sensible objects [*espèces du sensible*] (each being "in itself" or "accidentally"; "proper" or "common"). Whereas each sense has its proper sensible object [*idion*] (color for vision, sound for the sense of hearing, flavor for the sense of taste), "Touch, indeed, discriminates more than one set of different qualities": its object comprises several different qualities (ibid., 418a).

25. "But excess of intensity in tangible qualities, e.g. heat, cold, or hardness, destroys the animal itself. As in the case of every sensible quality excess destroys the organ, so here what is tangible destroys touch, which is the essential mark of life; for it has been shown that without touch it is impossible for an animal to be. That is why excess in intensity of tangible qualities destroys not merely the organ, but the animal itself, because this is the only sense which it must have. All the other senses are necessary to animals, as we have said, not for their being, but for their well-being" (Aristotle *Peri psuchēs* 435b14–20).

26. *Poésie* 64 (1993).

27. Nancy, *Muses*, trans. Kamuf. [Cited parenthetically in the text.—Trans.]

28. "[Ils] la *savent*"; the verb is *savoir* here, and not *connaître*, implying "They know her by heart," as opposed to "Ils la connaissent," "They are acquainted with her" (e.g., personally).—Trans.

29. Nancy, "Naître à la présence," in *Le poids d'une pensée*, p. 132. [See "The Birth to Presence," trans. Holmes, in *Birth to Presence*, pp. 3–4; slightly modified.—Trans.].

30. Nancy, *Corpus*, p. 93 (my emphasis). [Cited parenthetically in the text.—Trans.]

31. I would like to mention now already that I shall often, and no doubt rather freely, "speculate" about this project of Nancy's, of which I hitherto knew only the title, "La déconstruction du christianisme" ("The Deconstruction of Christianity"). My book was virtually completed when Nancy published the brief transcription of a talk with that title, which he improvised in Italy (see his "La déconstruction du christianisme," *Études philosophiques* 4 [1998]) ["The Deconstruction of Christianity," trans. Simon Sparks, in *Religion and Media*, ed. Hent de Vries and Samuel Weber (Stanford: Stanford University Press, 2001).—Trans.]. Now and then I shall allude to it, from the sidelines. Here, I would like to emphasize that after stating that "Christianity *as such* has been overcome," Nancy hurriedly adds (and this is what I subscribe to here, up to and including both uses of "perhaps"): "[Christianity] is in itself and through itself in a state of overcoming. This state of *self-overcoming* is perhaps quite proper to Christianity, perhaps its most underlying tradition, something that is clearly not without a certain ambiguity" ("Deconstruction of Christianity," trans. Sparks, p. 114).

32. See Nancy, *Sense of the World*, trans. Librett. [Cited parenthetically in the text.—Trans.]

33. *Le toucher: Jean-Luc Nancy* is the original title.—Trans.

34. In French: "rapport entre le sang et le sens, entre le 'coup de sens' et le 'coup de sang'" (p. 69).—Trans.

35. *Sang, cent* [one hundred], and *sans* are homophones; *sens*, with the addition of an audible "s" at the end, is their quasi-homophone.—Trans.

36. Spasm and distension: this passage confirms the gap between *extension* (*extensio*) and *spacing* of which I spoke earlier, toward the end of Chapter 2.

37. Let us not be held in thrall by this mechanistic or Cartesian aspect. Elsewhere Nancy expressly warns us against this interpretation, against "Descartes" being "wrong." He does this precisely in the course of an analysis of "touch" and "tact" "before any subject" (Nancy, *Corpus*, p. 85). The structure of *partes extra partes*, thus reinterpreted, and well beyond any concern about touch, which seems to intensify only later, runs through Nancy's whole œuvre, from 1978 onward approximately, and more particularly in all the places where Freud's Psyche

makes a comeback. For example, in *Le poids d'une pensée*: "The *psyche* is first psyche by its *extension, partes extra partes*, and by the opacity to itself in which it remains with respect to this exteriority-in-itself, or with respect to *the* to-*itself* [*cet*
à-*soi*] that constitutes it. ('Psyche is extended; knows nothing about it': this is
Freud's great saying.)" (*Poids d'une pensée*, p. 14). [See *Gravity of Thought*, trans.
Raffoul and Recco, p. 83. The translation of the Freud quotation is modified to
correspond with its rendition in the English Standard Edition of Freud's works.
—Trans.] See also this series in which *partes extra partes* stands *at the same time*
as a term within the sequence *and* as the rule, which is to say the form of the relation between all terms in the series. "Les iris," that utterly singular page of an extraordinary chapter about the ordinary, in sum, begins: "Yet we are touched,
something has touched some sensitive spot" (see Nancy, "Les iris," trans. Michael
Syrotinski, *Yale French Studies*, 81 [1992], p. 59).

    38. Elsewhere (e.g., in "Foi et savoir: Les deux sources de la 'religion' dans les
limites de la simple raison," in *La religion*, ed. Jacques Derrida and Gianni Vattimo [Paris: Seuil, 1996]; "Faith and Knowledge," trans. Samuel Weber, in *Religion*, ed. Jacques Derrida and Gianni Vattimo [Stanford: Stanford University
Press, 1998]), I have tried to take into account—in its generality, and first of all
concerning religion—this logic of immunity, and more precisely autoimmunity.
One could no doubt link it here with what Nancy says about festering immundity, which would be the expulsed, the abjected or rejected, the ejected of
the immune, or even autoimmune, process. Isn't it this law of the autoimmune
that commands all Christian thinking about the "flesh," often without the thinkers' knowledge? We'll encounter these questions again in a different form.

    39. This had already been written when I read the following remark in Nancy's
"La déconstruction du christianisme" ["The Deconstruction of Christianity"]:
"Let us add that, perhaps, we do not even know yet what Hegel's dialectical sublation really is, and perhaps we do not know what negativity is: in order to learn
it, it is necessary to dive into its heart, and risk finding that this heart may well
be a Christian heart, if I may say so" (*Études philosophiques* 4 [1998]: 507). [This
passage in the French version cited by J. D. has been emended from the version
published in English.—Trans.]

    40. On this point, see John D. Caputo, "A Number of Messianisms," in *The
Prayers and Tears of Jacques Derrida: Religion Without Religion* (Bloomington: Indiana University Press, 1997), esp. p. 139. See also John Schad, *Victorians in Theory* (Manchester: Manchester University Press, 1999). Schad, while referring to
Caputo as far as this point is concerned, also pursues Luther's phantom in Marx
and beyond him (see pp. 96ff.).

    41. Later, in Nancy's *Muses*, in the course of one of his most systematic analy-
ses of touch and self-touch, we once again come across this "verbal value" of
touch in connection with the figure of the touch: "*Le toucher*—perhaps it would
be better to say *la touche*, or else one would have to preserve the verbal value of

the word, as when one speaks of 'le sentir,' 'sensing'—thus has no 'primacy' or 'privilege' except insofar as it subordinates nothing to it" (*Muses*, trans. Kamuf, p. 17). This *de-hierarchizing* may be what lets the privilege of touch, acknowledged by Nancy, distinguish itself—at once *in* and even *of* the tactocentered or hapto-fundamentalist tradition evoked earlier, which I'll soon try to examine a little more closely (with Kant, Maine de Biran, Félix Ravaisson, Husserl, and so forth).

42. I.e., "Saisie dessaisie ou dessaisissante."—Trans.

43. A little later, a formula in parentheses justifies this excursion from *écriture*, writing, toward the *exscribed*—and there again I wonder how it will translate: "(*Écriture* is yet another misleading word. That which addresses itself to the body-outside [*corps-dehors*] in this way *exscribes itself*, as I try to write it, right at [*à même*] this outside, or as this outside.)" (Nancy, *Corpus*, p. 20). The word "body" itself, finally, in which this ex-scribing of *Corpus* both overinvests and disinvests, is yet another misleading word, a "late" product of "our old culture" (ibid., pp. 9–10). There is nothing but body: even "'psyche' is *body*" as soon as it is "extended" (ibid., p. 22). Nancy notes this at the point where he again cites the "most fascinating remark, and perhaps (I say this without exaggerating) the most decisive coming from Freud . . . in this posthumous note" (ibid.). And if there is nothing but body, well, "'Body' is, perhaps, the unemployed word par excellence. It is, perhaps, in any language, the word *too many*" (ibid., p. 21). Note that he says "perhaps" twice.

44. See also, on p. 21: "*the breaking of all language where language touches sense.*"

45. With regard to this autoimmune, globalatinizing exappropriation [*exappropriation auto-immune et mondialatinisante*], permit me to refer again (a couple of times doesn't constitute a habit) to my essay "Faith and Knowledge" (in *La religion*, ed. Derrida and Vattimo).

46. One day these texts on "Hoc est enim corpus meum" (and thus Nancy's, in particular) will unavoidably have to be to reread *with*—in a challenging configuration *with*—all those that Louis Marin has so lucidly devoted, throughout his immense work, to so many problematic (theological, historical, philosophical, semantic, and logical) dimensions of the Eucharist. This task, though necessary, is more than I can undertake here and beyond the scope of this book.

47. We'll come to the chapter titled "Glorious Body" (Nancy, *Corpus*, pp. 54ff.) later. Let us merely note for now that, in it, a certain "deconstruction" ironically recognizes the signature of God himself—or at least of the "creator's power." In truth, deconstruction = creation. "The creator's power has to do with the original deconstruction of any recognizable image" (ibid., p. 56).

4. The Untouchable, or the Vow of Abstinence

Novalis, "Logologische Fragmente" (1798), in *Fragments: [Extraits] choisis et traduits par Armel Guerne* (Paris: Aubier Montaigne, 1973), pp. 54-55; trans.

Peggy Kamuf. Evidently the line was "slightly modified"—cf. Novalis, *Schriften: Die Werke Friedrich von Hardenbergs*, ed. Paul Kluckhohn and Richard Samuel, vol. 2: *Das Philosophische Werk*, 1 (Stuttgart: Kohlhammer, 1981), S. 541.

1. I.e., "Il y a *la* loi du tact."—Trans.
2. I.e., "Il y a *là* loi du tact."—Trans.
3. According to Husserl, this loss of intuition, this formal symbolism is a moment of crisis, like an amnesia of sense. But here the formulas in question are not deprived of intuition by accident or during a crisis from which they might emerge simply with the reactivation of the originary intuition of sense. On the contrary, the radical and essential impossibility of such fulfillment is what they "aim" at, or "mean to say," their "sense."
4. I could not find any really explicit reference in Aristotle to the blow and the caress, the more or less elliptical treatment of which, after Levinas, by Henri Maldiney, Didier Franck, and Jean-Louis Chrétien, for example, will be dealt with later.
5. One can easily see that it is difficult to reduce the (human or nonhuman) kiss, and in particular the kiss on the mouth, to a simple case of some kind of "lingual touch"—which makes for serious problems already in the Aristotelian tradition. In his book *L'appel et la réponse* (Paris: Minuit, 1992), Jean-Louis Chrétien notes that even if Aristotle only aims at a "view of the flesh as a whole" and does not refuse to "evoke the tactile function of a determined part," he "comes back several times to lingual touching and justifies in detail that, compared to that of other living beings, the human tongue is the most tactile, *haptikōtatē*, marking this as an argument in favor of man's higher sensibility." Chrétien then adds: "One cannot fail to find it surprising and disconcerting that lingual touching is evoked more often than manual touching, even when it is a question of describing in what way human touching prevails over the touching of other animals" (p. 114).

Fair question, but it can only take shape if one follows the most constant, the steadiest and most powerful tradition (which we shall have to debate later on), and presupposes that the principle of touch must first of all be incarnated in the hand, especially in the human hand—a precision generally but too hastily held to be pleonastic. Furthermore, what ensues in the same passage should relieve the author's surprise since it is in the very name of this absolute privilege and of what brings the hand close to the soul that Aristotle seems only to set the hand *apart*, where, in truth, of course, he puts it *above*. And here is the continuation of this passage: " . . . of other animals. For Aristotle the hand is the prehensile hand—the hand that takes, squeezes, and holds, and thus the empty or vacant hand, the hand that can become anything because it is nothing, and in that way is like the soul (*Peri psuchēs* 3.8)."
6. Nancy, *Corpus*, p. 82.
7. Levinas's writings about the caress, followed by Husserl's and Merleau-

Ponty's. Then, in particular, Didier Franck's *Chair et corps: Sur la phénoménologie de Husserl* (Paris: Minuit, 1981), singling out his chapter on "The Caress and the Shock" ("La caresse et le choc," pp. 158ff.), as well as Chrétien's *L'appel et la réponse*.

8. See Nancy, "Le poids d'une pensée," in *Le poids d'une pensée*, trans. as "The Weight of a Thought," in *Gravity of Thought*, trans. Raffoul and Recco. Quotations from "Weight of a Thought" have occasionally been slightly modified or rendered in Peggy Kamuf's translation of the same passages in Jacques Derrida, "*Le toucher*: Touch / To Touch Him."—Trans.

9. Nancy, "Weight of a Thought," trans. Raffoul and Recco, p. 75.

10. Jean Paulhan, *La preuve par l'étymologie* (Paris: Minuit, 1953).

11. See what is said about "earthquake" and "tectonic gravity" in "Infime dépense de quelques grammes" ("Minute Expense of a Few Grams"), a chapter in Nancy's *Corpus* in which the haptical lexicon is particularly rich (p. 90).

12. Nancy, "Weight of a Thought," trans. Raffoul and Recco, pp. 77, 80; emphasis mine [slightly modified.—Trans.].

13. The words *exacting* and *demanding* are in English in the French text. —Trans.

14. See Emmanuel Levinas, *Le temps et l'autre* (Paris: Arthaud, 1947; reprint, Presses universitaires de France, 1983), pp. 82ff.; and *Time and the Other and Additional Essays*, trans. Richard A. Cohen (Pittsburgh: Duquesne University Press, 1987), p. 89.

15. Emmanuel Levinas, *Totalité et infini* (The Hague: Nijhoff, 1961); *Totality and Infinity: An Essay on Exteriority*, trans. Alphonso Lingis (Pittsburgh: Duquesne University Press, 1969). [Citations of *Totality and Infinity* appear parenthetically in the text.—Trans.]

16. For example, in *Adieu: A Emmanuel Lévinas* (Paris: Galilée, 1997) [see Jacques Derrida, *Adieu to Emmanuel Levinas*, trans. Pascale-Anne Brault and Michael Naas (Stanford: Stanford University Press, 1999).—Trans.]. In "Violence and Metaphysics" (in *Writing and Difference*, trans. Alan Bass [Chicago: University of Chicago Press, 1978], p. 85 and passim), I broached Levinas's thematic handling of the caress—this movement carrying toward the untouchable, *epekeina tēs ousias*, beyond being, or beings—but also, and correlatively, a certain (obsessive and at times rather phobic) mistrust with regard to the tactile, and in fact to any contact. A vow of abstinence has to be anything except a contact phobia—quite the contrary, if I may say so!

17. "To touch and to touch oneself [*toucher et se toucher*] (to touch oneself = touched-touching)[.] They do not coincide in the body: the touching is never exactly the touched. This does not mean that they coincide 'in the mind' and at the level of 'consciousness.' Something else than the body is needed for the junction to be made: it takes place in the *untouchable*. That of the other which I will never touch. But what I will never touch, he does not touch either, no privilege

of oneself over the other here, it is therefore not the *consciousness* that is the untouchable . . . " ("Working Notes," in Merleau-Ponty, *Visible and the Invisible,* trans. Lingis, p. 254). We'll come back to these matters later.

Since the untouchable here is neither mind nor consciousness but, verily, body proper and in the flesh, one has indeed to think the logic of an untouchable remaining right at, right on the touchable, if one may say so still. This touchable-untouchable (which we try to hedge in from all sides, as it were, by approaching it without being able to approach too much, yet from multiple sides and ways) is not someone, nor is it what certain cultures term an "untouchable." But this "untouchable" with its *prohibition* against being touched could not be announced, named, and identified in this way except inasmuch as—let me stress again— there is some touchable-untouchable in general, before any religion, cult, or prohibition. Any vow of abstinence—hence avowing both the touchable and the untouchable—experiments with the touchable *as* untouchable, in a betrayal that is originary and therefore unforgivable, or *imprescriptible*, as is said of crimes against humanity in France today: outside the statute of limitations.

18. Speaking of my unspeakable temptation, I should confess to being tempted: to go all the way and say that the caress not only touches or borders on the messianic, but that it is the only capable, possible, and signifying experience for the messianic to show through. The messianic can only be stroked.

19. Levinas writes further: "Its [Eros's] movement consists in going beyond the possible" (p. 261), and "A *not yet* more remote than a future, a temporal *not yet*, evincing degrees in nothingness" (p. 264).

20. Since this is explicitly an analysis of the flesh, the body proper experienced as "carnal," and inasmuch as it is not reduced to the face, one should no doubt question these texts within a wide configuration, which is still to come (for Levinas, of course, does not refer to these texts as such): configured with Husserl (especially in *Ideas II*, which Levinas later comments upon), with Merleau-Ponty (especially in *Signs* and *The Visible and the Invisible*), with Didier Franck (especially in his "Incarnation of Another Body [L'incarnation d'un autre corps]," "Pairing and Resemblance [Accouplement et ressemblance]," and "The Caress and the Shock [La caresse et le choc]," in *Chair et corps*), and with Chrétien in *L'appel et la réponse*. A few specific elements of this "configuration" or rather "trend" [*mouvance*] will be provided later.

21. I am emphasizing "exorbitant" because of the strange recurrence of this word in Levinas and its regular reappearance in different contexts in the writings of others. See Chapter 9, "Tangent III."

22. I.e., "sans qu'on ait l'air d'y toucher."—Trans.

23. Levinas's emphasis. For my part, I'd have emphasized the "without's," "as if's," and all the "not's" that deliberately disorient the ontophenomenological syntax, even if dialectical. This is what Levinas describes—while delimiting it,

with a gesture familiar in Heidegger—as a "contradiction" for "formal logic" alone. Thus, for example: "Voluptuosity, as profanation, discovers the hidden as hidden. An exceptional relation is thus accomplished in a conjuncture which, for formal logic, would arise from contradiction: the discovered does not lose its mystery in the discovery, the hidden is not disclosed, the night is not dispersed. The profanation-discovery abides in modesty, be it under the guise of immodesty: the clandestine uncovered does not acquire the status of the disclosed" (*Totality and Infinity*, p. 260). The least one can say is that this complicates the task of what Levinas titles a "Phenomenology of Voluptuousness" in *Time and the Other*.

24. I have already suggested this in the foreword ("Avances") to Serge Margel's book *Le tombeau du dieu artisan* (Paris: Minuit, 1995).

25. See Apuleius, "The Most Pleasant and Delectable Tale of the Marriage of Cupid and Psyche," in *The Golden Ass*, bk. 5, trans. William Adlington (1566), http://icg.harvard.edu/chaucer/canttales/clerk/cup-psy.html (accessed December 17, 2004).—Trans.

26. This may be a good place to recall (as we'll do later from another point of view) that Henri Maldiney has an original way of orienting a certain thinking of the untouchable in Merleau-Ponty toward a thematics of the caress, which would not be the tactile exploration of a thing:

> The revelation of flesh culminates in the caress, where the Being of the flesh and the carnal experience coincide in the felt-Being [*l'être-senti*] of the body of the other which is exactly revealed as flesh. . . . According to this intentionality of pure agency from which the caress is suspended, what does the caress intend in its very touching? It intends the *untouchable*: that of the flesh that I will never touch.
>
> The untouchable, and as well the invisible, are an intrinsic dimension of the flesh of the world that I touch and that I see. Merleau-Ponty says that it is the invisible of the world that makes the world visible. The invisible is not added to the visible in order to make with it a total. (Henri Maldiney, "Flesh and Verb in the Philosophy of Merleau-Ponty," in *Chiasms: Merleau-Ponty's Notion of Flesh*, ed. Fred Evans and Leonard Lawlor [Albany: State University of New York Press, 2000], p. 62)

27. Here Levinas emphasizes the word *manière*, perhaps to suggest a way and a figure of the hand.

28. This non-signifyingness is not an insignificance opposed to significance, any more than the beyond of the face ceases to imply the face. This is the precaution one must not fail to take when one is so gravely inscribing a certain "*inversion* of the face" and a certain "*disfigurement*" on the side of femininity: "In this inversion of the face in femininity, in this disfigurement that refers to the face, non-signifyingness abides in the signifyingness of the face" (*Totality and Infinity*, pp. 262–63). If one reads what follows, one comes across the motif of gravity: "feminine beauty" would become "weightless grace" only if it let itself be

"converted" by the artist's hand, when "the beautiful of art *inverts* the beauty of the feminine face" (p. 263; Levinas's emphasis).

29. I am leaving out of the picture the question of Levinas's treatment of the animal—on purpose, since it is the object of a separate study in a different book (see "L'animal que donc je suis," in *L'animal autobiographique: Autour de Jacques Derrida*, ed. Marie-Louise Mallet [Paris: Galilée, 1999], p. 264n1).

30. A few years later, in 1965, in the course of a remarkable analysis of some passages in Husserl's *Ideas II* (which we'll soon in turn turn to), Levinas took an interest in the structure of the sentient-sensed from another point of view—one that is different but could be interesting when tested against these analyses of the caress. This also goes with *a certain manner of the hand, the manual*. And about these *Empfindnisse* effacing by way of their very indeterminacy "the sentient-sensed and subject-object structures, which the word *Empfindung* suggests," Levinas adds in a note: "One hardly dares to create a neologism to translate this notion: the term *sentance* could perhaps express the diffuse character of this notion" ("Intentionnalité et sensation," in Emmanuel Levinas, *En découvrant l'existence avec Husserl et Heidegger* [Paris: Vrin, 1967], p. 157). [My translation.—Trans.]

Didier Franck also refers to this in *Chair et corps*, p. 97. It is on the very same page where Levinas twice alludes, within the Husserlian analysis, to a "kind of fundamental" and immediate *iteration* "whose sensation is the event itself" that he proposes the word *sentance*. This constitutive iteration makes of the *Empfindnisse*'s extension something other than a simple spatial extension. It opens an intentional experience *of* space *in* space.

31. We'll return to the question of the *Son* later in a more Christian context. I purposely interrupt this analysis at the point where we ask ourselves, as we go from love and Eros to fecundity, whether Eros has ended and acknowledged its own death, mourning itself; and whether filiation (especially paternity, sons and brothers, which are here the only themes of this analysis of fecundity) opens toward a happy and legitimate issue for this tragic failing in solitude. This is a problem I have approached in other texts dedicated to Levinas's thinking ("Violence and Metaphysics," in *Writing and Difference*, trans. Bass, pp. 79–153; *Psyché*; and *Adieu to Emmanuel Levinas*, trans. Brault and Naas). See, here, the chapters in *Totality and Infinity* following those just evoked, from "Fecundity" to "Filiation and Paternity."

It is possible—I'm not certain—that the questions posed by these three texts intersect with those that Luce Irigaray raises in "The Fecundity of the Caress: A Reading of Levinas, *Totality and Infinity*, 'Phenomenology of Eros,'" the chapter she devotes to Levinas in *An Ethics of Sexual Difference*, trans. Carolyn Burke and Gillian C. Gill (Ithaca, N.Y.: Cornell University Press, 1993). "Before orality comes to be, touch is already in existence," she observes (ibid., p. 187) at the outset of a reading intertwined with a meditation on God's becoming outside touch [*hors tact*] and on the "memory of touching," "the most insistent and the most difficult to enter into memory" (ibid., p. 215).

32. Levinas never speaks of perjury, it seems to me, nor of oaths—at least not in these terms. I tried in *Adieu to Emmanuel Levinas*, by another route leading to the same thing, to demonstrate this kind of quasi-transcendental inevitability of perjury.

5. Tender

1. See Levinas, *Totality and Infinity*, trans. Lingis, p. 279.

2. In an interview given a quarter of a century later, Levinas expresses concerns about his own use of the word "love." As if he were retracting it, wanting to efface the symmetry or the reversibility that the word seems to suggest, and above all the "concupiscence," that is, the concupiscent desire for what Christian language calls the flesh—but not the erotic. "I hesitate to use the word 'love,' I'm very wary, I often say that I've never used the word 'love'; the word 'responsibility,' in the way I use it, is love's stern name—love without concupiscence, love without reciprocity—in a way, an irreversible relationship. . . . I must logically go through the unreflected responsibility of this erotic society—this society without concupiscence—and take into consideration my insertion into a society whose members I proceed to compare, in order to be within the objectivity called for by justice, and that grounds justice. I define love as a notion of logic—is this naïveté perhaps?—and put it in the register of knowledge, while specifying gender, species, and individual." See "Entretien Lévinas-Ricœur," in *Lévinas: Philosophe et pédagogue* (Paris: Nadir, 1998), pp. 16–17. [My translation.—Trans.]

3. I.e., "le tendre ne s'éprouve qu'à tendre"—Trans.

4. See Nancy, *Experience of Freedom*, trans. McDonald: "For the gift is never purely and simply given. It does not vanish in the receipt of the gift—or of the 'present.' The gift is precisely that whose 'present' and presentation are not lost in a realized presence. The gift is what comes-up [*sur-vient*] to the presence of its 'present.' It is thus kept, in this coming-up and surprise of the gift, as gift, as the giving of the gift. In this it is an offering, or withdrawal, of the gift in the gift itself: the withdrawal of its being-present and the keeping [*retenue*] of its surprise. It is not a question here of the economy of the gift. . . . The offering is the inestimable price of the gift" (pp. 146–47 [slightly modified—Trans.]). Indeed, it comes down to a certain "freedom." On the topic of freedom, see the text by D. Giovannangeli, which also deals with Nancy, in *Le passage des frontières* (Paris: Galilée, 1994), p. 68. The question remains of whether the value of "keeping" or "guarding," which is recurrent and decisive in this whole passage and indispensable to distinguish between the gift and the offering, the offering in the gift, allows one to eschew economics. One may doubt it, as suggested earlier (see Chapter 2, "Spacings").

5. See Nancy, *Sense of the World*, trans. Librett.

6. Jean-Luc Nancy, *L'intrus* (Paris: Galilée, 2000), p. 13, trans. Susan Hanson as "L'Intrus," *CR: New Centennial Review* 3 (2002): 2. [The text, first circulated on the Internet, was then first published in *Dédale* 9–10 (1999).—Trans.]

7. Nancy, "L'Intrus," trans. Hanson, p. 10.

8. Ibid., p. 11.

9. See Jean-Luc Nancy, "The Sublime Offering," trans. Jeffrey Librett, in *Finite Thinking*, ed. Sparks, pp. 211–44.

10. "One must change sense, pass from sight to tact": this phrase is emended in Librett's translation. Its place is on page 233, second paragraph, (ending of the) third sentence. It occurs in *Une pensée finie*, on page 179. It has been reinserted here in Peggy Kamuf's rendition.—Trans.

11. Nancy, "Sublime Offering," trans. Librett, p. 233 [short passage added—Trans.].

12. George Berkeley, *Philosophical Works, Including the Works on Vision* (London: Everyman, 1993), p. 54. See also (e.g., on p. 295) the passages on "experience" and "connexion," which produce the same common names for ideas or objects (either visible or tangible) that remain radically heterogeneous and irreducible to one another.

13. Ibid., pp. 61–62.

14. Ibid., p. 296, "The theory of vision . . . vindicated and explained."

15. In "Deconstruction of Christianity," trans. Sparks, cited earlier, Nancy says at the same time that we must find *something else*, and that that is "the thing itself" to be thought: "[T]he question is whether we can . . . locate at the heart of Christianity a root [*provenance*] more original than Christianity itself, a root that might allow another possibility to arise" (p. 116). Earlier, he writes: "Let us say, then (*cum grano salis*, this would probably be my way of being phenomenological), that Christianity or the Christian is the very thing—*the thing itself*—that has to be thought" (p. 113).

16. Jean-Luc Nancy, to whom I had spoken about my long-standing wish to write on his thinking about touch (and who since then, with a gentle irony, has gone on putting out ever more tactile antennae of his corpus), wrote to me in August 1991:

> [Someone] . . . has written to me about Christianity (in relation to certain of my texts—but without establishing any "positive" relation), and he said in passing, "Our faith no longer has any notion of what the divine touch might be—for Christianity is indeed a religion of the touch, whatever one might like to do about that (Jesus lets himself be touched and this is not without meaning)." Well here, dear Jacques, is something that can revive a certain mischievous remark, which has on occasion shown up, about my "Christianity."

The announcement of the "deconstruction of Christianity" then followed.

17. See also Mark 1: 40–42, and Luke 5: 13. [English Bible quotations are from the Revised Standard Version, slightly modified.—Trans.]

18. In *Memoirs of the Blind*, trans. Brault and Naas, I tried to follow the path of this Christic touch and more generally this relation between the tactile and light, between hand, finger and eye.

19. About touching and healing the ear, see Luke 22: 51.

20. See also Luke 8: 43–54 about this same episode.

21. There again, touching signifies the moment of pardon, by virtue of love ("And he said to the woman, 'Your faith has saved you; go in peace'" [Luke 7: 50]).

22. "Jesus saith unto her, Touch me not" is the King James Version; "Jesus said to her, "Do not hold me" is the Revised Standard Version of John 20: 17. —Trans.

23. In the Epistles (Corinthians, Colossians, Timothy, Hebrews), the motif and the lexicon of touch are more often associated with a prohibition: do not touch; let that remain untouchable. Since Thomas Didymus has been mentioned, we could attempt a reading (one among many other possible ones) of Maurice Blanchot's *Thomas l'Obscur* as an abyssal, meditative fictive recollection of this evangelical episode played back in this way. From the start, the book teems with examples concerning this touchable-untouchable, always between *life* and *death, words* and *animals*: "Desire was this same corpse which opened its eyes and knowing itself to be dead climbed awkwardly back up into his mouth like an animal swallowed alive. . . . He knew with terrible certainty that it [his thought], too, was looking for a way to enter into him. Against his lips, in his mouth, it was forcing its way toward a monstrous union. Below his eyelids, it created a necessary sight. . . . Hands and corpses were taken away. Alone, the body of Thomas remained, deprived of its senses. And thought, having entered him again, exchanged contact with the void" ("Thomas the Obscure," trans. Robert Lamberton, in *The Station Hill Blanchot Reader: Fiction and Literary Essays* [Barrytown, N.Y.: Station Hill Press / Barrytown, Ltc., 1999], p. 61). In the famous reading scene, at the beginning of chapter 4, words are watching Thomas like beasts of prey that let themselves be *touched* by a look: "In relation to every symbol, he was in the position of the male praying mantis about to be devoured by the female. They looked at each other. The words, coming forth from the book which was taking on the power of life and death, exercised a gentle and peaceful attraction over the glance which played over them" (ibid., p. 67). And further, in the same chapter: "His hands sought to touch an impalpable and unreal body. . . . His head was forced to touch the evil, his lungs to breathe it in. . . . It was in this state that he felt himself bitten or struck, he could not tell which, by what seemed to him to be a word, but resembled rather a giant rat, an all-powerful beast with piercing eyes and pure teeth" (ibid., p. 69).

24. Jean-Luc Nancy, "Une pensée finie," in *Une pensée finie*; "A Finite Think-

ing," trans. Edward Bullard, Jonathan Derbyshire, and Simon Sparks, in *Finite Thinking*, ed. Sparks, pp. 3–30.

25. Nancy, *Experience of Freedom*, trans. McDonald, p. 7 [slightly modified—Trans.].

26. See the entire conclusion of the chapter "Are We Free to Speak of Freedom?"; ibid., pp. 1–8.

27. Ibid., p. 8.

28. Ibid., p. 7 [slightly modified—Trans.]. This sensible, more precisely tactile, figurality, regularly marks the exposition of *Experience of Freedom*, especially where reaching a "limit" is at issue.

29. Nancy, "Sublime Offering," trans. Librett, p. 233 [short passage added—Trans.].

30. See Nancy, *Logodaedalus*.

31. Nancy, "Sublime Offering," trans. Librett, p. 232.

32. Ibid., p. 233

6. Nothing to Do in Sight

1. First published in *Critique* (January–February 1988) (as "Le rire, la présence"), then reissued in *Une pensée finie* and *Birth to Presence*, trans. McVarish, pp. 368–92, this text, "Laughter, Presence," is at once (and at least—since I shall not venture to sum it up or just reduce it in this way) a magnificent reading of Baudelaire's "The Desire to Paint," and of the "laughter" in it that Baudelaire contrives to make us hear and see: "the laughter of a wide mouth, red and white and alluring, that makes one dream of the miracle of a superb flower blooming on a volcanic soil" ("Laughter, Presence," in *Birth to Presence*, p. 370). "Laughter, Presence" is also a powerful meditation about art, *the* arts and sense, *the* senses of art, arts and the senses. [Baudelaire's "The Desire to Paint" appears in Charles Baudelaire, *Paris Spleen*, trans. Louise Varèse (New York: New Directions, 1947); Emily McVarish's version as it appears in *The Birth to Presence*, pp. 368–92, is quoted.—Trans.]

2. Nancy, "Laughter, Presence," trans. McVarish, p. 389 [slightly modified—Trans.].

3. Ibid., pp. 388–89.

4. Nancy, *Being Singular Plural*, trans. Richardson and O'Byrne. [In the passage that follows, citations of *Being Singular Plural* appear parenthetically in the text.—Trans.]

5. One's heart at the heart of the other's heart. A man's heart or a woman's: Nancy has no inkling of which, he says, about the heart that sur-vives in him henceforth. A man's or a woman's? This is the place for a reminder: in "normal" conditions and before any virtual transplantation, only a woman can feel the

beat of someone else's heart in her. The word for it is "pregnancy." In "miraculous" conditions, in the extraordinary story of Flesh and Incarnation—but without transplantation—it is announced as an Annunciation: two hearts in you. Between Man and God, Jesus's Sacred Heart then begins to beat within Mary, one of our Marys.

May I decently give in to a temptation and bring up an almost secret recollection? (I like to remember it, happily, like a shared grace.) On the eve of the *operation* of which we spoke earlier, when Nancy was about to change hearts, I heard myself tell him on the phone, from California: "Don't worry, I'll wake up with you."

And in a certain way, though I knew it to be more easily said than done, I thought I could recognize in this, to the letter, a figure of truth, dare I say much larger than I—a literally tangible figure of the heart's truth, as well as the truth of an incommensurable gratitude, toward who accepts and receives, toward the friend who doesn't reject and whose body consents to keep the heart of another man or another woman, toward who (through this incredible *survival*, and in a better way) lets us give thought to the bottom of the heart, its inmost depths, farther than the depths of what so much recollection and memory gives us as a legacy, wherever we are told about the "heart," from the Bible to Pascal to Martin Heidegger—memory, precisely, there where it joins with thinking, with the grace of gratitude, with love or friendship.

6. Georges Bataille, *Histoire des rats*, in *Œuvres complètes*, vol. 3 (Paris: Gallimard, 1971), p. 114. "A Story of Rats," in *The Impossible: A Story of Rats, Followed by Dianus and by the Oresteia*, trans. Robert Hurley (San Francisco: City Lights, 1991), pp. 25–26; very slightly modified.—Trans.

7. No offense is meant against the singularity of this laugh (answering a certain Baudelaire—rather than Bataille), but how can we not let it ring together with the laughter that seems to come forth on the last page of *Une pensée finie*? At the end of "Dei paralysis progressiva" [trans. Thomas Harrison, in *Birth to Presence*, pp. 48–57], which also tells of Nietzsche's end (death, jubilation, paralysis: "'one can die from being immortal'"), one can hear the "obligation" to sing —to sing, says Nietzsche the Crucified to Peter Gast, "a new song": "Sing me a new song" (*Birth to Presence*, p. 56).

There again laughter—silent laughter this time—*laughs touching*. But it laughs the touching-without-touching of the limit—attaining without touching it. Nancy writes: "To him the heavens are no longer the heaven one reaches after passing through death. Here, too, death shrinks into insignificance, now no longer because it precedes itself in paralysis, but because the life which will *attain* it, which is always already in the process of *attaining it, does not, in it, touch* on the moment of mediation" (ibid., p. 57; I emphasize "attaining" as well as the strange syntax of this "does not, in it, touch."—J. D.). What attains, without

touching inside, traces a kind of writing, or a way of writing and signing, here—
what Nancy a little later terms "a singular trace [*tracé*], a finitude whose limit
puts into play each time anew the whole spacing of the world." Death, jubilation, paralysis: "the end is endless" (ibid., p. 57).

8. Plato *Phaedo*, trans. Benjamin Jowett, 65b.

9. Plato *Republic*, trans. Benjamin Jowett, 10.611e.

10. Blaise Pascal, *Pensées and Other Writings*, trans. Honor Levi (Oxford: Oxford University Press, 1995), p. 122 [*Pensée* no. 505].

11. Plotinus *Enneads* 6.9.7, Loeb ed., trans. A. H. Armstrong (Cambridge,
Mass.: Harvard University Press, 1988).

12. Ibid.

13. Ibid., 5.3.17.

14. Ibid., 5.3.10. In *L'appel et la réponse*, p. 134, Jean-Louis Chrétien cites another passage in the *Enneads* as well (4.4.23 and 3.23) and specifies: "For Plotinus
or Saint Augustine, who profit from progress made in the study of nervous physiology, Aristotle's explanation is obsolete. But Plotinus says that the organ of
touch is the whole body, *pan to sōma*, and this keeps it apart from the other
senses. Saint Augustine writes that the very sense of touch is diffuse throughout
the body. And Marsilio Ficino [writes]: 'Tactus, qui per omnia membra univer-
salis est animae sensus.'" See also Chapter 13 on this point.

15. Aristotle *Metaphysica* lambda [12], 7.1072b.19–21, trans. W. D. Ross, in *Basic Works of Aristotle*, 689ff. This passage is quoted by Chrétien in *L'appel et la
réponse*, pp. 150–51. The latter follows the Thomist lineage or interpretation of this
"figure" and especially insists on the primacy of the intelligible. This "clearly asserted" primacy would mark at the same time the irreducibility of transcendence
and a "radical difference from 'my absolute contact with myself'" of which Merleau-
Ponty speaks [in *Phénoménologie de la perception* (Paris: Gallimard, 1945), trans.
Colin Smith as *Phenomenology of Perception* (London: Routledge, 1962), p. 343.—
Trans.], and from an auto-affection." We'll come back to this later.

16. Henri Bergson, "Introduction to Metaphysics," in *The Creative Mind*, trans.
Mabelle L. Andison (New York: Philosophical Library, 1946), p. 195.

17. Ibid.

18. Ibid., pp. 35–36. My emphasis. Bergson does say "contact" and "coinci-
dence." The stakes are rather weighty—we'll keep taking the measure of this.
Bergson does not say (not here in any case) "partial coincidence," as Merleau-
Ponty does in his article "Bergson in the Making," in *Signs* (trans. Richard C.
McCleary [Evanston, Ill.: Northwestern University Press, 1964]). This reading of
Bergson by Merleau-Ponty, at this point of "contact," is examined later: see Chap-
ter 7, "Tangent I."

19. Gilles Deleuze and Félix Guattari, "The Smooth and the Striated," in *A
Thousand Plateaus: Capitalism and Schizophrenia*, trans. Brian Massumi (Min-

neapolis: University of Minnesota Press, 1987), pp. 492–93. Despite these references, Deleuze and Guattari are intent on taking "some risks" and "making free use of these notions" (p. 493).

20. Ibid., p. 494.

21. Ibid. My emphasis.—J. D.

22. See Hélène Cixous, "Savoir," in *Veils*, trans. Geoffrey Bennington (Stanford: Stanford University Press, 2001). [Cited parenthetically in the text.—Trans.]

23. I.e., *amiraculés.*—Trans.

24. In the same book [i.e., Cixous, *Veils*], rather than by vision and the veil (revelation, unveiling of the truth), it is by way of *a touch* that I distinguish the prayer shawl, or tallith, in its animal-like figure: "A prayer shawl I like to touch more than to see, and to caress every day, to kiss without even opening my eyes or even when it remains wrapped in a paper bag into which I stick my hand at night, eyes closed. . . . Before seeing or knowing, before fore-seeing and fore-knowing, it is worn in memory of the Law" ("A Silkworm of One's Own: Points of View Stitched on the Other Veil," in *Veils*, p. 43).

In [Jacques Derrida] *La dissémination* (Paris: Seuil, 1972) reading and writing and the very experience of text call on this interlacing of a woven web and what remains to be *touched* no less than seen: against a kind of criticism that is deluding itself "in wanting to look at the text without touching it, without laying a hand on the 'object'" (*Dissemination*, trans. Barbara Johnson [Chicago: University of Chicago Press, 1981], p. 63).

25. Deleuze and Guattari, *Thousand Plateaus*, pp. 492–93.

26. Ibid., p. 493. My emphasis.—J. D.

27. Ibid., pp. 474–75.

28. Nancy emphasizes "*here* . . . 'Hoc est enim corpus meum'"—he, incidentally, very often makes use of this "here" in a remarkable, differentiated way. His "here" deserves a study of its own. My own underscoring of "privilege given to immediacy" and of what Nancy opposes to it, namely, "local, modal, fractal"— also emphasized—can easily be understood.

But if I have underscored "properly," it is because, while grasping its pedagogical and rhetorical necessity, I continue to harbor doubts about the possibility or the sense of such a "properness" of writing or its body. To say it without any detours, I propose to debate the compatibility between this "properly of it" and the logic of the paragraph surrounding it. This concession should also be "more deconstructed"—it already appears twice at the beginning of the same paragraph in the definition of exscription: "its other-border-proper," "the other-border-proper." Beyond pedagogical concessions, this is a serious matter indeed. It has to do with an irresistible desire of appropriation (which is the "my body" itself, the very "here"). It has to do with its law, but also this *same* law that must—in order to make this desire hatch—destine it also to expropriation—or hand to this desire expropriation as a promise, or hand this desire over to the promise of expropriation. This promise is always a threat: exappropriation. And it should stop me from simply speaking, as I just did, of a "same" law. The word "same" itself, selfsame ipseity itself (*mesme, medisme, meïsme, metipsimus,* superlative of *metipse*), is as deconstructible as the word "proper." And the French word *proche* ("proximate"), and the French word *prochain* ("next," "neighbor," "fellow man."). But try to speak without them!

29. Nancy, "Laughter, Presence," trans. McVarish, pp. 389–90, 392 [very slightly modified—Trans.].

7. Tangent I

1. I.e., "*Faudrait-il* pouvoir *le toucher?*"—Trans.
2. Nancy, "Sublime Offering," trans. Librett, p. 233.
3. Nancy, "Laughter, Presence," trans. McVarish, p. 389.
4. Without reconstituting the enormous thicket formed by this debate, let us select as evidence some remarks on the said "question of the hand," "the figure of the hand" ("like my hand"), attributed by Diderot in his *Lettre sur les aveugles à l'usage de ceux qui voient* to "our blind man," who is asked what he means by a mirror: "'An instrument,' answered he, 'which sets things in relief at a distance from themselves, when properly placed with regard to it. It is like my hand, which, to feel an object, I must not put on one side of it.'" And Diderot goes on: "This blind man's only knowledge of objects is by touch. . . . Sight, he therefore concludes, is a kind of touch which extends to distant objects and is not applied to our face" ["Letter on the Blind for the Use of Those Who See," in *Diderot's Early Philosophical Works,* trans. Margaret Jourdain (Chicago: Open Court, 1916), p. 72.—Trans.]. This proposition, "sight is a kind of touch," is taken up again literally by Maine de Biran, who deems it both true and insufficient. The end of Diderot's *Lettre sur les aveugles* returns to the analogy of the hand: "If you trace on my hand with a point . . . my hand would become a sensitive mirror; but the difference is great between this canvas and the organ of sight. I suppose the eye is a living canvas of infinite delicacy; the air strikes the object. . . . If the skin of my hand was as sensitive as your eye, I should see with my hand as you see with your eyes, and I sometimes imagine there are animals who have no eyes, but can nevertheless see" (ibid., pp. 155–56).
5. See, esp., "Carnival of the Senses" in Élisabeth de Fontenay, *Diderot: Reason and Resonance* (trans. Jeffrey Mehlman [New York: Braziller, 1982]), where she recalls this philosophy of touch, or rather this touch *as* philosophy ("And I found that of all the senses the eye was the most superficial, the ear the most haughty, smell the most voluptuous, taste the most superstitious and inconstant, touch the most profound and philosophical" [pp. 157–58]), and precisely warns

against hastily attributing this "recognition of the theoretical importance of the sense of touch" to the "materialist cause" (p. 167). "The great victor in this carnival of the senses established on the ruins of the castle of the eye and consciousness is touch—Diderot termed it the organ of the 'tight' [*l'organe du 'serré'*]" (p. 166). [I have restored and translated the phrase "l'organe du 'serré,' comme l'appelle Diderot," which does not appear in the published translation.—Trans.] This same chapter cites more than one text referring (or reducing, as we shall later say) the sense of touch to the hand ("'It is not because man lifts his eyes to heaven, like all birds, that he is king of the animals,' we read in the *Histoire des deux Indes*. 'It is because he is armed with a supple, industrious, flexible, and helpful hand'" [p. 167]), in the tradition of Anaxagoras, who already links the human to the manual: "Man thinks because he has hands" (p. 162). I would also like to refer to the invaluable book by Martin Jay, *Downcast Eyes: The Denigration of Vision in Twentieth-Century French Thought* (Berkeley: University of California Press, 1993). (I feel particularly close to what the latter wrote on the score of "phallogocularcentrism," although, in this rather unstable logic, which is prone to reversals, a deconstructive thinking of spacing just as regularly has to call on the visible against a certain interpretation of the audible.) See also *Modernity and the Hegemony of Vision*, ed. David Michael Levin (Berkeley: University of California Press, 1993); and *In Visible Touch*, ed. Terry Smith (Sydney: Power Publications, 1997).

    6. René Descartes, *Discourse on Method, Optics, Geometry, and Meteorology,* trans. Paul J. Olscamp (Indianapolis: Bobbs-Merrill, 1965), p. 67. I should quote the First Discourse in its entirety and closely analyze its whole rhetoric (particularly the "two or three comparisons" that Descartes proposes in order to account for the rays of light which "enter into the eye" [ibid., p. 66]). In "Eye and Mind" (trans. Carleton Dallery, in *The Primacy of Perception: And Other Essays on Phenomenological Psychology, the Philosophy of Art, History and Politics*, ed. James M. Edie [Evanston, Ill.: Northwestern University Press, 1964]), Merleau-Ponty gives a gripping summary of this: "The question being so formulated, it is best to think of light as an action by contact—not unlike the action of things upon the blind man's cane. The blind, says Descartes, 'see with their hands.' The Cartesian concept of vision is modeled after the sense of touch" (p. 170). There is a chance, as the saying goes, that things are more complicated than that, if not altogether different. In this passage, Descartes is only proffering a "comparison"—the first, among others. An expressly pedagogical comparison is not necessarily what Merleau-Ponty here terms a "model," and Descartes certainly does not say that the blind "see with their hands." More precisely, he writes that "one might almost say that they see with their hands, or that their stick is the organ of some sixth sense given to them in place of sight" (*Discourse on Method, Optics . . .* , trans. Olscamp, p. 67).

Merleau-Ponty's proposed interpretation of the *Dioptrics* pertains to the tradition of Diderot's "Letter on the Blind for the Use of Those Who See": "'And what are eyes, do you suppose?' asked Monsieur de—. 'An organ,' replied the blind man, 'on which the air has the effect this stick has on my hand.' That answer amazed us. . . . Madam, only turn to Descartes' *Dioptrics*, and there you will see the phenomena of sight illustrated by those of touch, and the plates full of men busied in seeing with sticks. . . . that great philosopher was, in this respect, no more superior to the blind man than a common man who has the use of his eyes" (Diderot, "Letter," p. 73).

As for this stick of the blind, Martin Jay precisely recalls (*Downcast Eyes*, pp. 74–79, 34ff., 98ff., and passim) the long sequence of Descartes's predecessors (beginning with Simplicius's commentary on Aristotle's *Peri psuchēs*). He further recalls (pp. 34–35), with Robert Mandrou (see the latter's *Introduction to Modern France, 1500–1640: An Essay in Historical Psychology*, trans. R. E. Hallmark [London: Edward Arnold, 1975]), that touch remained the dominant sense, the master sense until the eighteenth century.

7. On this point, see Merleau-Ponty, who recalls Fichte and Schelling and points (accurately, I think) toward what ties the thinking about effort to the "idea that the will is the condition of the self" (*Incarnate Subject*, trans. Milan, p. 70).

8. Pierre Maine de Biran, "Introduction," in *The Influence of Habit on the Faculty of Thinking*, trans. Margaret Donaldson Boehm (Baltimore: Williams & Wilkins, 1929), pp. 47–83. [Edition cited by Jacques Derrida: Maine de Biran, *Influence de l'habitude sur la faculté de penser*, ed. Pierre Tisserand (Paris: Presses universitaires de France, 1954).—Trans.]

9. Maine de Biran, *Influence of Habit*, p. 52. [Further cited parenthetically in the text.—Trans.] I here leave aside any systematic study of works that thus begin with the sense of touch, at least in an analogous fashion (like Aristotle), and give a justification for doing that. That was Kant's gesture, as we saw. It will also be Hegel's, for example in the *Encyclopedia of the Philosophical Sciences*, though only with regard to the philosophy of nature (¶¶ 358ff.). Things change, of course, and so does, for the feeling soul (¶¶ 399ff.), the order of the senses, in the philosophy of spirit. It is also the question of habit—Maine de Biran's question—that Hegel poses just after that, as well as the question of plasticity. See Catherine Malabou, *L'avenir de Hegel: Plasticité, temporalité, dialectique* (Paris: Vrin, 1996).

10. This passage from a note does not appear in the translation used here. It is printed in a recent edition of Maine de Biran's work, *Mémoires sur l'influence de l'habitude*, ed. Gilbert Romeyer-Dherbey (Paris: Vrin, 1987), as part of the "Notes rédigées par Maine de Biran en marge de son exemplaire du mémoire imprimé, ou sur feuilles insérées dans l'ouvrage." See p. 292n5.—Trans.

11. Bonnet's sentence appears on the title page of the essay in the edition used, following the "Report of M. Destutt-Tracy." The official question "proposed by

the Class of Moral and Political Sciences of the Institut National," also appearing on the title page, is: "To determine what is the influence of habit upon the faculty of thinking; or, in other words, to show the effect which the frequent repetition of the same performances produces on each of our intellectual faculties" (Maine de Biran, *Influence of Habit*, p. 41).—Trans.

12. Variants of the title exist. *Influence de l'habitude sur la faculté de penser* was the cover title, used as the title proper in the translation by Margaret Donaldson Boehm. It is reproduced in facsimile on the cover of the 1987 Romeyer-Dherbey edition.—Trans.

13. Merleau-Ponty, *Incarnate Subject*, trans. Milan, p. 64.

14. Merleau-Ponty, *Phenomenology of Perception*, trans. Smith. [Cited parenthetically in the text.—Trans.]

15. The emphasis is mine. Among all the questions that these passages raise, those tied to the words "assumption" [*reprise*] and "almost" are doubtless among the more frustrated.

16. Merleau-Ponty, *Signs*, trans. McCleary, pp. 183–85. The underscoring is mine, except for the words "because" and "seeing," emphasized by Merleau-Ponty who gives no reference for "partial coincidence." But even when he recognizes "non-coincidence" or "partial coincidence" or "fusion," as he increasingly does in all his last writings, even when he states that intuition is not "*simply coincidence or fusion*," he noticeably maintains the principle of an intuition, and even an intuition of coincidence. Even with a "non-coincidence," "I" still "coincide." That is what Merleau-Ponty nicknames "absolute knowledge," as we have just read.

17. Pierre Tisserand [the editor of the edition cited by Jacques Derrida—Trans.] says about touch that for Maine de Biran it is "the philosophical sense since it gives us the perception of resistance; and the scientific sense since it is the sense of measure and educates the eye. Sight thus becomes a sort of remote touching . . . " ("Introduction de l'éditeur," in *Influence de l'habitude sur la faculté de penser* [Paris: Presses universitaires de France, 1954], pp. xxxvi–xxxvii.) Further, in the same tradition, Jules Lagneau says: "Touch is the philosophical sense, that is, the sense of reality" (Lagneau, *Célèbres leçons et fragments* [Paris: Presses universitaires de France, 1950], p. 151 [p. 208 in the second edition, 1964]; cited by Chrétien in "Le corps et le toucher" ["Body and Touch"], in *L'appel et la réponse*, p. 113). Concerning Lagneau's hand, I shall add this detail: Lagneau situates the *idea* of the object, such as it is *conceived, before* and as the *condition* of the tactile perception of resistance. The origin of objective resistance is fundamentally untouchable, beyond or before touch: "It is the idea of an object that produces in us the perception of resistance. Even the sensations of double touch resulting from the movement of the hand seeking to reunite the parts by way of the object would not suffice to reveal to us the existence of the object that is resisting. It is

necessary that *we conceive some other thing beyond what we are touching*" (p. 151 in the 1950 edition). Lagneau later writes: "Touch, the sense of reality, educates the other senses, especially the eye, sight being truly the sense of exteriority" (p. 153 in the 1950 edition).

18. The translator of the text, Margaret Donaldson Boehm, notes: "[Pierre] Tisserand [editor of the 1954 edition of *Influence de l'habitude sur la faculté de penser*] writes me that for Biran a *tête sonore* is a head in which occurs the inner speech which accompanies the idea. In speaking the thought to ourselves, the speech resounds in our head. It is what is now known in psychology as an auditory image." Maine de Biran also calls them *vocal* heads; he extends this analysis to animals and among other things cites Buffon's *Discours sur la nature des oiseaux*. This is not the only anthropo-zoological incursion. What Maine de Biran proffers about the relation between hearing and the vocal organ finds itself confirmed in the observation of certain animals, certainly, but also, *a contrario*, in the example of the wild boy of Aveyron. The latter, according to Maine de Biran, was deaf not because his ear could not hear but because he did not have the ability to speak and lacked the organ that makes hearing *active*. A savage does not hear himself speak; he does not touch himself with his voice.

19. On Kant's hand, see Chapter 3. On Husserl's hand, see Chapter 8. On Heidegger's hand, see "*Geschlecht* II: Heidegger's Hand," trans. Leavey, in *Deconstruction and Philosophy*, pp. 161–96. On the hand and the eye, see [Derrida] *Of Grammatology*, trans. Gayatri Chakravorty Spivak (1976; rev ed., Baltimore: Johns Hopkins University Press, 1997), pp. 83ff., and *Memoirs of the Blind*, trans. Brault and Naas.

20. *La souche*, literally, is the stump, but here "stock" or "line."—Trans.

21. The wording of this note does not appear in the translation used. The note appears in the 1987 Romeyer-Dherbey edition among the "Notes rédigées par Maine de Biran en marge de son exemplaire du mémoire imprimé, ou sur feuilles insérées dans l'ouvrage." See pp. 293–94n10.—Trans.

22. Not all human hands are the same. Difference with Heidegger's hand here: for the latter, the privilege of the hand carries beyond an act of knowledge and a motor action (grasping, *begreifen*, conceiving, taking, gripping). This prehensile or manipulating gesture is still the gesture of the monkey or the human as a simple animal or as *animal rationale*. See "*Geschlecht* II: Heidegger's Hand," trans. Leavey, in *Deconstruction and Philosophy*.

23. Kant, *Anthropology from a Pragmatic Point of View*, trans. Dowden. This is also about a long footnote, which I shall tackle separately in a forthcoming book.

24. My translation. This note does not appear in the translation used. Its place is on p. 61, at the end of the second paragraph, after "it is in virtue of this that it opens a feeding ground for intellect and furnishes it with its more substantial nourishment." In the Romeyer-Dherbey edition, it is on p. 140.—Trans.

25. Maine de Biran, *Influence of Habit*; p. 141 in the Romeyer-Dherbey edition.—Trans.

26. If I may point this out again in passing, in *Of Grammatology* (rev ed., trans. Spivak, pp. 83ff.), it is around this *question of the hand*, this "history of writing . . . as an adventure of relationships between the face and the hand," this "representation of the *anthropos* . . . a precarious balance linked to manual-visual script," a "balance . . . slowly threatened," around this question of hominization in general, and "the question of the *name of man*" that a deconstruction is organized, which distances itself from the (Luthero-Heideggerian—to say it rather too hastily) *destructio* mentioned earlier (see Chapter 3). The reference to Leroi-Gourhan's work, though disagreeing at times, plays an important part in this, as it does also in Bernard Stiegler's original problematic, developed so powerfully and compellingly, in *La technique et le temps* (Paris: Galilée, 1994–96) (and more particularly in the first volume, chap. 3, pp. 153ff.).

27. Félix Ravaisson, *De l'habitude*, ed. P. Millot (1894; Paris: Fayard, 1984), pp. 21–23. On the Aristotelian tradition in which one can place the author of the *Essay on the Metaphysics of Aristotle* (1837), see Christiane Mauve, "Ravaisson lecteur et interprète d'Aristote," in *L'antiquité grecque au XIXe siècle: Un exemplum contesté* (Paris: Harmattan, 1999). On Ravaisson's place in the history of the French philosophical institution and its spiritualistic trend, see Christiane Mauve and P. Vermeren, "Le dernier des métaphysiciens contre le bouffon de la philosophie: Une stratégie du spiritualisme universitaire en France: Félix Ravaisson, l'éclectisme et les disciples de Victor Cousin," *Corpus* [philosophical journal] 3 (Oct.–Nov. 1986), where the reader will find references to the indispensable work dedicated to Ravaisson by Dominique Janicaud (*Une généalogie du spiritualisme français: Aux sources du bergsonisme: Ravaisson et la métaphysique* [The Hague: Nijhoff, 1969]) and François Laruelle (*Phénomène et différence: Essai sur Ravaisson* [Paris: Klincksieck, 1972]).

28. See Ravaisson, *De l'habitude*, p. 67.

29. Ibid., p. 24.

30. Ibid., p. 25.

31. Nancy, *Corpus*, p. 76.

32. Ravaisson, *De l'habitude*, p. 48; my emphasis.

33. Ibid., pp. 25–26.

34. Ibid., p. 13.

35. Ibid., p. 34.

36. Ibid., p. 14; my emphasis.

37. See Xavier Bichat, *Recherches physiologiques sur la vie et sur la mort* (Paris, 1800); id., *Physiological Researches on Life and Death*, trans. F. Gold (Boston: Richardson & Lord, 1827).

38. Ravaisson, *De l'habitude*, pp. 36–37.

39. Ibid., p. 34, on a "law of grace."

40. Ravaisson cites Augustine's *Intimior intimo nostro*. But how would he have handled Augustine's discourse about a sense of touch that he recognizes to be diffused throughout the body, to be sure, but whose temptations regarding carnal concupiscence he does not denounce, as he does those of sight, hearing, taste, and smell? And we wonder especially what Ravaisson would have done with the absolute privilege that Augustine recognizes for *concupiscentia oculorum*, rightly translated, he says, by "general experience of the senses" (*generalis experientia sensuum*): "The general experience of the senses therefore it is . . . which is called the lust of the eyes: for that the office of seeing, wherein the eyes hold the prerogative, do the other senses by way of similitude usurp unto themselves (*sibi de similitudine usurpant*), whensoever they make search after any knowledge (*cum aliquid cognitionis explorant*)" (*St. Augustine's Confessions*, vol. 1, trans. William Watts [Cambridge, Mass.: Harvard University Press, 1979], 10.35, p. 177).

41. Ravaisson, *De l'habitude*, p. 45. There is as well a "divine secret" with regard to the "transmission of life" (p. 39). And the "secret of education" (p. 44) must regulate virtue, customs, and morals in accordance with this divine secret. For though habit is a virtue (p. 9) and "virtue is first an effort, a fatigue" (p. 44), it is called upon to overcome the said fatigue in pleasure, art, and grace, saintliness and innocence. "It [virtue] through practice alone becomes an attraction and a pleasure, a desire that forgets or does not know itself; and little by little it moves closer to the saintliness of innocence. There is the whole secret of education. Its art is to attract us to the good, and our propensities [*penchants*] tie us there. A *second nature* is thus formed" (p. 44). The references to Aristotle on this page again link the thinking of movement to the thinking of desire or "propensities." No movement of the spirit without desire.

Beyond its conventional usage, the recurrence of the word *secret* ["secret" or "secrecy"] also points to a process of interiorization, spiritualization, and therefore *dissimulation*, which is essential for this history of life, this history of habit where "extremes touch," and proceeds while concealing its meaning, and dephenomenalizing itself, if one may say so. In its "spiral," it "represents the return of Freedom to Nature, or rather the invasion of the realm of freedom by natural spontaneity": the "tendency to persevere in the act itself which constitutes Being" (ibid., p. 49). We shall later identify a kind of French filiation in this Christianization of Aristotelian desire (*orexis*) (see Chapter 11 on Jean-Louis Chrétien).

8. Tangent II

1. I.e., "le toucher figure—et la technique est de la partie."—Trans.

2. Husserl, *Ideas II* [hereafter cited parenthetically in the text—Trans.]. The analyses dealing with touch in this work have more than once been the object of

a certain attention in France. I'll come back to this later in gratitude. Clearly, these writings, like all such steps forward, even now await reading again, and rereading, with infinite patience.

3. *Leib* is translated as "Body" by the translators of *Ideas II*; J. D. terms it *corps propre*, rendered here as "body proper."—Trans.

4. This gesture of "For example . . . my . . . hand" appears elsewhere, notably in one of Husserl's manuscripts from 1932, dedicated to kinesthetic perspectives; "Nehmen wir die Hand als Beispiel" [Let us take the hand as an example], Husserl notes. Ulrich Claesges cites this in *Edmund Husserls Theorie der Raumkonstitution* (The Hague: Nijhoff, 1964), p. 113, which analyzes a large number of unpublished texts, frequently of later date than those collected and transcribed in *Ideas II*. Especially in the chapter "Taktueller Raum und Leibbewusstsein" [Tactile Space and Body Consciousness], Claesges deals there with the questions that are tackled here specifically from the perspective of the historical heritage from which Nancy's thinking takes off, albeit limited to aspects of the treatment of the relation between sight and touch in *Ideas II*, where the argument seems more systematically, thoroughly, and painstakingly developed than anywhere else. To my knowledge at least, Husserl never returned to and reconsidered the *thesis* (for it is a thesis as much as a description—such at least is my hypothesis) that accords such a "privilege" [*Vorzug*] to touch in *Ideas II*.

5. Since *This Sex Which Is Not One* (trans. Catherine Porter with Carolyn Burke [Ithaca, N.Y.: Cornell University Press, 1985]), as we know, Luce Irigaray has been following and interpreting what is at stake in "woman's autoeroticism" and the violence to which it is subjected when "The *one* of the form, of the individual, of the (male) sexual organ, of the proper name, of the proper meaning . . . supplants, while separating and dividing, that contact of *at least two* (lips) which keeps woman in contact with herself, but without any possibility of distinguishing what is touching from what is touched" (p. 26). Throughout several of her books, we can follow the unfurling of this logic, dealing with what the feminine would be in the interpretation of a "re-touching," which is to say an auto-affection not reducible to its masculine interpretation. For example:

> So, when she touches herself (again), who is "she"? And "herself"? Inseparable, "she" and "herself" are part the one of the other, endlessly. They cannot really be distinguished, though they are not for all that the female same, nor the male same. . . . And even if "to touch oneself," for the masculine gender, is defined as that which begins to set up the distinction subject-predicate, subject-object, in the most archaic fashion, i.e., in the relation of attribution: x is (to, in, . . .) y—which still allows passivity to have a place in auto-affection, or else a suspension between activity and passivity in the attribution of being—it will never be known who/what is x, who/what is y in the female." (Luce Irigaray, *Marine Lover of Friedrich Nietzsche*, trans. Gillian C. Gill [New York: Columbia University Press, 1991], pp. 90–91)

This re-touching, which always has to do with more than one or more than two lips, purportedly thwarts any oppositional logic, and passes beyond any terminal or terminological limit, and therefore any discrimination: "But when lips kiss, openness is not the opposite of closure. Closed lips remain open. And their touching allows movement from inside to outside, from outside to in, with no fastening nor opening mouth to stop the exchange" (Luce Irigaray, *Elemental Passions*, trans. Joanne Collie and Judith Still [New York: Routledge, 1992], p. 63).

The re-touching of lips itself can thus be remarked in a structural analogy between the top and the bottom—an analogy that reaches homonymy in certain languages (French, in any case): "Two lips? Retouching, unclosed enclosure of the body. The envelope of the skin is neither sutured nor open onto a 'canal' that takes in or rejects, but partially open onto the touch of two mucouses, or of four, at least: the lips above and the lips below" (Luce Irigaray, *To Speak Is Never Neutral*, trans. Gail Schwab [New York: Routledge, 2002], p. 242).

6. Although in principle they are indissociable, for obvious reasons, here I have to leave aside these problems (as well as those of passive genesis, the parallel between transcendental phenomenology and pure psychology, life or the "livingness" [*vivance*] of the living present) that I more than once broached elsewhere.

7. Slightly modified.—Trans.

8. Husserl recalls this difficulty at the beginning of his introduction to the "Constitution of the Spiritual World" (p. 181).

9. In the section on the spiritual world, under the heading "motivation," the example of the hand reappears, associated with the foot this time. It deserves a separate analysis, but precisely in its spiritual sphere, where the movement of the hand or the foot seems more human than ever, if one may say so, which is to say "freer" than ever. And it is then a question of motor activity more than tactile sensation. One has to follow the arguments that lead Husserl, in the course of an analysis of the "I can" and the "I do," to go from the "real [*reell*] psychophysical process" to the intentional relation. I move my hand or foot (later on, the word "dance" comes up), I push, I pull, I offer resistance to a thing, I strike a ball or a stone—all these movements we term *mechanical* are a physical-real process, and the "Object, 'this man,' 'this animal,' partakes of this event in virtue of his 'soul'" (p. 229). Husserl often refers to the *freedom* of the "I can"—to the "consciousness of the free 'I can'" (p. 270) in relation to kinesthetic processes. In a number of manuscripts collected and translated into French under the title *De la synthèse passive* (Grenoble: J. Millon, 1998) [p. 104 and passim], he does this especially for sight. "*Here*, however," Husserl adds, then, "we are not concerned with this real [*reell*] psychophysical process, but with the intentional relation. I, the subject, move my hand, and . . . the same holds for the 'I hit the stone.' The Bodily member, the hand, *appearing* to consciousness in this or that way . . . is an Object for the subject and is, as it were, a *theme* of his freedom, of his free action" (*Ideas II*, p. 229).

10. "Along with" is used in the English text.—Trans.

11. Husserl often comes back to examples of illusions or hallucinations that, at the moment when the "real" or material thing "vanishes from being" or comes clean as a sort of ghost, nevertheless leave intact, and even permit freeing in oneself, like a spontaneous reduction, the properly phenomenological contents of consciousness, without faith this time, without "belief," as he puts it in English, in the passage about a "lady whom we do not know" and a "waxwork figure" (Husserl, *Logical Investigations*, trans. J. N. Findlay [London: Routledge, 1982], 2: 609). We may compare this example with the one Husserl offers as a memory from his youth (during his years as a student in Berlin), when he took a simple figure, a deceptive, mechanical doll (there again, a lifeless Psyche!) for a strange young woman holding a catalogue in her hands and looking with interest at the same thing he is examining. (This story appears in a manuscript translated in the compilation *De la synthèse passive*, trans. Bruce Bégout and Jean Kessler [Grenoble: J. Millon, 1998], p. 53). Regarding what phenomenology has to say about hallucinations, illusions, and perceptual deception ("something . . . perhaps even a great deal," Husserl specifies), see his *Ideas I*, i.e., *Ideas Pertaining to a Pure Phenomenology and to a Phenomenological Philosophy*, I, *General Introduction to a Pure Phenomenology*, trans. F. Kersten (The Hague: Nijhoff, 1982), ¶ 88, p. 215.

12. Once more, this "(animal being)" in parentheses will have come to our notice. This time it is not even an allusion to the nonhuman animal's animalness but to man himself *as* animal. "'Man' (animal being)" translates "'Mensch' (animalisches Wesen)."

13. Therefore, when Husserl means to say "flesh," he says *Fleisch* [flesh, *chair*]. Flesh is not all of the living body proper that many have fallen into the habit of translating as *chair* (flesh) in French. No doubt, this came about after Merleau-Ponty extended it in a more or less unlimited way when he spoke of the *chair du monde* [flesh of the world], even if this use of the term now spills beyond the latter's discourse, in occasional attempts to set oneself free from it.

Didier Franck, who also translates *Leib* as *chair*, may be right when he notes that it is "absurd" "to translate *Leib* as 'body proper' [*corps propre*], as is often done, for a great variety of divergent reasons. In the sphere of the proper, all bodies are proper; the difference does not lie between two types of body but between bodies in general and *Leib*" (*Chair et corps*, p. 94n12). No doubt—but how, then, is one to translate *Fleisch* (for example, in the text just quoted)? This *Fleisch* is just a definite part of the *Leib*, the living body, "my body," and moreover, we can designate it in the body of another living being, human or not. Above all, how are we to avoid the heavy connotations in French of the word *chair*, its rhetorical use, its idiomatic history and dominant code? Outside a purely objectivistic frame of reference (for example, in the language of surgeons, butchers, or painters), its moralizing and primarily Christian connotations (concupiscence, sins of the flesh, incarnation, etc.) are rather difficult to erase. This is especially so in the areas tackled by those in France who have adopted this translation, then given this word credit well beyond the value of a simple translation. Can we—shall we, some day—come to a point when, by means of much performative rewriting and terminological decision-making, we can efface these connotations, assuming that this is what we want? Is this not a question to add to the agenda Nancy calls for under the heading "deconstruction of Christianity," a task no doubt as necessary as it is im-possible? We shall have to come back to these translation problems, which are not merely "translation-problems."

14. This is so especially when Husserl opposes the noncoincidence of my seeing body with my seen body, as opposed to the self-coincidence of my touching-touched body; and, one recalls, when he says, "What I call the seen Body is not something seeing which is seen, the way my Body as touched Body is something touching which is touched" (*Ideas II*, p. 155); or when he speaks of the coincidence of the "visual Body" with the tactile body proper, grounded upon the self-coincidence and the coincidence of "other things (or phantoms)" "which are constituted both visually and tactually" (p. 159).

It is difficult to see (1) how such a coincidence might be possible, for the reasons just noted; and (2) especially, even if it were possible, within one of the "senses," how this coincidence so full of itself and fully identical with itself could make room for a secondary "coincidence" between different senses, for example (this is Husserl's example), between the visual and the tactile. On the contrary, it seems that it is a certain noncoincidence with itself that allows the articulation, conjuncture, or joining (however inadequate and interruptible) between several heterogeneous sensible experiences, between more than one sense, and each time more than a sense that is inadequate and nonidentical with itself and calls for a vicariant supplement. We could perhaps displace, turn around, and parody Maine de Biran's "How could the hands say to the eyes: *Do as we do*, if the eyes were immovable?" quoted earlier [in Chapter 7; Maine de Biran, *Influence of Habit*, p. 62n3]: how could the visual secondarily come to "coincide," attempt to "coincide," with the tactile if the tactile were not already different from itself, motioning toward surrogacy and wanting adequation—an ever inadequate want, therefore, calling for the technical?

15. The senses of the French *sens* include the sense of way or "direction." —Trans.

9. *Tangent III*

1. See Emmanuel Levinas, "Intentionnalité et sensation," in *En découvrant l'existence avec Husserl et Heidegger* (Paris: Vrin, 1967), pp. 156ff.

2. Nancy, *Corpus*, pp. 64–67.

3. See Chapter 7.

4. Merleau-Ponty, *Visible and the Invisible*, trans. Lingis, p. 147. [Subsequently cited parenthetically in the text.—Trans.]

5. The consequences of this motif in Christian ontotheology linking God, death, and the flesh can be followed in Nancy's "Deconstruction of Christianity," pp. 120, 130). In it, Nancy recalls in particular the "Christian roots" and provenance of nihilism and the "death of God" (the formula is Luther's).

6. Merleau-Ponty, *Signs*, trans. McCleary. [Subsequently cited parenthetically in the text.—Trans.]

7. In a remarkable article, "Monde, chair, vision," in *Chair et langage: Essais sur Merleau-Ponty* (La Versanne: Encre marine, 2001), to which we shall turn again later on, Françoise Dastur puts it clearly: the word and the motif of a "reflection" of the body proper can be found in Husserl, at least in his *Cartesian Meditations* (Dastur, "Monde, chair, vision," p. 95n4). See Françoise Dastur, "World, Flesh, Vision," trans. Theodore A. Toadvine Jr., in *Chiasms: Merleau-Ponty's Notion of Flesh*, ed. Fred Evans and Leonard Lawlor (Albany: State University of New York Press, 2000). [Quotations are from the published translation of Dastur's text in *Chiasms*, except for this note on Husserl, which does not appear in the translation, and of which the translation is my own. In later passages, I have modified the translation very slightly, and, for consistency, incorporated Joan Stambaugh's terminology from Heidegger's *Being and Time*. J. D. quotes Dastur's essay as it appears in Jacques Colette et al., *Maurice Merleau-Ponty: Le psychique et le corporel*, ed. Anna-Teresa Tymieniecka (Paris: Aubier, 1988).—Trans.] The same page rightfully also gives a reminder *to* Merleau-Ponty—or *against* him, as the Merleau-Ponty who might be tempted to reduce this—of the "'striking' difference" that Husserl inscribes "between the visible sphere and the tangible sphere, because an eye does not appear to one's own vision, nor can the visual sensation of color appear as the localized sensation of the lived body. If there is indeed therefore at least an experience of *double* contact, something touching which is touched, there is not in contrast a similar 'reflexivity' of vision, nor something seeing which is seen. This is why one cannot assimilate seeing and touching by speaking 'metaphorically' of a gaze that would 'palpate' things" (ibid., p. 39) [slightly modified; Husserl's terms here are taken directly from the translation into English of *Ideas II*: see pp. 155ff.—Trans.]. Dastur then evokes the "experience of the mirror" (ibid.) as it is described in Husserl's note mentioned earlier (see Chapter 8). See also Chrétien, *L'appel et la réponse*, p. 121, on this issue.

We are thus always led back to the tropological question, to the "metaphor" or metonymy of the senses: in everyday language, in the writings of philosophers, or—and this is the whole question—in the body of the "things themselves," in the very thing itself termed the body, or bodies (proper or not), and in the experience of these body-things that might make such a tropologics possible or even inevitable, without, however, justifying it. But what, then, does "justifying" mean?

8. At the very same moment when he denies any anthropological presupposition, as will be shown in detail later, Merleau-Ponty everywhere accords an exemplary importance to the experience that consists in shaking someone's hand. Now, does it serve any purpose to recall the cultural limits of this ritual gesture, which even in Europe or the West, moreover, is not evenly and homogeneously applied—any more than the kiss as a form of greeting, in fact. I shall mention a single example that I was lucky to experience during a recent trip to New Zealand: the greeting signaling hospitality known as *hongi*, by the Maori, consists in *touching* noses, with a double or triple pressure, while sometimes also shaking hands—both hands—and sometimes weeping and collecting the shared tears. It is said that *hongi* brings to mind the moment when Tane created the first woman by breathing the spirit of life into her nostrils. But this explanation is rare or mostly forgotten. See "Hongi (Pressing Noses)," in Anne Salmond, *Hui: A Study of Maori Ceremonial Gatherings* (Auckland: Red Methuen, 1975). I thank Laurence Simmons for giving me this text to read, as well as *Touch*, the remarkable (poetic, fictional, autobiographical) book by Gabriel Josipovici (New Haven, Conn.: Yale University Press, 1996). Among other things, in a valuable two-page appendix, the latter brings to our attention the idiomatic values in English of "touch," "touching," "stay in touch," and "touché!" He does not mention "keep in touch," which seems more American to me.

9. Nancy, *Sense of the World*, p. 82.

10. See earlier remarks in Chapters 6 and 7 and passim.

11. Nancy, *Sense of the World*, pp. 82–83; slightly modified—Trans.

12. It is already possible to follow this development in Merleau-Ponty's "The Philosopher and His Shadow" [in *Signs*, trans. McCleary] (beyond our indications here): "Thus the problem of *Einfühlung*, like that of my incarnation, opens on the meditation of sensible being . . . it is from the 'fundamental and original presence' of sensible being that the obviousness and universality which are conveyed by these relationships of essences come" (Merleau-Ponty, *Signs*, p. 171). Merleau-Ponty always relies on what Husserl actually says about an originary sensible intuition that is the foundation of ideal identities: ("'the things one of them sees and those the other sees are the *same*'" [ibid.]) and draws the conclusion that there is an originary sensible intuition *of others as there is of oneself*, something Husserl would never do. Merleau-Ponty no doubt pretends that he is making an objection to himself, an objection that might resemble ours ("The other person's life itself is not given to me with his behavior. In order to have access to it, I would have to be the other person himself" [ibid.]). What counts here, however, is that he rejects it without delay: "But things seem this way to us because we are making use of a mutilated idea of Nature and the sensible world" (ibid., p. 172).

13. Ibid., p. 184, quoted in Chapter 7.—Trans.

14. Edmund Husserl, *Cartesian Meditations: An Introduction to Phenomenology*, trans. Dorion Cairns (The Hague: Nijhoff, 1960), p. 139.

15. Nancy, *Being Singular Plural*, pp. 200–201n53 [slightly modified—Trans.].

16. Ibid., p. 61 [slightly modified—Trans.].

17. Dastur, "World, Flesh, Vision," in *Chiasms*, p. 41. Jean-Louis Chrétien also pays attention to this displacement: "As much as he possibly can, Merleau-Ponty continually draws together seeing and touching: ' . . . since vision is a palpation with the look [*regard*], it must also be inscribed in the order of being that it discloses to us. . . . ' [*Visible and the Invisible*, p. 134]—lending one and the other a comparable quasi-reflexivity, which Husserl bestowed solely on the sense of touch" (Chrétien, *L'appel et la réponse*, pp. 120–21).

18. Dastur, "World, Flesh, Vision," p. 40.

19. See Martin Heidegger, *Being and Time*, trans. Joan Stambaugh (Albany: State University of New York Press, 1996), p. 138.

20. Heidegger's own term is *Vorrang*, translated as "priority" by Stambaugh and often as *privilège* by French translators.—Trans.

21. Heidegger, *Being and Time*, p. 413n22 (*Sein und Zeit*, p. 363). "Making present" [*présentation*] translates *gegenwärtigen*, Kant's thesis and term in his "Transcendental Aesthetic," cited by Heidegger in a note (*Being and Time*, p. 413n20; *Sein und Zeit*, p. 358). Another note (*Sein und Zeit*, p. 363), as Dastur points out, aims at Husserl, where the latter uses the same word to "characterize sense perception."

22. Dastur, "World, Flesh, Vision," p. 40. Didier Franck quotes and takes into account, at a particularly important point in his book, the translation *in extenso* of the note to page 363 in *Sein und Zeit* [*Being and Time*, p. 413n22], which is mainly aimed at Husserl. In it, he announces a "series of questions" that "overflows the framework" of his work, "while pointing to one of its distant aims" (*Chair et corps*, pp. 24–25). With respect to Merleau-Ponty and the word "exorbitant," precisely or eerily chosen with respect to the place the eye is given, Luce Irigaray also speaks of the "exorbitant privileging of vision." ("Merleau-Ponty accords an exorbitant privilege to vision. Or else, once again, he expresses the exorbitant privileging of vision in our culture.") She does so in a reading of *The Visible and the Invisible* ("The Invisible of the Flesh: A Reading of Merleau-Ponty, *The Visible and the Invisible*, 'The Intertwining—The Chiasm,'" in *An Ethics of Sexual Difference*, trans. Carolyn Burke and Gillian C. Gill. [Ithaca, N.Y.: Cornell University Press, 1993], p. 174), equally oriented by her concern about "retouching" and "two lips" (ibid., p. 166), mentioned earlier (see Chapter 8 n. 5). But this time, it is around the phrase "two lips" as Merleau-Ponty himself inscribes it in a different way in *Visible and the Invisible* (ibid., p. 136; Irigaray's translators note: "At this point in Lingis's English translation, 'laps' is sub-

stituted for 'lips,' a typographical error that seems to mime what Irigaray calls the invisibility of the feminine" [ibid., p. 166].—Trans.).

See again here Jay, *Downcast Eyes*, esp. chap. 9, as well as Cathryn Vasseleu's recent book, *Textures of Light: Vision and Touch in Irigaray, Levinas and Merleau-Ponty* (London: Routledge, 1998). Vasseleu also wrote: "Touch, Digital Technology and the Ticklish," in *Touch Forum* (Sydney: Artspace, 1996). This short and remarkable four-page article—with which I am becoming acquainted as this book is already in production—announced the 1998 book. But, like this entire issue of this publication (consisting of forty-six pages, hardly accessible in Europe, as rich as they are condensed), the article is outstanding in the way it insists on the question of *technology* (Vasseleu reminds us that Marshall McLuhan said about the sense of touch that it is the sense of the electronic age) at the same time as the prohibition, phobia, or delirium of touching, according to Freud in *Three Essays on the Theory of Sexuality* or *Totem and Taboo*. These two motifs (the technological and the psychoanalytical ones, the metonymic supplement, and touch as abstention or abstinence) are what I am attempting to think *together* here.

23. On the "world-poor" (*weltarm*) animal world and so forth, see Martin Heidegger, *The Fundamental Concepts of Metaphysics: World, Finitude, Solitude*, trans. William McNeill and Nicholas Walker (Bloomington: Indiana University Press, 2001).—Trans.

24. Heidegger, *Being and Time*, p. 328.

25. Ibid., citing Kant, *Kritik der Reinen Vernunft*, B33; see *Critique of Pure Reason*, trans. Smith, p. 65.

26. In an older text in which I question the "privilege given to vision," there is no citation of these words by Heidegger (but rather Nietzsche's *Twilight of the Idols* [trans. Anthony M. Ludovici (New York: Russell & Russell, 1964), p. 67], the Apollonian ecstasy that "acts above all as a force stimulating the eye, so that it acquires the power of vision"), but the reference to Heidegger is clearly readable, though rather ambiguous, in the course of a long development dedicated to the history of philosophy as "photology," "metaphor of darkness and light (of self-revelation and self-concealment)," "heliocentric metaphysics," and so forth. At the center of the argument is the question about force, where it is difficult to find in a thinking of the gaze and in phenomenology "a concept . . . which would permit the conceptualization of intensity or force." See "Force and Signification" (the text is from 1963), reprinted in *Writing and Difference*, trans. Alan Bass (Chicago: University of Chicago Press, 1978), pp. 27ff. On the logic of "heliotropic" hegemony, see "White Mythology," in *Margins: Of Philosophy*, trans. Alan Bass (Chicago: University of Chicago Press, 1982). See also "Envoi," in *Psyché: Inventions de l'autre* (1987; rev. ed., Paris: Galilée, 1998), 1: 123ff.

On this motif of "force" and the related aporias in Husserl's phenomenology, Didier Franck also asks himself: "But when has phenomenology ever given itself the means to describe forces and think them?" (*Chair et corps*, p. 98). And further: "What is this force? How is one to understand the connection between incarnate presence and force? In phenomenology, is there any means whatever to answer these questions? We cannot be sure." He goes on to localize in Husserl's text what links this question of force to a universal teleology and sexual drives implying or intertwining the other's flesh in the ego's flesh (ibid., pp. 152ff.).

27. Dastur, "World, Flesh, Vision," p. 45 [slightly modified. Dastur here adds, in a note: "These [i.e., 'infinitesimal and radical displacement'—Trans.] are the terms by which Derrida expresses his own relation to the Hegelian discourse" [cf. Derrida, *Margins*, trans. Bass, p. 14.—Trans.]. Henri Maldiney also shows how the theme of noncoincidence becomes increasingly insistent (especially in *The Visible and the Invisible*, in fact), whether it is a question of touching and the touched, or in parallel, seeing and the seen. See Henri Maldiney, "Chair et verbe dans la philosophie de M. Merleau-Ponty," in Colette et al., *Merleau-Ponty: Le psychique et le corporel*, ed. Tymienieka, esp. pp. 73–74 and 87; and "Flesh and Verb in the Philosophy of Merleau-Ponty," trans. Claire E. Katz, in *Chiasms: Merleau-Ponty's Notion of Flesh* (Albany: State University of New York Press, 2000), pp. 51–76.

Jacques Colette, writing in the same vein ("La réflexivité du sensible," in *Merleau-Ponty: Le psychique et le corporel*), explains why, in *Visible and the Invisible*, "the reflection of the touching hand by the touched hand" remains "the model of all reflection," and then it "is a matter of surreptitiously introducing minimal amounts of noncoincidence in the homogeneous density of the immediate sensible present. This is necessary because the putting in contact of oneself with oneself is ungraspable, intangible—except if, in it, one inserts reflexivity in effect, the reflexivity that knows and recognizes the duality of presentified and presentifying consciousness" (pp. 44–45).

Maldiney and Colette then underscore the motif of an "imminence" and a "presentiment" announcing what is never attained, which is to say, coincidence, pure reflexive reversibility, the presence of Being, and so forth. Shouldn't one have started with this impossibility?

28. Maurice Merleau-Ponty, *The Structure of Behavior*, trans. Alden Fischer (Boston: Beacon Press, 1963).

29. E.g., Merleau-Ponty, *Phenomenology of Perception*, trans. Smith, pp. 8off. [Subsequently also cited parenthetically in the text, abbreviated as *Phen. Percept.*—Trans.]

30. See also ibid., pp. 143ff., 214ff., 237.

31. See Derrida, *Memoirs of the Blind*, trans. Brault and Naas, pp. 52ff., which also deals with the relations between the hand, the eye, and their prostheses, where I quote at length from and interpret these texts by Merleau-Ponty, in their relation to "tactile" things, among others.

32. It seems somewhat difficult, therefore, to follow Henri Maldiney when he further stresses this an-anthropological allegation or denial in quoting these same lines: "The *logos* of the world is not the *logos* of anyone and the philosophical *logos* is not an interpretation of the world by me nor by man. Instead, it is a revelation of Being in man, right in [*à même*] an open passivity" (Maldiney, "Flesh and Verb in the Philosophy of Merleau-Ponty," p. 73).

33. Is it still useful to emphasize this? In the instant when a "hiatus" is said to be "spanned [*enjambé*] by the total being of my body," this example of the hand still prevails—of my hand as the hand of a man. And this occurs at the very point where reversibility, so often put forward elsewhere, now seems to be in dispute; and noncoincidence seems to affect all the senses.

It was from these pages—without any cited reference—that Nancy extracted the sentence by Merleau-Ponty ("What we are calling flesh, this interiorly worked-over mass, has no name in any philosophy" [*Visible and the Invisible*, p. 147]) that he quotes, or rather keeps at arm's length, or even denounces, as was recalled earlier (see the beginning of Chapter 9), on the subject of that "toward which strains a philosophy of the 'body proper'" (Nancy, *Corpus*, p. 66).

As for the verb "palpate," in *Phenomenology of Perception*, it designates a figure of the gaze, a certain way of looking: "Blue is that which prompts me to look in a certain way, that which allows my gaze to palpate it in a specific manner" [Merleau-Ponty, *Phen. Percept.*, p. 210; slightly modified—Trans.].

34. For example: "If my left hand is touching my right hand, and if I should suddenly wish to apprehend with my right hand the work of my left hand as it touches, this reflection of the body upon itself always miscarries at the last moment. . . . But this last-minute failure does not drain all truth from that presentiment I had of being able to touch myself touching" (*Visible and the Invisible*, p. 9).

10. Tangent IV

1. In French: "A lieu et tient lieu: a lieu tout en tenant lieu, a lieu pour tenir lieu—par le fait de tenir lieu et en vue de tenir lieu: a lieu de tenir lieu: tenant lieu d'avoir lieu."—Trans.

2. Thank you.—Trans.

3. See Husserl, *Cartesian Meditations*, ¶ 60.

4. Nancy, *Being Singular Plural*, p. 200n53 [slightly modified—Trans.].

5. Franck, *Chair et corps*. [Subsequently cited parenthetically in the text. —Trans.]

6. The phrase "analytics of incarnation," which is rather appropriate to define *Chair et corps* ("Flesh and body") from the outset, appears toward the end of the book in a note aiming to define a task to come "that our work intends to make necessary" (Franck, *Chair et corps*, p. 149). See also ibid., p. 193: an "analytics of

flesh of which we have tried to establish the necessity." This "analytics of incarnation" is also part of a program that "overflows" phenomenology and of a "deduction" (toward which we will come back later) that Husserl, according to Franck, has "never set . . . to work" (ibid., p. 171).

7. These formulas appear very early (ibid., p. 40) and are then relayed by numerous equivalent expressions throughout the book.

8. Franck does refer to *Visible and the Invisible* in his chapter "Flesh and Body in Perception" (Franck, *Chair et corps*, pp. 41ff.), for example, about the absolute here, which as absolute origin is not part of the space of interchangeable heres and theres ("Flesh is the stage director of perception"). Another reference to Merleau-Ponty (ibid., p. 141) ultimately concerns a problem analogous to the one of the absolute here, in this instance the one of the Earth, in its protoprimordiality, which does not move, as Husserl said at one point. ["Die Ur-Arche Erde bewegt sich nicht": this phrase appears in Derrida's *Edmund Husserl's Origin of Geometry: An Introduction*, trans. John P. Leavey Jr. (Stony Brook, N.Y.: Nicolas Hays, 1978), p. 85. Dorion Cairns, in his *Guide for Translating Husserl* (The Hague: Nijhoff, 1973), translates *Ur-Arche* as "original ark."—Trans.] In the interval, another reference in a note conveys the concern that I share with Franck, even if I am tempted to respond to it less firmly than he does (we'll come back to this), about the translation of *Leib* as "flesh" (*chair*). Here is the note: "'The body (*Leib*) is nothing less but nothing more than the things' condition of possibility' (Merleau-Ponty, *Signs*, p. 173). 'Body' here is the translation of *Leib*" (Franck, *Chair et corps*, p. 47). See also, ibid., p. 168, a note referring to Merleau-Ponty on the subject of what resists eidetic variation, whether it is the archefacticity of the flesh or historicity, in a word, a certain radical *con-tingency* on which Franck's book focuses and which we shall tackle again later on.

9. See *Husserliana*, vol. 15, text no. 22, pp. 378–86, "Teleologie. Die Implikation des Eidos transzendentale Intersubjektivität im Eidos transzendentales Ich. Faktum und Eidos."—Trans.

10. "And so, should we think that this contact, as contact from oneself to oneself first of all, constitutes this very support? Perhaps, since the flesh is originarily constituted in tactility. Without this contact, no localization in general could take place." (Franck, *Chair et corps*, p. 140). Here, in addition to the texts that have been cited, Franck adds a note in which Husserl "qualifies the tactile layer as 'originary core layer'" [*Urkernschichte*] [*couche archi-nodale*]. [See *Husserliana*, 14: 484.—Trans.]

11. See Edmund Husserl, *On the Phenomenology of the Consciousness of Internal Time: (1893–1917)*, trans. John Barnett Brough (Dordrecht: Kluwer, 1991). "Lectures" corresponds to *Vorlesungen* in the first title: *Vorlesungen zur Phänomenologie des inneren Zeitbewusstseins* (Halle: Niemeyer, 1929).—Trans.

12. Chrétien, *L'appel et la réponse*, p. 106. After making a comment about Aris-

totle and speaking of an "untouchable within touching itself, a film or membrane that keeps the skin apart from things, and that we are not feeling," Chrétien adds: "For this slipping away [*dérobement*], in the sensations themselves, of the mediation, Aristotle seeks to account: this is the phenomenal grounding of the belief in the immediacy of contact." Chrétien also calls this slipping, this "minimal spatial removal [*éloignement*]," a *veil*, a self-veiling: "Prejudices about touch are ordered in keeping with its own veiling [les préjugés sur le toucher s'ordonnent à son propre voilement]." In other words, the truth of touch weaves, slips into, and retains this veil, the text or textile of its very phenomenality. We'll come back to this interpretation of the "intervallic" by Chrétien.

13. "Dürfen oder müssen wir nicht eine universale Triebintentionalität voraussetzen, die jede urtümliche Gegenwart als stehende Zeitigung einheitlich ausmacht und konkret von Gegenwart zu Gegenwart forttreibt derart, dass aller Inhalt Inhalt von Trieberfüllung ist und vor dem Ziel intendiert ist, und dabei auch so, dass in jeder primordialen Gegenwart transzendierende Triebe höherer Stufe in jede andere Gegenwart hineinreichen und alle miteinander als Monaden verbinden, während alle ineinander impliziert sind—intentional?" (Edmund Husserl, "Text Nr. 34," in *Husserliana*, 15: 595).—Trans.

14. "In der strömenden Urpräsenz haben wir unabänderlich immer schon Leibwahrnehmung, und so in der Zeitigung der imma-nenten Zeit geht durch diese ganze Zeit kontinuierlich hin-durch mein Leib-Wahrnehmen, synthetisch identisch denselben Leib allzeitlich konstituierend." See Husserl, Manuscript C 6, Leaf 5b (p. 7 in transcription). I very much thank Ronald Bruzina for contacting Dieter Lohmar—currently editing these manuscripts for publication—who kindly sent this text in the form in which it will appear once published. —Trans.

15. We can follow these two movements (Franck, *Chair et corps*, pp. 191–93, in particular) after the analyses of two "lacunae" in the "Lectures on Time": (1) the temporal horizon of a protention "preceding, in time, the arche-impression, which is to say the origin of time," and (2) the originarily altered character, the mark of what is alien to the ego (*ichfremd*) in the constituting flesh: should arche-impressions come from the other, the "contradiction" in the relations between the ego and time would be lifted: "The ego can draw its origin from time, of which it is the origin; the same flux may be constituting and constituted if there are two egos that are carnally connected, and if absolute transcendental subjectivity is intersubjectivity." These movements are in fact announced or recalled throughout the book. Here we find again all the paradoxes of the constituting-constituted; they have occupied me for a long time, and Nancy, for his part, states in the passage that I have just cited: "The constitution is itself constituted" (Nancy, *Being Singular Plural*, p. 200n53).

16. "The absolute of constitution is thus con-tingent, and as phenomenology

sets about exhuming and reactivating the most archaic layers of constitution, as it sinks deep toward its own foundations, it lets an adverse [*advers*] and anarchic grounding come forth, a phenomenon of which it no longer recognizes the phenomenality; it lays bare an archefacticity that it pretended to reduce.

This archefacticity, which is the originary con-tingency of the flesh and the will never fall within an intentional analytics, seems by the same token to offer itself as a theme for an existential analytics, which can be understood as a hermeneutics of facticity and attempts (by way of an ecstatic [*ekstatique*] interpretation of intentionality) to displace as radically as possible the primacy of the subjectivity of consciousness. *The flesh, both proper and unproper, gives time.* . . . Not only is it incarnation that essentially constitutes perception, but also the flesh does not let itself be brought back to temporality as to its principle. It could therefore not take place in an analytics of *Dasein* that is entirely oriented and dominated by temporality" (Franck, *Chair et corps*, p. 193). See also p. 169n31.

This limit in *Being and Time* had earlier been given a sort of complementary explanation or interpretation. It is because reckoning with the flesh—fleshly, or sexual, difference—would have jeopardized the privilege of temporality that Heidegger is said to have kept to a sexually neutral *Dasein* (see Franck, *Chair et corps*, p. 171). But it is especially the book's first chapter that calls into question the *order* in which *Sein und Zeit* unfolds—the starting point of the question of Being in an existential analytics; fundamental ontology; the destruction of traditional ontology lastly guided by temporality, and so forth. According to Franck, this "concerns" his way of proceeding, in its *order*, in a way, and does not necessarily "reverse, criticize" it (ibid., p. 26). To be sure, Franck writes (p. 27) that Heidegger himself later wrote, in *On Time and Being*: "The attempt, in *Being and Time*, section 70, to derive human spatiality [of *Dasein*—Trans.] from temporality is untenable" (Heidegger, *On Time and Being*, trans. Joan Stambaugh [New York: Harper & Row, 1972], p. 23).

On this question of the neutrality of *Dasein*, and the dissemination (*Zerstreuung*) of *Dasein* in space, a dissemination that spatializes or spaces out, I take the liberty of also referring the reader to [Jacques Derrida,] "Geschlecht, différence sexuelle, différence ontologique," in [id.,] *Psyché* ["Geschlecht: Sexual Difference, Ontological Difference," *Research in Phenomenology* 13 (1983)].

17. Franck, *Chair et corps*, pp. 58ff.

18. See also Chapter 8.

19. Elsewhere, regarding death, Franck also speaks of "the absence of any thematization of the flesh" in Husserl (*Chair et corps*, p. 130). We could no doubt complicate, if not dispute, such assertions—just by reading *Ideas II* (and many other texts by Husserl), as well as the references that Franck himself makes to certain important and difficult texts by Heidegger on the sense of "Leib" and "Leibhaftigkeit" (ibid., pp. 21n4, 27nn26–32). Doesn't Franck himself explain in what

way "no one may easily subject to any unifying law the whole set of Heidegger's writings on the flesh" (ibid., p. 27)? Admittedly, this is not the same as saying, as he did several pages earlier, that in Heidegger, "just as in Husserl, the question of the sense of the flesh does not arise" (ibid., p. 21). Moreover, some of Heidegger's texts (e.g., those quoted in ibid., p. 27nn31–32) point toward the effort he made (whether or not he accomplished it, that is a different question) to give thought to *Leib* beyond the body and the living organism as well as "psychical" flesh— and probably beyond the flesh grasped in a Christian sense.

20. See Franck, *Chair et corps*, p. 20. [In this passage, Franck quotes from Heidegger's *Prolegomena zur Geschichte des Zeitbegriffs* (Frankfurt a/M: Klostermann, 1979) [*Gesamtausgabe*, vol. 20], pp. 53–54; *History of the Concept of Time: Prolegomena*, trans. Theodore Kisiel (Bloomington: Indiana University Press, 1985), pp. 40ff.—Trans.]

21. Heidegger, *History of the Concept of Time*, pp. 40ff.

22. Edmund Husserl, *Idées directrices pour une phénoménologie*, trans. Paul Ricœur (Paris: Gallimard, 1950); cf. Edmund Husserl, *Ideas: General Introduction to Pure Phenomenology*, trans. W. R. Boyce Gibson (London: Allen & Unwin, 1931); referred to here as *Idées*, trans. Ricœur; *Ideas I* (trans. Boyce Gibson); and *Ideen I*, for the German text (*Ideen zu einer reinen phänomenologie und phänomenologischen Philosophie* [3d printing] [Halle: Niemeyer, 1928]).—Trans.

23. One of the two sentences in question is the following (twice quoted by Franck, *Chair et corps*, pp. 19, 164): "Thus essential insight *is* intuition, and if it is insight in the pregnant sense of the term, and not a mere, and possibly a vague, representation (*Vergegenwärtigung*), it is a *primordial* dator Intuition, grasping the essence in its 'incarnate' (*leibhaften*) [modified from 'bodily'—Trans.] selfhood" (Husserl, *Ideen I*, ¶ 3; *Ideas I*, pp. 55–56 [one term modified—Trans.]; *Idées*, trans. Ricœur, p. 22 [modified by Franck as stated—Trans.]). The fact that Husserl puts the word *leibhaften* in quotation marks signals or underscores the fact that it does not, properly speaking, mean "incarnated in some flesh" or even "in the flesh" (as Franck transcribes it in his commentary on p. 164, this time—which is something we may surmise when dealing with an essence in its ipseity or selfhood ["das Wesen in seiner 'leibhaften' Selbstheit"]).

In Husserl's other sentence (*Ideen I*, ¶ 39; *Idées*, trans. Ricœur, p. 126; *Ideas I*, p. 127), quoted by Franck on p. 19, Husserl emphasizes "*Bewusstsein der leibhaftigen Selbstgegenwart eines individuellen Objektes*," translated by Ricœur as "conscience de la présence corporelle en personne d'un objet individuel," and by Franck as "la conscience de l'autoprésence incarnée d'un objet individuel" [and by Gibson as "the consciousness of *the embodied (leibhaftigen) self-presence of an individual object*"—Trans.]. But isn't it clear, here, that for Husserl, this isn't about the body, or the flesh, or "anybody," or incarnation? Nothing but immediately present ipseity in general, as in the earlier example? Moreover, the phrase has to do with the "proper" of any "perceiving" "consciousness," even if what it perceives is neither living nor personal.

24. I tried to study this thematic role in *Edmund Husserl's Origin of Geometry* (trans. Leavey): see pp. 76ff., 88ff., and passim; and in *Speech and Phenomena: And Other Essays on Husserl's Theory of Signs* [trans. David B. Allison (Evanston, Ill.: Northwestern University Press, 1973)—Trans.]: see pp. 16ff., 34ff., and passim). I remain unconvinced that Husserl speaks a nonmetaphorical language intentionally aiming at some flesh or incarnation when he uses *leibhaftig* (and not *Leib* or *Leiblichkeit*) to designate an intuition or a perception of the thing itself (essence or individual).

25. See Franck, *Chair et corps*, p. 134.

26. I tackle this problem of *Körper* and *Leib* from a point of view that is both different and analogous in, for example, *Edmund Husserl's Origin of Geometry*, trans. Leavey, pp. 97ff., and *Speech and Phenomena*, trans. Allison, p. 81, precisely about hetero-affection at work in the pure auto-affection of the living present. As just pointed out, my perplexity stands all the less for any kind of criticism (unless it is preemptively a self-criticism) that I myself have had to translate *Sprachleib* as "linguistic flesh" [*chair linguistique*] ["linguistic living body," in the cited translation, p. 161—Trans.] and *die sprachliche Verleiblichung* as "linguistic incarnation" [*incarnation linguistique*] ["linguistic embodiment," in the cited translation, p. 161—Trans.] (see my introduction to Husserl's *Origin of Geometry*).

27. "Apperzeption eigener Leib und fremder Leib gehören wesentlich zusammen" (Husserl, *Zur Phänomenologie der Intersubjektivität: Texte aus dem Nachlass: Erster Teil: 1905–1920* [The Hague: Nijhoff, 1973], *Husserliana*, 13: 344).—Trans.

28. And so everything here plays itself out in the determination of the affect of *affection* as touch, tactile or contact effect. We could say the same for the determination of *impressions*. In order to show in what way "the temporalization of sense is, from the outset, a 'spacing,'" I had, for my part, attempted to analyze the hetero-affection at the heart of this "primordial impression" and of "a pure auto-affection in which the same is the same only in being affected by the other, only by becoming the other of the same." A certain *Verflechtung* also came about there, a primordial "intertwining" from which I was trying to draw a certain number of consequences. Cf. Derrida, *Speech and Phenomena*, trans. Allison, pp. 83ff.

29. Some might wonder what justifies this naming and why the relation of my flesh to another would be first and foremost or essentially a relation of "sexual difference," if we assume that there is only one, and that its signification does not merely come to specify a carnal difference. This question visibly worries Franck, who, in the preceding chapter, dedicates a note to the possibility that "in a certain way, carnal difference precedes sexual difference." But at this point, he also programmatically refers to the "analytics of incarnation that our work intends to make necessary" (Franck, *Chair et corps*, p. 149).

30. Ibid., p. 170; *Husserliana*, 13: 375.

31. See Chapter 9.

32. See Edmund Husserl, *The Crisis of European Sciences and Transcendental Phenomenology: An Introduction to Phenomenological Philosophy*, trans. David Carr (Evanston, Ill.: Northwestern University Press, 1970), ¶ 55, p. 187. On animals, see also Franck, *Chair et corps*, p. 91. In the quoted passage from *The Crisis*, Husserl writes among other things: "Among animals, men stand out, so much so, in fact, that mere animals have ontic meaning [as such] only by comparison to them [*erst von ihnen her*], as variations of them" (Husserl, *Crisis*, ¶ 66, p. 227).

33. "Zugleich ist es klar, dass eine Natur ohne Leiber, also ohne Menschen undenkbar ist" (Husserl, *Zur Phänomenologie der Intersubjektivität: Texte aus dem Nachlass: Dritter Teil: 1929–1935* [The Hague: Nijhoff, 1973], *Husserliana*, 15: 639). —Trans.

34. I refer again to Stiegler's *La technique et le temps*, which lays out this problematic in closest proximity to Husserl—and in a debate with phenomenology, notably the phenomenology of time.

11. Tangent V

Note: The chapter title includes passages from Jean-Louis Chrétien, *L'appel et la réponse*, p. 153, quoting John of the Cross, *The Living Flame of Love*. The translation of Chrétien's text is my own, and passages from John are from *The Living Flame of Love: Versions A and B*, trans. Jane Ackerman (Binghamton: State University of New York Press, 1995), henceforward cited as *Flame B* (or *Flame A*)— slightly modified here, on p. 125 of Ackerman's text.—Trans.

1. Nancy, "Deconstruction of Christianity," trans. Sparks, p. 124. This passage announces a series of reflections about the "particular historico-philosophical context" where that which makes itself known to faith is "infinite distancing" or "the infinite opening of the sense of *ousia* thought as presence, *parousia* of itself" (ibid.; slightly modified—Trans.).

Not only does the figure of the "heart" appear in the lines that I just cited for reasons that are all too obvious, Nancy also speaks about the "heart of this movement of opening up" (ibid., p. 117), the "evangelical living heart of Christianity" (p. 123), and about penetrating "into the core, into the essential movement of kerygmatic or evangelical Christianity" (p. 123); and further—in the sense of another figure—about the "*act* of faith that each of the faithful can proclaim in his or her heart, something that I have not been concerned to examine here" (p. 125).

On "deconstruction" and "Christianity" in general, see [Jacques Derrida,] "Comment de pas parler: dénégations," in [id.,] *Psyché*; [id.,] "How to Avoid Speaking: Denials," trans. Ken Frieden, in *Languages of the Unsayable: The Play of Negativity in Literature and Literary Theory,* ed. Sanford Budick and Wolfgang Iser (New York: Columbia University Press, 1989); [id.,] "Passions," trans. David Wood, and "Sauf le nom," trans. John P. Leavey Jr., in [id.,] *On the Name,* ed. Thomas Dutoit (Stanford: Stanford University Press, 1995); [id.,] *The Gift of Death,* trans. David Wills (Chicago: University of Chicago Press, 1995); [id.,] "Faith and Knowledge," trans. Samuel Weber, in *Religion,* ed. Jacques Derrida and Gianni Vattimo [Stanford: Stanford University Press, 1998]; and, last but not least, to Hent de Vries's admirable *Philosophy and the Turn to Religion* (Baltimore: Johns Hopkins University Press, 1999).

2. Merleau-Ponty, *Visible and the Invisible,* p. 255.

3. Henri Maldiney, "La dimension du contact au regard du vivant et de l'existant," in *Le Contact,* ed. Jacques Schotte (Brussels: De Boeck, 1990), p. 177. [My translation; cited by Chrétien in *L'appel et la réponse,* p. 102.—Trans.]

4. See Derrida, "*Le Toucher*: Touch / To Touch Him," trans. Kamuf.

5. In *L'appel et la réponse,* see "Le corps et le toucher" [Body and Touch], pp. 102ff. Later, after this 1992 episode, in *Le sens du monde* [*Sense of the World,* trans. Librett], it was Nancy's turn to greet the work of this remarkable philosopher, whom he did not yet know when he wrote his own chapter on "Touching." Nancy noted: "On 'touching' in general, I have discovered too late to make use of it that I am following some paths parallel to those of Jean-Louis Chrétien, 'Le corps et le toucher,' in *L'appel et la réponse* . . ." (*Sense of the World,* p. 185n64).

Parallel paths indeed! We shall indeed be receptive to what makes the two stroll along in parallel, side by side, one by the other's *side*—and thus, lest we should ever forget it, the *other side.* And these parallels sometimes intersect and touch, too! But we shall nevertheless lean over and peruse the abyss that may separate the two paths. They are certainly alike. And yet, while remaining as different as possible, in this case they also look like two (incompatible) ways of being or not being Christian.

Subtitle: how to be or not to be Christian, or more crudely, The Importance of (not) Being Christian—as if this were possible.

6. It may be out of modesty that Chrétien abstains from citing Franck, since he published his book more than ten years after Franck's, in a series edited by the latter. It is difficult to avoid hearing an implicit reference to Franck (rather than to Merleau-Ponty) in a passage such as the following, in which I emphasize the word "*human* life" so as to announce or call to mind the *limit* I think is important: "The phenomenology of touch does not make up some regional and particular study attending to one function of the living among others. From the outset, a phenomenology of life, of the body and the flesh, can only constitute itself by way of a phenomenology of touch, and this amounts to saying how serious it is. Touching is not first, or last perhaps, just one of the five senses: for Aristotle it is the sense that is necessary and sufficient to allow an animate body

to appear; it is the perpetual condition of possibility of *human* life and thus also of other possible senses that will always be part of a body that is tactile" (Chrétien, *L'appel et la réponse*, p. 104).

7. At this point, Chrétien appropriately notes of "Aristotle's thinking": "It comes down to the most radical and patient consideration of touch in the history of philosophy" (ibid., p. 102). It is no wonder, then, that by way of Aristotle's lexicon of *aporia* (which we started with and have just followed in Didier Franck as well), the *aporetic* tradition of this haptology is so insistent, and expressively so, in Chrétien (e.g., ibid., pp. 102, 104, 105, 108, and 147).

8. Chrétien often calls on Rilke, the thinker and poet of the hand, of hands, our "frightened hands" [*ängstliche Hände*], but first of all clasped hands—joined in caresses no less than in prayer. It is always a matter of demonstrating the transitivity of touch, and showing that all these hands that touch and are in touch accede to the very thing that exceeds touch and touch beyond self-touch. Still, after he has quoted and interpreted Rilke's second Duino elegy (which, according to him, "sets off contact with oneself against the caresses of lovers," that is, the poverty of self-touch against the hyperbole of touching-the-other), Chrétien reaches this conclusion: "Self-touching could not be the truth of touching" (ibid., p. 140).

9. Ibid., p. 151. Here, Chrétien has just quoted Aristotle (*Metaphysica* lambda [12], 7.1072b.19–21, and he makes the following comment: "While this spiritual touch no longer presents any medium or distance; while, as pure act, it is no longer of the order of affection; while unlike carnal touching, which is always mediate, it is totally immediate, it is nevertheless unfailingly transitive."

10. Aquinas: "Hence the intellect of the first sphere becomes actually understanding through some kind of contact (*per contactum aliquem*) with the first intelligible substance. . . . anything that is divine and noble, such as understanding and taking pleasure, which is found in the intellect having the contact (*in intellectu attingente*), is found in a much higher degree in the first intelligible object with which it is in contact (*in intelligibili primo quod attingitur*)" (Aquinas, *Commentary on the Metaphysics of Aristotle*, vol. 2, trans. John P. Rowan [Chicago: Regnery, 1961], [12.8.2542–43,] p. 893).

11. See Chapter 7.

12. Aristotle *Metaphysica* lambda [12], 7.1072b.19–21.

13. See Chapter 4. Chrétien does not quote Levinas on the subject of the caress any more than he cites Franck. He does so only on the subject of contact in sleep (which is often different, and generally comes later): "Sleeping is like coming into contact with the protective virtues of places; seeking sleep is seeking this contact through a sort of groping [*tâtonnement*]." The passage is quoted by Chrétien in *L'appel et la réponse*, p. 136, from Emmanuel Levinas, *De l'existence à l'existant* (Paris: Fontaine, 1947), pp. 119–20. [My translation. However, a published

translation of the book exists: Levinas, *Existence and Existents*, trans. Alphonso Lingis (The Hague: Nijhoff, 1978).—Trans.]

14. Thomas Aquinas, *The Disputed Questions on Truth*, trans. Robert W. Schmidt (Chicago: Regnery, 1954), vol. 3, [qu. 28, art. 3, resp.], p. 368.

15. John of the Cross, *Flame B*, in *Living Flame of Love*, trans. Ackerman, p. 127; quoted in Chrétien, *L'appel et la réponse*, p. 152.

16. John of the Cross, *Flame B*, in *Living Flame of Love*, trans. Ackerman, pp. 123, 125 [slightly modified—Trans.].

17. As cited in ibid., p. 127.—Trans.

18. See Chapter 4.

19. "Earlier chapters established the intersection of seeing and hearing—doesn't this presuppose the fundamental sense of touch? Chapter 4 is a study of the latter: its axis is a phenomenological reading of Aristotle, for whom man is a tactile being, since no one has given more thought than he to issues of touch. His questions, his replies, his aporias, in this place as in many others, determine the whole history of philosophy. Throughout these analyses it appears that the body, in tactility, does, and can, listen" (Chrétien, *L'appel et la réponse*, pp. 12–13).

20. Much later in the article these assertions are repeated and amplified; e.g., see p. 147.

21. To credit a logic that is not simply formal, it doesn't seem arbitrary in respect to this process, and the law it obeys, to invoke Merleau-Ponty's reference, in denying the anthropological character of his own discourse on the flesh of the visible and the flesh of the world (analyzed earlier as a denial in Chapter 9), to "Logos also as what is realized in man, but nowise [*nullement*] as his *property*" (Merleau-Ponty, *Visible and the Invisible*, p. 274).

22. Chrétien then cites Rémi Brague's book on "Aristotle and the question of the world" (*Aristote et la question du monde: Essai sur le contexte cosmologique et anthropologique de l'ontologie* [Paris: Presses universitaires de France, 1988]): "Man is the animal that possesses to the highest degree the sense that is to the highest degree common to all animals. His place at the top of the scale of the living pertains to the more perfect realization in man of what every living being, as living being, possesses" (pp. 260–61). [My translation.—Trans.] On the "superiority" of the sense of touch, see also Chrétien, *L'appel et la réponse*, pp. 122, 123 (in Aquinas), 124–25, 128, 130, and so forth.

23. See Félix Ravaisson, *De l'habitude*, ed. P. Millot (1894; Paris: Fayard, 1984).

24. "It follows that the soul is analogous to the hand; for as the hand is a tool of tools [*cheir organon estin organōn*], so the mind is the form of forms and sense the form of sensible things" (Aristotle *Peri psuchēs* 3.8.432a; trans. Smith). —Trans.

25. His "whatever the case may be" [*quoi qu'il en soit*] then leaves the discussion suspended and moves it to the hypothesis concerning what may be inter-

esting to keep, from a Christian point of view, for a thinking of the flesh: "Whatever the case may be, if one seeks to specify the excellence of human touching by
way of the feeling in the fingers, by way of a possibility that only man might possess, won't one be led to lose one of the other senses of universality, that is, the
sense of the flesh?" (Chrétien, *L'appel et la réponse*, p. 115).

26. Aristotle *Metaphysica* 12.7, 1072b.

27. I.e.: "la main de l'à-dieu."—Trans.

12. "To self-touch you"

1. French text: "Comment passer de '*le* toucher' à '*te* toucher'? Toi?"

2. Nancy, "La déconstruction du christianisme," p. 507; "Deconstruction of
Christianity," trans. Sparks, p. 116.

3. To my knowledge, in one place at least of his *Corpus*, Nancy does mention
Aristotle without giving a reference (where exactly does Aristotle say this?) but
about the senses *in general*—and feeling pleasure: "Aristotle knew it when he
said that each sense feels *and* knows itself to feel, each one separately, without
general control, each one in retreat, as sight, hearing, taste, smell, touch; each
one has pleasure and knows itself in this pleasure, in the absolute separation [*écart*]
of its pleasure: the theory of the arts is wholly engendered from there" (*Corpus*,
p. 103). In *Ego sum*, as has been noted [in Chapter 2—Trans.], a very brief allusion to Aristotle deals only with the localization of the soul in an organ. This organ is not determined. (See "Unum quid," in *Ego sum*, p. 161.) See the discussion
of this problem in the preceding chapter, dealing with Chrétien's book.

4. See what was said earlier about this apropos of Husserl in Chapter 8.

5. Nancy, *Corpus*, pp. 31ff. It is thus necessary to reread the whole chapter titled "Expeausition." Note simply here that in the following chapter, "Thinking,"
sex is defined in this way: "It isn't the name of some thing that might be exposed:
it is the name of touching exposition itself. 'Sex' touches upon the untouchable"
(ibid., p. 35).

6. Nancy, "Deconstruction of Christianity," Simon Sparks, p. 125.

7. Nancy's *L'intrus* (The Intruder) was cited earlier. Such a "cardiography"
would not be limited to the essay titled "Le cœur des choses" (in Nancy's *Une
pensée finie* [Paris: Galilée, 1990], pp. 197ff.; "The Heart of Things," trans. Brian
Holmes and Rodney Trumble, in *The Birth to Presence* [Stanford: Stanford University Press, 1993], pp. 167ff.). But it would begin perhaps with that text, with
its very typical manner of starting out from an idiom, touching thereby the end
of its language, the tip of its tongue ("This immobile heart does not even beat.
It is the heart of things. The one we speak of when we say 'to get to the heart of
things'"); from there it goes, in all directions, to the bottom of things, here to the
bottom of the heart, of his heart, his other heart, his heart of the other, of all

hearts. "The Heart of Things" is one of the principal places in which Nancean thought exposes "the exscription of sense."

8. Jean-Luc Nancy, "The Unsacrificeable," trans. Richard Stamp and Simon Sparks, in *Finite Thinking*, ed. Sparks.

9. [Deut. 10: 16: "Circumcise therefore the foreskin of your heart, and be no longer stubborn."—Trans.] "After Saint Paul, Augustine, and the entire tradition, Pascal writes: 'Circumcision of the heart, true fast, true sacrifice, true temple: the prophets showed that all this must be spiritual. Not the flesh that perishes, but the flesh that does not perish'" (Nancy, "Unsacrificeable," p. 58, citing Pascal, *Pensées*, trans. A. Krailsheimer [Harmondsworth, U.K.: Penguin Books, 1966], ¶ 268, p. 109).

If there is so much at stake between Judaism and Christianity regarding circumcision (literal or spiritual, of the body or the heart, as figure of spirituality, of the touchable or untouchable heart), can one say for all that that what separates Christianity from Judaism, the syncope between them, there where they cannot touch each other, the Judeo-Christian noncontact is precisely the relation to touching? Can one say that the Jew requires (sensible or literal) touching whereas the Christian spiritualizes it and thus loses it? That would be somewhat simple and, in part, the part of spirit, already a conventional, Christian interpretation, if not Christianity itself. For Christianity, inversely, is also intent on inaugurating a religion of sensibility, even of touching. Hence, it would also accuse the Jews of giving in to the sublime or cold hardness of insensitive or untouchable transcendence, and so forth. We should come back to this—and say more about a certain hardness, for example, the hardness about which Hegel speaks when he speaks about Jews and the nonreconciliation and nonforgiving of which they are the figure. And further of the ruggedness of hands, the insensitivity of sensibility itself, if not of the "insensible sensible," which has earned its warrant of philosophical nobility (in Kant, Hegel, Marx, and so on).

An infinite chiasmus remains: Jews like to touch more than Christians who like to touch more than Jews. Accordingly, Jews bring the Letter into play against the Spirit, and thus the touchable against the untouchable. But Jews are also the ones keen on Separation, on Scission, on the Untouchable Invisible, and the unrepresentable sublime. Inversely, (Pauline) Christians put into play the Spirit (thus the untouchable) against the Letter, but they are also the ones keen on a return to the sensible, Incarnation and mediation, and thus on the Touchable Visible. Jesus: the Touched-Touching. And Muslims are the hyperbolic heirs of this endless contradiction, that is, contradiction of the very Infinite itself. As usual, God *self*-contradicts himself. And this is a habit we have *contracted* in our turn. "This contradicts itself" [*ça se contredit*]—what could this possibly mean, exactly, in good English [French]? Isn't it as undecidable as "it touches (itself)" [*ça se touche*]?

10. Nancy, "Unsacrificeable," trans. Stamp and Sparks, in *Finite Thinking*, ed. Sparks, p. 63.

11. Ibid. [slightly modified—Trans.].

12. Nancy, "Unsacrificeable," trans. Stamp and Sparks, in *Finite Thinking*, ed. Sparks, p. 53 [slightly modified—Trans.].

13. For Aristotle, touch is also "the sense for food," among other things: "all animals have one sense at least, viz. touch, and whatever has a sense has the capacity for pleasure and pain and therefore has pleasant and painful objects present to it, and wherever these are present, there is desire, for desire is just appetition (*epithumia*) of what is pleasant (*hēdeos orexis*, desire of what is pleasant)" (Aristotle *Peri psuchēs* 2.3.414b.3ff., trans. Smith). Jean-Louis Chrétien cites this passage in *L'appel et la réponse*, p. 117.

14. The buccal mouth, let us recall, and not the oral mouth. "Buccality is more primitive than orality." We should reanalyze, from a different point of view, a rhetorical one, the very fine pages that conclude Nancy's "Unum quid" in *Ego sum*. What opens and situates itself then may be the question of rhetoric in general— here by way of a rather singular metonymy, the one that gives rise—at the moment one speaks it—to every metonymy, which is to say the mouth and the face. Already Nancy was drawing the consequences, for Descartes as for Freud, of the fact that "The psyche is extended, knows nothing about it" ("Unum quid" in *Ego sum*, p. 161). "*Os, oris*, the mouth of orality, is the face itself taken as metonymy for that which it surrounds. . . . But *bucca* is the puffed-out cheeks, the movement, contraction and/or distension of breathing, eating, spitting, or speaking. . . . The mouth is the opening of ego; ego is the opening of the mouth. And there, what comes to pass is that it spaces itself out [*ce qui s'y passe c'est qu'il s'y espace*]" (ibid., p. 162). See the discussion of "Unum quid" in Chapter 2.

15. Jean-Luc Nancy, *L'impératif catégorique* (Paris: Flammarion, 1983).

16. Jean-Luc Nancy, "Elliptical Sense," trans. Jonathan Derbyshire, in *Finite Thinking*, ed. Sparks, p. 109.

17. Nancy, "Finite Thinking," trans. Bullard et al., in *Finite Thinking*, ed. Sparks, p. 5.

18. Aside from everything that has previously been devoted to this question, this takes us back—albeit differently—to Bergson, who no doubt attempted to resist the authority of the optical and to subtract the concept of intuition from sight, in that which connects it with duration. In any case we have seen how he does this at least in a figurative way (but the figure is our question here) for intuition when it finds itself at the center of and the source of a philosophical thinking "worthy of the name." His statement is famous: "A philosopher worthy of the name has never said more than a single thing [Heidegger insists on this uniqueness in his own way—J. D.]: and even then, it is something he has tried to say, rather than actually said. And he has said only one thing because he has

seen only *one point*: and at that it was not so much *a vision as a contact* [my emphasis—J. D.]" (Henri Bergson, *The Creative Mind*, trans. Mabelle L. Andison [New York: Philosophical Library, 1946], p. 132). And this philosopher, as soon as one takes on the spiritual world, has known, according to Bergson, how to speak this language rich in images, which knows it says things in their proper sense, where abstract language unconsciously says things in their figurative sense.

Nancy, a "philosopher worthy of the name," may be thinking only one thing, Bergson would say, which is to say of touch, of course; but this time, then, just this once, he would have done it in contact *with contact*, contact itself, and this changes and undoes everything. For (again in matters of punctuation and punctuality) if he has "seen only one point . . . " in what was "not so much a vision as a contact," then it is that there is no "the" sense of touch, nor "contact"—and furthermore that this point is especially not a point, an indivisible place, a touchable limit, but a *spacing*—forever. To be sure, an exact punctuality is divisible; it knows how to divide itself and it knows that it is divisible—in its spacing as in its very finiteness. In this, there is some very divisibility "even" of the point. And from the said undecidable divisibility, a decision comes forth, stops short, makes its point—if there ever is any. We have just read: "Discerning is where touching and vision touch. It is the limit of vision—and the limit of touch" (Nancy, "Elliptical Sense," trans. Derbyshire, p. 109).

19. Nancy, "Finite Thinking," trans. Bullard et al., in *Finite Thinking*, ed. Sparks, p. 8.

20. Particularly in the long and richly complex note with the following conclusion: "There is only sense in touching that. But in touching that, there is only finite sense" (ibid., p. 323n14).

21. Ibid., p. 29, quoting Rimbaud, "Le cœur supplicié."

22. Nancy, *L'intrus*, trans. Hanson as "L'Intrus." (Since I have also mentioned that Nancy does not know whether his new heart is a man's heart or a woman's, I need to specify here that in a note to *L'intrus*, he adds a reference to a certain drawing by Sylvie Blocher: "Jean-Luc with a woman's heart.")

23. Nancy, "L'Intrus," trans. Hanson, pp. 13–14, modified; my emphasis. [The bracketed sentence is from the original version of the essay and has been added here: Derrida quotes from the first publication in French of *L'intrus*, on the Internet, remarking in a note on this "technical form of private publishing, termed *e-mail*."—Trans.]

24. Nancy, "Elliptical Sense," trans. Derbyshire, pp. 109–10, modified. One could follow the semantics of touching in its most literal form throughout the book.

25. Ibid.

26. Ibid.

27. Ibid., pp. 110–11 [very slightly modified—Trans.]. About all the connecting threads that go from this question of the untouchable's touch and exscription,

there are also many other relevant passages in this book. In the original edition of *Une pensée finie*, see pp. 18, 55ff., 137, 143, 207, 208, 211, 241, 243–44, 247–49, 254, 258, 263, 267, 268, 271, and passim. See also Nancy, *Le poids d'une pensée*, pp. 10–11, 14, and passim.

28. Jacqueline Risset, *L'amour de loin* (Paris: Flammarion, 1988).

29. Ibid., p. 25.

30. Who will have known better than Nancy how to think-live what "consenting to the body and bodies" may mean? In the plural, to more than one heart? To consent in and to the plural. I ask myself this and don't find any answer to it in "my life."

31. Chrétien, *L'appel et la réponse*, p. 145.

32. Nancy, "L'Intrus," trans. Hanson, p. 7 [my emphasis—J. D.].

13. "And to you"

1. Nancy, "L'Intrus," trans. Hanson, p. 7.

2. Nancy, *Experience of Freedom*, trans. McDonald, pp. 119 and 120.

3. Plotinus, "Free Will and the Will of the One," *Enneads* 6.8.19, Loeb ed., trans. A. H. Armstrong (Cambridge, Mass.: Harvard University Press, 1988), p. 291. [Derrida cites Plotinus, *Traité sur la liberté et la volonté de l'Un* [*Ennéade* VI, 8 (39)], trans. Georges Leroux (Paris: Vrin, 1990).—Trans.] In commenting on this passage, Georges Leroux notes something important for us at the point where Nancy names this "generosity of being" "freedom": "There is no compelling necessity at the origin of essence, but rather a generous spontaneity that Plotinus here dares to name freedom (*Ennead* VI 8)" (ibid., p. 387). See also the discussion in Chapter 6 of this book.

4. Plotinus, "Free Will and the Will of the One," *Enneads* 6.8.18, pp. 285, 287.

5. [Here Nancy cites Kant's *Religion Within the Limits of Reason Alone*.—Trans.] Nancy, *Experience of Freedom*, trans. McDonald, p. 124.

6. Ibid., pp. 200–201.

7. Nancy, "Finite Thinking," trans. Bullard et al., in *Finite Thinking*, ed. Sparks, p. 25 [slightly modified—Trans.].

8. Ibid., p. 24 [slightly modified—Trans.].

9. See Chapter 4.

10. With regard to the contagious and contaminating, immunity and immunosuppression, see e.g. Nancy's *L'intrus* and *Corpus*, p. 91. The latter is thus also a book about organ transplantation, AIDS, and even autoimmunity and all that follows. A text like this one (*this* one, indeed) is itself exposed in this way and cannot have any preventive system, index, or supposedly exhaustive way of treating things, to protect itself against the contamination that immediately goes beyond its bounds. We are touching the limit—and testing or tasking it.

11. Nancy, "Cœur des choses," trans. Holmes and Trumble as "Heart of Things," —Trans.

12. Nancy, "Shattered Love," trans. Lisa Garbus and Simona Sawhney, in id., *Finite Thinking*, ed. Sparks, pp. 245ff.; "The Heart: Broken," in ibid., pp. 255–257.

13. On the contact (with self), on self-love, the love of self, and *philautia*, see Nancy, *Finite Thinking*, pp. 259ff. The being-*touched* of the subject in love signifies here its being opened up, wounded, broken in its integrity, struck, as in fencing one may be "touché": "Love re-presents *I* to itself broken (and this is not a representation). It presents this to it: he, this subject, was touched, broken into, in his subjectivity, and he *is* from then on, for the time of love, opened by this slice, broken or fractured, even if only slightly" (Nancy, "Shattered Love," trans. Garbus and Sawhney, pp. 260–61).

14. Novalis, *Fragments*, ed. Guerne, pp. 54–55 [trans. Peggy Kamuf]; on the heart, see ibid., pp. 94–95.

15. Ibid., trans. Kamuf, pp. 44–45 [modified—Trans.].

16. Nancy, *Le poids d'une pensée*, p. 3; "Weight of a Thought," trans. Raffoul and Recco, p. 75.

17. See Jean-Luc Nancy, "Notre probité!" in id., *L'impératif catégorique* (Paris: Flammarion, 1983); "'Our Probity!': On Truth in the Moral Sense in Nietzsche," trans. Peter Connor, in *Looking After Nietzsche*, ed. Laurence A. Rickels (Albany: State University of New York Press, 1990), pp. 67–88; and Nancy, "Le katègorein de l'excès," ibid.; "The *Kategorein* of Excess," trans. James Gilbert-Walsh and Simon Sparks, in *Finite Thinking*, ed. Sparks, pp. 133–51.

18. Nancy, *Le poids d'une pensée*, pp. 115–24.

19. Nancy, "Weight of a Thought," trans. Raffoul and Recco, in *Gravity of Thought*, p. 80 [very slightly modified—Trans.].

20. Jean-Luc Nancy, *La naissance des seins* (Valence: École régionale des beaux-arts, 1996) [my translation—Trans.]. Among others things this is a meditation, at the same time lyrical, thoughtful, and analytical. It runs through a kind of anthology and iconography while also multiplying its touches—always in accordance with the "grammar" that we have been trying to formalize ("turn the tongue again toward what has touched it" [p. 6]; "toward a limit of language but a limit to touch, a fragile film of a skin" [p. 9]; "with language right at the thing—how to touch, hold, handle, weigh, and preserve it so as to give it" [p. 11]; "the derivative indefinitely going on the tangent—what touches in order to distance itself, what touches while distancing itself . . . system of flight and contact" [p. 19]; "Always weighing out imponderables. Thought weighs—this is the meaning and sense of its name" [p. 26]; "in order to touch to the extent of this loss" [p. 33]; "We are exactly between the two" [p. 42]; "This is how one touches truth: one turns and deviates from it to observe its silence" [p. 70]).

21. Nancy, *La naissance des seins*, pp. 46–47.

22. Ibid.
23. Ibid. Nancy underscores *exactement* ("exactly").
24. Nancy, "Weight of a Thought," trans. Raffoul and Recco, pp. 75–76.
25. Ibid., pp. 80–81.
26. See ibid., pp. 79–80, on exscription and the impenetrable (that which would set up an obstacle to traversal or perforation). See also Nancy, *Experience of Freedom*, pp. 103–4: *"thinking touches the impenetrable resistance of freedom"* (that is, also that of "language," of the *"singularity* of thinkers and thoughts," "of the *body* that thinks"). I would have liked to insist on the impenetrable according to Nancy, and on the impenetrable Nancy. By associating this motif with that of his exactitude, I would have shown that his taste for the impenetrable (of which there are countless signs in his texts) lets one divine in Jean-Luc Nancy a degree of hardness. His tenderness, his generosity, his exactitude, his punctuality, his attentive availability to all others, to all virtual differences, always ready for anything, are not necessarily contradicted by a certain hardness, by adamant rigor—resolution, duty, courage, and knowing (when necessary) how to be or to appear severe, inflexible, insensitive, or untouchable. His punctuality (in the divisibility-indivisibility of its point) penetrates and remains impenetrable and incalculable; it remains as the fair, inflexible *beam* [*fléau*] of the scales, fatally befalling what weighs. What a blow [*quel fléau*]. I am abstaining from a long exegesis of Kantian hardness (*Härte*) according to Hegel, who, as a good Christian, of course, thinks about and criticizes it.
27. Nancy, "Weight of a Thought," trans. Raffoul and Recco, p. 76.
28. Nancy, "Elliptical Sense," trans. Derbyshire, p. 110.
29. Nancy, "Weight of a Thought," trans. Raffoul and Recco, pp. 76, 80.
30. Ibid., p. 79.
31. Ibid., p. 81 [slightly modified—Trans.].
32. Ibid., p. 80 [slightly modified—Trans.].

Salve

1. Nancy, *Experience of Freedom*, trans. McDonald, p. 7 [modified—Trans.]. On the self-touching of thoughts as freedom, of a thought that "touches . . . , in itself and of itself, *this limit that is its very freedom,*" see also ibid., p. 59. It is a difficult thought because this experience is that of a nonsubjective, even unconscious, freedom. The self-touching that forms its space or spacing also exceeds subjectness, the subject/object opposition, responsibility as egological or subjective, even intentional, consciousness, and as responsible decision. This has to affect a whole politics, a whole problematic of the political. About the problems that are important for us here, see also ibid., pp. 44, 47, 59, 89, 100ff.

2. Nancy, "Sublime Offering," trans. Librett; "L'offrande sublime," in *Une pensée finie.*

3. Nancy, "L'offrande sublime," p. 187. [This passage trans. Peggy Kamuf.— Trans.]

4. Nancy, *Experience of Freedom*, trans. McDonald, p. 44.

5. Ibid., p. 47 [slightly modified—Trans.].

6. "[I]t is not a question of rejoining an 'intact' matter: we are not opposing immanence to transcendence. . . . There is no intact matter—if there were, there would be nothing. On the contrary, there is tactility, posing and deposing, the rhythm of the coming and going of bodies in the world. Tact unbound, parting and imparting itself" (Nancy, *Corpus*, p. 102).

7. I.e., "un salut exespéré."—Trans.

8. I.e., "Un salut sans salvation, un salut juste à venir."—Trans.

Index of Names

The index of names (other than Jean-Luc Nancy's) was compiled by the translator.

MERIDIAN

Crossing Aesthetics

Deborah Esch, *In the Event: Reading Journalism, Reading Theory*

Winfried Menninghaus, *In Praise of Nonsense: Kant and Bluebeard*

Giorgio Agamben, *The Man Without Content*

Giorgio Agamben, *The End of the Poem: Studies in Poetics*

Theodor W. Adorno, *Sound Figures*

Louis Marin, *Sublime Poussin*

Philippe Lacoue-Labarthe, *Poetry as Experience*

Ernst Bloch, *Literary Essays*

Jacques Derrida, *Resistances of Psychoanalysis*

Marc Froment-Meurice, *That Is to Say: Heidegger's Poetics*

Francis Ponge, *Soap*

Philippe Lacoue-Labarthe, *Typography: Mimesis, Philosophy, Politics*

Giorgio Agamben, *Homo Sacer: Sovereign Power and Bare Life*

Emmanuel Levinas, *Of God Who Comes To Mind*

Bernard Stiegler, *Technics and Time, 1: The Fault of Epimetheus*

Werner Hamacher, *pleroma—Reading in Hegel*

Serge Leclaire, *Psychoanalyzing: On the Order of the Unconscious and the Practice of the Letter*

Serge Leclaire, *A Child Is Being Killed: On Primary Narcissism and the Death Drive*

Sigmund Freud, *Writings on Art and Literature*

Cornelius Castoriadis, *World in Fragments: Writings on Politics, Society, Psychoanalysis, and the Imagination*

Thomas Keenan, *Fables of Responsibility: Aberrations and Predicaments in Ethics and Politics*

Emmanuel Levinas, *Proper Names*

Alexander García Düttmann, *At Odds with AIDS: Thinking and Talking About a Virus*

Maurice Blanchot, *Friendship*

Jean-Luc Nancy, *The Muses*

Massimo Cacciari, *Posthumous People: Vienna at the Turning Point*

David E. Wellbery, *The Specular Moment: Goethe's Early Lyric and the Beginnings of Romanticism*

Edmond Jabès, *The Little Book of Unsuspected Subversion*

Hans-Jost Frey, *Studies in Poetic Discourse: Mallarmé, Baudelaire, Rimbaud, Hölderlin*

Pierre Bourdieu, *The Rules of Art: Genesis and Structure of the Literary Field*

Nicolas Abraham, *Rhythms: On the Work, Translation, and Psychoanalysis*

Jacques Derrida, *On the Name*

David Wills, *Prosthesis*

Maurice Blanchot, *The Work of Fire*

Jacques Derrida, *Points . . . : Interviews, 1974–1994*

J. Hillis Miller, *Topographies*

Philippe Lacoue-Labarthe, *Musica Ficta (Figures of Wagner)*

Jacques Derrida, *Aporias*

Emmanuel Levinas, *Outside the Subject*

Jean-François Lyotard, *Lessons on the Analytic of the Sublime*

Peter Fenves, *"Chatter": Language and History in Kierkegaard*

Jean-Luc Nancy, *The Experience of Freedom*

Jean-Joseph Goux, *Oedipus, Philosopher*

Haun Saussy, *The Problem of a Chinese Aesthetic*

Jean-Luc Nancy, *The Birth to Presence*